Chinese Warlord

The Career of Feng Yü-hsiang

Chinese Warlord

The Career of Feng Yü-hsiang

James E. Sheridan

Stanford University Press, Stanford, California

Stanford University Press
Stanford, California
© 1966 by the Board of Trustees of the
Leland Stanford Junior University
Printed in the United States of America
Cloth SBN 8047–0145–8
Paper SBN 8047–0146–6
First published 1966
Last figure below indicates year of this printing:
79 78 77 76 75 74 73 72 71 70

For Sonia

Preface

The warlords of twentieth-century China have received little scholarly attention. Doubtless the chief reason is simply that the aggregation of unexplored Chinese historical problems is vast, whereas the assault force of scholars is very small; warlords are but one of innumerable important topics that have been neglected. Moreover, scholars tend to work on history's successes, and the warlords were destined for oblivion. Perhaps it is also because the warlords were so numerous, their relations so constantly in flux and so utterly confusing, the sources so treacherous, that it seemed hardly worth the trouble to study that disordered subject when many other topics lay conveniently at hand. Whatever the reason, the warlords have been among history's forgotten men.

It is good that this situation is beginning to change, for despite our ignorance about the warlords we can be sure that they were of great historical significance. Their wars and intrigues, their government and misgovernment, formed the context in which more conspicuous currents of recent history arose. The Nationalist and Communist movements, for example, must have been profoundly influenced by the warlord environment in which their early growth took place. Certainly the history of imperialism in China was influenced by the warlords. One can even trace the Kuomintang's defeat on the mainland in some measure to warlord influence on the party. These and other historical problems will be clarified when the nature of modern warlordism is better understood. A first step is the study of individual warlords, such as Feng Yü-hsiang.

This book is the biography of a warlord, not of a man; available sources do not justify an attempt to present Feng in all his human dimensions. I have focused on the political and military events that were important in Feng's career, or in which his actions influenced Chinese political life. In particular, I have emphasized events that bring out the warlord character of Feng's attitudes and activities. In Chapter I some of the chief characteristics of warlordism are set forth rather tentatively. I plan to devote a future study to a more comprehensive and analytic survey of the dynamics of warlordism.

A number of place names were changed during the period covered by this book. I have used the names proper to the particular time under discussion. For example, Peking and Chihli are used for the years before 1928, at which time these names were changed to Peiping and Hopei respectively, and the new names are used for events after that year. Money matters offer no such simple solution. Various metal and paper currencies, both Chinese and foreign, circulated during the warlord era. Chinese sources use the word *yüan* and English sources use the dollar sign, but these are not meaningful indications of value, for the actual value of *yüan* or dollar varied greatly, depending on the precise kind of money in question. Thus most money figures in this book provide only a general idea of the sums under discussion.

It is a pleasure to thank the many people who contributed in one way or another to this book. I had the good fortune to begin my study of Chinese history under the very best of mentors, Professor Joseph R. Levenson; his stimulating teaching drew me into Chinese studies, and his kindness smoothed the way. Some chapters of this book derive from a dissertation written under Professor Levenson's supervision and criticized constructively by Professors Woodbridge Bingham and Robert Scalapino. Professor Chen Shih-hsiang was unfailingly patient and gracious in helping me with translation problems. Sections of the manuscript profited from the painstaking and extraordinarily perceptive criticism of Professor Robert Wiebe. Mr. Howard Boorman kindly helped me check several details.

Many persons supplied me with personal recollections, documents, books, and the like. During 1958–59 I interviewed separately six of Feng's former officers; some preferred not to be identified, and I ultimately decided to leave them all anonymous. Mr. Chang Yüan-hsi accompanied Feng to the United States in 1946, and told me of that trip during an interview in Taipei in 1959. In Yokohama in 1959, Mrs. Kristian Hannestad, who tutored Feng in English for several months in 1925, graciously told me about her memories of that period. In 1960 in San Francisco, Mr. Paul C. Hodges told me of his experiences as a teacher and physician in China during nine years of the warlord period. Mr. Hugh Yu-tinn shared with me his recollections of the warlord era and also loaned me helpful material. Mr. Jen

Yu-wen (Chien Yu-wen) not only furnished me with some books by and about Feng, but also wrote me several letters about his experiences with Feng and the Kuominchün. Mr. Richard Lindheim provided me with copies of some of the press releases Feng Yü-hsiang issued in New York. Dr. and Mrs. Walter Lowdermilk, who were hosts to Feng and his wife when they came to the United States in 1946, recalled those days for me in conversations in Berkeley in 1961. In 1959 in Tokyo, I had a series of talks with Mr. Matsumuro Takayoshi, Feng's adviser in 1924–25, who was extraordinarily courteous, cooperative, and helpful. Mrs. Robert Moynan sent me books and photographs relating to Feng that would have been impossible to obtain elsewhere; the photograph in this book of Feng's troops at a baptismal service is used with Mrs. Moynan's kind permission. Professors Earl Pritchard and Donald Lach provided me with material left by Professor Harley MacNair. Mr. Ernest T. Shaw, who was in Peking during the early 1920's, supplied me with copies of correspondence that he wrote at that time relating to Feng Yü-hsiang. Mrs. Elizabeth Stelle, who was a missionary in China for many years, sent me a written statement of her recollections of Feng Yü-hsiang and Li Te ch'üan, to which Miss Grace Boynton and Miss Alice Huggins also contributed. Mr. Mark Wheeler sent me a volume of Feng's poetry not otherwise available. Professor C. Martin Wilbur shared with me some extremely helpful information uncovered during his own research. In 1964 in Evanston, Illinois, Mr. K. C. Wu told me some of his memories of Feng. Each of these persons is appropriately cited in the Notes, but I wish here to express my appreciation and gratitude to all of them.

I also want to thank the following persons, who provided me with information about Feng or warlordism, but whom I have not had occasion to cite specifically in the Notes: Charles L. Boynton, Lyman V. Cady, Rowland Cross, Samuel N. Dean, Stella Miner Flagg, Elmer Galt, Ku Meng-yü, William A. Mather, Miriam Ingram Pratt, Frederick Pyke, C. H. Robertson, Mrs. Charles A. Stanley, and Francis F. Tucker.

While doing research in the Far East, I received much aid and cooperation from Chinese and Japanese scholars. Mr. Lo Chia-lun and his staff at the archives of the Committee for the Compilation of Kuomintang Historical Materials, on Taiwan, helped me find essential material. The staff of the library of Academia Sinica was also very helpful, and Professor Kuo T'ing-yi gave me bibliographical assistance. In Tokyo, Japanese scholars showed me every conceivable courtesy. I especially wish to thank Professor Ueda Toshio, Professor Ishikawa Tadao, and Mr. Fuji Shozo. Mr. Horii Etsuro gave me essential help in the use of Japanese sources in Tokyo.

Mrs. Margaret Uridge and Mrs. Jeannot Nyles of the Interlibrary Borrowing Service of the University of California were of invaluable aid in obtaining materials for me in this country and abroad. Mr. Eugene Wu helped me exploit the riches of the Hoover War Memorial Library at Stanford. The librarians of the American Board of Commissioners for Foreign Missions responded quickly and efficiently to various requests; Mrs. June Russell, former assistant to the librarian of the American Board, was especially helpful in guiding me to the Louella Miner letters. All quotations from Louella Miner's letters, and the photograph of Feng and his family, are used with the kind permission of the American Board, which is now a part of the United Church Board for World Ministries.

My research in the Far East, and some of my work in this country, was done under grants from the Ford Foundation. I am tremendously grateful to the Foundation for this aid, and for the consideration and flexibility with which the grants were administered. Of course, the conclusions, opinions, and other statements in this study are my own, and are not necessarily those of the Ford Foundation. I appreciate the generosity of Northwestern University in allowing me time for research and writing as well as money for research expenses.

I am indebted to Stanford University Press editors John Farrell, Aidan Kelly, and Jesse G. Bell for their careful editing and unfailing cooperation. I am grateful to Linda Grove for conscientiously verifying the accuracy of my English-language references; and to Lorna Gallagher and Ruth Oldberg for typing portions of the manuscript.

Unfortunately I can think of no way to associate these friends and helpers with the numerous deficiencies of the book. Those are my contribution.

JAMES E. SHERIDAN

Contents

Four pages of illustrations follow p. 250

1. Emergence of the Warlords   1
2. A Soldier of the Manchus   31
3. From Soldier to Warlord   49
4. Military and Civil Administration at Ch'angte   74
5. Tuchün   97
6. Plots in Peking   120
7. Tupan of the Northwest   149
8. Defeat   177
9. The Northern Expedition   203
10. End of the Kuominchün   240
11. The Last Years   268
12. The Moral Warlord   283

Appendix   297

Notes   305

Annotated Bibliography   357

Glossary   373

Index   376

Chinese Warlord

The Career of Feng Yü-hsiang

1. Emergence of the Warlords

In Chinese history, the term warlord ordinarily designates a man who was lord of a particular area by virtue of his capacity to wage war. A warlord exercised effective governmental control over a fairly well-defined region by means of a military organization that obeyed no higher authority than himself. From 1916 to 1928, virtually all of China was divided among many such regional militarists, big and small; those years are therefore commonly termed the "warlord period," although warlords and warlordism remained important in Chinese politics long after 1928.

Regionalism and Militarism in the Late Ch'ing

Military regionalism did not, of course, come suddenly into being in 1916; rather, it was the culmination of a process that had begun about a century earlier. Indeed, regionalism always was latent in China, even when the central government operated at maximum effectiveness. Communication and transportation facilities never were adequate to the task of binding all parts of the vast country to its political center. There were strong local and regional variations in language, habits, and traditions. Although the Chinese traditionally took great pride in Chinese culture, incentives to national patriotism were few and weak, whereas provincial and local loyalties were powerful.[1] As long as the central government was vigorous and reasonably efficient, there was little to arouse this latent regionalism; in any event, the central authority could check such tendencies whenever they appeared. Conversely, a decline in central power both stimulated the growth of regionalism (as an alternative to anarchy) and lessened the government's ability to restrain that growth. During the nineteenth and early twentieth centuries, the Manchu Court suffered just such a decline.

During that period, Western commercial and industrial powers used force or the threat of force to wrest economic and territorial concessions from the Manchus. Manchu prestige declined under these military and diplomatic defeats, the treasury was drained, and the very premises of Chinese society were undermined by new institutions and ideas introduced by the Westerners. At the same time, the state was also beset by domestic revolt. By the early nineteenth century, agrarian distress was widespread, and in the time of the Tao Kuang emperor (1821–50) revolts began to erupt all over the empire.

The Ch'ing military organization—enfeebled by inactivity, extreme decentralization, and especially corruption—could do little to meet these crises.[2] Consequently, local armed forces sprang up to defend local interests. The central government, unable to prevent the formation of such forces, could only try to control those elements of local power whose interests most nearly coincided with its own. It succeeded in enlisting the support of some local forces, mostly led by gentry, in quelling local uprisings. But when the discontent in the countryside was mobilized by the Taipings into a great wave of revolution, local forces were no longer effective. A new type of armed power was necessary.[3]

Under this stimulus, some of the local forces were brought together into larger, regional armies. The first army of this type, which set the pattern for later ones, was the Hunan Army (Hsiang-chün), organized by Tseng Kuo-fan in 1853. In obedience to an imperial order to recruit and train the Hunan militia to fight the Taipings, Tseng organized an army based on existing local forces. He expanded his army by local recruiting and by incorporating new local forces, always indoctrinating the latter to ensure that they became an integral part of the larger organization. By 1856, the Hunan Army numbered about 60,000 men, and after this date it evidently grew even larger. For a number of years, Tseng's forces operated successfully against the Taiping rebels as the central government's only effective military support.[4]

At the beginning of the 1860's, Tseng assigned a subordinate, Li Hung-chang, the task of organizing a new regional army to supplement the Hunan Army. It was called the Anhwei Army (Huai-chün), and its nucleus was formed by the spring of 1862. By 1864, it numbered 70,000 troops. It eventually superseded the Hunan Army as the most powerful regional force, and in fact remained the largest and strongest army in China until almost the end of the century.[5] Although the Anhwei and Hunan armies were not the only regional forces, they were the most important, both as military organizations and as manifestations of the growth of regional power.

The regional nature of the armies was implicit in their recruitment. Tseng's army was composed almost entirely of Hunanese until 1856, and Hunanese remained predominant after that date. Li's army at the outset was recruited largely from Anhwei. The leaders also sought authority over the sources of revenue in their regions, and the central government increasingly conceded financial control as it came to recognize the Court's dependence on the regional armies. Li and Tseng also acquired regional administrative authority, which facilitated the creation of personal political machines.[6]

The Hunan and Anhwei armies were personal as well as regional, for they were virtually the private instruments of their commanders. An important criterion for selecting key officers was their personal loyalty to the commander-in-chief. These officers in turn selected subordinates loyal to them, and so on through the ranks. The troops' ultimate focus of loyalty was thus not the central government, but the army's commander-in-chief. At the same time, the commander's authority was qualified by the fact that the soldiers owed their most direct and strongest allegiance to their immediate superiors. For example, men of the local forces that were incorporated into the regional armies were primarily loyal to their own leaders, and only through them to the regional army leader, thus creating a hierarchy of loyalties. In sum, the Hunan and Anhwei armies were recruited and maintained regionally, and were bound together by a complex of interrelated ties of regional feeling and personal loyalties.[7]

When the Taiping Rebellion was finally stamped out, regional leaders controlled the only effective armies in the country. From then on, the Ch'ing government was without direct control over the major military activities of China.[8] Regional leaders not only had political authority in their own domains, but were leading figures in the councils of the nation, the most conspicuous being the head of the Anhwei Army, Li Hung-chang, who represented China before the world for three decades. Economically, the provincial leaders had a stranglehold on regional finances.[9] The balance between central and regional power was unequivocally and permanently altered.

It is true that this regional power was used to support the central government.[10] Regional leaders, though they sought and acquired the substance of regional power, did not aspire to formal independence or seek the overthrow of the dynasty. Financial and other limitations combined with rivalry among the various leaders to inhibit any such aspirations. Moreover, the Ch'ing dynasty, though racially alien, defended a Confucian social order against the challenge of anti-Confucian rebels and Western barbarians, and regional leaders saw this cause as their own. But it was their power, limited not so much by the central government as by their own commitment to the social order identified with that government.

In the decades following the Taiping Rebellion, the Manchu government tried one expedient after another to regain effective control of the nation's military, but to no avail. Indeed, regionalism was an important factor in the Chinese defeat in the Sino-Japanese War of 1894–95. Provincial autonomy had reached the point where it was difficult to obtain troops, funds, or supplies from provinces not directly involved in the fighting. As Li Hung-chang put it at the time, "One province, Chihli, is dealing with the whole nation of Japan."[11] Five years later, during the Boxer Rebellion, there was another startling example of the extent of provincial independence. While imperial troops fought Allied armies in Chihli, the high provincial officials Liu K'un-i, Chang Chih-tung, and Yüan Shih-k'ai, together with other officials in the south, remained aloof from the struggle and observed an agreement with the foreign powers.[12] The Manchus were unable to reduce this remarkable regionalism before the dynasty fell in 1912.

The fiasco of China's war with Japan in 1894–95 produced one important change on the Chinese military scene: it prompted the move toward military modernization that resulted in the famous Peiyang Army.* After China's defeat, the court recognized the need to modernize China's military arm, and asked Yüan Shih-k'ai to draw up a program for training a new and modern army. Yüan was a protégé of Li Hung-chang; between 1885 and 1894, he had made a good reputation serving as China's commissioner in Korea, and after the war he had shown interest in military reform. Yüan submitted detailed plans for an army organized and trained on the German pattern. The court approved, and about 5,000 troops were turned over to him for training. In December 1895, Yüan, then 36, began training these troops at Hsiaochan, a small market town between Tientsin and Taku that had formerly been a station of the Anhwei Army.[13]

Within a decade, he had created the most formidable army in China. During that period, in 1901, he succeeded Li Hung-chang as Commissioner of Trade for the Northern Ports, and his troops then became the Peiyang Army. By 1906, this army was variously estimated

---

* The name "Peiyang" comes from Pei-yang ta-chen, the Commissioner of Trade for the Northern Ports. This position, which was held by Li Hung-chang from 1870 to 1901 and thereafter by Yüan Shih-k'ai, entailed various military responsibilities; the forces involved came to be known as the Peiyang Army. Although this name was current under Li as well as Yüan, in current usage it refers nearly always to Yüan's army.

at 50,000 to 80,000 men, well-equipped and with Western-style training. However, Yüan's success made him enemies in some court circles, and he was eased out from direct command of his troops in 1906–7. Two years later, after the death of the Empress Dowager had removed his most powerful friend, Yüan was dismissed from office and retired to his home in Honan, where he lived quietly until the outbreak of revolution in 1911.

Despite these setbacks, Yüan lost little effective control over the Peiyang Army. The reason was that the Peiyang Army was a personal army, just as the earlier regional armies had been. The critical element in Yüan's control was the very same one that had allowed the earlier army leaders to control their forces—the loyalty of the officers. Yüan evidently tried also, with some success, to inculcate direct loyalty to himself in the ranks,[14] but he gave far greater attention to the more important task of keeping the loyalty of his commanders. He was extremely careful in the selection of his officers; for example, he seldom used returned students, whose heterogeneous training and background might make it difficult to bind them to him. He cultivated a teacher-student relationship between himself and his chief subordinates, a type of connection that today is still strong in East Asia, and was much more so at the beginning of the century.[15] Yüan made the relationship meaningful by seeing to it that both his military and civilian subordinates received rapid promotion.[16] In this fashion, he rewarded past loyalty and hinted at what future loyalty might bring. He was also careful to protect his lieutenants. For example, when a furor erupted because a soldier struck a foreigner, it was necessary to transfer the division commander; but Yüan reinstated him in his command as soon as the affair quieted down.[17] In such ways, Yüan successfully cultivated the loyalty that bound his officers to him during his absence, a loyalty that permitted him to resume command without difficulty when the revolution came.

In 1912, Yüan's Peiyang Army was the most powerful military organization in China, but it was certainly not the only one. Attempts at military modernization had added to, not replaced, the complex, antiquated, and decentralized Ch'ing military structure. The weakness of the court vis-à-vis the provinces had prevented the abolition of the old forces. Consequently, a great mishmash of military units were scattered over the country. Some were fairly new, with touches of modernity, and others were quite old-fashioned; but virtually all were under provincial authorities, and had more or less the character of personal armies.

There was a natural line of development from the personal armies of the mid-nineteenth century to the Peiyang Army. However, in the course of that development, the character of the armies changed in important ways. The first regional armies were created by civil officials who had risen in the Ch'ing bureaucracy in the traditional fashion through the examination system. Although they understood well the uses of the military power they had created, they were not fundamentally military men. They were active and successful in many fields besides the army. Their values, like their offices, were primarily civilian, and accorded little dignity to military activity. The regional leaders were willing to adopt certain Western techniques and devices, but only on a limited scale. Some Western concepts were used in training, and some Western equipment was employed; that was all. A good indication of the limits imposed by their traditional, anti-Western orientation was their refusal to grant command positions to graduates of newly established Western-style military academies.[18] Because of this discrimination, which continued as late as the 1880's, the new learning of these graduates was largely unused. In short, the early regional forces were fundamentally traditional armies led by civilians with a profound commitment to the preservation of Confucian society.

Although the creators of the first regional armies were civil officials who had risen in the traditional fashion, their military successes opened up a new road to power for men who had neither their academic background nor their extensive civilian experience. It became possible to rise to high position through service in the regional armies. Twenty of the forty-four governors-general appointed between 1861 and 1890 rose to prominence as regional army commanders. During the same period, over half the 117 governors appointed had served as officers in the regional forces. About one-fourth of the governors held neither of the two highest civil service degrees; most of this group rose to power through military service.[19] For a time, men of this sort were still eager to don the robes of civil officials, for the prestige of officialdom was not dead. However, as the old century yielded to the new, military success gradually came to be considered sufficient in itself.

A number of circumstances conspired to that end. In the first place, the pressing need for modernization finally forced the abolition of civil service examinations in 1905. This confirmed that the old road to power was a dead end. At the same time, the long-standing contempt felt by educated Chinese toward a military career was fading. As part of its military modernization program, the Ch'ing government purposefully tried to raise the prestige of military service. The disciplined behavior of the best of the new forces contrasted well with the actions traditionally expected of soldiers, and helped the reputation of the military. The school system that emerged as part of the Manchu reform program after the Boxer catastrophe stipulated that pupils wear uniforms and that military drill be taught in all schools, including missionary institutions.[20] In a country where the military had so long been viewed with disdain, this was a remarkable innovation.

At the same time, the continued pressure of foreign imperialism kindled the beginnings of patriotism and a martial spirit. Foreign observers noted the growth of these feelings particularly during and after the Russo-Japanese War, when the Chinese vicariously relished the victory of fellow Asians over a European power.[21] A large proportion of the Chinese students in Japan after 1905 chose to study the art of modern war.[22] Finally, a military career was respected in the West, and as willingness to imitate the West grew, that Western attitude also acted to alter Chinese conceptions. A military career was perhaps not yet completely respectable, but it was becoming so.

Around the turn of the century, as a result of the army's increasing power and prestige, and the simultaneous diminution of the central government's authority, army leaders no longer used their military eminence to gain civilian posts; instead, they devoted themselves exclusively to the military. Many of the army leaders of the time had been trained for a military career, as distinguished from the commanders of the first regional armies, for whom military activity had been an adjunct of a civilian occupation.

Although Yüan Shih-k'ai held civilian posts, he and a number of his senior officers exemplified this trend toward professionalism. Moreover, they did not share the profound commitment of the early regional leaders to the preservation of traditional civilization, and thus to the perpetuation of Manchu rule as the bulwark of Confucian society. This was partly due to the fact that they were soldiers rather than Confucian scholar-officials. In any event, Confucian society was changing so rapidly under the impact of foreign and other pressures that its preservation was clearly an unrealistic goal. In addition, and more immediately important, Yüan's personal prospects were bleak. The ruling circles at court after 1908 disliked and feared him, and though he was at the peak of his powers, he could see little likelihood of regaining his former authority under normal circumstances. No earlier regional leader had ever suffered such a blow to his personal ambition, and thus none had ever experienced the same temptation to use his military power for personal ends.

The upshot of these social and personal factors was that Yüan and his officers were not restricted by the values and loyalties that had prevented the earlier regional leaders from asserting their independence. The early regional armies were personal armies, but the Peiyang Army was the first to become a personal army only, in the sense that it had no commitment to suprapersonal principles and goals. To that extent, it represented the beginnings of warlordism.

In sum, the last century of the Ch'ing dynasty witnessed two related developments. On the one hand, the central government steadily weakened under the blows of domestic rebellion and foreign wars; as the central power declined, regional economic and political autonomy increased. On the other hand, the influence of military men steadily grew, not only because armed force was needed to deal with internal revolt and foreign threats, but also because of the increasing respect accorded the military by proponents of nationalism and Westernization. These were two aspects of a single phenomenon. That is, as regional power increased, it tended to flow into the hands of military men. By 1911, these men had little commitment to the Confucian order; their major commitment was to personal advancement by military means.

The Warlord Period

The most powerful man to emerge from the Revolution of 1911 was Yüan Shih-k'ai. He was legally head of state, and he personally controlled, in the Peiyang Army, the most formidable military organization in China. With these two supports, Yüan was able to maintain effective rule over most of a fairly unified country until a few months before his death in 1916. But ominous signs appeared during those years. The number of men under arms climbed as provincial leaders, and Yüan himself, steadily recruited soldiers. More important, Yüan repeatedly used his armies for domestic political purposes. To the extent that he used military force to gain his ends, he undermined the office of the presidency, and intensified the weaknesses of the political parties and republican civil authority in general. His reliance on force or the threat of force had the effect of rendering the already puny Republic virtually impotent, and of strengthening the arm that he flexed, the military. Since the republicans could not restrain Yüan by political means, they also turned to armed force. A republic of militarists came into being. The preponderant military strength of the Peiyang Army allowed it to dominate the other militarists, and thus China was assured of a kind of unity as long as the Peiyang Army remained unified. But Peiyang cohesion depended on the personal loyalty of the army's chief officers to Yüan Shih-k'ai. When Yüan died in June 1916, the keystone of the army's unity disappeared, and army authority reverted to the top commanders. The Peiyang hierarchy began to break down into its constituent hierarchies, still on the basis of personal loyalties. Non-Peiyang military units had also been organized on this basis. Now, freed from the domination of unified Peiyang power, they rose to challenge one another as well as Peiyang units. Thus began a period in which the political life of the country was dominated by incessant struggles among military men for regional or national dominance. This was the warlord period of modern Chinese history.

The constant strife, the ceaseless shifts and changes, that characterized this period make the political-military history of Chinese warlordism extraordinarily complicated and confusing. Nevertheless, it is possible to outline the main events, which fall into three phases.

Early Warlordism. The early phase of warlordism began with the death of Yüan Shih-k'ai in 1916 and lasted until the first great military expression of the Chinese nationalist movement, the Northern Expedition, which started in 1926.[23] This was the period of "pure" warlordism, when wars and political maneuvers were solely the work of military men in quest of power and wealth. Although they rationalized their wars and policies with patriotic and altruistic slogans—many of which may even have been sincere—none of them represented any important segment of the population, nor were their struggles the expression of genuine national or social movements.

The political and military events of this phase were extremely complex. Confusing military and political maneuvering occurred on various overlapping levels. On the one hand, there was a series of contests between major warlord groupings for control of Peking and the machinery of the national government. On the other hand, within each of these groupings there were ambivalent tendencies. There was competition for control of the group, and those who hoped to profit from such control sought to strengthen and perpetuate the group as a group, irrespective of other considerations. But there was also a strong desire to maintain provincial or regional autonomy, particularly among those who were not closely connected with leading warlords. Thus there were forces working for the maintenance of warlord groups and other forces working for their disintegration. At the same time, there was rivalry between the North, where the Peiyang clique was strongest, and the South, where non-Peiyang militarists predominated.

Owing to these various conflicts, the situation was very unstable and in constant flux. From the death of Yüan Shih-k'ai in June 1916 until the spring of 1926 there were six different heads of state.* This includes neither the brief imperial restoration in 1917 nor the three periods of several months each when a caretaker, or regency, government existed while decisions were being made regarding a new head of state. In the same period, over twenty-five successive cabinets were formed.[24] These rapid political changes to some extent reflected the shifting balance of power among the leading military cliques.

The dissolution of Peiyang unity actually began several months before Yüan Shih-k'ai died. Toward the end of 1915, Yüan undertook to restore the monarchy with himself as emperor. Southern militarists opposed this move, and took up arms to force Yüan's resignation. Military action against Yüan began in the two southern provinces that were not controlled by the Peiyang clique: Yunnan and Kweichow. As a result of the war that followed, Peiyang leaders lost control of Kwangsi, Kwangtung, Szechwan, and Hunan. During this war another military leader, Chang Tso-lin, maneuvered to become tutu of Fengtien, and to have his candidate made tutu of Heilungkiang;† this created a firm foundation for the further development of an independent Manchurian military clique. Thus, by the time of Yüan's death, several important regions had already been severed from Peiyang control.

The extent to which republican government was a facade for military control was illustrated by the fate of Yüan's successor as President, the former Vice-President, Li Yüan-hung, who was not a leader of a Peiyang faction and had little military support. Actual power soon gravitated to Premier Tuan Ch'i-jui, a Peiyang leader. According to Li Yüan-hung's secretary, Li was seldom informed about important national affairs; he was not even told what took place at cabinet meetings.[25] His duty was presumably only to sign measures passed by Tuan's cabinet.

Immediately after Li assumed office, the first of a series of disputes broke out between North and South over which constitution was to be the basis for Li's succession to the presidency. Neither the Southerners nor the Peiyang clique objected to Li's being President, but the

---

* Li Yüan-hung served twice as President, both times being counted to make six terms.

† Military governors of the provinces during and after the Revolution of 1911 were given the title of *tutu*. After Yüan's death the title was altered to *tuchün*. Still later it was changed to *tupan*, but this title did not catch hold, and provincial overlords were generally called *tuchün*.

former wanted the office to be defined in accordance with the 1912 provisional constitution, whereas the latter preferred a constitution promulgated under Yüan Shih-k'ai's auspices in 1914. The earlier document provided more power for parliament, and the Southerners hoped that this provision would give them a voice in a government otherwise dominated by the Peiyang clique. When the navy declared for the South, Tuan Ch'i-jui yielded to the Southern contention, and the country was ostensibly unified by the fall of 1916.

Only a few months after this, another conflict developed over the question of whether China should declare war against Germany. Tuan Ch'i-jui, supported by some politicians and many of the Peiyang militarists, wanted to join the Allies against Germany. The other outstanding Peiyang leader, Feng Kuo-chang, supported Li Yüan-hung in opposing a declaration of war. Evidently counting on Feng's support, Li boldly dismissed Tuan as Premier on May 23, 1917. Tuan responded by calling upon the Peiyang militarists to oppose the President, and eight provinces declared independence of the central government. When Feng did not offer the military backing that Li apparently expected, the President sought assistance from an old-style militarist, Chang Hsün. Chang accepted Li's summons on several conditions, one of which was that parliament be dissolved. When that was done, Chang Hsün proceeded to restore the Manchu emperor to the throne on July 1, 1917.

There is little doubt that this restoration was no surprise to the other militarists,[26] including Feng Kuo-chang and Tuan Ch'i-jui, both of whom welcomed it for their own reasons. Tuan saw it as a means of eliminating Li and the parliament, affording him a chance to seize more power under the guise of protecting the Republic. Feng, then Vice-President, viewed the restoration as an opportunity to oust Li and succeed him as President. Therefore, the restoration had no sooner been announced than the Peiyang leaders combined against Chang Hsün, and the restored monarch was once again deprived of his throne a mere two weeks after regaining it.

At the conclusion of the short-lived restoration, Feng became President and Tuan again became Premier. Several weeks later a new conflict broke out when Tuan tried to take over Hunan province in opposition to the militarists of Kwangtung and Kwangsi, who would not allow that province to fall into Peiyang hands. A military government, in which six provinces of the South and Southwest ultimately participated, was organized to "protect the constitution." At the outset Sun Yat-sen was made the head of this government, but it was actually dominated by the warlords of Kwangtung and Kwangsi. Despite this opposition, Tuan pressed his plan to gain control of Hunan, and war broke out.

This North-South war dragged on for the next two years, gradually becoming obscured by wars within both camps. In the South, a series of local wars sputtered on and off until the Kuomintang was reorganized and began to assert a new revolutionary power in 1926. In the North, Peiyang militarists gradually divided into two large groups: the Anfu clique (often called the Anhwei clique), headed by Tuan Ch'i-jui; and the Chihli clique, led by Feng Kuo-chang until his death in 1919. After Feng's death Ts'ao K'un emerged as the nominal head of the Chihli faction, although effective military leadership increasingly fell to his chief subordinate, Wu P'ei-fu. Competition between these two cliques steadily sharpened, and culminated in war in the summer of 1920.

The Chihli-Anfu War was the first of several major struggles for the control of northern China. Chang Tso-lin, the warlord of Manchuria, cooperated with the Chihli faction, and the Anfu group was quickly defeated. This paved the way for a contest between the two victors in 1922, when the Chihli armies under Wu P'ei-fu defeated Chang's Fengtien army. This was known as the First Chih-Feng War. Although the Chihli militarists gained northern China, they did not have the strength to oust Chang Tso-lin from his Manchurian stronghold, where he retired to regroup his forces.

The Second Chih-Feng War broke out in the autumn of 1924. It ended almost immediately when one of the chief Chihli leaders, Feng Yü-hsiang, turned against Wu P'ei-fu and brought about his rapid defeat and flight. Feng and Chang Tso-lin were now the two major warlords in northern China, and within a year of Feng's turn against Wu, he was at war with Chang. Feng was defeated, and Chang acquired complete control of the government at Peking. That was the situation when the National Revolutionary Army started its historic march, the Northern Expedition, to wrest the country from the warlords.

While the warlords were preoccupied with struggle for power and position, the context in which their struggles took place was changing. Chinese nationalism was burgeoning, and for the first time became linked with a revolutionary social movement. The nationalist movement began among students, but spread quickly to a wider public. It was nourished not only by indignation over the political and economic concessions that foreign powers had wrung from China, but by currents from abroad, especially the fact and theory of the Russian Revolution. In 1919, when the Versailles peacemakers ignored Chinese demands and turned German concessions in Shantung over to Japan, Chinese anti-imperialist indignation found expression in the great May Fourth Movement. Two years later the Chinese Communist Party was formed, and in 1924 the Kuomintang was reorganized along Bolshevik lines with Russian assistance; both parties preached Chinese nationalism, and they soon allied to seek their common goals.

Both parties were strongly anti-imperialist, and both received ardent support from students and intellectuals. By the early 1920's, however, Chinese nationalism was fed by stronger currents than the agitation of intellectuals. Among these currents was the growth of industry in China. During World War I, the industrial output of Western nations was devoted to their war effort. Chinese producers suddenly found themselves free from the crushing pressure of foreign competition, and native industry expanded rapidly. Growth was especially fast for producers of cotton textiles, flour, matches, cigarettes, cement, canned food, bean oil, and even coal and iron. As a result of this expansion, Chinese commercial and industrial leaders gained strength and confidence; in particular, they saw a great future if only national unity and independence could be achieved under a government that would protect their interests. At the same time, a small urban working class grew up, and a militant labor movement came into being with surprising speed. Peasant unions were also organized, and joined with the labor movement to seek new status and rewards.

The Communist-Kuomintang alliance channeled these new economic forces into the nationalist movement, thus fusing anti-imperialism with social revolution. For the first time in the history of China, political parties had mass support and represented national aspirations. The first step toward the realization of those aspirations was a military expedition to eliminate the warlords and unify the country under a revolutionary government. When this was attempted, warlordism moved into its second phase.

Warlordism Under Attack. This second phase was very short, lasting from the beginning of the Northern Expedition in 1926 to the establishment of the Nationalist government over a nominally unified country in 1928. These years were characterized by warfare between the National Revolutionary Army (together with allied forces) and warlords who opposed it, individually or in coalition.

In the late spring of 1926, the Kuomintang-Communist alliance launched a military campaign to eliminate the warlords and unify the country. The National Revolutionary Army moved steadily and rapidly north from its base in Kwangtung, its successive victories being as much the achievement of its propaganda vanguard as of actual battle. Many warlords chose to join the revolutionaries rather than fight them. By the end of the year, Wuhan was in Nationalist hands, and in early 1927 Shanghai was occupied. The Northern Expedition then halted temporarily while the two allies settled internal differences.

The Kuomintang-Communist alliance, beset from the outset by contradictions, had become increasingly strained during the northward march. The Communists aimed ultimately at a far more radical social revolution than the Kuomintang, and Communist agitation among peasants and urban laborers alarmed Kuomintang conservatives. Moreover, with the Communist Party growing rapidly, and Communists occupying key positions in the Kuomintang and the government, there arose the specter of a Communist takeover of the Kuomintang. Personal rivalries between rightist and leftist leaders within the Kuomintang added another element to the latent split between the two wings of the revolutionary movement.

This latent split emerged as a complete and open rupture after the revolutionary forces reached the Yangtze. The Communists and the Kuomintang left wing dominated the government, which was moved from Canton to Hankow. In April 1927, Chiang Kai-shek, who headed another Kuomintang government at Nanking, suddenly attacked the Communists and their organizations, killing hundreds of leftists, crushing the Communist-led labor movement, and virtually shattering the Communist Party in China. Russian advisers were ousted from the country in July. Sun Yat-sen had died in 1925, and to the split with the Communists in 1927 was added a struggle for leadership of the Kuomintang. By the end of the year, that contest had been won by Chiang Kai-shek, who emerged as head of the army and of the party.

After those important changes, the Northern Expedition was resumed under Chiang's general command in April 1928. Chang Tsolin, the warlord of Manchuria, headed the coalition of northern warlords that opposed the Kuomintang advance. The campaign included some hard fighting, but the revolutionaries advanced steadily, and in two months it was all over; Chang Tso-lin fled, and the National Revolutionary Army occupied Peking. The nation, it was said, was unified.

Residual Warlordism. It has often been asserted that the success of the Northern Expedition in 1928 marked the end of the warlord period, which is commonly described as lasting from 1916 to 1928.

This is misleading. Many warlords continued to command personal armies, control territory, and retain tax revenues after 1928; and in general warlordism remained a conspicuous feature of political life under the Nationalist government.

Such residual warlordism was at least partly the product of the National Revolutionary Army's policies during the Northern Expedition. Many warlords chose not to fight the advancing army as it marched north, but to join it with their forces intact. The Kuomintang leadership "reorganized" such units, not by changing their structure or shifting key personnel, but by giving them numbers to identify them as units of the National Revolutionary Army; that was all. Units that joined in this fashion—with no genuine commitment to Kuomintang principles or the goals of the revolution, or to anything but their own self-preservation—ultimately far outnumbered the original National Revolutionary Army. By the time the army reached the Yangtze, thirty-four warlords and their troops had joined it.[27] Within six months after the beginning of the Northern Expedition, the army was nearly three times its original size, primarily as a result of the adherence of warlord units.[28] By April 1928, on the eve of the expedition's last stage, the National Revolutionary Army consisted of fifty separate armies. Well over half of them had originally been warlord armies;[29] and in a very real sense they continued to be, despite their changed status.

Top officials of the Nationalist government certainly had few illusions that the end of the Northern Expedition meant the elimination of the warlords. For example, the Minister of Finance, reporting on the state of the country's financial unification in early 1929, said:[30]

There is today little if any improvement from conditions existing during the period of warfare. Thus the national revenues from such provinces as Hunan, Hupeh, Kwangtung, Kwangsi, Shensi, Kansu, Honan, Shansi, and Suiyuan, not to mention those from the Three Eastern Provinces [Manchuria], Szechwan, Yunnan, and Kweichow, are entirely appropriated by the localities mentioned. In the provinces of Hopei (Chihli), Shantung, and Fukien, the revenue officials are at least commissioned by the Central Government, but in other provinces they are appointed by local and military authorities and most of them fail even to render accounts.

When the government attempted to transform its nominal authority into genuine control, the result was war. In the spring of 1929, government forces engaged a group of warlords called the Kwangsi clique. Shortly thereafter, a pair of warlords—Feng Yü-hsiang and Yen Hsi-shan—challenged the government and there began a sporadic but bloody war that lasted until the fall of 1930. In subsequent years, there were no warlord wars on this scale (the war with the Communists cannot be considered in this category), but there were smaller outbreaks. There was also continuing political competition between the Nanking government and regional militarists as the former sought to make its authority genuinely national.

The extent and nature of residual warlordism after 1928 is a subject that merits serious investigation. To what degree did it render the government less able to counter the Communist challenge and the Japanese invasion? Or was it perhaps a symptom, rather than a cause, of weakness? Was its existence a measure of the extent to which Kuomintang nationalism under Chiang Kai-shek had become attenuated and adulterated? Many such questions might be asked, and hopefully will one day be answered. Here it is enough to note that the government's control after 1928 was sufficiently loose and qualified to allow residual warlordism to exist, and thus to offer defeated warlords—such as Feng Yü-hsiang—the hope that they might someday rise again.

Warlords and Warlordism

Although the warlord period lasted for years, and warlordism came to dominate the entire country of China, there are very few monographs relating to individual warlords or to events in specific geographic regions during the warlord period.[31] General statements on these subjects are therefore more hazardous than most, particularly since there is enough information already available to indicate that there was probably greater diversity in warlordism than has usually been assumed. Nevertheless, some tentative generalizations must be attempted.

The Warlord. As mentioned at the beginning of this chapter, a warlord was one who established and maintained control over territory by the use of his personal army. All warlord armies, of course, were personal. Indeed, they were often referred to in terms of the commander's name rather than whatever formal designation they might have had; the troops of Feng Yü-hsiang, for example, were often called the Feng-chün, or army of Feng. Identification sometimes extended to unit commanders, a reflection of the hierarchy of loyalties mentioned earlier. Thus, a soldier might say that he was from the Li division or the Wang brigade of the army of such-and-such a general.[32]

The personal nature of warlord armies derived primarily from the late Ch'ing trends in that direction; the Peiyang Army was the outstanding example, and it was this force that provided the nuclei for many of the leading warlord armies. The personal character of the armies was intensified by their physical and organizational separation from each other. Units of Western armies of that period normally could not act independently, but employed a communications system by which the services of several units could be coordinated. Communication facilities in China were not adequate for that kind of organization; hence army divisions were organized as complete and independent entities.[33] A division could be severed from the national army organization without organizational difficulties or reduction of the division's fighting potential. Personal authority over one's troops, therefore, implied the capacity for independent military action.

In the years following the death of Yüan Shih-k'ai, political, military, and social conditions had conflicting effects on the personal nature of warlord armies. As the central government lost all semblance of true national authority, and local and regional warfare became chronic, warlords could manipulate their armies with no consideration for higher authority, civilian needs, ordinary morality, or the armies themselves. In a sense, this was the acme of personal authority. At the same time, the extensive social and economic disorder fostered by the warlords themselves furthered the breakdown of traditional moral values that were already under attack from other quarters. The warlords were looking out only for themselves, and this attitude quickly spread to their subordinates. As a result, the hierarchies of loyalty came to be based less and less on ethical considerations and more and more on mercenary ones; service was increasingly conditioned upon expectation of reward. Defections became common as officers sought more profitable opportunities, either on their own or under a new and more promising master. Discipline in the ranks deteriorated, and payment by money or the right to pillage was sometimes necessary to exact obedience. In a word, loyalty—given with more and more conditions attached—became increasingly uncertain, and the warlord's authority was correspondingly diminished.

Soldiers for these personal armies were obtained in several ways. Probably the most important was ordinary recruitment. Recruits were plentiful, despite the possibility of death or injury from fighting in wars in which they had little personal interest. The turmoil created by warlord conflicts was one reason for their availability. A large number of jobless and hungry men in the cities and countryside were willing to join an army in order to be clothed and fed, and perhaps paid. At the very least they expected an occasional opportunity to loot, and the roving life of a soldier may have promised to inject some romance into an essentially barren existence.[34]

Besides normal recruitment, it was common practice for a warlord to incorporate into his own army troops of a defeated antagonist, a practice illustrative of the "loyalties" of the time. Sometimes bandit gangs were similarly absorbed after their defeat, or simply as a result of a deal between a warlord and a bandit leader.[35] In some instances, forced conscription was employed, but the large number of available recruits generally made this unnecessary. However, porters, drivers, and laborers were often forced into temporary service.[36] The more intelligent and ambitious warlords attempted to train their men into reasonably efficient and disciplined organizations. Other warlords did little in this regard, and their forces, although sometimes huge in numbers, were weak and inefficient.

Territorial jurisdiction was the second essential characteristic of a warlord. The extent of the territory could vary tremendously. Major warlords sometimes controlled areas as large as or larger than the chief states of Western Europe, with many millions of inhabitants. Petty warlords might control two or three districts, or perhaps only a very few villages. Historically, the petty warlords were very important, and though specific allusions to them are few, it should be remembered that there were sometimes many pockets actually ruled by minor warlords within the area ostensibly controlled by a major warlord. The customary terminology of warlordism ignores this phenomenon and is consequently misleading. When a warlord occupied the capital of a province, especially if he did so with the approval of the government in Peking, it was customary to consider him in control of that province. Journalists and historians have continued to err in this fashion, and maps of warlord-controlled areas—including maps in this book—follow the same practice, largely because so little is yet known about the configuration of control outside the capital area.

Control of territory was important for obvious reasons. It provided a warlord with a military base for defensive and offensive purposes, a source of foodstuffs and other supplies, and a source of revenue. A warlord needed funds for arms, ammunition, and other military supplies, and for personal enrichment. Most important, he needed money to pay his troops, without whom he could not control his territory. Unless he had funds to pay his soldiers—or an area that the soldiers could exploit in some fashion in lieu of pay—he could not control his army. His position thus rested on these two interrelated supports—army and territory. Or, to phrase it differently, a warlord needed an army to gain control of territory so that he could pay his army.

Because of the rapacity displayed by some warlords in the administration of their territories, the question arises whether "warlord" was simply a euphemism for "bandit." The chaos of the warlord period brought many bandit gangs into existence. Some were very large, equivalent to warlord armies. But bandits ordinarily did not control territory, and this was the essential difference. Bandits had to loot and run in order to survive as bandits; they had no semblance of legality and recognized no obligation to their victims. Warlords, on the contrary, could levy taxes; they were not forced to loot to maintain themselves, and many did not.

Moreover, warlords assumed the burdens of government for the areas they controlled. The governments they established were not always praiseworthy, but they were governments and usually maintained some degree of order. It has been asserted that many warlords were simply bandit chieftains who amassed great power.[37] To the extent this was true, it can be said that a bandit became a warlord at the point where he acquired acknowledged control over a specific area and assumed the tasks of governing it. Actually, however, none of the most important warlords became warlords in this fashion. Virtually all the major ones came out of the regular army, though some had been bandits before their army service.

The origins of the outstanding warlords were diverse. Many rose from very low estate; others had the advantages of wealth and education. Chang Tso-lin was a brigand in the pay of the Japanese during the Russo-Japanese War. He then became an officer in the regular Chinese army, went to Manchuria in 1911, and rose to be military governor of Fengtien.[38] Yen Hsi-shan, a battalion commander in the Manchu army, was head of a revolutionary faction in an army garrison in Shansi when the Revolution of 1911 broke out. He ousted the Manchu authorities and became military governor of the province, a position he held against all comers for two decades.[39] Wu P'ei-fu was an officer in the Peiyang Army, and became a protégé of his division commander. As the commander rose, so did Wu. He ultimately became effective head of the Chihli clique, although his patron was still nominally his superior.[40] Some men, like Feng Yü-hsiang and Ts'ao K'un, rose from the ranks. Others, such as Tuan Ch'i-jui and Feng Kuo-chang, were early leaders in the army modernization program directed by Yüan Shih-k'ai. But regardless of their diverse origins, most of them began their careers in the regular army.

Notwithstanding the military reforms of the late Ch'ing period, very few Chinese officers had the experience and training of the ordinary military leader in the West.[41] In lieu of extensive training, the

Chinese warlord depended on boldness, shrewdness, a certain resourcefulness, and a talent for personal leadership. An English diplomat with some forty years' experience in China asserted that under other conditions "China could have easily produced some very great military leaders from among the War Lords."[42]

Perhaps the cliché most persistently applied to the warlords is that they "sought power." This phrase suggests that they sought power for exclusively selfish ends, such as the accumulation of wealth. Certainly this was often true, but there were many exceptions—warlords who combined personal ambition with social and national concerns. Indeed, into this category fall most of the best-known warlords, notably Feng Yü-hsiang, Yen Hsi-shan, Ch'en Chiung-ming, Chang Tso-lin, and Wu P'ei-fu.

Some warlords were illiterate, their schooling limited to the storyteller's booth or theatrical performances. But they had great self-confidence and native intelligence. There were few mediocrities among them. On the basis of an intimate knowledge of the Chinese scene, Pearl Buck has written:[43]

Without exception, the war lords I have known have been men of unusual native ability, gifted with peculiar personal charm, with imagination and strength, and often with a rude poetic quality. Above all, they carry about with them, in them, a sense of high drama. The war lord sees himself great— and great in the traditional manner of heroes of ancient fiction and history who are so inextricably mingled in the old Chinese novels. He is, in effect, an actor by nature, as Napoleon was. The war lord is a creature of emotion; cruel or merciful, as the whim is; dangerous and unstable as friend or enemy; licentious and usually fond of luxury.

The warlord personality, with its flair for the theatrical, made the period colorful even while it was tragic. The common people, who suffered most from the warlords' acts, were nevertheless fascinated by them. They could tell innumerable stories about a warlord's temper tantrums, his extravagances, his reckless courage, his bold idiosyncrasies. There were tales explaining his origin: he was the personification of some god, some star, some magic creature.[44] Warlords assumed something of the stature of folk heroes.

Warlordism. The term warlordism refers to the aspects and conditions of warlord rule. One such aspect has already been mentioned: the growth of an essentially mercenary spirit as the loyalty of a warlord's subordinates came increasingly to be conditioned on his prospects of success.[45] In earlier years, the relationship between a military or civil official and his subordinates had been more or less analogous to that between a teacher and his students. A talented subordinate advanced thanks to his superior, not by usurping his superior's position or by finding a more powerful patron. Indeed, the warlords tried to cultivate this type of relationship with their subordinates, and with some success. Some of them effectively exploited regional and provincial loyalties also. But as the warlord period progressed, these loyalties began to break down.

As a result, the offer of money and position to entice officers to switch sides (a tactic known as using "silver bullets") became an important weapon in the warlord wars. It was essential, of course, that the defecting officer bring his troops with him, thus weakening his former leader while strengthening his new one. When the stakes of war were high, the bribes offered to officers were proportionately huge.* Less mercenary methods were also employed. As a result of the constant shuffling of military units, friends and relatives sometimes found themselves in opposing armies. In such cases, a commander might send men to lure their kinsmen or comrades away from an enemy force. "Conditions in our army are much better," they might argue. Or, "Come to our side, and we can all be together."[46] These tactics—particularly the use of "silver bullets"—brought about many defections, some of great significance. The defection of key subordinates was a factor in limiting the size of the territory a warlord could successfully control. Wartime commanders had to keep in mind the possibility of treachery, which could turn apparent victory into sudden defeat. In 1924, on the eve of the Second Chih-Feng War, an official of the Chihli clique epitomized the situation nicely. "We shall undoubtedly win," he said. "It is simply a matter of waiting for treason."[47]

The importance of defections illustrates once again the individualistic character of warlordism: personal preferences, aspirations, policies, and whims were little hampered by ideological or social restraints. Consequently the elimination of a single key person could drastically alter the total power situation, and murder was therefore a common warlord tactic. A favorite method was to invite an intended victim to a banquet, where he was seized and shot.[48]

Two or more warlords frequently found it expedient or necessary to combine in an alliance or confederation. For example, warlords of roughly equal strength might unite to resist the threat of a more

---

* An officer who participated in the critical war of 1929–30 between Chiang Kai-shek and the alliance of Feng Yü-hsiang and Yen Hsi-shan told this author that he received several offers during the conflict; the smallest was $100,000 cash for himself, plus regular payments for the support of his troops.

powerful nearby warlord, or a number of small warlords might come into the orbit of an important militarist in hopes that the alliance would achieve gains in which all would share. It was also possible for a single warlord organization to expand to the point where the leaders of its constituent elements were for all practical purposes independent, thus transforming a relationship of subordination into one of alliance. Indeed, this was essentially what took place in the two wings of the Peiyang Army after the death of Yüan Shih-k'ai. Generally, warlord alliances could realistically plan only short-term cooperation, for the warlord system was subject to so many and such sudden changes that the long-range future was always uncertain.[49]

Perhaps the most obvious characteristic of warlordism was war. Not all warlords were ambitious to expand their holdings, but all were interested in maintaining what they had against those who sought more. And since there were always those who sought more, local and regional wars were frequent.

The control of Peking was a prize sought by the most powerful northern warlords. There were several reasons for this. First, those who controlled the capital controlled such national administrative machinery as continued to function, and thus had a basis for claiming the allegiance of the country. Secondly, until 1928, foreign nations dealt with the Peking government as the government of China. Therefore, the warlord of Peking could assert a claim to any surplus from the customs collections and the salt gabelle after loan and indemnity charges defrayed from these sources had been met. Finally, there was always the hope that one might contract foreign loans in the name of the nation. These attractions were responsible for some of the major warlord conflicts in northern China. At the outset of the warlord period, the chief militarists themselves assumed high office in the Peking government, but this was seldom done after the early 1920's. Warlords, however, wanted the stamp of legitimacy, and the Peking government was invariably called upon to formalize changes wrought by warfare. This meant, of course, that whenever the distribution of armed and territorial power altered, there soon followed corresponding changes in the composition of the Peking government.[50]

There exists a widespread impression that wars between Chinese warlords were something like televised wrestling matches in the United States: a good deal of grunting and groaning, of posturing and grimacing, but little serious attempt to hurt each other. Many writers —especially "old China hands" but also scholars and Chinese authors —have written of the "comic-opera Chinese wars."[51] The essence of such opinions was expressed in an after-dinner statement attributed to a Chinese admiral. "China's wars," he said, "are always civil."[52] There is a great deal of truth in that remark. The commanders of opposing forces were sometimes friends or former colleagues, and they were willing to deal gently with each other. If one army was clearly superior to another, the latter deemed it useless to fight bitterly to a foreseen defeat. Men in the ranks who had joined the army to find a bit of security and opportunity were little interested in fierce fighting that offered neither.

Nevertheless, warlord wars were seldom as frivolous as some old China hands make them out to be. A French writer, for example, contemptuously labeled the First Chih-Feng War a "comic opera,"[53] yet there were thousands of casualties in this war.[54] After the battle for Tientsin between Feng Yü-hsiang and Li Ching-lin in December 1925 —during Feng's war with Chang Tso-lin—4,308 soldiers were treated at a hospital in the suburbs of Peking.[55] Moreover, medical care in Chinese armies at that time was poor, and relatively light wounds could result in death owing to lack of treatment.*[56] In addition, wars seemed to become more violent as the warlord period progressed.

The most tragic characteristic of warlordism was the oppression, injury, and hardship that it inflicted on the Chinese people. During the warlord era there was little constructive governmental action, even in critical emergencies. When famine or plague struck, provincial warlord governments often failed to provide effective relief; their disorder and greed also rendered it difficult or impossible for foreign re-

---

* A report from the American consul at Hankow to the American legation at Peking in June 1927 indicates the state of medical care in the Chinese military at that time. It concerns soldiers of the National Revolutionary Army, who presumably were better cared for than those of most warlord armies, and it describes the results of an informal investigation conducted by several American businessmen who reported "distressing conditions among the wounded in the hospitals which they visited. While the majority of cases were not of a serious character, there were many seriously wounded men, a large number of whom were operative cases. Many of the patients were lying on bare stone floors without covering of any kind, unwashed, unattended, and the dressings on their wounds appeared never to have been changed. The sanitary arrangements of the places visited were intolerable and created a feeling of fear for the general health of the patients in the buildings, as well as that of the community. The whole atmosphere of the buildings visited was that of mismanagement, insanitation, discomfort, and thorough uncleanliness." Earlier in the report, the consul wrote that no apparent provisions had been made for taking care of wounded Nationalist soldiers besides supplying the troops themselves with first-aid kits, and that only after the fighting at Hsüchow, when some 500 wounded men a day were sent back from the front to Hankow, were any hospital facilities set up. (Despatch from F. P. Lockhart, U.S. consul at Hankow, to the Secretary of State, June 22, 1927, 893.00/9246.)

lief organizations to aid the suffering people. Moreover, confiscatory taxation, the forced planting of opium instead of food crops, the widespread banditry, the dislocation of communications, and other features of warlordism all conspired to produce famine or near-famine conditions. The American Red Cross quite correctly attributed the widespread famine of 1928–29 primarily to warlordism.[57]

The warlords tapped almost every conceivable source of revenue, and in the process worked tremendous hardships on the people. The land tax, which was completely in the hands of provincial military leaders after 1919, became an instrument of terrible exploitation.[58] The tax was increased in many areas. For example, after Chang Tsung-ch'ang became the warlord of Shantung, land taxes rose to five or six times their former amount.[59] In some areas, there was a proliferation of supplementary taxes, which after a few years became the normal taxes to which further supplements might be added.[60] Land taxes were sometimes collected far in advance.[61] Pearl Buck writes of one region where the warlord collected the land tax for ten years in advance, even though the area was swept by famine.[62]

When such a rapacious warlord was ousted from control of a region, his successor had the choice of collecting the taxes dating from the year reached by his predecessor, or declaring that the latter's exactions were illegal and starting collections from the current year. From the peasant's point of view, of course, the difference was academic; it all added up to his paying the taxes several times over. In Kwangtung there were even instances of people taxed for land held by their ancestors that was no longer in their hands.[63]

Many additional taxes were also created. After the terms of a foreign loan in 1913 had placed control of the salt gabelle in the hands of foreigners, regional authorities countered by adding other taxes to salt: a salt transportation tax, a price tax, and so on. In Szechwan there were twenty-six types of taxes added to the basic salt tax by 1924.[64] In Kwangtung there were areas where one was taxed for owning a pig, taxed if one's daughter married, taxed for owning geese, and taxed for many other reasons.[65] The government at Changsha imposed a tax on postal parcels coming from outside the province.[66] In Fukien, where tax collectors were particularly imaginative, door plates were among the many items taxed.[67]

Many special taxes were levied at irregular intervals for particular purposes, or ostensibly particular purposes. There were taxes for "university expenses," "military expenses," "self-government expenses," and so forth.[68] In 1927, Sun Ch'uan-fang, a warlord opposing the northern advance of the National Revolutionary Army, ordered all districts in the area under his control to pay a special land tax to finance a last desperate stand.[69] In Shantung there were a number of special taxes, including, when the harvest was particularly good, a "rich harvest tax."[70] The following list, which illustrates the extraordinary tax burdens of the time, shows the taxes levied in Amoy as of January 1924:[71]

pork tax
pig tax
pig slaughter tax
pig-rearing tax
pig-inspecting tax
surtax on pork for educational expenses
fish tax
tax on fish hongs
tax on fish shops
cockle, crab, and prawn tax
sea product tax
night soil tax
fruit tax
bamboo shoot tax
tobacco and wine tax (stamp duty)
wine tax (local wine)
onion and garlic tax
oyster shell tax
lime tax
narcissus bulb tax
chicken and duck tax
sanitation tax (for cleaning streets)
brothel license fee
brothel tax
brick and tile tax
lumber tax
lower-class prostitute singing tax
street lamp tax
surtax for electric lamps
police tax
cotton tax
hawker's tax
cotton yarn and cotton thread tax
flour tax
bean, sugar, and oil tax
license fee for prostitute on call

transportation, or sea protection tax
tax on employees of fishing boats
superstition tax (on candles, paper money for funerals, etc.)
trade tax
householders' protection tax
opium-smoking lamp tax
license fee on opium smoking
license fee on milk
passenger tax for water police
pig seller's tax
tax on opium cultivation
shoe tax
gambling tax (on gambling houses)
fuel and rice tax
water boat tax
cow and horse sanitation tax
vegetable tax
shop tax
theater tax
paper tax
tea tax
tinfoil tax
sugar malt tax
firecracker tax
deed inspecting fee
deed-stamping fee
land tax
field tax
likin
beancake tax
examination fee for prepared medicine
license fee for discharging goods from steamer
piece goods tax
rice and wheat vermicelli tax

The warlords exploited many other sources of revenue in ways that directly or indirectly imposed hardships on all classes of the Chinese population. Railroads were a major source of revenue, and were taxed for all they were worth.* Heavy freight charges plus special taxes and surtaxes were even wrung from exasperated foreigners, contrary to treaty arrangements, by the simple expedient of not having freight cars available for those who did not pay.[72] Transit taxes, or likin, were exacted time after time on a single shipment of goods.[73] For example, a shipment of paper worth $1,350 when landed at Shanghai was shipped up the Yangtze to Chengtu. It passed through eleven tax stations, the last being at the very gates of Chengtu, and the illegal taxation collected on it by regional authorities totaled $2,150.[74] In some cases, warlords acquired revenue by establishing state monopolies over the manufacture of certain goods.[75] Forced loans, for which bonds were issued that were presumably redeemable over a period of years, were sometimes exacted from certain sections of the populace.[76] Contributions were forced from chambers of commerce by threatening to loot their cities.[77] Opium monopolies were auctioned off. Many of the so-called Opium Suppression Bureaus were actually warlord agencies for taxing opium in the guise of fines.[78] Warlords sometimes issued their own currency; in at least one province, these provincial notes were stamped to the effect that they would be redeemed for silver "after the war."[79] Finally, there were foreign loans. Tuan Ch'i-jui, for example, received large sums from the Japanese—the so-called Nishihara loans.[80]

Besides having to pay innumerable direct and indirect taxes, the people were forced to serve warlord armies as porters, and to provide carts and animals for transport purposes. At the beginning of the Second Chih-Feng War, for example, Wu P'ei-fu demanded 4,000 carts from several districts, each cart with a driver and two donkeys.[81] An American consul at Foochow gave the following description of the movement of 20,000 men from Fukien into Chekiang in the middle of 1924:[82]

Units of troops stationed in various parts of the Province had to be brought to Foochow, and other units sent to take their place; for it must be understood that armies in China are personal armies, and when one military com-

---

* Not infrequently, two or more warlords would control sections of a railroad. This could lead to a virtual standstill of traffic, for each warlord was unwilling to permit rolling stock to enter an area controlled by a rival or a potential rival. Therefore, nothing moved; at least nothing moved very far. This occasionally created serious situations. For example, in January 1925 when Peking badly needed fuel and food, which were ordinarily shipped to the city in large quantities over the Peking-Hankow Railroad, the warlord of Honan refused to permit railroad cars on this line to leave his own domain. Incidentally, the warlord of Honan at that time was supposed to be a close ally and subordinate of the warlord of Peking.

mander moves his forces out of a certain region, all the troops owing personal allegiance to that commander, no matter where stationed or scattered, must go with him, and their places [are] subsequently taken by troops owing allegiance to his successor in power. Thus, the movement of 20,000 troops from Foochow into Chekiang Province involved the moving, over a greater or less territory, of very nearly if not quite double that number of troops. When it is noted that, in this region totally devoid of railways and almost equally devoid of roads capable of allowing vehicular traffic, to move 5000 men requires not less than 200 boats, if the transportation is by water, or 1500 human load-carriers, if by land; that troops are billeted on the populace; that boats and carriers are seized and used without compensation; and that the troops are generally unpaid and do more or less general foraging and looting along the way; it can be seen what a strain on the economic life of this region the simple movement of 20,000 troops constituted. Two other elements in this situation must be noted. One is that there was imminent danger of a conflict between the forces moving out of Foochow and those taking over the reins of power; hence trade had to fear not only seizure of transport facilities but also the possibility of reprisal for appearing to assist one faction or the other. The second is that the commander moving out had virtually to be "bought out" with a promise of continued financial support, the amount being $200,000 monthly—$200,000 a month for the support of an army outside the Province in addition to an at least equal sum for the support of that remaining, to be borne, of course, by the trade.

The practice of using peasant carts and labor for temporary purposes was not new in China. In earlier periods, however, the peasant received money for his services; the military also made some attempt to be reasonable about how long they used a peasant and how far from home they took him.[83] This solicitude decreased as the warlord period progressed.

The people suffered directly from the abuse of disorderly troops. Soldiers in pairs or small groups held up peasants and townspeople on the roads outside towns, and sometimes in the towns themselves.[84] Rudeness and physical abuse were common. When warlords fought, there was always the possibility that either the victors or the defeated would loot nearby communities; so cities and towns in a war zone would take on "a curious, shut look, waiting, tense. The richer families send their women and children away, and day after day the streets are full of this procession of the rich, fleeing. The poorest, the riffraff who have nothing to lose, take on an expectant look, their dreams filled with looting."[85]

The following is an eyewitness description of the looting of Huchow, a large town near Shanghai, in the fall of 1924. The American Consul-General at Shanghai called the account from which this excerpt comes "reasonably accurate."[86]

[Two generals reached Huchow with 5,000 soldiers.] ... They began immediate negotiations with the Chamber of Commerce for a large sum of money in lieu of sacking the city. After much bargaining $100,000 was paid over to them and they went away. Later in the day other of the troops ... began to arrive on small boats they had been able to get, and by foot, thoroughly disgusted and worn out. Hearing of the neat little sum so readily paid to their comrades in arms, they at once demanded a like settlement. This was impossible at the time and they were put off.

[Early the next morning they began looting the city.]

Later I went out to the street and saw the people still running excitedly back and forth. The first place I noticed broken into was a shoe store. The board planks used to cover the windows had been broken off, the window smashed in and the place completely rifled and all the stock of shoes carried off. The next place was a watch and clock shop. It had met the same fate. The plate-glass window had been smashed, the show-cases completely broken up, and all the watches and smaller pieces of jewelry scooped into bags and taken away. The clocks, being large and heavy, were not taken. Walking down the street I passed many soldiers in more or less ragged uniform, staggering along under their loads of watches, dollars, and other small but valuable loot they had taken. In every case they had their guns in position ready for use. Many carried pistols with hammers cocked. One soldier ordered three women standing in a shop door watching the proceedings to hold out their hands, and took a small cheap silver ring roughly off one of the women's hands. He bent it a little, fitting it to his own finger as he walked away down the street.

Some of the soldiers went running through the streets shouting for the people to stand aside, which they did. This frightened them more than ever, which the soldiers especially desired. One had a large bag, larger than an ordinary 10 lb. bag of sugar, completely filled with dollars. As he ran, he stumbled and the dollars scattered over the ground in every direction. But he did not stop so much as to look round. Some bystanders tried to pick up some but two or three soldiers shouted out and stopped it. One man did pick up a dollar and ran down a side street evidently unafraid of the fire of the soldier. They would step up to a man on the street, point their guns at him and demand his money. If he refused they threatened [to] fire. He would inevitably hand out what little he had, perhaps two dollars, four dimes, fifteen coppers. But the dimes and coppers were refused. Nothing was accepted but dollars and banknotes. A number of the soldiers went to the city temple, drew their guns on the shopkeepers, peddlers, customers, tea-drinkers, etc., and ordered that their dollars and banknotes be put into handkerchiefs and towels spread on a table. More than $600 was thereby netted.

... Many shops finished by the soldiers were immediately entered by local ruffians and cleaned up of the less valuable property left. Large silk shops were looted, jewelry shops, silver and gold shops, and any place where valuable but light property might be obtained.

The Bank of China and the Bank of Communications were looted time and again by different crowds of soldiers coming in from time to time.

After a war in Kiangsu in 1924, an investigating commission reported that many houses had been burned, many people had been killed, and many others had lost all they owned. Peasants fleeing invading armies left fields unplanted or harvests unreaped. In a district of Hunan, it was reported that of all peasants drafted to serve as porters for the military, less than half ever returned home.[87]

The disorders caused by warlordism also facilitated foreign political and military interference in China. Between 1902 and 1914 foreign investment in China doubled, and in the following fifteen years it doubled again, reaching an estimated total of $3.3 billion. By the 1920's, foreign investors owned nearly half the Chinese cotton industry, the largest industry in the country. They owned a third of the railways outright and held mortgages on the rest. They owned and operated more than half the shipping in Chinese waters, and carried nearly four-fifths of China's foreign and coastal trade. China's adverse balance of trade grew to $1.5 billion by 1924, and to twice that sum in the next ten years.[88]

With this much at stake economically, foreigners inevitably became involved in warlord politics. Their involvement generally took the form of military aid and subsidies, and was accordingly welcomed by the leading warlords, some of whom set up special offices to handle such matters. Foreigners viewed their outlays as an investment, and one that might pay handsome dividends if the man they backed were to succeed in unifying China under his leadership. Japan, for example, was particularly interested in Manchuria, and supplied the Manchurian warlord with advice, weapons, and other assistance. The Japanese also furnished large sums to Tuan Ch'i-jui early in the warlord period, which Tuan used to build up his army. Japanese intelligence agents kept a close watch on Feng Yü-hsiang when he stepped into national politics, and had some fleeting hopes of cultivating a pro-Japanese attitude in him.

The Soviet Union was also openly involved in Chinese domestic politics. Although Soviet aid went chiefly to the Kuomintang-Communist alliance until the 1927 split, when the Russians were expelled from the country, Feng Yü-hsiang was at the same time receiving material aid, organizational assistance, and military advisers from the Soviet Union. The British were widely rumored to be supporting Wu P'ei-fu. There were also unconfirmed reports that British interests provided funds and rifles to Chang Tso-lin in 1925, at the time he was fighting Feng Yü-hsiang, who was backed by the Russians.[89]

Foreign nationals served in virtually every important warlord camp, usually acting as advisers and military instructors. (Doubtless many were intelligence agents for their own nations.) Feng Yü-hsiang, for example, had at least one German, one Italian, and one Japanese officer in his army besides his Russian advisers. One of the chiefs of

Chang Tso-lin's arsenal at Mukden was an Englishman, who, incidentally, designed an improved mortar for Chang's use. One of the Britisher's chief aides was an American. There were many other foreigners working for warlords.

Another foreign activity in China was supplying arms and munitions to the various warlords. Foreigners brought arms into the country in small packages and by the shipload. An Arms Embargo Agreement was signed by most of the major powers in 1919, but several countries did not sign it, and few others took it seriously.[90] Arms merchants of all nationalities continued to find plenty of customers along the China coast.[91]

The supply of arms by foreigners caused great resentment among Chinese intellectuals. As one of them wrote:[92]

In all the civil wars, the rifles and field guns come from abroad. The bullets and shells come from abroad. Bombs and powder and hardware all come from abroad. The money [for the wars] comes from abroad. It has gone so far that in recent years the flour and military provisions have come from abroad. Only the blood and flesh of our dead countrymen who kill one another on the battlefields are Chinese.

Although some warlords had nationalistic ideas and aspirations, warlordism as a social phenomenon was the essence of anti-nationalism. Nationalism aspired to a unified nation; warlordism throve on division. It inhibited the growth of new intellectual and economic forces that could develop the productive capacities of the nation's physical and human resources. Nationalism demanded the elimination of foreign controls and privileges; warlordism facilitated foreign military invasion, political intervention, and economic exploitation. Nationalism called for pride in the nation's past and present, and hope in its future; warlordism fostered demoralization and hopelessness at home, and destroyed the prestige of the nation abroad. Nationalism meant patriotism; warlordism meant self-seeking. Warlordism, indeed, could exist only at nationalism's expense.

However, warlordism was the context from which the most important Chinese nationalist movements arose. The Kuomintang was reorganized and expanded at the height of the warlord period. At almost the same time, Chinese Communism was born and began its early development. A whole generation of Chinese intellectuals came of age under warlord governments. The cumulative influence of warlordism on millions of Chinese children and adults is incalculable, but clearly enormous. The precise nature of that influence is obscure, and must remain obscure until we know more about the major warlords themselves. Feng Yü-hsiang was one such warlord.

2. A Soldier of the Manchus

There is a saying in China that "a great man does not talk about his lowly birth." In an earlier period, this maxim may have reflected a genuine value, but by the time Feng Yü-hsiang became prominent such notions were viewed with increasing disfavor. In theory, at least, China was entering the period of the exaltation of the common man. The old saying was no longer applicable; a man's lowly birth might even be a political asset, and Feng was not reticent about the humble environment from which he came. The surroundings of his early life were also rather fitting, for this future warlord spent the years from his birth in 1882 to 1912 in and around the camps of the regional armies.

Childhood

At the time Li Hung-chang organized the Anhwei Army, one of the local forces that came under his general command was led by Liu Ming-ch'uan, and was called the Ming-tzu chün, or Ming Army.[1] Feng Yü-mou, the son of an impoverished peasant family, joined this army to escape a life of ill-paid work as a bricklayer, hired laborer, and servant. In the army, he gradually advanced to the rank of platoon commander.

The Ming Army participated in several rugged campaigns: first against the Taipings, then against the Nien rebels, and finally, under Tso Tsung-t'ang, against Muslim rebels in Shensi during the 1870's. After that, the army went to Shantung. There Feng married a young Miss Yü, and a year later their first son was born. When the Ming Army was disbanded the following year, Feng took his family back to Anhwei; but soon afterward they returned to his wife's home in Shantung. They were very poor, and life was difficult; Feng again sought to improve his circumstances by joining an army, this time the Anhwei Army. In 1881, he was sent to Hsingchichen in the province of Chihli. The next year his wife gave birth to their second son, whom they named Chi-shan. It was he who grew up to be known as Feng Yü-hsiang. Feng Yü-hsiang's mother ultimately bore five more sons, but only these first two lived to manhood.[2]

Shortly after the second son was born, the family moved to Paoting, and when he was two years old they moved again, this time to a small town a mile or so outside Paoting named K'angkechuang. Young Chi-shan spent most of his boyhood until the age of fourteen in this area, and thereafter continued to speak with a Paoting accent. It was not an easy boyhood. Money was always scarce and trips to the pawn shop were frequent; even the family bedding was pawned on occasion. Food had to be purchased on credit at times, and interest rates were high.

Perhaps the family income would have been more adequate if some of it had not gone for opium; but both Feng's parents were addicts. Years later, the memory of their vain attempts to break the habit was still seared into Feng's mind. His childhood memories in general were somber; as an adult, his only happy recollections were of theatrical shows put on by troupes of traveling players. Such shows were almost the only formal entertainment available to the villagers.[3]

When the boy was ten years old, he was suddenly given a profession and a new name, both of which were to identify him for the rest of his life. The troops among whom his father served were known as the "Father and Son Soldiers," thanks to the practice of listing officers' sons on the payroll even when they were too young to drill or perform other military duties. There were only a limited number of such positions, and the competition to obtain them was understandably keen. In 1892 there was a sudden vacancy, and friends of Feng's father who happened to be at headquarters immediately acted to enroll his son. But they either had forgotten or did not know his given name. Fearing that someone else might fill the vacancy if they took time to inquire, one of the men put on a bold front and confidently wrote down the name "Feng Yü-hsiang." In this way, Feng simultaneously acquired a name and entered upon the career that would make that name famous throughout China.[4]

Feng's mother died about this time, and the boy henceforth could usually be found in the army camp with his father. Although he studied briefly with a tutor to acquire the only formal education he ever had, his real school was the army. The year after his enrollment, he was given a spear and practiced throwing it at a target. When his father was ordered to Taku to help build gun mounts there, Feng went along, helping in the work and following his father on patrol.

By the time he was fourteen, he was already as tall as some of the adult soldiers in the camp. At that age, when the troops returned from Taku to Paoting in 1896, Feng entered the army as a full-fledged soldier.[5]

The Young Soldier

As a regular member of the Anhwei Army, Feng began to receive training in military drill, as well as some lessons in extra-military activities. One evening soon after he had become a soldier, some of his friends persuaded him to gamble. He lost far more than he was able to pay, and spent three years paying the winners off in small monthly installments.[6] A few months after he had paid his debt he was again persuaded to play, and again he lost. Penniless and unhappy, he picked up a knife with his right hand and threatened his left: "If you gamble again, I'll cut you off!" This threat was not sufficient, and a few months later he again gambled and lost. Once more he threatened his hand with a knife, and this time the hand must have been impressed, for Feng apparently never gambled again.[7]

It was just after Feng became a regular soldier that he also learned "what a fearful thing wine is." His friends cajoled him into drinking so heavily that he was ill for several days with a most impressive hangover, including "bubbles all over [his] body." He understandably resolved never again to drink "even a single glass."[8]

These peccadilloes—and perhaps a few more that Feng was not so ready to confess—seem the natural consequence of a young boy's association with older soldiers. But Feng was no ordinary boy, and these few incidents apparently represent the extent of his ventures into petty dissipation. He was intelligent and industrious, and devoted most of his time to work and study. He seems to have believed that the contrast between his energy and conscientiousness and the more ordinary qualities of his fellows would lead to rapid advancement.

Among other things, Feng's ambition led him to rise early and cry out commands to a deserted drill field. In those years, only a very limited number of men in the Anhwei Army were qualified to lead military drill, and drill leaders were given extra pay in proportion to the number of men they could handle. Feng was then probably an ordinary infantryman, although he may have served as a cook for a short time.[9] Whatever his status, he sought to improve it by becoming a drill leader. Every morning before dawn, Feng went to the empty drill field and marched imaginary soldiers in precision maneuvers. The field rang with his cries: "Attention!," "Present arms!," "At ease!," and so on. Feng said he did this for the incredible period of four years, during which he "accomplished an astonishing amount."[10] One of his accomplishments was to become known as the man with the high voice who disturbed everyone's morning sleep. But he also achieved his goal, for by 1901 he was assistant drill instructor.[11]

In a modern American army, Feng would be known as an "eager beaver," or worse. Soldiers of the Anhwei Army found a different label for him; they called him "wai-kuo tien-hsin," or "foreign snack," the idea being that as a Chinese soldier he was destined to be killed by foreigners anyway, so his noisy industriousness was wasted effort.[12]

In 1900 Feng had his first fleeting contact with foreigners. When Boxers became active in the Paoting area, the troops stationed there were ordered to suppress them. The officers, however, admired the Boxers' anti-foreign activity, and ignored their orders. Boxer drills were openly conducted in the vicinity of Paoting until April, when an order came through commanding the military to train the Boxers. Soon afterward, Boxers, with assistance from the military, burned a number of Christian churches in the region; and at least once Feng went along and watched the blaze. When the Allied armies finally broke through to Peking, they sent troops to Paoting, and the Chinese military units departed. Feng was assigned to rear-guard duties, and was one of the last soldiers to leave the city. Fearing capture by foreign troops, he hid for several days in the home of a friend, and then walked to the village some 70 miles away where his unit was quartered.[13]

In the following year, 1901, Feng became very dissatisfied with conditions in the Anhwei Army. The food was bad and insufficient; Feng often had to supplement his rations with food bought with his own money. Officers were corrupt and found many pretexts to deduct portions of the soldiers' pay. Moreover, many officers were incompetent, and Feng lamented their inability to perform their duties properly.[14] One might speculate that he also lamented the inability of his superiors to recognize promising subordinates, for Feng's industry and ambition had thus far yielded discouragingly meager rewards. It was at this time that he came across a number of booklets used by Yüan Shih-k'ai in the training of his new army.[15] Feng was impressed by them, and when one of his friends left to join Yüan's army, Feng decided to follow his example. On April 27, 1902, Feng became a soldier in the third battalion of Yüan Shih-k'ai's Right Wing Guards Army.[16]

Not long afterward, he experienced what he later called the greatest disgrace of his life. Yüan Shih-k'ai, who had only recently been appointed Pei-yang ta-chen, moved his headquarters to Tientsin, and his troops followed. But one of the provisions of the Boxer Protocol was that Chinese troops could not be stationed within 20 li, about 7 miles, of Tientsin. Therefore some of Yüan's units changed into police uniforms in order to enter the city.[17] For Feng this was a humiliating illustration of the weakness of China vis-à-vis the West. At the time it engendered anti-foreign feelings in Feng, but a few years later these feelings turned against the Manchus.

Feng found conditions in the Right Wing Guards Army far superior to those in the Anhwei Army. Some of the officers were illiterate, but there were few who could not drill men. Marksmanship was taught, and though Feng disapproved of the methods used, he admitted that the results were good.[18] Moreover, Feng found the new army much more appreciative of his talents and energies. He seems to have been highly regarded by his superiors from the outset. Indeed, he was so valued that on one occasion, when outstanding soldiers were being selected to compose a special company, Feng's superior hid him from the selecting officer.[19] Feng's acknowledged ability, plus the fact that the army was being expanded, opened the way for steady promotion. A few months after he joined, he became second sergeant, and five months later first sergeant. By 1905 he had risen to platoon commander. Some of his promotions were obtained through examinations, in which Feng seems invariably to have made the highest marks.[20]

In 1905 the Right Wing Guards Army was reorganized to become the 6th Division of the Peiyang Army. Tuan Ch'i-jui was the division commander, and one of the brigade commanders was another Peiyang stalwart, Lu Chien-chang. Feng continued to demonstrate eagerness, industry, and ability, and he advanced steadily in rank. By the end of the year he was a company commander.[21] Even more important, he had attracted the attention and friendship of Lu Chien-chang. Lu liked Feng, and looked upon him as a promising young man. Although Lu had no daughter of his own, in 1907 he gave his wife's niece to Feng in marriage.[22] Few details are available about the relationship between Lu and Feng during those years, but it was to prove an extremely important connection for Feng during and after the revolution.

The next two years were largely devoted to training in Nanyüan, on the outskirts of Peking. Then, in 1907, Hsü Shih-ch'ang, one of Yüan Shih-k'ai's principal protégés, went to Manchuria as viceroy. He took with him the 3rd Division of the Peiyang Army and two mixed brigades that had been organized from elements of the 5th and 6th Divisions. Feng was one of those involved in the transfer, and he became company commander in the 1st Mixed Brigade, which was stationed in Hsinminfu.[23]

The following years in Manchuria were exciting and profitable ones for Feng. First of all, there was intensive study. Since his first days in the army, Feng had been attempting to educate himself, and now his efforts were supplemented by regular lecture courses that all officers were required to attend. In addition to theoretical studies, there was the practical work of leading men. Although there was no war at the time, there was fighting, most of it against the perennial enemy, bandit gangs. Bandits sometimes formed small armies, and occasionally had better discipline and more effective organization than the government troops. Army units often permitted the bandits to flee, and when battle did occur the troops did not always win.

Bandit chiefs even had a certain consciousness of rank. Feng once captured a bandit leader who refused to answer his questions on the ground that Feng was of too low a rank to interrogate him. This infuriated Feng, who had the bandit's head cut off and displayed for all to see. In the meantime, however, he had reported the capture; and when his superiors asked him to produce the captive, Feng—having exceeded his authority in ordering the execution—was in trouble. Fortunately, an even higher authority sent an order to execute the bandit, so, after a few days' wait, the execution was routinely reported.[24]

In this Manchurian period, which lasted until the autumn of 1911, Feng acquired many of the impressions and ideas that he later utilized to formulate his own training programs. Probably some of them came from classroom work, but it was always to actual conditions, events, and experiences that he referred when he later wrote down his ideas about training troops. For example, Feng saw that extensive gambling among the troops was bad for discipline, especially when the officers gambled with the men, and he concluded that gambling should be forbidden in the army.[25] He witnessed the inability of some soldiers to withstand the hardships of simple campaign conditions. They tired easily, and could not keep up with the bandits they were pursuing. They got cold at night, and lit fires that attracted bandit attacks. Feng decided that soldiers should be trained to a peak of physical fitness and be prepared to endure harsh conditions while on campaign.[26] He saw filthy latrines used by hundreds of men, and blamed the officers for ignoring the elementary principles of hygiene and sanitation; they alone were responsible, since the men could not be expected to know any better.[27]

Probably the most important general concept that developed in Feng's mind at this time concerned the position and obligations of an officer. He attributed most of the many ills he observed to incompetent officers and to the great gap between officers and men. The men's food was often poor and insufficient. This would not happen, Feng decided, if the officers ate with the men. Only by sharing the hardships of the men could officers be assured of loyal support, and a unit be assured of the best possible morale and fighting efficiency.[28] All these ideas sound elementary enough, and they cannot be considered revolutionary even for early twentieth-century China. But in most Chinese armies they were not put into practice, especially during the warlord period. Much of Feng's later fame derived from the simple fact that he actually implemented these principles.

During the years in Manchuria, Feng acquired many ideas about military organization and training, and he obtained a good deal of practical experience. At the same time, he was also having other experiences, and learning about other ideas—ideas concerning revolution. He began reading revolutionary literature, and even writing some. But before this, of course, he had to learn to read and write.

A Soldier's Education

Feng Yü-hsiang's father, although himself illiterate, shared the high esteem for education common to most Chinese at that time. As a consequence, he arranged for his eldest son, Yü-hsiang's brother, to attend school, despite the perennial financial difficulties of the Feng family. The boy went to school for five years and nine months, after which he left to join the cavalry. However, the teacher had already been paid for the entire sixth year, of which three months remained. It was decided to send Feng Yü-hsiang, who was then nine years old, to the school for those three months.[29] This was Feng's first experience with formal education.

Feng looked forward eagerly, if fearfully, to beginning school. When the day arrived, he put on his New Year's suit of clothes, and, with his father, who was dressed in his best uniform, set off for school. The schoolroom was one room in the teacher's home. The walls were splattered with ink and pitted with holes dug by mischievous children, but to young Yü-hsiang it was a place of opportunity. He kowtowed respectfully to the old man who was to be his teacher, and took the seat assigned him. He began his education by pronouncing characters as they were intoned by the teacher from the two primers of a Confucian education, *The Hundred Names* and the *Three-Character Classic*.[30]

In later years Feng remembered that the teacher liked to reprimand the pupils by tapping his pipe on their heads. He also recalled that the conversations between the teacher and his guests were more interesting than the lessons.[31] Little more remained in his memory, for he had to leave the school after his allotted three months. But he was enthusiastic about learning, and continued to study in and around the army barracks, with occasional assistance from a literate soldier. He made a writing brush by pushing a length of hemp through a stick of bamboo, and he practiced writing on slabs of metal or pieces of brick, using mud in lieu of ink.[32]

In 1893 Feng was allowed to attend another school for the entire year.[33] During that time, he read three classics of Chinese philosophy: *The Great Learning, The Doctrine of the Mean,* and *The Analects*. He also began to read the writings of Mencius. However, this was not reading in the Western sense of the word. Feng and his fellow pupils echoed the pronunciation of the teacher as he read the text aloud, but there was no attempt to teach them the meaning.[34] That was to come later. As it worked out, it came too late for Feng, who had to leave school at the end of the year. He had attended school for one year and three months, and that was all the formal education he would ever have.

It was about two years later that Feng formally entered the army as a regular soldier. The assiduity he displayed in the following years was not limited to the drill field. He read a remarkable amount for a semi-literate boy. For several years he read mostly novels, which were popular with boys his age in and out of the army, both for their content and because they were written in the vernacular, which made them far easier to read than more serious literature. Even so, they were not easy reading for Feng until he had painfully worked his way, with much rereading, through his first two choices: *The Investiture of the Gods* (Feng-shen yen-i), a Ming mythological novel, and *The Romance of the Three Kingdoms* (San-kuo-chih yen-i), the great Chinese novel of war and violence, friendship and treachery, set in the turbulent period following the Han dynasty. After his first reading of *The Romance of the Three Kingdoms,* Feng acquired a book of songs based on incidents in the novel; he compared the songs with passages in the book describing corresponding events, and in this way tried to understand more completely the meaning of the text.[35]

Work on these two novels evidently improved Feng's reading ability appreciably, for he subsequently read six books in quick succession. Three were of a popular nineteenth-century genre: novels idealizing the careers of historical officials. Full of violence and derring-do, these novels combined the Robin Hood theme with aspects of a modern detective story.* Feng later praised them for their representations of virtuous officials, in contrast to the other three works, which he criticized for their excessive concern with love affairs to the neglect of more edifying subjects.†[36]

During the last two or three years of the nineteenth century, Feng read and enjoyed some of China's most famous works of literature. These included *The Water Margin Novel* (Shui-hu chuan), better known in English as *All Men Are Brothers*; *Record of a Journey to the West* (Hsi-yu chi), part of which is translated by Arthur Waley in *Monkey*; and *Strange Records of the Liao Library* (Liao-chai chih-i), from which selections have been translated under the title *Strange Stories From a Chinese Studio*.[37] From these, Feng turned to two satirical novels that mock the ridiculous and vicious aspects of Chinese officialdom: *The Travels of Lao Ts'an* (Lao Ts'an yu-chi), and *The Unofficial History of the Literati* (Ju-lin wai-shih), translated into English as *The Scholars*. These works, Feng later said, "increased [his] love of literature."[38]

About the time Feng finished reading these novels, his education in military theory began. The first military book he studied was *The Detailed and Illustrated Book of Yüan Shih-k'ai's Training and Drill-*

---

* The pattern for this interesting genre was set by *The Judicial Cases of His Excellency Shih* (Shih kung an), published in 1838. This work, which sometimes bears the title *Strange Scenes of the One Hundred Judgments* (Pai-tuan ch'i-kuan), is based on the reputation of Shih Shih-lun, an official of the K'ang-hsi period, for efficiency, incorruptibility, and benevolence. The novel embellished and exaggerated these traits to fit the commoner's romantic conception of the ideal official who protects the poor and weak from the rich and powerful. Although the novel was not a genuine innovation in Chinese literature, its great success prompted a flurry of books on the same order. Feng comments on this work in *WTTSSH*, pp. 50–54, and Hummel, II, 653–54, has a biography of Shih Shih-lun. Feng took his courtesy name from one of the novels in this group. A character in *The Lasting Celebration of Peace* (Yung-ching sheng-p'ing) is named Ku Huan-chang (雇焕章). Feng changed the radical of the last character to make his courtesy name Huan-chang (煥璋), although many sources give it incorrectly as 煥章.

† These three works were *The Dressing Chamber* (Fen-chuang lou), *The Twice Flowering Plums* (Erh-tu mei), and *Spectacular Stories, Ancient and Modern* (Chin-ku ch'i-kuan). Although love affairs are central to the first two, it is surprising that Feng remembered the third as a work with so little content that it made "the reader's bones turn soft," for this celebrated collection of stories deals with a great range of subjects. Feng comments on these three books in *WTTSSH*, pp. 55–56.

ing Methods (Yüan shih hsün-lien ts'ao-fa yang-hsiang t'u-shuo). This was a bound set of small booklets that Yüan used in the training of his army. One of its sections was devoted to the qualities necessary for a general: bravery, humanity (*jen*), honesty, and the ability to train his men well and serve as an example to them.[39] Other sections described the requirements for noncommissioned officers, the important points soldiers must be made to understand, how the troops should behave on the march, and so on. Catechisms were commonly used as training devices, and the book included several of them. Two of these were as follows:[40]

Q. When the infantry attacks the enemy, what is the most important thing to do?
A. Fire [our] guns.
Q. Who gives instructions about firing guns?
A. The officers who lead the troops.
Q. What do they teach?
A. (1) How to estimate distance. (2) What size gun to use. (3) What to shoot at. (4) What method of firing to use. (5) When to fire. (6) [They] check to see if the soldiers are taking aim. (7) [They] check to see if the bullets are any good. (8) When to stop firing.
Q. When passing through villages in which there are many people, what rules must be observed?
A. Always look straight ahead, and not to the right or left.
Q. When the enemy is first sighted, what must the officers be most careful about?
A. Information about the enemy, and topography.
Q. What is meant by "information about the enemy"?
A. Whether the enemy is near or far; whether the enemy troops are few or numerous; what kind of troops they are [infantry, cavalry, etc.]; what positions they occupy. [Any information on] the actions of the enemy when marching or at rest is called "information about the enemy."

Before reading Yüan's book, Feng "had not known there was such a thing as military theory."[41] The discovery that there was, and it was available in Yüan Shih-k'ai's army, was a major reason for Feng's transfer to the Right Wing Guards Army. The move was immediately profitable in educational terms. Feng was among four men chosen from his company to attend a School for Officers and Soldiers in Hanchiashu, a village on the outskirts of Tientsin. Here he studied military strategy, fortifications, weapons, and topography. Feng and two of his classmates were particularly industrious, and sought out the teacher after class for instruction in arithmetic. There were classes every day, and Feng never missed one. He later appraised the instruction as "clear and basic," and his teacher as excellent.[42]

To supplement his instruction, Feng also read some military books not required by the school. While he was still in Hanchiashu, a fellow soldier introduced him to *The Study of Military Strategy in History*, a compilation by the late-Ch'ing regional leader Hu Lin-i of excerpts relating to military affairs from the *Tso Chuan*, the ancient commentary on *The Spring and Autumn Annals*, and from the *Comprehensive Mirror for Aid in Government*, Ssu-ma Kuang's great history of China.[43] Feng also read disquisitions on army etiquette, on leading troops, on scouting procedures for the infantry, and on other subjects.[44] In addition, he studied the writings of Sun-tzu, ancient China's most celebrated military writer, and declared them to be of great value.[45]

Feng asserted that "the period of greatest intensity in my search for knowledge" was the time he spent in Manchuria after 1907. His education there included military studies, for a school was set up so that all officers had to attend. Graduates of the War College served as teachers, and they taught such subjects as international law in wartime, the use of military maps, techniques of military command, and the history of the Russo-Japanese War.[46]

After Feng transferred to Yüan Shih-k'ai's army, his reading of nonmilitary books took a serious turn, away from the novels that had been his major literary diet until then. In Hanchiashu, where he was stationed from 1902 to 1905, Feng and a friend shared the expense of hiring a tutor. With this teacher Feng studied that portion of the Confucian canon called the Four Books—*The Analects, Mencius, The Great Learning*, and *The Doctrine of the Mean*. Feng was very pleased with the instruction, and claimed that he remembered each sentence for many years, but a few years later, in Manchuria, he complained that he still could not read literary Chinese with any proficiency.[47]

While in Hanchiashu, Feng also read several essays by the celebrated writer and reform leader Liang Ch'i-ch'ao, who, Feng declared, would have been a truly great scholar if he "had not taken the wrong road in his politics."[48] As a result of an allusion by Liang to *The Simplified Record of History* (Kang-chien i-chih-lu), a summary of a summary of Ssu-ma Kuang's *Comprehensive Mirror for Aid in Government*, Feng went out and bought all 16 volumes of that work.[49] This was apparently Feng's most ambitious excursion into the realm of Chinese history. He also read a book of letters and training songs written by Tseng Kuo-fan; later he used these songs in training his own troops, as did other warlords who appreciated their efficacy.[50] It was also just before going to Manchuria that Feng first read books dealing with non-Chinese affairs. There were two such books, which he obtained about 1904 or 1905. One was the *Comprehensive History of the World* (which Feng found confusing),[51] and the other was *Women of the Five Continents,* by an American missionary.[52]

After Feng went to Hsinminfu in 1907, he bought a dozen or so booklets containing biographical sketches of Admiral Nelson, George Washington, Peter the Great, and other famous figures. The booklets were written for children, and Feng found them "easy to read and easy to remember."[53] This was the extent of Feng's acquaintance with the world beyond the borders of China.

Feng's command of written Chinese was still limited in 1907, and he sought help from his roommate, an army doctor who was well grounded in Chinese literature. "When I read novels . . . ," he complained, "I understand every sentence. But when I read such works as the *Comprehensive Mirror* . . . , I find it all a jumble, and there are a number of places that I cannot understand. What should I do?" At the doctor's urging Feng diligently studied classical essays, and with the doctor's help he acquired a reasonable command of literary Chinese.[54]

In sum, as of 1911 Feng had read most of China's famous novels, had read some rather elementary books and booklets relating to military training, and had acquired some familiarity with a few works of Chinese philosophy and history. The classes conducted in the Peiyang Army presumably acquainted him with a few facts about Western military practices, but his knowledge of Western history and of Western civilization in general was extremely limited.

This last was probably the most significant of all Feng's educational shortcomings, for ideas of Western origin dominated the Chinese political and intellectual scene at the time he was closest to national power. He was potentially more receptive to the implications of these Western concepts than most of his warlord contemporaries, as later chapters will show. But educationally, Feng could never catch up. After the Revolution of 1911, his opportunities for study steadily diminished as he acquired increased responsibilities. Even more important, he did not know what to study, so that his continued assiduity did not pay the dividends it might have paid if it had been properly directed. In understanding the political and social movements that surged through postrevolutionary China, Feng was always a step behind.

The Soldier Becomes a Rebel

In the middle of November 1908, the Emperor Kuang-hsü died. Feng Yü-hsiang is said to have wept and gone into mourning over his death.[55] At that time he was still a loyal soldier, and the thought of revolution was far from his mind.

One day Feng was reading a book by Tseng Kuo-fan when a fellow officer, Sun Chien-sheng, entered his quarters. Sun glanced at the book, grimaced, and inquired whether Feng was "still hoping to become a loyal official and a filial son." Feng asked what was wrong with those goals. "I don't oppose anyone's becoming a filial son," declared Sun, "but I cannot approve of anyone's being a loyal official. You just wait here a moment and I will get you two books to read. Then you will know what I mean."[56]

The books that Sun Chien-sheng gave Feng, with earnest admonitions to keep them well hidden, were *The Diary of Ten Days at Yangchow* (Yang-chou shih-jih chi), by Wang Hsiu-ch'u, and *The Record of the Massacre at Chiating* (Chia-ting t'u-ch'eng chi-lüeh), by Chu Tzu-su. Each work describes the fall of a Chinese town to the Manchu invaders of the seventeenth century. They were bloody events; one modern source estimates that over twenty thousand people were killed at Chiating, and far more at Yangchow.[57] The two accounts given to Feng are replete with gory details, as in the following description of Manchu soldiers herding captured Chinese women at Yangchow:[58]

The women wore long chains around their necks . . . ; they stumbled at every step so that they were covered with mud. Here and there on the ground lay small babies who were either trodden under the hooves of horses or the feet of men. The ground was stained with blood and covered with mutilated and dismembered bodies, and the sound of sobbing was heard everywhere in the open fields. Every gutter and pond was filled with corpses lying upon one another. The blood turned the water to a deep greenish-red colour, and the ponds were filled to the brim.

Feng said he was roused to a fury by reading these two books. "Cold sweat broke out over my body . . . ," he wrote. "I involuntarily ground my teeth and swore to avenge [the massacred Chinese] and to restore the freedom of my people."[59] This incident, which occurred in 1908, combined with several others to turn Feng toward the path of revolution. Early in 1909 Hsü Shih-ch'ang left Manchuria and was replaced by Hsi-liang, whose arrogance and corruption angered Feng and some of his friends.[60] In August of that year, China signed an agreement giving Japan permission to reconstruct the Antung-Mukden Railway, a concession Feng resented.[61] But doubtless the most fundamental cause of Feng's change of heart was simply the influence of his associates.

In Manchuria, Feng was friendly with several officers who were anti-Manchu, although not active revolutionaries. They were "good-hearted, enthusiastic officers who ardently detested the obscurantism of the Ch'ing court."[62] Their ideas confirmed Feng's own observations of corruption in the Ch'ing government and army, and of Manchu inadequacy in the face of foreign aggression. From this point, it was but a short step to a completely anti-Manchu position.

This shared anti-Manchu feeling, and perhaps a common consciousness of educational deficiencies, led Feng and a few friends to join together in a study group that they named the Society for the Study of Military Arts.[63] The members met regularly, usually early in the morning, to study and discuss writings on various aspects of military activity. They also discussed current events, and members reported to the group on newspaper articles and editorials that they had read. They memorized passages of two or three hundred characters and practiced writing them. They also attempted to relate contemporary events to principles or theories that they were studying.[64]

We do not know how their time was apportioned between military topics and social and political issues, especially during 1909 and 1910. It is clear, however, that the group did not at any time have a concrete political program. Though the subjects they studied went beyond the "military arts," their purpose was mostly self-education, not political agitation.[65] It is doubtful that the group ever became as consciously revolutionary as Feng liked to recall in later years, although he and his friends became increasingly dissatisfied with the Manchus.

In the autumn of 1910, several units in Manchuria were brought together to create the 20th Division. Feng was a member of the division, as were the other five men he listed as original members of his study group. These were Shih Ts'ung-yün, commander of the 1st Battalion of the 79th Regiment; Wang Chin-ming, commander of the 2nd Battalion of the 79th Regiment; Cheng Chin-sheng, commander of the 2nd Battalion of the 80th Regiment; Wang Shih-ch'ing, commander of the 1st Battalion of the 80th Regiment; and Yüeh Jui-chou, whose rank and position are not clear.[66] Other sources list more members.[67] There seem to be two reasons for this. First, the very looseness of the study group, and its lack of any specific political program or policy, meant that "membership" was somewhat ambiguous; Feng wrote that over a hundred men were "sympathetic," which probably means little more than that they were friends of the members of the core group.[68] Second, when the Wuhan revolt broke out in 1911, it triggered several smaller revolts in northern China, among them the revolt at Luanchow, in which some members of Feng's study group participated;

writers bent on emphasizing Feng's early commitment to revolution have described many of the leading figures of the Luanchow revolt as members of the study group.[69] Actually, the study group as a distinct entity seems to have disappeared for all practical purposes in the fall of 1911, and Feng and his friends simply became involved in the larger and more complex revolutionary movement.

The first step in this process occurred in late September or early October 1911, when a portion of the 20th Division, notably the 78th and 79th Regiments, was sent southward from Manchuria to participate in the autumn military maneuvers.[70] Feng Yü-hsiang, who was in the 80th Regiment, remained at Hsinminfu in Manchuria. When the troops on maneuvers were in Luanchow, a town in Chihli on the Peking-Mukden railway line, word came that revolution had broken out in Wuhan. The Ch'ing court immediately ordered all troops to cease maneuvers and await orders.

The commander of the 20th Division was Chang Shao-tseng, one of several Japanese-trained officers appointed to high positions after Yüan Shih-k'ai was dismissed from office. Although not really a revolutionary, Chang had close friends in the revolutionary movement, and his own attitude was more liberal than that of the regular Peiyang officers. Moreover, the 20th Division was divided into two factions, one supporting the Manchu government and the other seeking its overthrow.[71]

When news of the Wuhan revolt reached Luanchow, the revolutionary faction wanted to advance on Peking, while the more conservative group objected. The result was a compromise: a telegram to the Ch'ing government enumerating twelve specific requests and generally urging the rapid establishment of responsible parliamentary government under the Manchu emperor.[72] On the day the Ch'ing government received this wire, news came that the province of Shansi had declared its independence. Faced with this revolt in the North, the court promptly acceded to the demands of the 20th Division.[73]

A week later, however, Chang Shao-tseng was relieved of his command and assigned to a position in the Yangtze provinces.[74] Chang hesitated; he disliked giving up command of his troops, but he was afraid to disobey orders and take a more revolutionary stance. Beset by both factions in the division, he finally solved the problem by fleeing to the foreign concession in Tientsin.[75] He was replaced by General P'an Chü-ying, who was anti-revolutionary. There may have been some shifting of troops from Luanchow, but the three battalions of the 79th Regiment remained. These were under the command of

Chang Chien-kung, Wang Chin-ming, and Shih Ts'ung-yün. The last two were members of Feng's study group.

Meanwhile, some members of the T'ung Meng Hui established headquarters in the French concession in Tientsin, and began to look for opportunities to extend the revolution to northern China. Their attention was promptly drawn to Luanchow, partly because it was a key station on the railroad line between Peking and Manchuria, partly because of the presence of a radical faction among the troops there.[76] In late November, the Tientsin revolutionaries met to discuss the prospects at Luanchow. One of their number was Sun Chien-sheng, the officer who had loaned Feng the two anti-Manchu books three years earlier. Sun had left Luanchow for Tientsin at the same time as Chang Shao-tseng, and had assumed a leading position among the Tientsin revolutionaries. He reported that the battalion commanders Shih, Wang, and Chang were all pro-revolutionary but were hesitant about taking action on their own. The revolutionaries decided to send men to Luanchow to look over the situation.[77]

Discussion then turned to Feng Yü-hsiang. Feng's regiment had just been transferred south of Shanhaikuan to a small town named Haiyang to guard against revolution. One of the T'ung Meng Hui plotters suggested that someone be sent to Haiyang to see if Feng's battalion could also be brought into the revolt, but Sun Chien-sheng objected. Feng, he said, did much talking and scheming, but he was uneducated, untrustworthy, and unreliable. He recommended postponing a decision until Shih Ts'ung-yün, who knew Feng best, could be consulted.[78]

Actually, Feng was already involved in some revolutionary activity. After the Wuhan revolt, Feng and some of his friends at Hsinminfu set about spreading revolutionary ideas among the troops at Hsinminfu. Most of their efforts went into printing and distributing broadsides. The content, probably copied directly from newspapers, included such things as the telegrams sent by various provinces proclaiming sympathy with the revolt. Some three or four hundred copies of each broadside were secretly delivered to the various barracks during the night.[79]

In mid-December, Sun Chien-sheng, Ling Yüeh, and several others of the Tientsin group went to Luanchow to persuade Wang, Shih, and Chang to revolt and establish a "Military Government of the Northern Army." The three officers promptly joined in the plot, and recommended that Feng also be included.[80] Several days later Wang Chin-ming went to Haiyang to arrange for Feng's cooperation. Feng agreed, and it was decided to act sometime between December 30, 1911, and January 8, 1912.[81] Feng was to be notified of the precise day, which would be decided by consultation between the Luanchow officers and the Tientsin revolutionaries.

Shortly after this, one of the Tientsin plotters, fearful that the government knew of the plans for revolt at Luanchow, urged that Wang, Shih, and Chang move at once.[82] On the evening of December 29, a telegram was sent from Luanchow to the capital urging the establishment of a republic. Feng Yü-hsiang's name was one of those signed to the telegram.[83] The government immediately sent Wang Huai-ch'ing, an official in the Luanchow area and an acquaintance of Shih Ts'ung-yün and Wang Chin-ming, to attempt to conciliate the commanders and prevent revolt.[84] When Wang arrived at Luanchow, however, he was forced to become leader of the new revolutionary government, and a telegram was issued in his name declaring an intention to attack Peking within 24 hours.[85]

But everything went wrong. Wang Huai-ch'ing escaped almost immediately and wired the government about the true state of affairs.[86] Troops were dispatched to attack the rebels. At the same time, certain troops that were supposed to support the Luanchow rebels failed to move, or moved too slowly. Moreover, Chang Chien-kung, the commander of one of the three battalions involved in the revolt, turned on his two fellow revolutionaries and attacked them from the rear.*[87] The revolutionary troops commandeered a train, but at Leichuang, a village south of Luanchow, they found the railway line cut and government troops lying in wait for them.[88] After bitter fighting that lasted two days, the rebels were defeated. Wang Chin-ming and Shih Ts'ung-yün were killed, together with most of their followers.[89] The Luanchow revolt was over.

Although Feng ever afterward pointed to his participation in this revolt as evidence of his early revolutionary respectability, he took no part in the fighting. Shortly before the revolt, his regimental commander had discovered that the regiment's printing machine—apparently something like a mimeograph machine—was in Feng's quarters, and had ordered his arrest when printed broadsides began to appear. He was under guard when the revolt occurred.[90]

Although an order was allegedly issued for Feng's execution, his punishment was in fact nominal, thanks to his close relationship with

* In 1929 one of Feng's officers came upon Chang Chien-kung in Kaifeng. He seized Chang and executed him for his betrayal at Luanchow. (Li T'ai-fen, p. 8.)

Lu Chien-chang, both as friend and as relative. Lu, one of Yüan Shih-k'ai's most trusted followers and an old-time Peiyang officer, interceded on Feng's behalf, and as a result of Lu's efforts Feng was only forced to resign. At Lu's suggestion, he returned to his home in Paoting to await developments.

3. From Soldier to Warlord

On March 10, 1912, Yüan Shih-k'ai was inaugurated as President of China. The revolution was over, and the Republic was launched. In that same month, Lu Chien-chang was ordered to recruit, organize, and train five battalions of troops. He immediately appointed Feng Yü-hsiang commander of the vanguard battalion, with orders to recruit and train some 500 men.[1] Feng's organization of this unit was the first step in the creation of his personal army, and it struck the keynote of his activities for the following eight years.

During that period Feng attracted some attention, and incidentally brightened the hopes of Christian missionaries in China, by adopting the Christian religion. He also played a part in several events of national importance. But the real focus of his efforts was on his army. Those efforts were twofold. On the one hand, he steadily expanded and assiduously trained the troops under his command. At the same time, he sought to find a path through the shifting maze of Chinese military politics that would assure the continued existence of his military force as a fairly independent entity, and also assure his own authority over it.

From Battalion to Mixed Brigade

The five battalions under Lu Chien-chang were called the Left Route Reserve Army, a rather misleading name for what was essentially a police force serving the political ends of the President. Until 1914 Lu was head of the Department of Military Law, and in that capacity he was responsible for ferreting out and executing Yüan Shih-k'ai's enemies, including many revolutionaries. The battalions under his command apparently constituted the military arm of his office. It was probably the anti-revolutionary character of Lu's activities at that time that accounts for Feng's reticence, and a dearth of information generally, about what Feng's forces did during the first few years of the Republic.[2]

As soon as Feng received his assignment as battalion commander, he proceeded to a district in south-central Chihli to recruit his men.[3] Most of the recruits whom he accepted came from families of peasants, laborers, or petty merchants.[4] Feng was rather particular in selecting soldiers, and preferred men who had no former military experience.[5] Within four or five days he had recruited a battalion of approximately 500 men, which he then took to Peiyüan, just north of Peking, for training.[6]

From the summer of 1912 to the autumn of 1913, the battalion was always in or near Peking.[7] During this time, Feng recruited some of the men who were to become his chief subordinates in the days of his greatest influence. These included Li Ming-chung and Han Fu-chü, whom Feng had known in prerevolutionary days, and Shih Yu-san, Sun Liang-ch'eng, Liu Ju-ming, and Sun Lien-chung.[8]

The first year of the Republic was marked by continual friction between President Yüan Shih-k'ai and the Kuomintang. The friction became more intense in the spring of 1913, and came to a head in July when the Kuomintang unsuccessfully attempted to oust Yüan in the short war known as the Second Revolution of 1913. In all Feng's writings, he is conspicuously silent about this revolt. The reason, of course, is that he did not participate in it. He was stationed in Peking at the time, and he followed the lead of Lu Chien-chang.[9] Although it is not known just what that involved, there can be no doubt that it was not pro-revolutionary.

During the Second Revolution, Lu's army was reorganized and expanded, and in the process Feng became a regimental commander. Just as a year earlier he had recruited the men for his battalion, his first task now was to obtain additional troops to fill out the regiment.[10] With several of his subordinates, Feng went to northern Honan for recruits, and within two weeks he had a full regiment of approximately 1,600 men.[11] He took his new men to Peiyüan and again began the work of transforming peasants into soldiers. During this expansion, Feng acquired several other men who were to make their careers in his army.[12]

In the spring of 1914, Feng's men got their first taste of battle when they were ordered to help in the pursuit of the White Wolf, a picturesque and intelligent bandit chieftain who began to roam north-central China in the wake of the Second Revolution. The White Wolf's band probably numbered between two and three thousand men, and occasionally was reinforced by outlaws from affiliated bands.[13] Though it is possible that he had ties with revolutionaries,[14] the raids and exploits associated with his name had little political significance, except insofar as they weakened the government and caused it to lose prestige.[15] His band sacked towns, killed and kidnapped foreigners as well as Chinese, and generally spread fear and havoc. The press was full of fact and rumor about his exploits.

By the beginning of 1914, the White Wolf had become a national problem. British and American legations made repeated representations to the Chinese government demanding that effective measures be taken against the brigands.[16] Yüan Shih-k'ai assigned several officers in succession the job of catching the White Wolf, but the bandit continued his marauding into the spring. In April, Lu Chien-chang was given command of the White Wolf campaign, and was also made commander of the 7th Division, which was specially organized for anti-bandit activities.[17] Feng Yü-hsiang's regiment had been expanded to a brigade just prior to this, and now it was made the 14th Brigade of Lu's new division.[18]

There were at least 12,000 troops involved in the pursuit of the White Wolf, and Feng's brigade played a central role. His men were better trained and in better physical condition than soldiers in most Chinese armies, and the forced march was their forte: they covered so much distance in forced marches that they were nicknamed The Flying Army.[19] It was probably Feng's soldiers that a news account in May said were of

a different calibre [from] those who were sent [after the White Wolf] elsewhere. We never read of 3,000 men making a forced march one week and leaving a big city the day after their arrival and a few days later giving more than a good account of themselves a good distance to the west of Sianfu.[20]

Such pressure forced the White Wolf to flee to Kansu. After a month or so he returned to Shensi, where he was maneuvered into battle and decisively defeated by Feng's men and other government troops in the summer of 1914. The White Wolf himself was killed in the fighting.[21]

In October 1914, Feng's brigade was again reorganized, this time becoming the 16th Mixed Brigade. Some five to six thousand men strong, the new unit consisted of two regiments of infantry, one battalion of artillery, one battalion of cavalry, and one machine-gun company.[22] As part of the reorganization, the new brigade was removed from Lu Chien-chang's division; it became an independent unit that received its orders directly from the central government. Of course, if the brigade were to participate in a large operation, Feng would come under the general command of the officer in charge. In any event, Feng could not flout the wishes of a high officer or official under whose regional jurisdiction he might find himself. Nevertheless, Feng acquired substantial independence, particularly in the policies he pursued within his brigade.[23]

The formation of the 16th Mixed Brigade was the last in the series of expansions and reorganizations that Feng's troops underwent during the first three years of the Republic. Feng commanded the 16th Mixed Brigade for the next seven years, and men from this unit constituted the loyal and experienced core of the forces he led in the critical decade of the 1920's.

Feng Becomes a Christian

During the early years of the Republic, Feng took the step that gave him a unique name in modern Chinese history. He became a Christian, although it was not until some years later that he became generally known as the "Christian General."

Feng had his first memorable contact with Christianity when he was a boy. Shortly after he joined the army, an epidemic broke out in Paotingfu, and Feng was among some troops who were ordered to walk through the city firing rifles to chase away the evil spirits responsible for the disease. Feng and some of his comrades thought the firing would be no less efficacious if they aimed at something, so they shot at a sign outside a Christian church.[24]

Some time later, Feng's idle curiosity led him to that same church to listen to sermons, which he admittedly did not understand. On one occasion, the preacher told his listeners that "if someone strikes you on the right cheek, turn your left cheek. If he takes your outer clothing, give him your inner clothing, too." Feng and some companions tried to put this dictum to the test by walking off with a table from the church. When the missionary demanded an explanation, the soldiers quipped that he should be offering the chairs and benches as well. The perplexed preacher did not rise to the occasion, but insisted the table be returned. Feng admitted that during this period he sometimes went to church just to raise the devil.[25]

What transformed Feng from a skeptic into a believer? Both Feng and missionary writers point to the favorable impression that selfless missionary service made on him. After unsuccessfully seeking effective medical care from Chinese doctors, he twice received it free from missionary doctors, who replied to his expressions of thanks by admonishing him to thank God.[26] Presumably Feng's gratitude and curiosity were both stimulated. These writers also attribute Feng's conversion to the persuasiveness of the Christian message, and cite these examples of its effect on him: he heard a particularly convincing sermon in Manchuria;[27] missionary literature aroused such an interest that he began regular church attendance shortly after the revolution;[28] he was deeply impressed by the meetings held by John R. Mott, a founder and leader of the international student Christian movement, who visited China early in 1913;[29] he joined a Bible class conducted by Liu Fang of the Methodist Episcopal Church, and finally, in 1914, was baptized in the Methodist Church by Liu.[30]

Feng was also very impressed by the behavior and values of Christians he observed. They did not smoke opium; whether poor or rich, they saw to it that their children were educated; there were no idlers among them; and Christian women did not bind their feet. "These few simple points," wrote Feng, "elicited my extraordinary admiration. At that time [about 1912–14] I thought that if all the people of China could act in a similar fashion, the nation would gradually find a way, and society would indeed gradually improve. Because of this, my attitude toward Christianity daily became more sympathetic."[31]

Feng Yü-hsiang was an emotional man, and it is certainly credible that he could be powerfully moved by the gentle selflessness of kind missionary doctors, by the emotional power of a well-structured sermon or an evangelical meeting, and by the industry and decency with which Christians lived in society. But Feng was also a devious and calculating man. One writer interprets his conversion as a completely cynical move. Feng, he writes, became a Christian for two reasons: to ingratiate himself with foreign imperialists, who held the reins of power in China; and to manipulate his superstitious troops with the help of pseudo-Christian symbolism, after the manner of the Taiping leaders.[32] This explanation unquestionably touches on a key factor in Feng's turn to Christianity: the religion's link with Western political and military power in China. In later years, when he was no longer connected with organized Christianity and there was some doubt whether he could still be properly described as a Christian, Feng admitted that

During the last years of the Manchu dynasty, revolutionaries were being arrested right and left. Therefore many of us became Christians in order to avoid difficulties. Moreover, that faith had its good points. It proposed universal love, sacrifice, no smoking or drinking, no gambling or chasing women, that children learn to read, and that girls not bind their feet.[33]

This statement not only summarizes the chief attractions that Christianity had for Feng, but also suggests the sequence in which these attractions were felt. Initially drawn to Christianity because it offered certain practical advantages, Feng discovered intrinsic values in the religion as he became increasingly familiar with the actions and attitudes of Christians. Although it is true that Feng ultimately used Christianity to infuse his army with a unique élan and to intensify its loyalty to him, it is impossible to know when he started thinking in these terms.

In sum, it can be said that Feng accepted Christianity because it fulfilled several needs. It offered the possibility of personal protection and advantage. Its adherents exemplified social practices and individual virtues that Feng thought commendable. (Although the social injunctions of Christianity were not so different from those of Confucianism, Feng considered Christianity more successful in realizing its goals in the daily lives of its adherents.) Moreover, Christianity may well have satisfied emotional and intellectual needs in Feng, notably in its ritual aspects and in its practical implications for behavior. He was more interested in what Christians did than in what they thought. His concern with Christian doctrine seldom went beyond moral platitudes that had as much Confucianism as Christianity in them. According to one of Feng's close associates during the mid-1920's, Feng at that time, over a decade after his conversion, "did not understand the higher concepts of Christianity."[34] It would probably be equally accurate to say that he was simply not interested in them.

Yüan Shih-k'ai's Monarchical Movement

At the time the 16th Mixed Brigade was organized in the fall of 1914, rumors were already circulating in Peking that an attempt would be made to restore the monarchy with Yüan Shih-k'ai as emperor.[35] In 1915 these rumors were confirmed when a society was organized to bring the monarchical movement into the open. The work of this society finally resulted in the convening of a rigged national assembly, which drew up a formal demand that Yüan Shih-k'ai become emperor. On December 12, 1915, Yüan accepted the proposal, and January 1, 1916, was declared the first day of the reign of the Hung-hsien monarchy.

While Yüan's supporters were organizing, members of the Kuomintang and of the Progressive Party were taking steps to oppose them. The leaders of the opposition were scattered, and the first stirrings of their activity occurred in several cities. But revolutionary efforts came to be concentrated in Yunnan, where an army was formed under the general leadership of Ts'ai Ao, a protégé of Liang Ch'i-ch'ao and a man long prominent in military circles in the Southwest. This army later came to be known as the National Protection Army. On December 23, 1915, the opposition leaders wired Peking that they would declare their independence from the central government on the 25th if the plans for the reestablishment of the monarchy were not canceled. Yüan Shih-k'ai did not accede to this demand.

The National Protection Army was divided into three units for military action. One was to remain in Yunnan. Another, under Tai K'an, was to go eastward to Kweichow. And the third, led by Ts'ai Ao himself, was to invade Szechwan. The province of Kweichow, which had figured in the plans of the revolutionaries even earlier, declared its independence shortly after Tai K'an's troops reached the provincial capital. Tai therefore sent part of his force to western Hunan, and led another portion north to cooperate with Ts'ai Ao in Szechwan. Although other provinces declared their independence from the central government, and thus their opposition to the Hung-hsien monarchy, it was in Szechwan that the bulk of the National Protection Army actually fought. In that fighting, Feng Yü-hsiang played an important part.

On May 1, 1915, Yüan Shih-k'ai appointed Ch'en Huan acting civil governor of Szechwan, and on June 22 he was ordered to serve concurrently as military governor.[36] Ch'en had been assistant chief of staff in the central government, and was one of Yüan's most trusted subordinates. Since he did not have his own armed force, three mixed brigades were transferred to Szechwan and placed under his command. Feng Yü-hsiang's 16th Mixed Brigade was one of these.[37]

Actually, Feng took only one regiment to Szechwan; the rest of the brigade remained in southern Shensi, where Feng had been stationed since shortly after the defeat of the White Wolf. There was a good deal of disorder in Szechwan at this time, and in the fall of 1915 the province was divided into five bandit-suppression districts. Feng was made responsible for one of these districts in the northern part of the province, and was engaged in the pursuit of bandits when the movement to restore the monarchy entered its final phase.[38]

Virtually all accounts of Feng's role in the anti-monarchical war assert that he supported Ts'ai Ao against Yüan Shih-k'ai, and to that extent confirm Feng's claim to long revolutionary respectability. Those accounts, however, derive from Feng's own version of the affair: a good example of the efficacy of writing one's own history. It may be true, as Feng maintained, that he was from the outset in complete sympathy with the National Protection Army, but his actions were not completely consistent with this attitude. Indeed, Feng's opportunistic behavior reflected the values of a nascent warlord, just as the conflicting factors he had to reconcile—his preference for a cause, his obligation to his superiors, his overriding desire to maintain his army's strength and independence—presented a typical dilemma of the warlord era. Feng resolved it by keeping a foot safely in each camp until the outcome of the struggle was clear.

Feng first became involved in Yüan's imperial drama late in 1915, when he received a wire from Shensi urging him to support Yüan as emperor; it was doubtless from Lu Chien-chang, who was then military governor of that province. At the same time, he received from Chengtu the draft of a telegram petitioning Yüan to become emperor; it was being circulated for all medium- and high-ranking military officers to sign, after which it was to be sent to Peking. Although Feng always claimed that he refused to support the petition, in fact he probably signed it.[39]

The next move, according to Feng, occurred on New Year's Day, 1916. Feng and his officers had received notification of the Yunnan rebellion the day before, and after discussing its implications they wrote three letters. One was to Ch'en Huan, explaining that Feng and his men could not fight the National Protection Army, and urging Ch'en to take a similar stand. Another was to Liu I-ch'ing, an adviser at Ch'en's headquarters, asking him to persuade Ch'en not to fight the Yunnan army. The third letter was to Ts'ai Ao himself. Feng says that this letter expressed admiration and respect for Ts'ai, as well as agreement with his goals. However, the letter continued, Feng's military power was very weak, he was surrounded, and he was being subjected to great pressures. Consequently, he could take no immediate action, but instead would try to avoid fighting with Ts'ai's forces until he could openly join with Ts'ai in overthrowing the monarchy.[40]

Four points should be noted about Feng's assertions. First, except for writings by Feng and his supporters, none of the other accounts of this period mentions any such letters.[41] Second, in Ts'ai Ao's collected telegrams the first allusion to communications from Feng is in a wire Ts'ai sent some three months after the letter in question was allegedly dispatched.[42] Third, in the fighting that took place in southern Szechwan during the first three months of 1916, Ch'en Huan seems to have considered Feng's unit one of his most reliable.[43] Finally, and most important, regardless of whether Feng sent the letters, the fact remains that he fought against the Yunnan forces during the next three months, and that he played a prominent role in the fighting at Hsüchow.*

Hsüchow is a town in southern Szechwan of great strategic importance for any invasion from Yunnan. The Yangtze River enters Szechwan at its southwestern corner, flows northeast past Chungking, and then turns east into Hupeh. The Min River, with its headwaters in northwestern Szechwan, flows southeast, passing near Chengtu, and joins the Yangtze at Hsüchow. Therefore, from Hsüchow an army can travel easily up a river valley to either of Szechwan's main cities. Moreover, the mountains on the Yunnan-Szechwan border are cleft by the valley of the Yangtze, providing a natural pathway into Szechwan from Yunnan. Hsüchow stands at the mouth of that valley. It is not surprising, therefore, that immediately after the Yunnan army raised the banner of revolt in December, a brigade was sent to attack Hsüchow as the first step in the invasion of Szechwan.[44]

Meanwhile, the central government was preparing for the defense of Szechwan. Yüan Shih-k'ai sent Ts'ao K'un's 3rd Division, Chang Ching-yao's 7th Division, and several other units to defend Szechwan and attack Yunnan.[45] Yüan also telegraphed Ch'en Huan to marshal all of his strength to defend Hsüchow and block the northward advance of the Yunnan army.[46] However, the unit that Ch'en charged with this task either was routed or only feigned resistance,[47] and the Yunnan army occupied Hsüchow on January 21.[48]

While this was going on, Feng was at Neichiang, about seventy miles north of Hsüchow, where he summoned the troops he had earlier left to suppress banditry in northern Szechwan.[49] Shortly afterward, he was ordered to oust the rebel invaders from Hsüchow.[50] Feng obeyed, and soon reported that on January 31 he had attacked and defeated a unit of Yunnanese troops about 15 or 20 miles northeast of Hsüchow.[51] About three days later he attacked the city itself, but he was forced to retreat after hard fighting that lasted a day or longer.[52]

Feng's account of the circumstances surrounding these battles is vague and incorrect. It merits examination, however, not only because it has long been accepted as the true story of Feng's role in Sze-

---

* Hsüchow was also called Hsüchoufu, or Hsüfu, and this last form was frequently transliterated into English as Suifu. Today it is called Ip'in.

MAP 1. Yunnan-Szechwan border region.

chwan, but because it illustrates a characteristic of Feng's retrospective writing: the presentation of unquestioned facts in a very questionable light.

According to Feng, before he started for Hsüchow he contacted Liu Yün-feng, the leader of the Yunnan troops occupying the city. He told Liu that he had already communicated with Ts'ai Ao, that he wanted to cooperate with the National Protection Army, but that he was surrounded by Yüan Shih-k'ai's troops and therefore could not openly proclaim his position at that time. Liu replied that Feng must either openly come out against Yüan Shih-k'ai or surrender. It was, Feng lamented, most unexpected that Liu would be so obstinate.[53]

After Feng started toward Hsüchow, according to his account, he sent his chief of staff to Liu Yün-feng to negotiate along the following lines. (1) The two sides would agree not to fight; if there were absolutely no alternative, they would fire their rifles into the air. (2) If the opportunity arose, Feng would issue a circular telegram declaring his sympathy with the National Protection Army. Feng's representative was also to explain that government troops were pressing him from the rear, making it necessary for him to make some pretense of carrying out his orders.[54] Liu, however, steadfastly insisted that Feng either oppose Yüan or surrender, and a third emissary from Feng failed to sway him.[55]

By this time, Feng's troops were approaching Hsüchow. Feng wrote:[56]

On the one hand, our troops advanced. On the other hand, I sent a man to inform Liu Yün-feng, and to request him to retreat voluntarily from Hsüchow and permit us to occupy [the town]. Then we would promptly retreat. I beseeched [Liu] not to misunderstand me. Then we advanced, firing toward the sky. We fired for a whole day. When we had advanced to . . . the vicinity of Hsüchow, Chiang Hung-yü [Feng's chief of staff] secretly hid our ammunition in a ravine, and spread the word that we were out of ammunition. Then I sent a man to inform Liu Yün-feng that we now wanted to retreat, and to ask him to hold his lines and stop retreating.

This version is completely misleading. Since Liu had rejected Feng's proposals, why would he retreat from troops firing into the air? That he did not is confirmed by Feng's later remark that "although we did not truly fight, nevertheless there were a number of killed and wounded."[57] He states that 60 of his men were wounded, and that he captured over a hundred wounded men from the Yunnan army.[58] Moreover, Feng's troops did not occupy Hsüchow. It is clear, in fact, that Feng suffered a defeat in his first attempt to take the city.[59]

Feng's troops may have attacked Hsüchow several more times during the remainder of February,[60] but Feng only mentions the decisive action of March 1, when he succeeded in capturing the city.[61] His description of this victory is designed to meet all possible criticisms, for it explains why it was necessary to attack Hsüchow vigorously, and at the same time asserts that there actually was no fight at all.

As Feng relates it, his superiors continued to press him to retake Hsüchow. Finally he decided that if he attacked the city with vigor he could "avoid an unexpected attack" by Chang Ching-yao, Ts'ao K'un, and Wu P'ei-fu, who was in Ts'ao K'un's division. Moreover, a victory over Liu would make him more amenable to Feng's suggestion of an informal truce.[62] But when Feng started for Hsüchow, he also sent a messenger ahead with a letter from Liu I-ch'ing, Ch'en Huan's adviser. This letter, Feng asserts, asked Liu Yün-feng to permit Feng's troops to occupy Hsüchow for three days, after which Feng would allow the Yunnan troops to reoccupy the town. And, wrote Feng, this is just what happened: Liu Yün-feng relinquished control of Hsüchow to Feng, who remained two days and then withdrew so that Liu could resume control.[63]

Actually, only the first part of this account bears much resemblance to the facts. Feng did attack Hsüchow with vigor, and managed to capture the heights overlooking the city.[64] But Liu's ultimate retreat from Hsüchow does not appear to have been prearranged with Feng. Rather, Liu's withdrawal was dictated by the logistics problems that beset the Yunnan army throughout southern Szechwan. Ts'ai Ao's entire invasion force had fewer than 4,000 poorly provisioned men,[65] and he was therefore forced to evacuate Hsüchow because he could not spare the reinforcements needed to hold it.[66] It is difficult to determine how severe the fighting was at Hsüchow before the Yunnanese decided to retreat. However, Feng's report to the government stressed the stubborn resistance he met; he claimed that over a thousand rebels had been killed and a hundred captured.[67] A presidential citation was issued on March 7 praising Feng for his "intense loyalty and bravery."[68] He was also made a baron of the third grade.[69]

Feng's was not the only government victory in early March. The Yunnan army had also been forced out of Luchow and Nach'i, across the river from Luchow, as well as several other towns.[70] However, on March 17, rebel troops counterattacked and reoccupied at least five towns in southern Szechwan, not including Hsüchow, thus demonstrating that they were still a force to be reckoned with.[71] Moreover, two other provinces had responded to the Yunnanese call to revolt.

Kweichow had declared its adherence to the revolution in January, and Kwangsi followed suit on March 15. It was only after these developments that Feng began earnest negotiations with the rebel forces, and he did so in cooperation with Ch'en Huan.

Feng had apparently initiated negotiations shortly before he recaptured Hsüchow. In a telegram probably written on March 2, Ts'ai Ao mentions that Feng had twice sent emissaries to him. Ts'ai wrote that Feng

proposes to overthrow Yüan and support Feng [Kuo-chang for President]. Moreover, he has assumed the responsibility of linking up with the northern army [and bringing them into the revolution]. Feng was cheated by Yüan Shih-k'ai after the Luanchow rebellion, and therefore hates him. His troops are for the most part revolutionary. He has accepted my order to rebel quickly and also to press Ch'en [Huan] to declare [his independence].[72]

As has been seen, Feng did not "rebel quickly." Indeed, although Ts'ai seemed to think that Feng had already joined him, Feng was still negotiating. In the middle of March, he asked two missionary doctors from the hospital at Hsüchow to arrange specific peace terms between himself and the Yunnan army, a request made with Ch'en Huan's approval.[73] The ensuing negotiations culminated in a one-week truce starting on March 31. This truce was later extended for a month, and for another month after that, to June 6. In fact, after Yüan Shih-k'ai abolished the monarchy on March 20 there was no more fighting between the National Protection Army and the Peiyang forces in Szechwan.[74]

However, the rebels were not satisfied with Yüan's abdication as emperor; they wanted him to resign the presidency as well. They were therefore eager that Szechwan join the column of revolutionary provinces. If Feng Yü-hsiang were to join the National Protection Army, the pressure on Ch'en Huan to do likewise would increase. At the time of the first truce extension Ts'ai Ao had hopes that Feng would act quickly.[75] However, Feng vacillated until May while Ch'en was negotiating with the rebels on behalf of Yüan's claims to the presidency. The rebels were adamant, and instead of yielding to Ch'en they finally won him over to their side. On May 3, and again on May 12, Ch'en Huan sent wires to Yüan urging him to resign. Yüan answered evasively, and on May 22 Ch'en Huan declared Szechwan to be independent. It was about the time of Ch'en's second wire that Feng first made public his adherence to the Yunnan cause.[76] Only then did he turn Hsüchow over to the Yunnan army and proceed to Chengtu.[77]

Feng later described these few months as the most difficult period of his life. He regretted that some people call a man an opportunist simply because he "gives a matter much consideration."[78] Nevertheless, it is clear that Feng played his cards very carefully during the anti-monarchical war. He made no decisive public move in favor of the revolutionaries until peace negotiations sanctioned by Yüan Shih-k'ai were in progress, thereby lessening the chance that he would be attacked by Peiyang forces under Ts'ao K'un; until the general trend of events seemed to be against Yüan and in favor of the National Protection Army; and until Ch'en Huan was committed to supporting the revolutionaries. A fourth consideration was probably also important, although its significance is difficult to gauge. On May 9 Ch'en Shu-fan, an official in northern Shensi, revolted and forced Lu Chien-chang out of the province. On the 16th, Ch'en Shu-fan declared Shensi independent.[79] Lu Chien-chang, Feng's friend and relative, supported Yüan Shih-k'ai, and his removal from the scene may have lessened the importance of loyalty to Yüan in Feng's mind. However, this is highly speculative, since Lu himself did not turn against Yüan.

If one accepts Feng's claim that he was sympathetic to the revolutionaries at the outset, the charge of opportunism seems even more valid. If he favored the rebels, there was nothing to prevent his agreeing to Liu Yün-feng's perfectly reasonable demand that he take an open stand against Yüan. Feng's excuse that he was surrounded by strong Peiyang forces was not quite accurate, for there were none in the direction from which the Yunnan army came. Feng clashed with the rebel troops at least twice, and we can assume that if he was close enough to fight them, he was close enough to join them.

But it is true that Peiyang troops in Szechwan outnumbered the National Protection Army. If Feng had joined the latter in January or February, or even in March, he would have been joining the underdogs, and their defeat might have meant the elimination of Feng's independent military power. In this connection, at least, events in Shensi doubtless exercised an influence. Units of Feng's 16th Mixed Brigade were still in Shensi, and as long as that province was in Yüan's camp Feng could expect that his defection might result in the loss of those units. They were, in a sense, hostages for Feng's good behavior. Once Shensi had declared itself for the Republic, however, they were hostages no longer—or rather their significance as hostages was exactly reversed.

In sum, there is little doubt that Feng was sympathetic to the Yunnan revolt. But historically that sympathy was of secondary importance, just as it was of secondary importance to Feng personally. The clear fact that emerges from Feng's actions in Szechwan is that his primary concern, from beginning to end, was to keep his military power intact. All other considerations were subordinated to that end.

The Restoration of P'u-i

About two weeks after Ch'en Huan declared Szechwan to be independent, Yüan Shih-k'ai died. At the end of that same month, June 1916, Ch'en left Szechwan; Feng Yü-hsiang departed at about the same time and proceeded to Shensi.[80] While there he received a wire from Tuan Ch'i-jui, who was at that time Minister of War and Premier, ordering him to station the bulk of his troops in the vicinity of Langfang, about halfway between Peking and Tientsin.[81] Feng remained at Langfang from the summer of 1916 to the spring of 1917, and devoted his entire stay to the reorganization, teaching, and intensive training of his troops.

In the spring of 1917, Feng was presented with a serious challenge to his military position. Tuan Ch'i-jui proposed to send a brigade of soldiers to Kansu, and to form that brigade by combining one of Feng's regiments with units from another division. Feng objected strenuously. He offered to lead his entire mixed brigade to Kansu if necessary, but he did not want it divided. Shortly after this altercation, Feng was relieved of his command of the 16th Mixed Brigade and ordered to serve as brigade commander in the 6th Route Patrol Defense Corps.[82] An officer named Yang Kuei-t'ang was given command of the 16th Mixed Brigade.[83]

The officers of the 16th Mixed Brigade promptly sent a series of telegrams to the central government urging that the order for Feng's transfer be rescinded. In the meantime, Feng did not leave his command because, as he explained later, his troops "would not permit him to go."[84] Indeed, his officers were making plans to go to Peking in person if their protests went unheeded.

The central government sent two officers, one after the other, to mollify Feng's troops. But the troops were adamant, and the Peking authorities, fearing mutiny, moved reliable units into positions where they could threaten Feng's brigade. Finally, Lu Chien-chang went to Langfang, where he first spoke privately with Feng and then addressed the troops. Lu apparently told them that there was little chance of successfully opposing Feng's dismissal at that time, and that they should acquiesce, biding their time until Feng could return to them.[85] After that Feng left peaceably to assume his new command, but with the understanding that not a man was to be transferred out of the 16th Mixed Brigade.[86]

Several reasons have been adduced for Feng's dismissal, none of which touches on what seems to have been the basic factor: Feng's indirect connection with Feng Kuo-chang through Lu Chien-chang.[87] By mid-1917, the Peiyang clique was already splitting into the two factions that were ultimately to be led by Feng Kuo-chang and Tuan Ch'i-jui; the rivalry of these two men was already apparent, and both were maneuvering for greater power. During the warfare in Szechwan, Feng Yü-hsiang had proposed to Ts'ai Ao that Feng Kuo-chang succeed Yüan Shih-k'ai.[88] This alone would have made Tuan suspicious. Moreover, it is possible that Feng's proposal was made at the suggestion of Lu Chien-chang, from whom Feng took his cue in factional matters at that time. Ch'en Shu-fan, who had driven Lu out of Shensi, was a member of Tuan's clique, and this brought Lu even closer to Feng Kuo-chang.[89] Seen in this light, Tuan's dismissal of Feng Yü-hsiang seems to have been a move against Lu, and particularly against Feng Kuo-chang.

Although this may have been the underlying reason, the immediate cause of Feng's dismissal was his strong opposition to any reduction in the size of his force by sending some of his men to Kansu. It was true that Feng's army was larger than a normal mixed brigade; it was about the size of a division.[90] In normal times, a reduction in personnel would not have been unwarranted. But these were not normal times.

Feng did not remain in his new position very long. He complained of the corruption and inefficiency of the 6th Route Patrol Defense Corps, and finally submitted his resignation. It was not accepted, and when a second attempt to resign also failed Feng pleaded illness. He was granted a leave and went to T'ien T'ai Mountain, a few miles west of Peking, to "recuperate." From there he maintained constant contact with his former subordinates in the 16th Mixed Brigade, and waited for an opportunity to regain his old command.[91] Elsewhere in China, events were already in progress that would provide him with that opportunity.

A number of top military men had been discussing the possibility of restoring the Manchu emperor since the early spring of 1917, if not earlier.[92] The opportunity to translate these discussions into action came that summer when President Li Yüan-hung sought to resolve his conflicts with parliament on the one hand, and with Tuan Ch'i-jui on the other, by dismissing Tuan as Premier. Tuan called on provincial military leaders to oppose the President, and eight provinces declared independence. Li asked Chang Hsün to mediate the dispute. Chang, perhaps the most reactionary of the warlords, had little use for the Republic; he even forbade his soldiers to cut their queues, the symbol of loyalty to the Manchus. He accepted Li's summons, but instead of mediating he dissolved parliament, and on July 1, 1917, he proclaimed the restoration of the Manchu emperor.[93]

Li had taken the bold step of dismissing Tuan because he thought he had the backing of Feng Kuo-chang and Feng's supporters. But Feng in fact coveted the presidency for himself and refused to support Li, who had to flee the capital. Similarly, Chang Hsün believed with some reason that his restoration scheme had Tuan's blessing.[94] But Tuan did not cooperate; he promptly resumed his old position in the government. Neither Tuan nor Feng had anything to gain from a restoration of the monarchy; they both sought power within the general framework of the Republic. Therefore, whatever impression they may have given Chang when the plot was in the talking stage, both leaders turned against him and the boy-emperor as soon as the restoration was announced. Their opposition deterred other military leaders, and the restoration was defeated.

The crisis created by the restoration afforded Feng Yü-hsiang his opportunity. His way of regaining command of the 16th Mixed Brigade was reminiscent of the method employed by Yüan Shih-k'ai in 1911: he demonstrated that his troops could be used only if he led them.

The bulk of the 16th Mixed Brigade was at Langfang, a town on the Peking-Tientsin railway. Other units of the brigade were also near Peking. They were therefore logical forces to move quickly against Chang Hsün. Tuan sent a wire to Yang Kuei-t'ang, Feng's successor, ordering his brigade to be the vanguard of the anti-restoration army. But Yang was not in Langfang to act on this order. Yang's assistant searched for him in Langfang, at his home in Peking, and at his concubine's residence in Tientsin, but Yang was not to be found. In the meantime, Tuan again wired orders. The brigade's chief-of-staff replied that Yang could not be located, and that they could not move without a commander. However, he told Tuan, the entire brigade would gladly follow the orders of their former commander, Feng Yü-hsiang.[95]

While this was going on, Feng was not idle. As soon as he received word of the restoration, he sent a man to Peking to raise funds by mortgaging some property.[96] He then left T'ien T'ai for Tientsin, where he discussed possible courses of action with Lu Chien-chang.[97] He then met with a representative of Tuan Ch'i-jui. It is impossible to know exactly what happened at that meeting. Feng says that Tuan offered to restore his rank because he feared that Yang Kuei-t'ang was supporting Chang Hsün.[98] More likely, however, Feng made it clear that only he could order the 16th Mixed Brigade into action in support of Tuan, a fact that was underscored by the "disappearance" of Yang Kuei-t'ang. Tuan had little choice and agreed to Feng's resuming control of the brigade; or, rather, Tuan agreed to Feng's resuming formal command, for it is clear that the brigade had never really been out of his control. Yang Kuei-t'ang mysteriously reappeared as soon as Feng was reinstated.[99]

Tuan formally announced the beginning of the war against Chang Hsün on July 5. On the following day, Feng, back at Langfang, issued a public statement denouncing the restoration and pledging his support to the Republic.[100] That same morning, he had his first encounter with Chang Hsün's troops a few miles north of Langfang. During the following week, Feng led his troops toward Peking, fighting several battles on the way. His brigade was one of the first units to enter the capital and decisively defeat Chang Hsün's troops.[101] Chang fled to the Dutch legation on July 12, and two days later Tuan entered Peking. The war against the restoration was over.*

On July 21, 1917, a presidential mandate formally reappointed Feng commander of the 16th Mixed Brigade.[102] By that time he had

---

* On July 14, according to Feng and all sources compiled under his auspices, Feng issued a circular telegram urging the elimination of the Manchu royal house. It asserted that the continued existence of the mock Manchu court within the Forbidden City was the basic cause of the attempted restoration of P'u-i, and that as long as it existed there would be other attempts. The wire recommended four specific steps. (1) The Treaty of Favorable Treatment, concluded between the Republic and the Manchu house at the time of the Revolution of 1911, should be abrogated, and the annual subsidy to the Manchus should be discontinued. (2) The name Hsüan-t'ung should no longer be used, and P'u-i should become an ordinary citizen. (3) The palaces and property of the imperial family should revert to the nation for public use. (4) Those who had perpetrated the attempted restoration should be punished severely. (*KMCKMS*, chap. 4, pp. 47–48.) That such a telegram was sent is confirmed by at least two other sources, but neither identifies Feng as the sender. (Wen-i pien-she she, chap. 4, pp. 18–19, and Chang Chuang-an, pp. 204–5.) They indicate, rather, that it was sent by the "entire body of the Peiyang military" (Pei-yang chün-chieh ch'uan-t'i). If so, it would not have been the only time Feng pictured himself as the leading figure in events in which he actually played only a subordinate or participating role. On the other hand, if the telegram was actually endorsed by most or all of the leading military men, it is surprising that it did not have a greater effect. In any event, the steps recommended by the wire were not carried out in 1917. Feng Yü-hsiang himself would carry them out seven years later.

FROM SOLDIER TO WARLORD

returned to Langfang, but he was not to remain there very long. Less than a month after his reinstatement, civil war broke out anew, and Feng was soon involved.

Bound to the Chihli Faction

Tuan Ch'i-jui had reassumed the office of Premier even before the restored monarchy was overthrown, and Feng Kuo-chang had installed himself as Acting President. Feng did not leave his position as tuchün of Kiangsu, however, until he had arranged for a suitable successor and generally prepared a strong power base. Li Shun took over as tuchün of Kiangsu, Ch'en Kuang-yüan replaced Li Shun as tuchün of Kiangsi, and Wang Chan-yüan became tuchün of Hupeh.[103] All these men had been associated with Feng Kuo-chang since the Revolution of 1911, when they were subordinate officers in his army.[104] Within the group of Peiyang military leaders as a whole, they supported Feng as opposed to Tuan. The three provinces they controlled constituted the basis of Feng's power.

The only new tuchün created by these arrangements was Ch'en Kuang-yüan, who until then had been commander of the 12th Division, stationed at Nanyüan. Tuan agreed to this addition to Feng Kuo-chang's strength because he received a quid pro quo: Feng agreed to Fu Liang-tso's becoming tuchün of Hunan. However, the appointment of Fu, formerly Tuan's Vice-Minister of War, touched off a new civil war between the North and the South.

The Southern battle cry was "Protect the Constitution," a phrase used by Sun Yat-sen to justify the establishment of a military government in Canton. But Sun was in the South at the tolerance of military leaders who were more concerned with the balance of military power than with constitutional niceties. They wanted Hunan to be under the control of the Hunanese, and to serve as a buffer between North and South; they had evidently obtained Tuan's assent to this arrangement as early as March 1917.[105] But when he reneged by appointing Fu Liang-tso tuchün of Hunan on August 6, 1917, it meant that his influence would spread to the very doorstep of Kwangtung and Kwangsi. The southern warlords were naturally willing to help Hunan resist Tuan's move, and this precipitated the war. The slogan "Protect the Constitution" was only a slogan, for the war, like all the wars of that decade, was actually a contest between warlords for regional and national power.

Among the Peiyang military leaders, only Tuan Ch'i-jui and his supporters favored this war, hoping that they could unite China under their control by military force. Feng Kuo-chang and his supporters were opposed to a military solution; they felt that the Southern warlords would recognize the suzerainty of the central government if the government in turn would recognize their regional authority. Although such an arrangement would not provide true unification, it would probably be about as effective as military subjugation, and much less dangerous to the central government. The war party and the peace party strove to outmaneuver each other, and Feng Yü-hsiang became directly involved in the struggle.

Near the end of 1917, probably in early December, Tuan ordered Feng to take his brigade to Fukien, and from there to attack Kwangtung.[106] Lu Chien-chang either accompanied Feng or joined him a few days after his departure; indeed, one report claims that Lu was officially commander-in-chief of the Fukien Reinforcements, Feng's brigade.[107] Feng and his troops started south, but they stopped when they reached Pukow, just north of Nanking in Kiangsu province. Feng remained there, a guest of Li Shun, until the end of January 1918.

Feng explains his extended stop in Kiangsu in terms of his reluctance to participate in a civil war that could only devastate the nation.[108] This may have been partly true, but it was not the whole truth. Feng's actions at that time were largely determined by the political goals of Lu Chien-chang, and were part of a pattern of complicated maneuvering and plotting.[109]

As mentioned above, Lu Chien-chang was ousted as tuchün of Shensi by Ch'en Shu-fan, who called himself a younger brother of Tuan Ch'i-jui.[110] Lu was also reportedly a sworn brother to Feng Kuo-chang and to Feng's chief adherent, Li Shun. Whatever his reasons, is it clear that at Pukow Lu influenced Feng Yü-hsiang in a way that served the interests of Feng Kuo-chang.

The sojourn of the 16th Mixed Brigade at Pukow aided Feng Kuo-chang in several ways. First, it precluded the brigade's serving in Fukien and Kwangtung as an instrument of Tuan Ch'i-jui. Second, the brigade was a potential threat to Northern armies going to invade the South. An army from Shantung turned back rather than confront Feng's troops.[111] Finally, despite Feng Kuo-chang's professed peace policy, it is possible that there were tentative plans to use Feng's brigade to invade Anhwei, oust the Anhwei warlord, Ni Ssu-ch'ung, and install Lu Chien-chang as head of the province.[112] No such invasion occurred, however, and early in 1918 Feng left Kiangsu at the order of Feng Kuo-chang.

At the time Feng Yü-hsiang arrived in Pukow, Feng Kuo-chang had seemed to be gaining the upper hand over Tuan and his clique. Northern troops had been chased from Szechwan and from all of Hunan except Yochow, near the northern border between Hunan and Hupeh. On November 14, 1917, the leaders of the Northern troops defeated in Hunan circulated telegrams asking that the war be stopped. On November 17, similar wires were sent by the three Yangtze tuchüns who supported Feng Kuo-chang, and also by Ts'ao K'un, tuchün of Chihli and at that time considered one of Tuan's supporters.[113] In the face of these reversals, Tuan resigned as Premier, and his resignation was accepted by President Feng Kuo-chang. Tuan was replaced by Wang Shih-chen, who supported Feng's peace policy.

During the following two months, however, the situation changed. On December 3, tuchüns of the war party, including Chang Tso-lin from Manchuria, met in Tientsin and discussed military means for solving the North-South division.[114] On December 18, Tuan Ch'i-jui was appointed head of the Chinese forces presumably destined to participate in the war in Europe. In that capacity, he borrowed great sums from Japan, which he used to strengthen his own military power. At the same time, Tuan Chih-kuei, a leading figure in Tuan Ch'i-jui's faction, was made Minister of War.[115] Also, in early December two local militarists in central Hupeh declared their independence, and late in January 1918 Southern armies occupied Yochow, which until that time had been the only important point in Hunan still held by Northern forces.[116] These two events aroused concern in Wang Chan-yüan, tuchün of Hupeh, for the security of his province, and he evidently asked Feng Kuo-chang for armed assistance, thus reversing his former position in favor of conciliation.[117] Moreover, in January, Ni Ssu-ch'ung and Chang Huai-chih, both supporters of Tuan Ch'i-jui, persuaded Ts'ao K'un to urge a resumption of hostilities.[118] Finally, Hsü Shu-cheng, Tuan's right-hand man, went to Manchuria in January to arrange for Fengtien troops to enter China proper in support of Tuan's policies.[119]

In the face of these pressures, Feng Kuo-chang issued a presidential mandate on January 30 appointing Ts'ao K'un to lead a punitive expedition against Southern troops in Hunan and Hupeh.[120] At about the same time, Feng ordered Feng Yü-hsiang to lead his brigade out of Pukow and go west as part of the expeditionary force charged with rescuing Hupeh.[121] Feng and his men left Pukow at the end of January aboard some six or eight steamships.[122] On February 5, the first of these vessels reached Wuhsüeh, a town in the southeast corner of

Hupeh about 20 miles upriver from Kiukiang. At that time the river was too shallow for most steamers to go any farther, and this was evidently the reason why the brigade disembarked at Wuhsüeh.[123] Local observers expected the troops to continue westward with little delay, but the brigade remained in Wuhsüeh, where on February 14 Feng Yü-hsiang issued a circular telegram that attracted nationwide attention.

In his telegram, Feng deplored the civil war that had so long been ravaging China. It was senseless, he said: one could be neither proud of victory nor ashamed of defeat when fighting one's own brethren. To be sure, the President was the highest officer in the land, and should ordinarily be obeyed. But when Feng Kuo-chang, who as everyone knew wanted peace, ordered war, the situation was different: the President had clearly been coerced, and his order should be opposed. The telegram concluded with an appeal to all troops to stop advancing and fighting, and make peace a reality out of pity for the suffering nation.[124] Four days later Feng issued a similar telegram calling for a cease-fire, the convening of the national assembly, and peace.[125]

On February 25, a presidential mandate was issued reprimanding Feng Yü-hsiang for not obeying orders, for circulating telegrams advocating peace, and for forcibly appropriating salt and likin revenues in Hupeh. As a consequence of these offenses, Feng was deprived of his post and his case was referred to Ts'ao K'un for investigation. The commander of the 2nd Regiment of Feng's brigade replaced Feng as brigade commander.[126]

On March 1 the brigade responded with a telegram to the government asking that Feng not be relieved of his command. Feng had not taken the salt revenues, said the telegram, and he was not the first person to propose peace. Moreover, in advocating peace he spoke for every man in the brigade. The government should either cancel Feng's dismissal, the telegram concluded, or "shoot all 9,553 of us."[127] Meanwhile, Feng continued to command the brigade as if nothing had happened.

Shortly after the brigade sent its telegram, Ts'ao K'un also requested the government not to remove Feng from his command, but rather to give him an opportunity to atone for his offense.[128] On March 18, a presidential mandate was issued. In consideration of the wire from Ts'ao K'un, and another from the tuchün of Hupeh recommending "extraordinary leniency" toward Feng, Feng was deprived of his army rank of lieutenant general, but temporarily permitted to remain in his post under the control and order of Ts'ao K'un.[129]

It is easier to describe this sequence of events than to explain it, for one thing because we do not know whether the leading figures in Feng Kuo-chang's faction were at odds with one another, or were actually cooperating behind a facade of discord. It is doubtful that Feng Yü-hsiang's Wuhsüeh declarations were inspired by sympathy for the Southerners in general or Sun Yat-sen in particular, as has been averred,[130] or motivated solely by aversion to civil war. More likely, they were an extension of the policy implicit in his stopping at Pukow. On one level, they were directed against Anhwei in the hope of promoting the interests of Feng Kuo-chang and Lu Chien-chang. On another level, they conformed with the peace policy that had been publicly promoted by Feng Kuo-chang until the end of January, and that apparently still had his private support.

Two of Feng's chief officers have stated that Lu Chien-chang instigated Feng's Wuhsüeh declarations, and one of them has said that the move was aimed at Ni Ssu-ch'ung.[131] Ni himself interpreted it this way. He reported to the government that Feng's troops were preparing to attack the capital of Anhwei, while Kiangsu forces were concentrating to invade the province from the east.[132] Again, as at Pukow, it is not certain how seriously an invasion of Anhwei was considered by Feng and Lu.* At the very least, however, their move prevented Anhwei troops from leaving the province to fight in Hupeh or Hunan.[133] It thus prevented the spread of Anhwei military influence in Hupeh, a development that Wang Chan-yüan would certainly have found unwelcome. Moreover, it inhibited the extension of hostilities, and to that extent was in line with the peace policy.

Feng's Wuhsüeh declarations were made with the approval of Li Shun, and were supported by the other Yangtze tuchüns.[134] One may therefore infer that they also were supported by Feng Kuo-chang, and that his earlier acquiescence in the war policy had not reflected his

---

* The NCH, Feb. 23, 1918, p. 421, carried the following report: "Apart from a lengthy telegram which was circulated on February 14 by General Feng Yü-hsiang, he also took an oath in company with officers in the following form: 'Traitor Nyi Tsze-chung, the instigator of the rebellion, has trampled upon all law and discipline. The President was in duress and Parliament was throttled. Hostilities between brethren have been recklessly started to the great calamity of China, and the Powers are laughing at us. How can our country become strong if this traitor is not removed? We hereby denounce him and will punish him for his crimes with the valiant forces at our disposal. Let all of us be of one mind, never forgetting and never swerving from our purpose.'"

true feelings. This, perhaps, accounts for the government's lenient treatment of Feng Yü-hsiang.

Unfortunately for the cause of peace, no other warlords followed Feng's lead. Ts'ao K'un and his chief subordinate, Wu P'ei-fu, though among the least ardent supporters of the war policy, were not disposed to join the peace movement at this time; indeed, Wu reoccupied Yochow on March 17. Moreover, Fengtien troops had entered Chihli in late February, and on March 21 they started for Hunan and Hupeh. Feng Kuo-chang's peace policy was completely shattered, and on March 23 Tuan Ch'i-jui was again appointed Premier. Feng Yü-hsiang was left without support.

Isolation was dangerous for a warlord, particularly for one with as few resources as Feng Yü-hsiang. He had no alternative but to adopt a conciliatory attitude. When Tuan returned to power, Feng sent him a congratulatory message, a move that foreigners declared established Feng's reputation as a humorist forever.[135] More important were his new ties with Ts'ao K'un and Wu P'ei-fu, which were rendered formal by the President's mandate of March 18 officially making Ts'ao Feng's superior officer. This arrangement was welcome to Ts'ao as representing a great increase in his potential military power. For Feng it provided a convenient way out of an impossible situation.

Having extricated himself from such dangerous circumstances, Feng showed no further aversion to civil war. In mid-April his brigade left Wuhsüeh for western Hunan to fight against Southern troops.[136] After sporadic fighting during May and early June, Feng's brigade occupied Ch'angte on June 22.[137]

Sometime before this, Lu Chien-chang had left Feng and gone to Tientsin, where he was invited to Hsü Shu-cheng's office for discussions. Hsü Shu-cheng—"Little Hsü"—was perhaps the leading figure in the Anhwei clique after Tuan Ch'i-jui himself. Lu Chien-chang visited Hsü on June 15. A few moments after he arrived he was taken by Hsü's soldiers into the garden and shot to death.[138]

It is generally accepted that though Tuan Ch'i-jui was ready to take some action against Lu, he had not intended anything as drastic as assassination.[139] But once the act had been committed, he stood by his subordinate. Knowing Lu's relationship with Feng Yü-hsiang, the commander of a powerful brigade, he immediately took steps to mollify Feng. On June 18, two days after the official announcement of Lu's "execution," a presidential mandate restored Feng's military rank.[140] About the same time Feng was made Defense Commissioner of Ch'angte,* and soon afterward he was given an award by the government.[141] Naturally, Lu was not mentioned in any of these orders, but the concatenation of events speaks for itself; Lu assisted Feng even in death. Feng said nothing publicly about Lu's murder.

In the six years since the establishment of the Republic, Feng had successfully weathered a series of threats to his army and his personal status. He had survived largely by shrewd opportunism. He had feelings, often strong feelings, about some of the issues that arose during those years, but they were consistently subordinated to his overriding goal: keeping the greatest possible control over the military force he had trained.

In the final analysis, however, the ability to come out on the winning side was a tenuous and uncertain means of achieving that goal. In the context of Chinese warlordism, the best defense of one's armed force was that armed force itself. Feng was certainly aware of this, and since the revolution he had steadily expanded the number of men under his command. He had seized every opportunity offered by time and circumstance to train his troops, to mold them into a vigorous and powerful fighting machine with a strong personal loyalty to himself. He had been reasonably successful in those efforts. Nevertheless, the demands made upon Feng by the political-military struggles of the early republican period inevitably interfered with his training programs. He and his troops had been shifted from one end of the country to the other, and had been involved in a series of crises that made systematic training all but impossible. Feng's troops had acquired valuable experience, but they needed formal training, education, organization, and indoctrination. For this purpose Feng needed a period of relative peace, a fixed location, and freedom from outside interference. All three of these needs were met when he became Defense Commissioner of Ch'angte, a position he occupied for the following two years.

---

* Feng Kuo-chang was upset about Lu's murder, but was pressured into signing a presidential mandate explaining that Lu had incited rebellion and had connections with bandits in several provinces. The mandate was issued on June 16. (Hsieh Kuan-lan, No. 41, p. 7. See also *NCH*, June 22, 1918, p. 684.)

4. Military and Civil Administration at Ch'angte

Feng Yü-hsiang is best remembered by his former subordinates for his competence in training troops. Their memories are corroborated by the widespread praise Feng's troops received from foreign observers impressed by their discipline and overall high caliber. This praise tapered off after 1927, when his army came to include many units not trained by him and not committed to his regulations. Of course its reputation for discipline continued, and not undeservedly, but the troops who sustained that reputation were nearly all veterans of Feng's training process.

Many characteristics of that process were apparent before Feng went to Ch'angte. But the constant expansion during those early years, when his army grew from the 500 recruits of 1912 to over 10,000 men in 1918, left little time for the kind of intensive training procedures that Feng devised and applied at Ch'angte.

It was also at Ch'angte that Feng had his first extended experience in public administration. As a military officer, Feng was presumably responsible for military affairs in the three districts, or *hsien*, assigned to him. But during the warlord period, such an assignment inevitably entailed exercising civil authority as well. His civil administration at Ch'angte was characterized by the insistence on public order, the puritanism, and the penchant for public works programs that he later displayed in the administration of larger areas.

MILITARY TRAINING AND MORAL INDOCTRINATION

Recruiting

In trying to distinguish Feng's army from other warlord armies, some writers have focused on Feng's recruiting policy. They say he recruited peasants and workers exclusively, in a conscious effort to bar former soldiers and others likely to have degenerated into "good-for-nothings."[1] Although it is unquestionably true that Feng was more particular about recruits than many of his contemporaries, the view that he demanded recruits of a standard high above the norm for the time is exaggerated. Indeed, Feng's criteria for selecting men were essentially those set down by the Department of the Army. Speaking of his recruiting trips in the autumn of 1913, Feng described as acceptable men who were peasants or workers of good family, between the ages of 19 and 26, without venereal disease, and of about 5' 7" minimum height. "Anyone whose face was yellow or whose flesh was emaciated, who was spiritless, or whose height was insufficient, we did not want."[2] Feng was perhaps more conscientious than many other warlords in applying recruiting standards, but the real difference between his troops and those of most other warlord armies resulted from his rigorous training program.

In theory, recruits to Feng's army or to any other Chinese army were to serve for three years. But in practice, a man's term of service was very indefinite, as the following comment of one of Feng's chief officers indicates:[3]

When a man came to join the army, the recruiter would ask him why he wanted to join, and that was about all. After he became a soldier, if he had some good reason for going home, like the illness of a parent, he could request leave. He might get off for a month or even two, assuming there was no war or imminent war. After his leave expired, he had to return to the army. If he decided that he no longer wanted to be a soldier, he could request a long leave and remain at home if he got it. The authorities were naturally very reluctant to grant such permission, but if a man was determined and there was no war immediately in the offing, he could sometimes get it because he was considered a potential deserter anyway.

Thus enlistment was not conceived of as a fixed "hitch," but rather as a less definite relationship whose duration depended on various fluctuating factors, ranging from a soldier's personal situation to the current needs of the army.

Most volunteers apparently had few home ties to bind them, and the inducements that led them to join served to keep them in. The army quickly became a home and a way of life. Of course, that way of life varied from one warlord army to another. In the worst of them, it was a life of dissipation, looting, and petty extortion. In Feng's army, by contrast, it was a life of rigorous discipline, hard work, and continual training.

Although it was common practice during the warlord period to absorb soldiers from defeated enemy units, this was not an important source of men for Feng before he went to Ch'angte. In the second half of the 1920's, however, he increasingly resorted to that practice.

Military Skills and Knowledge

There is little material available on the precise nature and quality of the technical military features of Feng's training program, although it is clear that he did not neglect these aspects.[4]

At Ch'angte, Feng established a Military Training Corps, with a section for officers and another for noncommissioned officers. A small degree of literacy was the standard of admission to either section. In groups of 120 men, those who qualified went through a three-month program during which they studied military tactics, techniques of leading troops, topography, weapons, military history, fortifications, and regulations. The Military Training Corps continued in existence after the brigade left Ch'angte, and the course of study was gradually expanded, until by 1924 the complete training period was two years.[5]

One of Feng's units that attracted much attention in later years was the Ta-tao-tui, the Big Sword Unit. It was apparently established in 1917, though it may have been in existence earlier.[6] It was initially called the Pistol Unit, and each man was outfitted with a rifle, a pistol, and a large sword. The unit was manned by troops handpicked for their fighting ability, and in subsequent years their exploits, particularly with their flashing blades, made them respected and feared throughout China as the Big Sword Unit. They later accomplished heroic feats against the Japanese. As Feng's army came to include more than one brigade, each one apparently had a Big Sword Unit. The men of these units wore patches on their uniforms that read:[7]

When we fight, we first use bullets; when the bullets are gone, we use bayonets; when the bayonets are dull, we use the rifle barrel; when this is broken, we use our fists; when our fists are broken, we bite.

Such fierce determination was certainly a military asset, but it reveals nothing of their technical capacities. However, it is reasonably certain that the level of military knowledge and skill in Feng's brigade was higher than in most other units of the period. It is perfectly certain that in terms of general military competence and effectiveness, Feng's brigade was superior to many other units of comparable size because of the other aspects of his training program, notably body-building and strict discipline.

Body-Building

When Feng served in Manchuria before the Revolution of 1911, he had been impressed by the inability of some troops to withstand physical hardship and fatigue. Determined that his own troops should display no such weakness, Feng from the outset emphasized physical fitness in training them. Besides the formal training prescribed by army regulations, Feng's men regularly practiced such things as weight lifting, vaulting wooden horses, and running obstacle courses. Special classes were also organized for boxing and gymnastics.[8]

As Feng moved from place to place during these early years, he continued his training program at every opportunity, and body-building was always a prominent feature. For example, while at Langfang during the winter of 1916–17, he organized trench-digging contests, in which units vied with one another in trying to shovel frozen ground.[9] In line with this Spartan approach, Feng thought rain or snow provided ideal conditions for military maneuvers.[10]

Feng had come to Langfang from Szechwan, and during the long and arduous trip he had found his noncombatant officers something of a burden. Supply officers, medical officers, and various clerical officers were, in Feng's words, "civilians through and through. First, they could not march. Second, they could not ride horses. Third, if an emergency occurred, they could not protect themselves. On this long and difficult march, how was I to treat them? Even I, the brigade commander, was carrying a load; how could I give them sedan chairs to ride in?" Therefore, at Langfang Feng instituted a policy of giving officers of this type both military and physical training, with the result that they were soon able to "jump off a horse and write [a report or dispatch], or jump on a horse and kill an enemy."[11] If examination showed that clerical officers had acquired sufficient military skill, they could be made regular military officers.[12]

There were also other men in the army whose duties were essentially nonmilitary: gunsmiths, blacksmiths, buglers, cooks, animal tenders, and the like. There were about 200 such men in every regiment, and Feng undertook to turn them into competent soldiers. In this way, every man in the brigade, regardless of his normal duties, acquired "the skill needed to kill an enemy."[13]

After the brigade was settled at Ch'angte, the civil officers were organized into a physical-exercise unit. Every officer had to participate in such activities as weight-lifting, gymnastics, running obstacle courses, and various sports. There were periodic examinations, with rewards for progress and punishments for lack of it. Of course, the regular military officers and all the soldiers also participated in similar physical activities. Most of Feng's troops could not swim when they joined the army, and learning how was also part of their training.[14]

Most men in the brigade seem to have acquired commendable ability in physical activities, particularly vaulting, gymnastics, and running obstacle courses. Feng insisted that the officers train with the same rigor that was demanded of the men, and preferred that the officers excel. He frequently demonstrated the athletic prowess of his army to visitors, and on such occasions teams made up solely of officers sometimes participated. A foreign observer at Ch'angte described one such exhibition:[15]

The usual pole jumping, vaulting, and bar exercises were carried out with great agility mingled with quite a good amount of freak displays, none of which resulted in failure. The close was an obstacle race commencing with a long jump over a ditch; a run along narrow baulks bridging across a pit; the swarming of first a brick wall, then a higher wooden barrier, and ending in a final run up a steep mound. The men started in batches of four. There was rarely more than a second or two between the first to reach the goal and the fourth. Nineteen seconds is reckoned a first class time. The entire display was by officers.

Another activity that was emphasized at Ch'angte was the rapid march with full pack. Indeed, this was "the most common type of training." The men frequently marched on the city wall surrounding Ch'angte. About twice a month week-long marches were made outside the city. Carrying packs weighing around 65 pounds, the men would march about 25 miles the first day, gradually increasing the distance until a day's march was 40 or 45 miles.[16] In a country where communications and transportation facilities were undeveloped, the ability to march rapidly for long periods of time was an obvious asset, and Feng's men came to excel in such tests of endurance. For example, on one occasion Feng's Big Sword Unit ran approximately 80 miles in 24 hours.[17]

Education

Most of the men who joined Feng's army were illiterate, or semiliterate at best.[18] Moreover, they knew no trade or craft; indeed, this ignorance was one factor that drove many into the army. As soldiers of Feng Yü-hsiang, however, they received both academic and vocational training, although the former was on a fairly elementary level.

Feng's attack on the problem of his soldiers' illiteracy began as early as the first or second year of the Republic, when he wrote a lesson book designed to teach 800 basic characters.[19] This booklet was still in use during the Ch'angte period, but by then the program to develop literacy was being considerably broadened. Two officers were assigned to compile a soldier's reader that included over a hundred essays, or excerpts from essays, by ancient and modern writers. They were evidently arranged according to difficulty of vocabulary and grammar so that each man could find his own level of competence and work from there. The teaching method was to explain the content and language of an essay or passage, then demand that it be memorized and written out from memory. Examinations were given every month. Since Feng wrote that there were special classes for those interested in literary Chinese, it is possible that the excerpts taken from classical literature were rewritten in colloquial language. For the students of literary Chinese, a reader was compiled of excerpts from the *Book of History*.[20]

Feng also set up classes in English and Japanese while at Ch'angte to assist the officers in translating and interpreting foreign military books and documents.[21] Feng admitted, however, that progress was very slow, and there was little indication in later years that his officers had achieved any proficiency in these languages.

Besides the educational program for his troops, Feng set up a secondary school in Peking for the sons of his officers. Established in 1917, it was associated with, and probably housed with, the Methodist mission in Peking. In 1919, he bought a house for the school and named it "The School for Officers' Sons of the Sixteenth Brigade." The curriculum was comparable to that of ordinary schools, with the addition of courses in the Bible and in handicrafts.[22] Schools were also set up to provide a basic education for the wives and other dependents of officers.

Shortly after the brigade arrived in Ch'angte, Feng addressed his officers on the importance of instituting vocational training in the army. He said there were three reasons for this. First, China needed skilled workers. Second, when soldiers left the army, they often had no way to make a living and frequently turned to banditry. This would not happen if they had a trade to fall back on. Third, many soldiers became crippled from war wounds, and it was imperative that they learn some skill with which to support themselves. Therefore he proposed to establish workshops in his army for the production of simple commodities and the training of officers and men.[23]

In these workshops, Feng's men were taught such skills as the manufacture of stockings, towels, and stationery, as well as tailoring, rattan weaving, and bookbinding. Later, printing was also added. Outside teachers were employed at first, but as officers and men became proficient they began to instruct each other, and the teachers were dismissed. Officers below a certain rank and all the men had to study at least one of these trades. Feng himself spent an hour or so each day in one of the shops. Many of the commodities produced were used by the army, and a store was set up to sell the surplus to the general public. A portion of the proceeds was distributed to the soldier-workers.[24] A foreign visitor to Ch'angte described the work as being done in a "most satisfactory manner," and said that the commodities produced were "most evidently strong and honestly made."[25]

In addition to these workshops, there were classes in carpentry, metal work, photography, and gun repair. Each civil officer was supposed to study at least one of these subjects, but it is not clear whether military officers and men were required or allowed to participate.[26]

Indoctrination

In later years, Feng often referred to the "political education" his troops received before and during their stay at Ch'angte. This description is somewhat misleading, for the indoctrination Feng's men received up to about 1926 was more moral than political, although this stress on morality had both political and military implications.

Feng's concern for the moral education of his men appeared very early. About 1915, he wrote a booklet entitled *The Book of the Spirit* (Ching-shen shu), consisting of eighty inspirational and admonitory statements organized into three chapters.* "The Spirit of Morality" emphasized the cultivation of personal character; it urged the reader to be serious in speech, cautious in action, diligent in study, and so on. "The Spirit of Patriotism" brought Confucianism to the support of the nation by asserting that the "sacrifice of one's own small self is the principle of humanity [*jen*] and righteousness [*i*]." "The Spirit of Military Discipline" stressed the role of discipline in personal and social achievement.[27]

A couple of years later, Feng compiled another short book for the edification of his men. This one consisted of moralistic historical tales, very simply written and with a few lines of commentary to ensure that the moral was not missed. For example, he wrote of the scholar who was said to have fastened sharp darts on the back of his chair to keep himself from falling asleep while studying. Chinese history abounds

* In 1926 Feng added a fourth chapter, "The Spirit of Revolution."

with stories pointing up the value of study, the importance of loyalty, the cleverness of great generals, and so on. It was stories like these that Feng included in his anthology.[28]

Feng's troops were also subject to several regulations that had moral overtones. They were not allowed to smoke tobacco, to say nothing of opium.* Drinking and gambling were likewise prohibited. Soldiers were admonished to abstain from profane or obscene language. They were forbidden to visit brothels, although this was a somewhat superfluous injunction since Feng usually closed the brothels wherever he went; he did so in Ch'angte.

Feng's attitude toward the personal behavior of his men was not quite as moralistic or fanatical as it has sometimes been made to seem. Each of these rules was clearly relevant to the morale, health, or discipline of the men. Indeed, with the exception of smoking, all of the activities prohibited by Feng are condemned or forbidden in any modern army. During the warlord period, when many soldiers were in poor physical condition, had little spirit, and antagonized the populace by their unruly behavior, Feng's troops were set apart by their adherence to his rules. Feng was not unaware of the military advantages and the favorable public image that resulted from his regulations, and they were probably motivated more by such pragmatic considerations than by any inordinate preoccupation with "sin," his interest in Christianity notwithstanding.

Feng has described his years at Ch'angte as the "period of my greatest enthusiasm for Christianity." He felt that "if the tenets of Christianity were intensively propagandized in the army, it would be of great benefit. Therefore, I determined that prayer should be one method of spiritual training in the army."[29] Daily religious services

---

* Feng has been quoted as saying that there was no rule against smoking in his army. Evidently he was trying to impress his listeners with an image of his men as clean-living Spartans who voluntarily abstained from smoking. Actually, smoking was proscribed, although some of Feng's high officers smoked secretly. At least it was a secret as far as most of the men were concerned. Feng discovered his officers smoking on more than one occasion, but usually dismissed the infraction with a facetious remark. Chien Yu-wen, a political officer under Feng in the mid-1920's, in *Hsi-pei tung-nan feng*, p. 25, tells the following story: "Feng did not smoke, and he did not like his subordinates to smoke. Army regulations on smoking were very strict. However, there were quite a few high officers who smoked secretly. On one occasion, Feng went to the room of his private secretary where he smelled smoke. Feng, as if reading an eight-legged essay, said: 'Your room is both smoky and stinking. It is stinking, and it is also smoky. Being smoky, it is stinking; being stinking, it is also smoky. Smoky, smoky; stinking, stinking. Stinking, stinking; smoky, smoky. It is smoky, and it is stinking; it is stinking, and it is smoky.' And turning his head away, he went out."

were held, Bible classes were organized, and the men were encouraged to read their Bibles and pray on their own. Every Sunday all the officers and men were assembled to hear religious services. Chinese preachers were employed, and many foreign missionaries were invited to come to Ch'angte at Feng's expense. By these means, the men were thoroughly exposed to Christian teachings. Although baptism into the Christian faith was encouraged, it was not compulsory. Indeed, those who were baptized did not gain any practical advantages over those who were not. For example, the promotion process took no account of a man's religion.[30]

Many of Feng's men did convert to Christianity, and foreign missionaries who baptized some of them were impressed by their knowledge of Christian teachings. It is difficult to tell just how many converted by the end of the Ch'angte period. One estimate says that two thousand of Feng's men were baptized Christians in 1919.[31] By the time the brigade left Ch'angte in the summer of the following year, it is probable that at least twice that number were Christians.[32] It is also likely that the percentage of Christians was higher among the officers than among the men.

It was Feng's program for encouraging Christianity among his troops at Ch'angte that first attracted the widespread attention of foreign missionaries. They were generally ecstatic about the "Christian General," whom they looked upon as an example of the power of the Christian message, and as a great potential force for the further Christianization of China. Feng accepted the assistance of the foreign missionaries and tolerated their enthusiasm, but it seems clear that his motives for promoting Christianity among his troops were in the main military.

From a military point of view, there was much to be gained from Feng's converting his troops to Christianity. In the first place, he was able to exploit the Christian belief in an afterlife to make his troops less fearful of death,* and hence bolder in battle.[33] Second, Feng's army acquired greater solidarity from its Christianization. For one thing, those who took their new faith seriously were not likely to defect to another army where they might be persecuted for their alien beliefs. Moreover, their common faith also brought the men closer to their leader, Feng Yü-hsiang. The bonds of respect, obedience, fear, and habit were thus supplemented by a spiritual bond. By virtue of

---

* Feng praised the Buddhist belief in reincarnation for having the same utility. (*WSH*, pp. 305–6.)

his superior rank and his longer experience as a Christian, Feng's relation to his Christian troops was not unlike that of a pastor to his "flock." Although Feng recognized that this relationship tended to strengthen the direct ties between him and his soldiers, he knew that the critical element in his control of the army was still the loyalty of his officers. Therefore he was particularly concerned to convert them. A few months after Feng left Ch'angte, he told a foreign missionary working in his brigade: "Remember that your chief work is not to try to convert the rank and file of my army, but to use your strength in trying to get all my officers filled with the Spirit of God, for as soon as that takes place the lowest private in the army will feel the effect of it."[34] If an officer refused to accept the faith, Feng sent other officers to talk with the man informally, pointing out the values and attractions of Christianity. Finally, the Christian influence supplemented Feng's other means of maintaining disciplined conduct.[35] Men were less likely to gamble, drink, seek out prostitutes, abuse shopkeepers, and generally cause trouble when such misbehavior violated not only army regulations, but also their religious beliefs.

Discipline and Loyalty

During the warlord period, when soldiers were often considered a greater menace than bandits and thieves, the appearance of well-disciplined troops was always somewhat of a surprise. In this respect, Feng's troops surprised people wherever they went, and in time they acquired a modicum of fame in China for their discipline alone. Foreign missionaries were always happy to see Feng take over jurisdiction of the area where they were working, not only because of his Christianity, but also because they knew that public order would be established and that they need not fear depredations by his troops. Both the quality of Feng's discipline and its rarity in China were reflected in letters from foreigners in Wuhsüeh at the time Feng stopped there early in 1918. After he had been there only a few weeks, foreigners customarily referred to his troops as "the model brigade."[36]

This excellent discipline was the cumulative result of many aspects of Feng's training and leadership. Moreover, most of these same aspects also nurtured the loyalty of Feng's men to the brigade and to Feng himself. In particular, the moral education Feng gave his men was conducive to both loyalty and good behavior. Feng's position as "spiritual leader" of his men has already been mentioned as a factor increasing their respect and his authority. Among other features of

Feng's training program that helped to develop discipline and loyalty was the rapport he was able to establish with his officers and troops. Feng took great pains to learn the names of as many of his soldiers as possible, and to become familiar with their family backgrounds and personal characteristics. In 1913, when he commanded a regiment of about 1,600 men, he knew the names of about 1,400 of them. When his men were ill, housed in poor quarters, or discomfited in any other way, Feng personally visited them and did whatever he could to ameliorate conditions. When strolling through camp, he would frequently sit down and chat with the men about their personal problems, their "gripes," their ambitions, current local and national issues, or any other subject that interested him or them.[37]

Feng held frequent inspections, usually twice a week, and if he observed any shortcomings, he discussed them in great detail with the officer in charge of the unit. During these inspections, he courteously asked the soldiers about their living conditions, food, and so on.[38]

Attending to the personal problems of the men was a principle of leadership that Feng believed in very strongly.[39] His concern for their welfare extended even to their home life. On one occasion, he is said to have had an officer beaten because he refused to reconcile with his estranged wife.[40] This concern usually expressed itself in a more benevolent fashion. If a man needed extra money for a wedding or a funeral in his family, Feng would provide it. He also had a program for sending part of each man's pay to his parents.*[41] Parents of soldiers killed in combat were entitled to receive money from Feng, and soldiers disabled as a result of their wounds were supposed to receive a monthly pension.[42] However, during most of Feng's career he was short of money, and it seems that these provisions were seldom carried out.[43]

Besides the informal contact Feng had with his men in camp, he frequently made speeches to them. He was a marvelously eloquent speaker. Emotional and shrewd, colorful and down-to-earth, he could hold his men entranced for one or two hours at a time. Although he often repeated essentially what he had said many times before, his men never tired of listening.[44] His eloquence and dynamic personality could move even relatively sophisticated audiences, but his humble

---

* Feng's account represents this as a unique program that exemplified his concern for his men and their families. Actually, it was evidently standard army policy, although it is doubtful that it was thoroughly carried out in any army. The *CYB*, *1919*, p. 322, in describing the conditions of army service, states: "Arrangements are made for the payment of a portion of a soldier's wages to his family...."

origins and service as a common soldier gave him an understanding, a simplicity, and an earthy quality that made him especially effective in speaking to the simple peasants who comprised his army.

By these means, Feng established a direct personal tie with his men. The part played by his officers in maintaining the loyalty of the army was, of course, crucial, but Feng's insistence on a direct relationship between himself and his men was conducive to the development of a strong personal loyalty. This, in turn, nourished discipline, for the men willingly obeyed orders that they knew emanated ultimately from their respected commander-in-chief.

Another factor that contributed to discipline and loyalty in Feng's army was the just treatment the men received. During the warlord period, corporal punishment was common in Chinese armies, and many officers abused their authority in this respect. This was true of the junior officers in Feng's newly recruited units in 1912 and 1913, who often resorted to physical violence with little provocation. Coupled with the rigorous training the men underwent, such abuses created a good deal of discontent, and many soldiers tried to desert. In an effort to curb this practice, Feng warned his officers against arbitrary mistreatment of their men and limited their authority to administer corporal punishment. Although he conceded that it could not be completely abolished in the conditions of the time, he specified the circumstances when it would not be tolerated in "Eight No-Hitting Rules." Officers were not to strike a man if he had been working hard; if he was a new recruit; if he was a first offender; if he was sick; if he had just eaten or was hungry; if he was depressed or sad; if the officer was angry; or if the weather was either very hot or very cold. Morale improved, and the number of desertions decreased after these rules were applied.[45] Nevertheless, corporal punishment was still creating problems at Ch'angte, where some soldiers developed ear trouble from being beaten with sticks; Feng ordered his officers thereafter to use only their hands to administer beatings.[46] He repeatedly urged them to treat their men with compassion and understanding.[47]

There was no favoritism in Feng's army. Officers and men alike knew they would be judged on the basis of their achievements, and not on such things as family connections, regional background, or religion. Feng scrupulously avoided anything that smacked of nepotism. When a relative approached him for a position, he refused, saying, "In my army it is only necessary to have one person by the name of Feng."[48]

Another important feature of the army was that there was little distinction between the officers and men in their dress and living conditions. Officers' uniforms were the same as enlisted men's except that the officers wore epaulets. Officers and men ate the same food, were subject to the same regulations, and generally shared the advantages and disadvantages of army life.* There was consequently little resentment from the ranks when an arduous assignment was made, because the men who gave the orders shared whatever hardships were involved. For example, when Feng's brigade left Szechwan in the summer of 1916, they had to transport large quantities of ammunition over rugged terrain. They could find no porters, and consequently the load was divided equally among officers and men, including Feng himself. Carrying loads weighing around 85 pounds, the men marched about 25 miles a day, but there were no complaints, since the officers shared the burden.[49]

Feng's long-range military ambitions were evident in his early efforts to develop a competent and devoted officer corps. During the early republican period, competent officers were more essential than ever to the development of an able army, since they had such a powerful influence over the generally illiterate and ignorant men. Realizing this, Feng organized intensive training classes for battalion commanders, company commanders, squad commanders, and noncommissioned officers at Peiyüan in 1913. Feng, who personally taught two courses, made a great effort to supplement classroom work with practical work in the field. Most of the men who became the medium- and low-ranking officers of the 16th Mixed Brigade were trained at this time.[50]

Late in 1914, when the 16th Mixed Brigade came into being, Feng set up a model company to develop potential leaders among his troops. It consisted of 130 selected men and was led by Li Ming-chung. In addition to the regular training program, the model company

---

* The utter simplicity of Feng's own uniforms and living habits became an essential part of the colorful public image he projected, and is mentioned in many contemporary accounts. Mr. Ernest T. Shaw, who was with the American Board Mission in China in the early 1920's, mentions an example of this trait in one of the letters he has kindly supplied this writer: "Recently Mr. Gailey [of the Peking YMCA] was going north and it happened that General Feng was coming about the same time, so he invited Mr. Gailey to come along with him in his special car. When Mr. Gailey and his coolies arrived at the station, they threw his baggage into a box car, then Mr. Gailey asked to be shown to the General's private car. 'Here it is over here!' they said, and led him over to another box car! He and the General rode together in it for twenty-four hours!"

studied principles of tactics and strategy. Feng was particularly concerned with their political education because of its bearing on their
loyalties, and he personally lectured the company on political topics
nearly every day.[51] Many of the men who led his army during the critical struggles of the mid-1920's were products of this model company.

In view of the importance of loyal officers, the absorption of defeated units was often a dubious gain. Units that surrendered easily
or defected to Feng could be expected to surrender or defect just as
easily to Feng's enemies. Feng's procedure in incorporating an enemy
unit was to retain its officers in their commands for a short time. During this period he treated the officers and men very well, and tried to
gain their confidence and respect. He then replaced the officers of the
incorporated unit with his own officers, and subjected the replaced
men to several months of training. After that they were assigned to
other units as subordinates of reliable officers. Of course, if any of
these new officers were considered incompetent or untrustworthy,
they were discharged.[52] As mentioned above, Feng did not absorb
defeated units on a large scale until the 1920's, when he found it im
possible to integrate the new troops with the old.

Training and Indoctrinational Devices

Some of the devices and methods Feng used in his training programs have been mentioned earlier, but there were many others.

One characteristic of Feng's training from the first was his use of
training songs, an old practice in Chinese armies. Frequently, when
Feng perceived shortcomings in his troops, he would compose lyrics
admonishing them, which were set to music and which all the officers
and men were required to learn. They were frequently sung on
marches, thus lifting the soldiers' spirits while drilling elementary
precepts into their heads. In 1912 and 1913, Feng's troops learned
songs dealing with proper behavior in battle, the techniques and
principles of firing a rifle, and tactical uses of terrain during a battle:[53]
In succeeding years, Feng wrote other songs to meet special situations
as they arose. For example, before starting the march into Szechwan
in 1915, he wrote a "Song for Marching Over Mountainous Terrain."
After Feng began to attend Christian services regularly, he put some
of his lyrics to hymn music.[54]

Songs were used not only to teach military methods, but also to inspire good behavior. There was a song about the necessity of loving
the common people, and another that listed the causes of the "na-

tion's shame." When Feng's battalion was stationed in Peking early in 1913, songs were written to discourage carousing. On those infrequent occasions when the men were allowed on the streets, they had to sing such songs as "We Must Not Drink or Smoke," or "We Must Not Gamble or Visit Whores." It is not surprising that many residents thought Feng eccentric.[55]

Religious and patriotic hymns were also part of Feng's program for uplifting his men through song. A foreign visitor to Feng's camp described a session at which such hymns were sung:[56]

There is a choir of some 16 men who sing in unison (or almost so) with clear, strong voices. . . . The men, too, join in, and one listens with surprise to some hundreds of voices rolling out "Onward Christian Soldiers" or "Stand Up, Stand Up for Jesus" or the National Anthem. This general singing is no perfunctory addition to drill: the faces of the men show the heartiness of the singing as unmistakably as the continuous full-voiced shout. The resources of softer singing have not yet been explored by the Christian soldiers of the Sixteenth.

It is not surprising that this visitor heard the singing of the National Anthem, for it was sung daily as part of Feng's attempt to inculcate patriotism in his men.[57] The patriotism Feng taught was rather vague. He identified the nation with the people; hence to love one's country one must love the people. In addition, he said, one must resist foreign encroachments, particularly those of Japan. Feng bitterly resented Japan's ultimatum of May 7, 1915, which forced China to accept the humiliating Twenty-One Demands. Thereafter, the belts of Feng's officers and men bore the inscription "In Memory of the National Humiliation of May 7." His soldiers also performed plays with themes encouraging resistance to Japan.

Plays were a common device used by Feng to train and indoctrinate his men. The officers and men wrote the plays, produced them, and acted in them. Designed to teach such virtues as sincerity, bravery, humaneness, and righteousness, the plays incidentally disseminated some elementary hygienic and scientific information. The content of a play was normally explained to the audience before the performance, a practice that greatly facilitated understanding.[58]

Feng often attempted to combine education with recreation, as in the case of these plays. At Langfang, for instance, recreation clubs were organized, and they also became an important feature of the Ch'angte program. Furnished with musical instruments, sports equipment, books, newspapers, and magazines, these clubs were places where the men could enjoy themselves while improving their physical fitness, their literacy, and their general knowledge.[59] Special activities supplemented those of the recreation clubs. In 1919, for example, a team from Feng's army participated in a large sports meet in Ch'angte. Summer retreats for officers were often held in cool mountain settings, where they could relax, amuse themselves with games, books, music, and painting, and hear lectures on "edifying subjects."[60]

Important Features of Feng's Army

What sort of army did this training produce?

In the first place, all the officers and men, combatants and noncombatants alike, were in excellent physical condition and could withstand sustained hardship. Moreover, all were taught military skills, so that, in a sense, there were no noncombatant personnel. It was an industrious army; the men were kept busy learning and working. They not only studied the skills of soldiering, but also acquired an elementary education and learned a simple trade.

The army was extremely well-disciplined. A soldier was not only expected to abide by rigorous discipline from the moment he joined, but also subjected to a process of moral indoctrination that, among other things, cultivated disciplined behavior. The men were taught that loyalty, decent behavior, frugality, good fellowship, and respect for learning were both good in themselves and good for the nation. In addition, a large proportion of the officers and men were converted to the Christian faith; the army was a Christian army. It was also patriotic; the army was taught to respect the Chinese people and to oppose both foreign nations and domestic politicians who attempted to exploit them.

It was a loyal army. Because of its many distinctive features, the men felt they were part of a unique organization; they were proud of the 16th Mixed Brigade, and loyal to it. Most important, they were loyal to Feng Yü-hsiang personally. Feng assiduously cultivated this loyalty through his detailed attention to the needs and thoughts of his men, the force of his personality and example, the justice of his administration, and his role as their religious guide. Officers and men alike respected Feng and trusted him. Nor did they find any inconsistency or contradiction between this personal loyalty to Feng and their patriotic devotion to the country. In the final analysis, Feng's opinion was always accepted as to what practical actions were patriotic and moral. One of Feng's officers has described the commander-in-chief's relationship with his men this way: "Everyone had a kind of mysterious trust in Feng. The power and influence of his personality were able to reach down to the lowest-ranking soldier in his force, so that the whole army was like a single body in which Feng was the head and the heart."[61]

Finally, it was at this time a small army. Of all its features, perhaps this was ultimately the most important. However accomplished it might be militarily, it was still only an expanded brigade. A larger army was necessary if Feng was to become a warlord of the first rank. He ultimately acquired a larger force, but he was caught up in the great and decisive struggles of the 1920's before he could mold it into the kind of cohesive, able, and spirited organization that he created in the years before he left Ch'angte.

CIVIL ADMINISTRATION AT CH'ANGTE

In a country inured to corruption and reaction, Feng's generally reformist and constructive civil administration attracted attention and was a source of his later fame. It was at Ch'angte that Feng had his first opportunity to exercise civil authority, and his administration there displayed several of the traits that marked his later civil rule.

Establishment of Order

The first task that faced Feng when he took over Ch'angte was the establishment of order. Hunan had been the scene of extended fighting, and in its wake had come depredations by bandit gangs and roving bands of undisciplined soldiers.[62] Feng immediately sent troops to quell these disorderly elements, and some vigorous fighting ensued. In one battle over 200 bandits were killed, and doubtless there were serious casualties among Feng's men. One bandit leader, rather than fight Feng's army, joined it; his band of several hundred men was organized into a new battalion. Peace and security were soon established in the area, although lawlessness continued to rage just outside Feng's jurisdiction.[63]

There is no question that Feng established law and order in the vicinity of Ch'angte and in the areas he controlled in later years. It is possible, however, that the disorder he suppressed was actuated by legitimate social and economic grievances. Throughout Chinese history, the word "bandits" has had an ambiguous meaning. Unsuccessful peasant uprisings against rapacious governments, for instance, have often been dismissed in official histories as outbreaks of banditry.

It seems safe to assume that this "bandit" label was applied as indiscriminately during the warlord period as before.*

Anti-Vice Measures

As soon as he was settled in Ch'angte, Feng embarked on a program to stamp out three vices: narcotics, gambling, and prostitution.

Feng estimated that 5 per cent of the population of Ch'angte were dope addicts at the time of his arrival.[64] Feng was strongly opposed to narcotics by temperament and background—his parents had suffered from drugs—and because he considered them to be one source of national debilitation. He therefore prohibited the sale and smoking of opium, and had opium traders arrested. Although his measures were not completely effective, a foreigner reported in the spring of 1919 that it was becoming ever "more difficult to evade the law."[65] Feng's men confiscated whatever drugs they found, and the collected stocks were publicly burned just before the brigade left Ch'angte in the spring of 1920. The fire lasted three days and nights.[66]

In order to cure the addicts, Feng set up a sanitarium, stocked it with medicine, food, and other supplies, and employed a specialist to supervise it. Addicts were encouraged to come voluntarily for treatment, but those who were unwilling were brought by force. To facilitate their rehabilitation, addicts who had been successfully treated

* The actual situation may not have been what is implied by the statement that banditry was suppressed, and law and order established. This possibility is hinted at by the existence of the Society of the Red Spears. According to peasant tradition, the Society of the Red Spears originated in the province of Shantung about 1920. Very little is known about the society, whose name derived from its members' practice of carrying long spears decorated with red tassels. It was apparently formed to combat the oppression of warlord armies, banditry, and conditions of general disorder. Like many Chinese secret societies, it had a marked religious aspect, and was traditionalistic and xenophobic. Its motto was: "Against bandits, against militarists, against foreign devils, against opium, against cards and wine; for peaceful labor and life, and for the preservation of Chinese ancient traditions." ("Xenanskie 'Krasnye Piki,'" pp. 170–72.) The activities of the Red Spears were said to be "defensive rather than offensive." (Hugh, p. 38.) In short, the Red Spears may not have been as disorderly an element as they have sometimes been considered, and their opposition to a warlord may have been evidence of the warlord's misrule. One source says Feng had some contact with the Red Spears at about the Ch'angte period, but this is doubtful. (Jonathan and Rosalind Goforth, p. 153.) For one thing, it is not even certain that the Red Spears existed at this time. Moreover, their activities centered in the Shantung-Hopei-Shensi-Honan region. Later, Feng did fight Red Spears in Honan, although he was also reported to have been the only militarist who was able to cooperate with them. (Dailey, "Christian General," p. 66.) The whole question is obscure, but it certainly seems possible that many of the groups referred to as bandit gangs were actually something like the Red Spears.

at the sanitarium were sent to the same vocational schools that Feng's troops attended, where they were taught a trade so they could earn a living upon their release. In this fashion, Feng said, three or four hundred people were cured of drug addiction.[67]

Given the conditions of the time, Feng's anti-opium program was commendable, even by modern standards. It is possible, however, that it was lax toward the upper classes. Nowhere do accounts of Feng's program refer to any forcing of landowners, officials, merchants, or other relatively prosperous persons to go to the sanitarium or to discontinue the use of narcotics. The opium eradication campaign seems to have concentrated on the poorer classes, an inference that is substantiated by the associated program of teaching former addicts a trade.

Gambling was also forbidden. Of all Feng's social reforms, this was doubtless the most difficult to enforce, for gambling can take place in private homes, where surveillance is difficult. Feng's own writings suggest that little was done to make this prohibition effective.[68]

This was not true, however, of Feng's prohibition of prostitution. As soon as he came to Ch'angte, he declared prostitution illegal; brothels were closed, and prostitutes were given three days to leave the area. This move, which was taken to protect the morals and health of Feng's troops, incidentally cut off a source of revenue, for prostitution was a taxable enterprise.[69]

Public Works

Besides undertaking these reforms, Feng promoted a variety of constructive works in Ch'angte. He met regularly with community leaders and asked them about local needs. On a number of occasions, he used his troops to help meet these needs.

His soldiers repaired the city wall, which was dangerously weak where the river surged against it. They extended a wharf into the river, so that the large number of residents who obtained their drinking water there could have access to water less polluted than that by the river bank. They also widened and repaired some roads. There were many barren areas in the Ch'angte vicinity, and Feng tried to beautify them by having his men plant tree shoots. Finally, he had stone pillars, inscribed with edifying maxims, erected alongside the roads.[70]

As public works, these were perhaps modest achievements. But although they did not involve any fundamental or far-reaching improvements, they benefited the community, which could hardly ignore the spirit of public service they reflected. If they achieved nothing else, they added to the reputation of the 16th Mixed Brigade.

Relations with the Public

In the eyes of both Chinese and foreigners, the reputation of the 16th Mixed Brigade rested primarily on the behavior of its members in their day-to-day contacts with the civilian populace. From the time the brigade was created, Feng was scrupulous in maintaining good relations with the communities in which his troops were quartered.

While Feng's brigade was staying at Wuhsüeh, the peasants in that vicinity frequently remarked on Feng's sense of justice and fair play.[71] There was good reason for this. His men were honest in their dealings with the people. There was no thievery by the soldiers, and when troops found it necessary to occupy a portion of a man's land, he was compensated. Feng had food brought in from other towns to relieve the pressure on the local food supply. In a proclamation to residents of Wuhsüeh and the surrounding countryside, Feng urged them to continue business as usual, and at the same time he ordered his troops to pay fair prices in sound currency. A few days before the brigade was to leave Wuhsüeh, Feng ordered his soldiers to settle all debts they had contracted in the town, and to return all borrowed articles. Any businessman who could not obtain a settlement of just debts was invited to apply directly to Feng, who saw that he did not suffer any loss.[72]

Feng followed similar policies at Ch'angte.[73] Such exemplary behavior by a Chinese warlord was news, and one correspondent reported:[74]

Ch'angte is peaceful, kept so by the excellent rule of General Feng. It is really a pleasure to see "business as usual" progressing in spite of military occupation and is in decided contrast to the southern part of the province. The soldiers are not billeted on the people and live in public buildings and at Government expense. In addition to excellent discipline, General Feng provides for the moral uplift of his men.

Most communities where Feng stayed were sorry to see him leave, for things usually got worse when his troops departed.[75] Certainly foreign missionaries were always unhappy to see Feng transferred, but appreciation of the behavior of his troops and the merits of his administration was not limited to foreigners. When Feng left Ch'angte and was crossing into Hupeh, the gentry and merchants of one town came to meet him and ask him to take over the administration of their part of the country.[76] Even the Hunan leaders, who were chasing out all Northern troops from the province in mid-1920, said they did not regard Feng as an enemy, and promised they would not attack him under any circumstances.[77]

Treatment of Foreigners

Since Feng promoted "business as usual" and at the same time encouraged the spread of Christianity, he could hardly help but be popular with foreigners in China, most of whom were directly concerned with either business or religion. However, Feng was very jealous of the dignity of China, and foreigners who flouted Chinese laws or Feng's regulations, or who in any way offended Chinese sensibilities, found him a very difficult man to deal with. This first became clear at Ch'angte.

On one occasion, a Chinese Catholic who became involved in a legal suit took sanctuary in the church of an Italian missionary. The missionary would not surrender the man to Feng's subordinates, and Feng decided to handle the matter himself. Taking the seal of his office, he went to the church and, standing on the steps, chastised the missionary: "You have the audacity to hide a criminal, and thus limit the authority of my country's laws. This seal is useless, then; I might as well give it to you and let you take care of affairs." Then Feng began crying in a loud voice to the people who had gathered around the steps: "The Catholic Church is hiding a criminal! The Catholic Church hides evil men!" The missionary, fearful that this outburst might jeopardize his missionary labors, finally relinquished the fugitive.[78]

Feng denied that he was opposed to Catholics on religious grounds, but it is clear that he had a low opinion of Catholicism in China. One young man, Feng related, accepted the Catholic faith and then became overbearing and arbitrary in his behavior. Moreover, he was abusive to his father. Feng writes that he had the boy seized and then "ordered some pistol troops to strike his mouth with the bottom of his shoe in the presence of everyone. They struck him until his mouth was full of blood, and he wept and cried out to me to forgive him." Some Catholics were all right, Feng conceded, but it was nevertheless true that many "Catholics look upon themselves as a specially privileged class. They put pressure on the government to protect evil men, and they behave arbitrarily in many ways."[79]

To show that he was not anti-Catholic on principle, Feng also tells of occasions when he acted against Protestant missionaries who behaved in a discourteous or arbitrary fashion.[80] However, these incidents with missionaries were insignificant compared to the continual friction that existed between Feng and the Japanese in Ch'angte.

There were a number of Japanese residents and shopkeepers in Ch'angte, and for a while during Feng's stay there was a Japanese warship anchored off the city. The first of several incidents occurred when Feng entered the city in 1918. He found Japanese flags flying from some shops, indicating that these stores were under Japanese protection. Feng was indignant at this foreign presumptuousness; he had the flags torn down and prohibited any such display in the future. On another occasion, some Japanese seamen objected to having their bags inspected by Feng's men at the city gate, and a scuffle ensued. Feng refused to make the apology demanded by the Japanese until the Japanese agreed to apologize to the sentries.[81] Other minor incidents followed. But Feng's major problem with the Japanese came in the spring of 1919, when the wave of anti-Japanese feeling started by the May Fourth Movement reached Ch'angte.

There was anti-Japanese feeling in Ch'angte in any event, and late in May, stimulated by events in Peking, there were open moves against the Japanese. Students went into the streets to urge the people to boycott Japanese products and shipping. Near the end of the month, students attacked and looted Japanese shops in the city.[82]

As a result of these disorders, local Japanese residents sent representatives to demand punishment for the leaders of the attack, compensation for losses, an apology, and a guarantee against future outbreaks. Feng apparently rejected the first three of these demands, but when the Japanese naval commander contemplated sending marines ashore to protect Japanese citizens, Feng accepted responsibility for the security of their shops. He ordered his Big Sword Unit to station two men in front of each Japanese residence and business establishment. They were to permit nobody to enter or leave, in order, as Feng explained, to avoid any risks. After a few days of this, "birds could build nests in the doorways of the Japanese-owned shops and houses; there was no business at all."[83] The Japanese then requested that the special guards be removed, and absolved Feng from responsibility for their future safety.[84]

Unfortunately, some important features of Feng's administration at Ch'angte are obscure. What, for example, was Feng's position relative to local tax revenues? There is little doubt that his own men collected the taxes, and that Feng retained all or most of the revenue for his own purposes. However, there are no data to confirm this. It would also be helpful to know if any of the Ch'angte revenues reached

Chang Ching-yao, the tuchün of Hunan. Probably they did not; probably Chang, like many another provincial tuchün, controlled only those portions of the province near the capital. Feng was at that time most closely associated with Wu P'ei-fu and Ts'ao K'un, and his relations with Chang were tenuous and cool. Wu was also in Hunan, and he likewise wasted no affection on Chang, who occupied the position that Wu felt should have been his. Both Wu and Feng seem to have adopted a rather independent stance toward Chang, but more than this we do not know.[85] More specific information about Feng's policies toward local Ch'angte leaders would also be helpful. In short, beneath the glitter of Feng's more conspicuous acts and policies there were other features that, if known, would provide greater insight into the nature of his civil rule. It was the unique characteristics of his administration that attracted most attention and that were recorded in writing. Therefore, for the moment, these must remain the measure of Feng's administration, and, indirectly, the measure of the man.

5. Tuchün

Feng Yü-hsiang left Hunan in the summer of 1920 after two years of peaceful training at Ch'angte. The respite was over, and Feng now plunged back into rough-and-tumble warlord intrigues, from which he would emerge in two years as a leading force in national politics.

After a few months in Hupeh, the 16th Mixed Brigade went to Shensi, where Feng became military governor. He was a tuchün at last. But his stay in Shensi was brief, for when war broke out in the spring of 1922 between the Chihli and Fengtien cliques, Feng's men fought on the side of the former. After the war, Feng was rewarded for his participation by being appointed tuchün of Honan. His tenure here was also brief: six months later, he was forced to accept a promotion to a position in Peking that actually diminished his independence and power by depriving him of a provincial base and provincial revenues.

The army Feng led to Peking at the end of 1922 had expanded far beyond a single mixed brigade. He had become commander of the 11th Division in addition to organizing three new mixed brigades, and this enlarged force constituted one of the leading armies in China. Moreover, by the time he left Honan, Feng's name was famous throughout the country, and the exploits and reputation of his army were known and admired in every province. In short, the two years from 1920 to 1922 witnessed the transformation of Feng from a figure of local importance to a warlord of the first rank, albeit weakened by the lack of a territorial base.

Departure from Ch'angte

The tuchün of Hunan, Chang Ching-yao, was hated by the Hunanese. He was a greedy and brutal tyrant, whose indiscriminate fe-

rocity earned him the nickname of "Butcher Chang."[1] Chang's tyr-
anny was propped up by the formidable army of Wu P'ei-fu, which
had conquered the province in 1918 and had been assigned watchdog
duties there, a task its commander did not relish. Wu not only thought
his conquest of the province entitled him to be tuchün, but also found
Chang's rapacity offensive. Therefore he was perfectly willing to abandon his guardianship of Hunan at the first opportunity. When the
Canton government offered him $600,000 to leave the province so
that Southern troops could drive out Chang, Wu departed without
hesitation at the end of May 1920.

The Hunanese armies, led by a former military governor of the
province, T'an Yen-k'ai, immediately launched a vigorous attack
against Chang Ching-yao, and by early June most of the province was
in their hands. The Hunanese troops dealt swiftly and mercilessly
with the hated bandit-soldiers whom Chang had assembled as his
army, but they did not attack Feng Yü-hsiang. Feng was respected by
the Hunanese leaders, and, some time before, T'an Yen-k'ai had even
sent representatives to ask Feng to join the Southern forces. Feng had
discussed this proposal with his officers, and they decided to refuse.
Feng and his men were Northerners; they had no ties with the Southerners, and they feared they would lose their identity and perhaps be
singled out for blame if things went badly.* In the summer of 1920,
after all the Northern troops except Feng's had left the province,
T'an Yen-k'ai issued a statement pledging that the Hunanese would
not attack Feng, whom they did not regard as an enemy.[2] When Feng
prepared to depart from Ch'angte, T'an sent him gifts and instructed
the Merchant Association of Ch'angte to give Feng 100,000 yüan.
Feng said he kept the gifts but refused the money.[3]

On July 6 Feng and his troops left Ch'angte, and the reforms he had
instituted virtually disappeared with him.† Feng and his men headed

---

* Since a number of passages in Feng's books indicate sympathy with the aims of
the Southerners, I asked several of his former subordinates why he did not join the
South when he had the opportunity. Almost without exception, the first sentence of
the reply was "Feng's was a Northern army," spoken in a tone of voice that implied
that this explained everything. Of course, there were other factors, but the great difference in atttitude between the North and South in China was of greater importance than can readily be imagined by those unfamiliar with the prejudices and
stereotypes held by people of either region about those of the other.
† A few days after Feng's departure, a private letter was sent from Ch'angte that included the following paragraph: "High sounding proclamations have been issued in
the city stating that the good works initiated by General Feng would continue to
be carried on: opium smoking, gambling, licentiousness, etc. were to be prohibited.
So far these proclamations have produced nothing practical, and we appear to be

into Hupeh, and on August 1, 1920, arrived at Shenchiachi, on the northern outskirts of Hankow. The brief war that had begun in July between the Anfu and Chihli cliques was over by then, and the defeated Anfu clique had been ousted from control of the Peking government. Feng remained in Shenchiachi until November, when he again led his troops northward, this time to Hsinyang, in southern Honan.

Feng's brigade was quartered at Hsinyang for the following six months, until the spring of 1921. For Feng this was a period of much introspection and self-criticism, punctuated by frequent resolutions to improve his character. He chastised himself for being lazy, proud, and ambitious; indeed, Feng lamented, he even desired wealth. He felt these were bad traits and resolved to eradicate them.[4] He began to keep a diary as a means of self-improvement. He wanted to be a "resurrected man, leading a new life," and decided the way to do this was to follow a rigid schedule.[5]

As so often seems to be the case with such personal schedules, it was easier to devise than to follow,* and was soon abandoned because of the exigencies of unforeseen problems. Feng's most serious difficulties while in Hsinyang concerned finances. He did not hold any local or regional office in Honan, and therefore had no handy source of revenue. At the same time, the central government was very remiss in supplying Feng with the funds required to pay and maintain his brigade. As a consequence, Feng had trouble even providing a sufficient diet for his men. This problem was seldom out of his mind. Once he even dreamed about the dearth of supplies, and afterward he commemorated the dream in a poem:[6]

> The suffering of the North-South War is unceasing.
> A friendless army defends Hsinyang.
> In a dream, I lament the lack of supplies,
> And when I awake, the pillow is wet with tears.

Since Feng was in severe financial straits, it was not surprising that he should think of his army as "friendless." However, Feng's brigade was not singled out for financial discrimination; many other units

---

reverting to the old conditions. The [Southern] soldiers are, for the most part, a scraggy, undisciplined lot and are themselves the worst offenders against public morality." (*NCH*, July 31, 1920, p. 293.)

* Feng's schedule was as follows: 6 A.M., get up, pray, read the Bible; 7 A.M., period of introspection; 8 A.M., inspect the officers and men; 8:30 A.M., breakfast, followed by official business; 10:30 A.M., receive official visitors; after lunch, practice calligraphy; 2 P.M., official business; 3:30 P.M., read moral books; 5–7 P.M., exercise and sports; after dinner, study English and write in diary; 9:30 P.M., pray and go to bed.

were in a similar condition. The central government was finding it increasingly difficult to pay the burgeoning armed forces, and in the next few years the problem was to become even more acute. Militarists with regional authority used regional funds. Commanders like Feng, without regional jurisdiction, had to rely on the central government or simply create or usurp local sources of revenue. The latter course, however, was not always available. Everything depended on the distribution of authority in the province, for preempting revenue sources would inevitably cause friction or conflict with those who already claimed jurisdiction over the taxes. While Feng was at Hsinyang, he was eager to avoid this sort of conflict. He wired the government repeated requests for money and made personal visits to government authorities, but with little success. Therefore, early in 1921, Feng turned to banditry. The victim he chose was the Peking government itself. Learning that a train was to pass through Hsinyang carrying several hundred thousand dollars in government revenue, Feng simply had his troops stop the train and seize the money. Then he notified Peking of his action.[7]

A few weeks after Feng had made news by turning to train robbery, there occurred what was aptly called the "Honan Revolt Mystery." The incident is still somewhat mysterious, but it is clear that it was partly behind Feng's leaving Honan, which in turn led to his rapid rise to the position of tuchün.

The mysterious revolt occurred in the spring of 1921, when Chao T'i was tuchün of Honan. At that time, Wu P'ei-fu was the actual leader of the Chihli faction, although ostensibly subordinate to Ts'ao K'un. Wu's official position of Assistant Inspecting Commissioner of Chihli, Shantung, and Honan made him Chao T'i's superior; indeed, some of Wu's troops were stationed in Honan. Early in 1921, Chao dismissed Ch'eng Shen as commander of the 1st Division of the Honan provincial troops. Ch'eng wanted to overthrow Chao, but first he obtained Wu's permission because he knew that no permanent change in provincial authority was possible without Wu's cooperation. It is not known whether Wu promised Ch'eng direct assistance, but in any event Feng Yü-hsiang was brought in on the plot. The revolt occurred in April, when Ch'eng Shen moved against Chao T'i in the north, while Feng attacked in the south. Wu P'ei-fu also attacked, but he attacked Ch'eng Shen and simultaneously ordered Feng to return his troops to their barracks immediately. Ch'eng Shen was defeated, his troops were disbanded, and the revolt was over.[8]

The mystery, which is still unsolved, is what motivated Wu P'ei-fu's devious actions. The best guess is that the entire affair was connected with the evolving division of the Chihli group into two cliques, one centering around Wu and the other around Ts'ao K'un.[9] In any event, Feng's involvement in the episode put him in an awkward position. He could not explain himself publicly without discrediting Wu P'ei-fu, and it was difficult for him to remain in a province controlled by a man whom he had conspired to overthrow. Realizing this, Wu promptly had Feng transferred to Shensi.

Tuchün of Shensi

In 1916 Lu Chien-chang had been forced out of Shensi by Ch'en Shu-fan, who had been military governor of the province since then. Ch'en was a member of the Anfu clique, and after the An-Chih War, with the leaders of the Anfu faction out of power and the central government in the hands of Chihli and Fengtien interests, there was bound to be a reshuffling of territory and spheres of influence. Inevitably, Ch'en Shu-fan's days were numbered, particularly since he did not have firm control over all parts of the province. On May 25, 1921, the central government ordered Yen Hsiang-wen, commander of the 20th Division, to succeed Ch'en as tuchün of Shensi.

Ch'en Shu-fan acknowledged the mandate that dismissed him from office, but requested that the government delay the arrival of Yen Hsiang-wen for a couple of months. Ch'en's motives were twofold. He wanted time to marshal all of his military strength to prevent Yen's take-over, and if that should prove impossible, he hoped to delay long enough to profit from the opium harvest. Many provincial militarists openly promoted the planting of opium poppy in their provinces, and Ch'en Shu-fan was one of the worst offenders.[10] Opium was taxed heavily, and immense revenues were derived from this practice. Ch'en Shu-fan knew if he could retain his position for a few months, he could probably obtain over $10,000,000 from this source alone.[11]

When the central government realized that Ch'en Shu-fan would have to be forced from office, two additional military units were ordered to accompany Yen Hsiang-wen into Shensi. One of these was the 7th Division, under Wu Hsin-t'ien, and the other was Feng's 16th Mixed Brigade, whose assignment was good news to the people of Shensi.[12] After a few battles, Ch'en Shu-fan was chased from the provincial capital, and Yen Hsiang-wen took over as tuchün on July 7. Feng and his men then proceeded to Hsienyang, a few miles west of Sian, where they were to be stationed.

Feng Yü-hsiang's men had played the leading role in ousting Ch'en

Shu-fan from Sian. As a result, Yen Hsiang-wen wired the central
government praising Feng and recommending that the 16th Mixed
Brigade be converted into a division. On August 5, 1921, Feng received orders to reorganize his troops as the 11th Division of the central army. Feng, of course, was named division commander; he was
also ordered to serve concurrently as commander of bandit-suppression activities in western Shensi.[13]

Since Ch'en Shu-fan had ousted Lu Chien-chang from Shensi in
1916, Feng must have found his role in Ch'en's downfall gratifying.
But Ch'en was not the only one of Lu's old enemies then in Shensi.
The earliest opposition to Lu had been led by a former bandit named
Kuo Chien, who had expected to replace Lu as tuchün. Ch'en had
double-crossed Kuo, but the latter was finally able to gain control of
a couple of towns in western Shensi, and from these strongholds he
carried on a campaign of harassment against Ch'en. Kuo was still
there when Feng Yü-hsiang and Yen Hsiang-wen entered the province
in the summer of 1921, and he offered Feng assistance in fighting
Ch'en.[14]

Kuo had a very unsavory reputation and was considered something
of a protégé of Fengtien interests.[15] Moreover, his hold on the western
part of the province obstructed provincial unity. Feng Yü-hsiang and
Yen Hsiang-wen consequently decided to kill Kuo, and Feng was
given the job, an assignment he evidently did not find distasteful. By
executing Kuo, Feng not only eliminated an obstacle to a unified administration, but also revenged the murder of his father-in-law, Lu
Chien-chang.[16]

The murder plot nearly turned into a fiasco. On August 13, Kuo
was invited to dine with Feng and two of his subordinates. While
they were eating, a company of Feng's soldiers gathered behind a
wooden wall surrounding the house. After waiting longer than they
had anticipated for a signal, several of the soldiers began to peek over
the wall. In doing so they put so much weight on the wall that it collapsed, and the soldiers fell headlong into the yard. This alerted Kuo
to the danger, but when he tried to flee Feng grabbed him and held
him until the soldiers came running in. A few moments later, Kuo's
head was cut off and hung outside for the edification of passersby.[17]

The elimination of Kuo Chien did little to diminish the troubles
of Yen Hsiang-wen. In fact, the piratical activities of Kuo's followers
became even more serious. Moreover, Yen could control only a narrow strip through the central part of the province. Much of southern
Shensi was still under Ch'en Shu-fan, who had been ousted from Sian

but not from Shensi, and most of the province north of the Wei river
was controlled by the Ching Kuo Chün, under the command of Hu
Ching-i and Yü Yu-jen.* In western and southwestern Shensi there
were other pockets of independent control.[18] Moreover, banditry and
disorder were widespread. Within a few miles of Sian, wrote an observer in that city,[19]

. . . violence and robbery stalk abroad. Farmers are afraid to venture out of
doors with even a donkey, lest both man and beast be pressed into the service
of some warring faction. In certain districts, shops are closed, business has
been suspended, and many people are taking refuge in the city. The practice
of kidnapping is extremely prevalent and very heavy ransoms are demanded
for the victims, and law-abiding people are groaning for the day when peace
and some approach to justice will obtain in the land.

Perhaps these problems weighed more heavily on Yen Hsiang-wen
than on most warlords. More likely, he had other problems of which
we know nothing. In any event, Yen committed suicide on August 23,
1921. Two days later, Feng was ordered to succeed Yen as military
governor of Shensi.[20] Within twenty days Feng had risen from brigade
commander to tuchun.

Administration of Shensi

Feng was certainly willing to give Shensi the efficient government
that it had so long been without, but he faced the same obstacles that
had thwarted Yen Hsiang-wen. As noted above, disorder was rampant
even in the vicinity of Sian, and it was worse in other parts of the
province. The financial situation was impossible. The provincial gov-

---

* The Ching Kuo Chün, or Nation Pacifying Army, had existed for several years
in Shensi. In January 1918, one of Ch'en Shu-fan's subordinates revolted in Sanyuan, about 35 miles north of Sian. The rebels captured the city, and a young officer named Hu Ching-i promptly organized the rebel forces as the Ching Kuo
Chün. The rebel army rapidly grew to about 20,000 men; it soon controlled over ten
counties (hsien) in central Shensi. However, it was not a unified force. Hu Ching-i
was in his twenties and found it difficult to control the conflicting ambitions and
ideas of his officers. In May 1918, Yü Yu-jen, a native son of Shensi with much influence and prestige in the province, arrived at the headquarters of the Ching Kuo
Chün in Sanyuan. On May 20th, he assumed the position of commander-in-chief of
the Ching Kuo Chün. He expanded the army to over 30,000 men, and reorganized
it. It finally came to control fourteen hsien, with a population of 3,000,000 people.
Yü Yu-jen was a leader in the Kuomintang, and his control of the Ching Kuo Chün
led Sun Yat-sen to plan to make Shensi a center of revolutionary activity, but this
plan soon fell through. From October 1918 to March 1919, there was a series of
armed clashes between Ch'en Shu-fan's troops and the Ching Kuo Chün. When the
peace talks between North and South began in the spring of 1919, the contending
forces in Shensi also settled down to a sort of stalemate, which was maintained until
Feng entered the province in 1921. (Chang Yün-chia, pp. 86–96.)

ernment's authority extended over only a dozen or so hsien in the vicinity of Sian, and half the land tax for 1922 had already been collected in these. Feng's first task, therefore, was to attempt to unify the administration of the province.[21]

Nominal progress toward that end was made in September, when Hu Ching-i declared that the Ching Kuo Chün was no longer an autonomous army. With the approval of the Peking government, it became the 1st Division of the Shensi provincial forces. Presumably the army thereby came under the control of the provincial governor, Feng Yü-hsiang. Actually, it retained a good deal of independence, although Feng had personal ties with Hu Ching-i and therefore some influence over Hu's actions.[22]

Feng's next concern was Ch'en Shu-fan and his troops, who still occupied the southern part of the province. Feng assigned Wu Hsin-t'ien and his 7th Division the job of establishing control over this region. Wu began the campaign in November and brought it to a successful conclusion by the end of the year. Ch'en Shu-fan fled, and his troops dispersed.[23] However, disorder continued, undoubtedly exacerbated by Ch'en's dispersed troops. Moreover, control of the area by Wu's troops was not the same as control by Feng's own men. In essence, a friendly warlord had replaced an unfriendly warlord in southern Shensi.

Feng also undertook military operations against the soldier-bandits, including Kuo Chien's former followers, in the west of the province, and against other bandit groups operating east of Sian.[24] Although the soldiers did good work, progress was slow; bandits were diligently harried and many were killed, but the groups were not disbanded.

As a matter of fact, Feng was never able to unify the province during the half year or so he was in power there. Hu Ching-i and Wu Hsin-t'ien were nominally subject to Feng's orders, but if Feng had attempted to exert genuine control in the regions occupied by their units, military conflict almost inevitably would have resulted. Feng was deterred by the dangers of such a conflict, not the least of which was that he would probably be condemned by the leaders of the Chihli clique, who counted Hu and Wu among their followers. But the fact remained that as long as these areas were beyond Feng's control, the problem of establishing genuine order even in his own jurisdiction was complicated; for bandits could raid his areas and then flee with impunity to a nearby sanctuary. Shensi had simply been plagued too long by disorder and disunion for Feng to root them out quickly, especially when he was fettered by such considerations of warlord politics. Even without these constraints, however, banditry could not be eliminated by military action alone; fundamental economic and other reforms were necessary.

Although Feng's direct authority was limited to certain areas of Shensi, those areas did feel the impact of his reforming zeal. Prostitution was prohibited.[25] Women under the age of 20 were forbidden to bind their feet, and older women were advised to unbind them.[26] Feng wanted to forbid the planting of opium, but he could not sacrifice the revenues from the drug. For this reason he decided that he would continue to allow one or two hsien to plant opium for a limited period, after which it would also be forbidden there. In the meantime, the tax on opium in those areas was to be doubled.[27] Since Feng controlled few hsien to begin with, this was perhaps not as self-denying as it seems at first glance. In any case, the ruling against opium probably was not rigorously enforced except to punish flagrant offenders, whose fines became an important source of revenue.[28]

Feng's policies were not limited to prohibitions. He set up a fund for expanded public education, and he frequently inspected the schools.[29] He established a School for the People, where adults with no education would have an opportunity to study. He also set up a recreation area called the Sports Field for the People. In addition, he opened a hall where the public was periodically invited for lectures delivered by Feng or one of his officers.[30] On Sian's city walls and on houses and public buildings, Feng had proverbs and instructive pictures painted.[31] As in Ch'angte, he planted trees along the roads, repaired and maintained old roads, and built new ones. Foreigners traveling on the road from Sian to T'ungkuan, on the Honan border, noted the "wonderful improvement" of the road since Feng had come to Shensi.[32]

Feng's reforming zeal was not appreciated by everyone, as could be seen in a private letter sent from Sian shortly after Feng had left the province. "All the people are glad he is gone," the correspondent wrote, "and hoping that he will never come back. His goodness was so tyrannically oppressive that ordinary people were in terror of their lives while the city was undergoing the process of cleaning up at his hands."[33] Some people inevitably suffer in most reform programs, and Feng's programs were no exception.

Such disgruntlement was the least of Feng's worries during his stay in Shensi. At the end of December 1921, there was an extraordinary outburst of anti-foreign feeling in Sian. Student demonstrators filled

the streets displaying anti-foreign posters. All Chinese working for
foreigners were forced to leave the houses of their employers. Placards
announced that in India the English treated the natives like cattle
and used Indian women as prostitutes. The same situation was imminent in China, they warned. Signs were posted declaring that China
was about to be partitioned by the powers, and the people were
alerted that "foreign troops will soon be here."[34] In mid-January
there was more excitement. Small cakes containing what seems to
have been anti-foreign propaganda were delivered to households with
the request that each recipient make a similar delivery to ten other
homes,* a sort of "chain letter in pastry."[35]

Although foreign observers at the time tended to lump these two
phenomena together, they were probably different in both origin and
nature. The student movement in December grew out of anti-foreign
feeling that had been smoldering for some time, and was fanned by
fears and misgivings about the Washington Conference, which was
then in session. It was a patriotic movement of the type that had become rather common since May 4, 1919, and Feng did not take strong
action against it.[36]

The "chain pastry movement" of mid-January, on the other hand,
seems to have been an attempt by Ch'en Shu-fan's agents to turn anti-
foreign feelings against Feng, whose Christian religion gave him an
obvious link with foreigners. Rumors circulated that Feng intended to
force all Chinese to convert to Christianity, and that he was going to
persecute members of other religions.[37] Regardless of how it might
tend to confirm the rumors, Feng had to protect the foreigners in
Shensi; if they were abused or harmed, he would be held responsible.
Therefore Feng countered this movement with harsher measures.
Many arrests were made, several of the pastry messengers were executed, and the movement was stamped out.[38]

A Christian tuchün was, of course, an extraordinary phenomenon
in China, and the suspicious and xenophobic populace of Shensi
could hardly be unaffected by the rumors about Feng's proselytizing
intentions. To calm any fears, Feng issued a public statement pointing out that all his men, regardless of their religion, were treated
equally, and that religious freedom was guaranteed by law to all

---

* This was not a novel idea in China. According to popular tradition, when Chinese
revolutionists were plotting the overthrow of the alien Yüan dynasty, they communicated with one another by sending parcels of round cakes as festival gifts. Inside the cakes were secret messages. It was in this fashion, legend has it, that moon
cakes became a part of the Mid-Autumn Festival, or as it is more popularly known,
the Moon Festival.

people. Moreover, he asserted, although he and some of his men were Christians, this had no effect on his army's well-known patriotism. He concluded by asking the people to work together with him and his troops for the welfare of Shensi.[39]

Despite its unusual vigor, Feng's administration could not bring about extensive or permanent changes. The province's disunity was from the outset an insuperable obstacle. Moreover, Feng did not remain in Shensi very long. In the spring of 1922 another major war broke out, and Feng was obliged to leave the province. He left Shensi much as he found it. Shortly before he departed, a foreign journalist summarized the problems Feng faced and the disappointing results he had achieved:[40]

Shensi had known no peace since 1912. It had been the happy hunting ground of the biggest brigand armies in China, not to mention the so-called Southern troops [the Ching Kuo Chün] who claimed the support of the Kuomintang. It suffered under some of China's worst tuchüns, among whom Ch'en Shu-fan, the last, was not the least. Feng's expedition was regarded as a crusade; his assumption of the tuchünship as a sure promise of peace at last. The upshot of it is that Feng keeps order in about a third of the province and that traveling is just about as unpleasant and dangerous as ever.

If the journalist had been writing a couple of months later, he might have added that Feng's reforms in the Sian area were discontinued shortly after his departure.

The First Chih-Feng War

Although the war in 1920 against the Anfu clique had been waged and won largely by Wu P'ei-fu, Chang Tso-lin had also fought on the side of the Chihli clique. Even if he had remained neutral, his Manchurian armies would have made him a power to be reckoned with in the postwar arrangements. Therefore, after the fall of the Anfu-dominated government, position and influence in Peking and in northern China generally were distributed in a rough balance between the Chihli faction and Chang's Fengtien faction. It was this redistribution that put Shensi under the Chihli militarists, and indirectly created the opportunity for Feng to become military governor of that province. However, during the following year and a half, that balance was increasingly upset as Wu P'ei-fu extended his regional authority in northern China, and Chang Tso-lin came to dominate the Peking government.

The fruits of the 1920 victory were largely appropriated by Chang Tso-lin and Wu P'ei-fu's superior, Ts'ao K'un. Wu himself obtained no territorial base. But his opportunity came in the summer of 1921, when the Hunanese invaded Hupeh to "rescue" the people of that province from their tuchün, Wang Chan-yüan. Wang was forced to flee the province, but Wu P'ei-fu then stepped in, defeated the Hunan army, and was appointed Inspecting Commissioner of Hupeh and Hunan, with his own nominee as tuchün of the former province. This extension of Wu's power was doubly repugnant to Chang Tso-lin because it was at the expense of Wang Chan-yüan, with whom Chang had evidently established a loose alliance or informal understanding. However, Chang moved to gain complete control of the machinery of the Peking government. In December 1921, he forced the resignation of Chin Yün-p'eng, who had become Premier after the An-Chih war, and had him replaced by Liang Shih-i.

One of Liang's first acts was to pardon many of the leaders of the Anfu faction whom Wu had had legally condemned after the Chihli victory in 1920. Liang also withheld funds from Wu. Most important, Liang ordered the Chinese delegation at the Washington Conference to yield to Japan on some points regarding the Shantung question, in return for which Liang would obtain additional loans from Japan. Wu P'ei-fu promptly issued a circular telegram denouncing Liang's unpatriotic act. Public opinion strongly backed Wu, and other tuchüns, including Feng Yü-hsiang, issued statements supporting him. Liang could not remain at his post; he pleaded illness and took a leave that amounted to retirement. Since Liang was Chang Tso-lin's choice, his effective elimination weakened Chang and increased the friction between him and Wu. In January 1922, a "war of telegrams" began between Chang and Wu. Meanwhile, each was organizing his armies and making plans with his military allies. Finally, in April, war broke out in earnest.[41]

At the outset, Fengtien seemed to have the advantage. Chang Tso-lin had more men and matériel than Wu P'ei-fu. Moreover, his home base in Manchuria could be easily defended in case he was defeated in northern China, whereas Wu had no such bastion to which he could retreat. However, in terms of discipline and fighting ability, the armies under Wu P'ei-fu were superior. This superiority proved to be the difference, and the war lasted only about a week, after which the Fengtien army retreated to Manchuria.[42]

Feng Yü-hsiang's troops played an important role in that brief but hard-fought war. There was, of course, no question of which side Feng would fight on. His past and present ties were all with the Chihli leaders. There were pragmatic considerations as well. If he remained on the sidelines while the Chihli faction was defeated, he would be faced by the swollen and antagonistic power of Chang Tso-lin. On the other hand, if the Chihli militarists won, Feng would incur their animosity for failing to assist them. Moreover, he knew that participation on the winning side would offer an opportunity to advance in the warlord hierarchy.

In addition, like most Chinese, Feng opposed the pro-Japanese policies of the government and was eager to bring it down. Not only did the government toady to Japan, but, according to Feng, it had monarchical tendencies. Ten days before the fighting broke out, Feng described the upcoming war to his men as a struggle between republicans and monarchists. His men, he declared, would fight on the side of the Republic and the common people. Compared to such an important duty, he said, the governorship of Shensi meant no more to him than his slipper, which he took off and dramatically flung away.*[43]

Feng turned over the position of Shensi tuchün to a local militarist, and on April 20 he left Sian at the head of his own division and other Shensi units.[44] While marching toward Honan, Feng exhorted his men to observe good discipline and to put forth their greatest efforts. He repeated that their goal was the overthrow of Chang Hsün to prevent the restoration of the monarchy;† he emphasized that they would be fighting for a principle, not for anyone's personal gain.[45] On April 26, they arrived at Loyang, in western Honan. Feng remained in Honan with part of his forces to protect that province and the lines of supply and communication to Wuhan.

Only one brigade of Feng's 11th Division fought in Chihli. This brigade, under Li Ming-chung, went to the vicinity of Changtzutien, the scene of the fiercest fighting of the war, where it was instrumental in the Chihli victory that initiated the rout of Chang Tso-lin's army.[46] On the basis of their performance in this war, a Western military writer rated Feng's troops as the best in China at that time, but expressed his opinion that in a conflict between Feng's 11th Division and Wu P'ei-fu's 3rd Division, Wu's men would probably win because Wu was a superior strategist.[47]

---

* When Feng did this, or at least when he wrote about it, he may have had in mind the passage in Mencius (7A.35) in which we are told that Shun (a mythical sage emperor) "looked upon abdicating the Empire as lightly as upon discarding a worn-out shoe."
† Chang Hsün, who effected the short-lived restoration in 1917, was on the side of Chang Tso-lin in the First Chih-Feng War.

Revolt of Chao T'i

On the very day that Chang Tso-lin's armies suffered the defeat that led to their withdrawal from China, the Honan army attacked the Chihli forces in Honan. Chao T'i, against whom the confused and abortive Ch'eng Shen revolt had been directed just a year earlier, was still tuchün of Honan. Even before the outbreak of fighting in late April, Chao had taken an ambiguous stand. Although he ostensibly supported Wu P'ei-fu in the battle of the telegrams, Chao T'i secretly wired Chang Tso-lin that he was compelled to take such a position. Wu P'ei-fu discovered this, and although Chao claimed it was all part of a plot against him, this and other actions led Wu to suspect Chao's loyalty. This was a major reason for Wu's leaving Feng in Honan, where he could keep an eye on Chao while concurrently performing other important military duties.

Whereas Chao T'i's position was uncertain, his brother Chao Chieh, commander of the First Temporary Honan Division, was definitely opposed to Wu P'ei-fu. Moreover, both Chaos feared that, in view of Wu's suspicions, a Chihli victory might result in a change of administration in Honan. The events of May 3–4 were thus sufficient to swing them to an unequivocal anti-Chihli position. During the vigorous fighting in Chihli on May 3, word spread that Wu P'ei-fu had been killed in action. On the following day, Chang Tso-lin, unduly sanguine, announced a great victory. When reports of these events reached Honan, Chao T'i immediately had the Honan provincial senate issue statements denouncing Wu P'ei-fu and Feng Yü-hsiang for interference in Honanese affairs, and on the following day, May 5, Chao Chieh and others led 30 battalions against Feng's units in Chengchow.[48]

Although Chao's troops considerably outnumbered Feng's and the other Shensi units in Chengchow, they could not take the city. Feng, who was in Loyang when the attack began, hurried back to Chengchow with reinforcements, and the tide quickly began to turn. Moreover, Chao had by this time discovered that Wu, instead of being dead, had defeated Chang Tso-lin. Therefore, on May 8 he ordered his troops to stop fighting, and organized an arbitration commission. Wu P'ei-fu, beset with the problems arising out of the war with Chang Tso-lin, wanted a quick, uncomplicated settlement of the Honan question. He wired Feng that the disbandment of Chao Chieh's troops would be sufficient, and that Chao T'i could retain his post, at least temporarily.[49] This surprising leniency may have been partly due to the fact that Wu and Chao T'i were sworn brothers. It is even more likely that Wu was willing to keep Chao T'i in office because Feng was obviously the only man in a position to replace him, and Wu did not want Feng to become tuchün. Although Feng was a Chihli warlord and nominally subordinate to Wu P'ei-fu, he was not one of Wu's protégés. Feng had risen to power on his own before joining the Chihli ranks, and he acted with a degree of independence that did not sit well with Wu. Accordingly, on May 9 the central government issued an order depriving Chao Chieh of his post and ordering Chao T'i to investigate the case.[50] Feng, who certainly had his eye on the tuchünship of Honan, would not accept that tacit exoneration of Chao T'i. He ignored the government's order and continued to attack the Honan armies until, on May 10, a mandate was issued dismissing Chao T'i and appointing Feng Yü-hsiang tuchün of Honan.[51]

Wu P'ei-fu again showed surprising leniency toward the Honan rebels when on May 12 a mandate from the capital appointed Pao Te-ch'üan Associate Director of Military Affairs in Honan.[52] Pao was division commander of the 2nd Honan Division, and had led ten of the battalions that attacked Feng's men in Chengchow. When it became clear that the revolt would fail, Pao switched sides, sending Wu some money as a token of his new allegiance. Pao was now Wu's man, and it seems likely that his assignment in Honan was due to Wu's desire to have his interests represented in the administration of the province, especially in financial matters.[53] Having received this assignment, Pao remained in Kaifeng after the Chao brothers had fled.

When Feng entered Kaifeng on May 14, he was welcomed by leading citizens and high officials, including Pao Te-ch'üan. Pao's warm welcome to Feng, his enemy of a week earlier, exemplified the game-like quality of many warlord conflicts. Pao had gambled and lost; the game was temporarily over and Feng, according to all the rules, should have held no grudges. But Feng claimed to be fighting for the nation and the people. He taught this to his troops, and generally tried to minimize or conceal the warlord quality of the wars in which he took part. Moreover, Feng was loath to share authority in Honan with anyone, certainly not with an erstwhile enemy and, presumably, a tool of Wu P'ei-fu. Therefore, as soon as Feng entered the city, he had Pao seized and shot.[54] He thus secured exclusive control of the Honan administration, and at the same time showed his men that he was indeed fighting for principles and would not accept the cordiality of a man whose troops only a few days before had been killing his soldiers. After that dramatic entry—the second time in a week that Feng had defied a mandate from Wu P'ei-fu—Feng settled down in Kaifeng to govern Honan.

Army Expansion

Before Feng was even settled in his new quarters in Kaifeng, he ordered that 4,500 men be recruited.[55] This struck the keynote of Feng's military activities in Honan, and before he left the province in November 1922, he not only had filled out his division, but also had created three additional mixed brigades.[56] These were the 7th Mixed Brigade, under Chang Chih-chiang, the 8th Mixed Brigade, under Li Ming-chung, and the 25th Mixed Brigade, under Sung Che-yüan. At that time, Feng probably had over 20,000 men in his army.[57]

As usual, Feng devoted much attention to training his men and to converting as many as possible to Christianity. Every Sunday fourteen separate church services were conducted for his troops.[58] Twelve "preaching places" were erected, apparently out in the open so that large numbers could assemble. A foreign visitor who visited all twelve in one day estimated that he had seen 6,000 of Feng's soldiers listening to the sermons. Four Chinese preachers worked full time among Feng's men.[59]

One incident undoubtedly won some converts to Christianity in the surrounding community. When the autumn harvest was threatened by lack of rain, Feng called all Christians in Kaifeng to a special prayer meting at which he prayed for rain. The next day rain fell in torrents, and the people understandably declared that "Feng is wonderful in prayer."[60] In addition to this somewhat unconventional assistance, Feng also continued the policy of having his troops work on projects for community welfare.[61]

With the influx of so many recruits, Feng took pains to avoid clashes between them and the civilian populace. His men were not permitted in town unless they had specific business there. Feng urged them to study whenever they were not training or working. He repeatedly stressed the importance of self-education. To want to save the nation and help the people was a noble aspiration, he said, but it could never be attained without knowledge.[62]

Administration of Honan

Shortly after Feng had entered Kaifeng and taken up the duties of tuchün, he issued a statement outlining ten immediate aims of his administration:[63]

1. To aid those people who had suffered from the war, and to prevent anyone's losing his home.

2. To order the province's finances and tax structure, and to eliminate oppressive taxation.

3. To register the population as a means of preventing banditry.

4. To maintain order among the provincial patrol corps until they could be reorganized.

5. To investigate and arrest corrupt officials and other undesirable elements in order to provide the people with tranquil conditions.

6. To establish factories where the unemployed could find work.

7. To put roads and irrigation facilities in good order.

8. To institute free education.

9. To abolish opium smoking, gambling, and prostitution.

10. To enforce rules against wearing queues and foot-binding, in order to eliminate these customs.

Although Feng was tuchün of Honan for only five and a half months, during that time he took some steps to carry out most of these aims. Almost the first thing Feng did after assuming the tuchünship was to confiscate all the wealth and possessions of Chao T'i that he could find. There were many rumors about the private fortune that Chao had amassed while he was governor of Honan, one estimate putting it as high as $25,000,000.[64] This was perhaps an exaggeration, and in any case much of it was apparently in foreign banks. Feng tried to attach these foreign deposits, but there is no evidence that he was successful. However, he did confiscate all the property owned by Chao and his family in Kaifeng and elsewhere. Feng also found a large sum of money at the tuchün headquarters, and an even larger amount buried in a cement-covered cache in the garden of one of Chao's homes. These two finds were variously reported to total from 1,500,000 to 3,000,000 yüan. Part of this money was earmarked to implement the first of Feng's ten aims, namely aiding civilians who had suffered from the recent war.[65] Beyond the establishment of some housing for refugees, however, we do not know precisely what measures were taken.[66] Feng was never averse to advertising his achievements in such matters, and the dearth of detail doubtless reflects a lack of achievement.

Action on Feng's second aim—the ordering of provincial finances—was badly needed in Honan. As in many parts of China, financial conditions were chaotic. There were various kinds of coins and currency circulating throughout China, including foreign coins. They not only varied in intrinsic value, but appreciated or depreciated because of local or regional conditions.[67] From the standpoint of the mass of the Chinese people, the value of copper coins was the most important monetary fact of life, for they were paid in copper coins and used them for most transactions. In 1922, the extensive depreciation of copper coins became an important problem in China.[68] Some attributed this depreciation to the overproduction of such coins, whereas others attributed it to purposeful debasement of the coinage.[69] According to a report from Kaifeng just a few weeks after Feng became tuchün of Honan, the problem in that city was due to debasement. The writer came to this conclusion after actually weighing various denominations of copper coins, and explained the debasement as "one of Governor Chao's schemes to make money."[70]

Although Feng took measures to ameliorate these conditions, it is not known what they were. Feng himself has not discussed the question, and mention of it elsewhere is so cursory and contradictory as to lead to the inference that little was accomplished.[71]

However, there were two noteworthy features of Feng's financial administration. First, Feng's finance department publicly posted audited statements of public expenditures, the first time in sixty years such a policy had been followed.[72] Second, Feng refused to appropriate money to send to Wu P'ei-fu. According to Feng, Wu demanded an initial remittance of 800,000 yüan and 200,000 every month thereafter. Feng replied that he could not and would not demand such sums from the people.[73] More to the point, although Feng did not mention it, he needed all the funds he could find to maintain his expanding army and administer the province. But it is true that compliance with Wu's demand would have meant additional hardship for an already hard-pressed people. Feng's predecessor had already collected the land taxes for 1922, so Feng collected them for the upcoming year. It is doubtful that those who paid these taxes found Feng's reforms worth the price.

The problem of banditry in Honan was even more acute than it had been in Shensi. It had been acute since the early years of the Republic; Honan, for example, had been the main area preyed on by the White Wolf. By mid-1922 it was the most bandit-ridden of all

China's provinces. Kidnapping was especially popular, and it was becoming commonplace for bandits to seize foreigners for ransom. In late November 1922, fourteen kidnapped foreigners were being held for ransom in Honan.[74] Many of these kidnappings were reportedly the work of Chao T'i's troops, who hoped to embroil Feng with foreign powers, much as Ch'en Shu-fan's adherents had tried to do in Shensi.[75] Of course, many Chinese were also seized as hostages. They usually fared far worse than foreigners; it was not unusual for the kidnappers to send an ear or a finger of a Chinese victim to his family, with the promise that additional parts would follow if the ransom was not forthcoming. In addition to kidnapping, the bandits committed many other crimes and were responsible for extensive destruction and misery.[76]

As in Shensi, Feng was again limited in his bandit-suppression measures because he did not control all the province. Wu P'ei-fu's headquarters were in Loyang, in western Honan, and his troops were stationed in several places in the western and northern parts of the province. Feng's jurisdiction was not, of course, strictly delimited, but for practical purposes it consisted of approximately the region east of the Peking-Hankow railway, or about a third of the province.[77] Even in this area, his control was complete only in the immediate vicinity of Kaifeng.

Feng sent detachments of troops in several directions in pursuit of bandits. After two or three months, foreigners began to report that these efforts were achieving results. "Arrested bandits and outlaws are daily sent in to Kaifeng in chains, and hundreds of them are now in Kaifeng prisons," wrote one observer.[78] The consensus was that Feng had "done wonders," and that the regions he controlled were all "fairly cleared of bandits."[79] However, Honan continued to be bandit-ridden in those regions where Feng could not go.

Besides suppressing ordinary bandits, Feng also attacked the "bandits in office." Most of the important officials of the provincial government and the Kaifeng city government were replaced by Feng's appointees. The chief motivation behind this move was Feng's desire to fill all important posts with men he could count on, although it was rationalized as a move to eliminate corruption. Some corruption probably was uncovered; at any rate, some officials were jailed and some were shot. The provincial government's offices soon became "regular beehives of industry."[80]

A portion of the money hidden by Chao T'i and discovered by

Feng was used to pay the arrears in teachers' salaries, and for the general improvement of education. Feng also ruled that revenues derived from certain specified taxes would be allocated to education.[81] He invited the dean of Nankai University at Tientsin, Ling Ping, to administer educational affairs in Honan. Ling, who was a prominent scholar, accepted the newly created post of Commissioner of Education for Honan. He was said to have given "several months of peace and quietness to the schools."[82] A foreigner in Hsüchow reported that "the schools are better managed than ever since I have been in this city."[83]

Feng converted many Buddhist temples into schools, an act that naturally did not meet with universal approval. One of these schools was the Nourish Virtue School, which was for the exclusive use of the families of Feng's officers and civil officials. There were classes for both adults and children.[84] Feng was also said to have laid the foundation for the University of Honan, and to have established the first public library in the province at Kaifeng.[85]

His usual prohibitions against opium and prostitution were promulgated immediately after he took office, and were effective in the regions he controlled. He also forbade gambling, and when offenders were caught they had to walk around the streets carrying posters describing their crime.[86]

He took a somewhat unconventional approach to the sale of alcoholic beverages. He did not forbid the sale of wine; on the contrary, he ruled that the price for a catty of the best wine could not exceed a specified amount, which was about a fourth of the retail price and about half of what it cost to produce that much wine. Under this system, customers were plentiful, but suppliers soon became scarce.[87]

Feng forbade foot-binding, which was prevalent in Honan, and also decreed that all queues must be cut off. Police were stationed at the city gates with scissors, and when an unwary and conservative peasant entered the city he was seized and given a haircut. Queues were still very common in Honan at that time, and many peasants avoided the city rather than run such a risk. Nevertheless, queues fell "at an awful rate."[88]

Kaifeng and several other Honan cities were cleaned up. Streets were kept swept and watered, and garbage and other filth was regularly carted away. Food and fruit vendors, who customarily exposed their wares to flies and dust, now had to cover them with netting. Pictures were painted on walls and other conspicuous places depict-

ing, among other things, the evils of unsanitary conditions. All theatrical performances had to pass censorship, and were approved only
if they tended to cultivate public or private virtues. A curfew was
apparently imposed on Kaifeng, so that the streets "after nine o'clock
at night might have been the streets of a country village, they were
so quiet."[89]

Transfer to Peking

Feng's reforms in Honan were more extensive, more vigorously enforced, and somewhat more effective than they had been in either
Ch'angte or Shensi, although the general character of all three programs was very similar. The widespread improvement of conditions
under Feng's administration elicited equally widespread praise and
support of Feng. Early in October 1922, rumors began to circulate
that Feng was going to be transferred, and peasants, merchants, and
intellectuals were all disturbed; numerous telegrams were sent to
Peking requesting that Feng be permitted to remain in Honan.[90] Both
President Li Yüan-hung and Wu P'ei-fu denied that Feng was going
to be transferred, but on October 31 a mandate was issued ordering
Feng to proceed to Peking to become Inspecting Commissioner of the
Army. He was to turn his tuchünship over to Chang Fu-lai.[91]

Almost as soon as Feng left, conditions in eastern Honan began to
deteriorate. His successor promptly levied the taxes for 1924 and also
exacted a special tax for the upkeep of his troops.[92] Most of the
administrative reforms introduced by Feng were repealed, corruption
began to flourish, and social conditions reverted to what they had
been under Chao T'i.[93] Ling Ping, Feng's Commissioner of Education, left Honan to return to his position at Nankai University.[94]
Bandits again became active, and within a few weeks after Feng's departure the bandit problem in eastern Honan was "as bad as, if not
worse than, it [had] ever been."[95] By early 1923, conditions in and
around Kaifeng and the other areas of Feng's jurisdiction had returned to what they were before his arrival.[96]

Many Honanese were very resentful that their expressed desire to
retain Feng as tuchün had been spurned. There was much speculation
in Honan and elsewhere about what was behind Feng's transfer, but
there is little question that the main reason was the deterioration of
relations between Feng and Wu P'ei-fu.

Feng had been associated with the Chihli clique since early 1918,
when Ts'ao K'un intervened on his behalf at the time of Feng's Wu-

hsüeh declarations. Wu P'ei-fu at that time was simply Ts'ao's leading subordinate. Not until Feng became tuchün of Honan was he formally under Wu, who was then Assistant Inspecting Commissioner of Chihli, Shantung, and Honan. But by then Wu controlled Ts'ao's military arm, and Ts'ao's authority was largely nominal. Most of the Chihli militarists accepted Wu's leadership, and, within limits, so did Feng. But Feng tried to set the limits himself.

After the impressive showing of Li Ming-chung's brigade in the First Chih-Feng War, which provided a sample of Feng's military power, Wu wanted to expand Li's brigade into an independent division. But Feng thwarted this by hastily ordering the brigade's return before it could be detached from his army.[97] When Wu assigned Pao Te-ch'üan as Assistant Director of Military Affairs in Honan, Feng ignored the order and executed Pao. Feng also rejected office seekers referred to him by Wu. Perhaps most important, Feng refused to send Wu the funds he demanded.[98] Feng's independent attitude would have made him suspect in any case, but when he held the position of tuchün in the very province where Wu had his headquarters, Wu could only consider him a threat. This was not true of Feng's successor, Chang Fu-lai, who was one of Wu's staunchest supporters and a pliable subordinate.

Besides the strained relations between Feng and Wu, there may have been other reasons for Feng's transfer. Wu P'ei-fu's power within the Chihli clique was strongly resented by Ts'ao K'un's associates. As will be seen in the following chapter, they sought to elevate their chief to the presidency, a move Wu P'ei-fu opposed. Ts'ao's adherents needed a strong military force in the vicinity of Peking to support their scheme, and it is possible that they, rather than Wu, had Feng transferred for that purpose.[99] In any event, their attitude toward Feng was known to Wu. By November 1922, Feng had been labeled a Ts'ao K'un supporter, and this naturally increased Wu's apprehension.[100]

When Feng received his orders to leave Honan, he obeyed immediately, and within three days he and his men had left the province. Feng was ordered to take only one division with him, and to leave his three additional mixed brigades in Honan.[101] This, incidentally, tends to confirm the explanation that Feng's growing power relative to Wu's was the reason for his transfer. Feng was definitely unwilling to obey this order, and his hasty departure was designed to forestall its enforcement. From Honan, Feng went straight to the capital and stationed his troops in and around the city. By this time,

Feng was widely known in China as a tuchün, a Christian general, and a reformer. Many northern Chinese who were concerned about the deplorable state of affairs in their country saw in Feng's disciplined army, his emphasis on education, his reforms, and his concern for the common people evidence that Feng was a warlord of an unusual kind, one who might be able to bring order out of the chaos of Chinese affairs.* Feng was already a figure of national renown. Now he stepped to the center of the national stage—Peking.

---

* Just a month before Feng left Honan, *The Weekly Review*, an English-language weekly published by Americans, began distributing ballots for a public vote to determine the "twelve greatest living Chinese." Virtually all of the voting was done by Chinese, mostly by teachers and students. Although the editors do not report the total number of votes received, the final tabulations indicate that they probably numbered not less than 25,000. The results, published early in January 1923, showed Feng second to Sun Yat-sen. Obviously, not too much weight can be given to such a small sampling of opinion. On the other hand, it is interesting and not without significance that voters who put Sun Yat-sen first, and who thought primarily in terms of progressive civilians, as the list will show, should put Feng in second place. The results, with the number of votes received by each of the twelve, were as follows:

1. Sun Yat-sen	1,315	7. C. T. Wang	925
2. Feng Yü-hsiang	1,217	8. Chang Chien	915
3. V. K. Wellington Koo	1,211	9. Yen Hsi-shan	742
4. Wang Chung-hui	1,117	10. David Z. T. Yui	703
5. Wu P'ei-fu	895	11. Li Yüan-hung	671
6. Ts'ai Yüan-p'ei	969	12. Hu Shih	613

The figure for Wu P'ei-fu is the one the paper listed. Either it is incorrect or Wu is listed out of sequence.

6. Plots in Peking

Feng's most familiar sobriquet is "the Christian General." To some unimpressed by his piety, however, he is known as "the Betraying General." Those who think the latter term more fitting cite a string of incidents dating as far back as 1915, each allegedly an example of Feng's betraying his superiors. Actually, however, the acts that gave rise to this label occurred during 1923–24. At that time Feng was stationed at Nanyüan, near Peking, and his army was the most powerful single unit in that vicinity. Feng devoted much of his time to training programs, and the Nanyüan period resembled the Ch'angte years in this respect. However, Feng also was involved in capital politics. In 1923 he used his power to help force Li Yüan-hung from the presidency. In the following year he used it to 'overthrow Wu P'ei-fu and compel President Ts'ao K'un to resign. By 1925, as one wit put it, Presidents found it very uncomfortable to be around Feng Yü-hsiang.

The Army at Nanyüan

When Feng brought his army to Peking from Honan in late 1922, he stationed one regiment inside the city, one brigade to the east of it, and the remaining bulk of his troops at the great military camp at Nanyüan, a few miles south of the capital, where he undertook a comprehensive training program.

The Nanyüan training program was in many ways an expanded version of the Ch'angte program. The emphasis on body-building continued, with competition in gymnastics, obstacle courses, and various types of physical labor.[1] An educational program was set up that was more comprehensive and better organized than the one at Ch'angte. Notable additions were courses in the history of World War I and in Chinese philosophy, taken by middle- and high-ranking officers. There were also seminars in which such officers studied specialized subjects.[2]

In order to check on the qualifications and performance of his officers, Feng organized a Qualifications Examining Group, composed of brigade commanders and staff officers. They regularly checked the work of the officers, and had great influence over demotions and promotions. Unit commanders also submitted annual fitness reports, which further aided Feng in evaluating the performance of each officer in terms of class work, field work, stamina, and morale.[3]

At Nanyüan, Feng took great pains to show his soldiers that if they were killed or wounded in battle they would be honored as national heroes. The names of officers and men who died in battle were engraved on brass plaques that hung in the Soldiers' YMCA, as well as on a white marble stone conspicuously displayed on the great drill field. The YMCA walls also bore notices recognizing deeds of valor or other exemplary military behavior.[4] The men attended memorial assemblies addressed by high-ranking army and government officials, including a representative of the President.[5] An Association for the Study of Methods of Comforting was organized to explore ways of providing solace and assistance to families of deceased soldiers, and assisting crippled soldiers to make a living.[6]

Feng frequently stressed the importance of proper hygiene, and in this connection he instituted a program at Nanyüan not unlike the one the Chinese Communists later promoted on a much larger scale: a fly-killing campaign. Every summer the camp was divided into sections, with responsibility for catching flies in each section divided among the soldiers.[7]

The workshop program also operated on a larger scale than the one at Ch'angte. It was divided into twelve departments: rug-making, soapmaking, metalworking, woodworking, rattan-working, button-making, tailoring, towel-making, leatherworking, cloth-making, stocking-making, and shoemaking. Perhaps the most novel commodity produced was a rug in the shape of China. Most of the daily necessities of the troops were produced in these shops, and the products were also sold on the local market.[8]

At Nanyüan, these workshops placed somewhat greater emphasis on the dignity of labor than had been the case at Ch'angte, although even there this element had existed. In this regard, Feng liked to tell the story of an officer who went to Switzerland. While there he filled out some government forms, and in the blank for his occupation he wrote "Colonel." The Swiss official scratched this out and wrote "No occupation." According to Feng, the official was quite right. On the walls of the Nanyüan workshops hung such maxims as: "To be a soldier is a citizen's duty, not an occupation; to work is to have an occupation"; "To be a man, one must have a real occupation; to rely on others for one's food is shameful"; and "Labor is sacred."[9]

Educational facilities for the families of Feng's officers were also expanded at Nanyüan. The School for the Sons of Military Officers expanded its curriculum, and its enrollment grew to over 400. The Nourish Virtue School for Girls, attended by female members of officers' families, had been established at Ch'angte, and continued to operate when the army moved to Shensi and Honan. Conditions in these two provinces had evidently precluded Feng's giving much attention to the girls' school, but at Nanyüan he devoted much time and energy to it. Besides classes in reading and writing, there was instruction in the Bible, ethics, arithmetic, singing, hygiene, and various aspects of domesticity, including the delivery of children.[10] Feng frequently addressed the students, who numbered over 200.[11] A kindergarten was set up at Nanyüan for the small sons and daughters of officers, and an American woman was employed as director. Branches of all these Nanyüan facilities were established at T'ungchow to accommodate the families of the men stationed to the east of Peking.[12]

During the Nanyüan period, each regiment operated a School for the Common People. Qualified military and noncombatant officers of the regiment acted as teachers, and all the uneducated adults in the Nanyüan vicinity were invited to attend. Each school had some 30 to 50 students.[13]

Feng's troop-indoctrination program at Nanyüan combined elements of Christianity, Chinese tradition, and a vague but ardent patriotism. Feng invited a foreign missionary and a Chinese minister to organize an evangelistic campaign among his troops. They were assisted by fourteen students from Peking University plus the chaplains regularly assigned to Feng's army, of which there were at least six at that time. This campaign resulted in no fewer than 4,500 baptisms. A genuine attempt seems to have been made to limit baptism to those who could demonstrate some knowledge of Christian tenets, and who could obtain testimonials from their superiors that they were leading clean and moral lives.[14] Feng wanted genuine, not nominal, conversion. By the spring of 1924, when Feng's army totaled about 30,000 men, approximately half were baptized Christians; between 80 and 90 per cent of the officers were Christians.[15]

Feng's personal reading program at Nanyüan concentrated on the Chinese classics. The work he read most frequently was the *Book of Changes,* although the *Book of History* ran a close second. He usually was assisted by a teacher in reading these books. Feng often quoted from the Chinese classics when addressing his men, and the book he most frequently referred to and urged them to read for themselves was the Sayings of Tseng [Kuo-fan] and Hu [Lin-i] on Leading Soldiers.[16] Indeed, Tseng Kuo-fan was probably Feng's favorite author. Given the classical bent of Feng's reading, it is not surprising that in the summer of 1924 he urged a university graduating class to take the men of ancient China for their models.[17]

Occasionally Feng even held up contemporary militarists as models of what could be achieved through determination and ambition. He pointed to Tuan Ch'i-jui, Feng Kuo-chang, and Ts'ao K'un as men who had risen to high office from the ranks. He told his men, "If you will only fix your determination to save the country and the people, any one of you could become President or Premier."[18]

Saving the country and the people was the essence of the patriotism Feng preached to his men. But he never provided many details about how one went about saving one's country and fellow citizens, beyond stressing the obligation to perform public service and resist imperialism. During the Nanyüan period, Feng gave attention to both duties. In the summer of 1924, for example, there were extensive floods in northern China, and Feng's troops worked hard dredging rivers and building dikes.[19] To instill an anti-imperialist attitude in his men, Feng usually held a meeting on May 7 to commemorate Japan's imposing the Twenty-One Demands on China. In the men's living quarters there were maps of China as it had been in the early nineteenth century, with those areas that had since passed into foreign control colored a vivid crimson.*[20]

Feng's nationalism derived largely from a sense of the unity and coherence of the Chinese people; he spoke more about the people than the nation. Indeed, Feng fostered something of a cult of the lao-pai-hsing (the common people). This is reflected in many of the catechisms used in his army. Officers shouted out the questions to their units, and the men responded in chorus. Feng began frequent use of this device at Nanyüan. The following was typical:[21]

Q. Who supplies you with food and clothing?
A. The lao-pai-hsing!
Q. What must you do if somebody cheats or oppresses the lao-pai-hsing?
A. Overthrow him!
Q. What must you do if Feng Yü-hsiang oppresses the lao-pai-hsing?
A. Overthrow Feng Yü-hsiang!

* A similar practice was followed by the Nationalist government in the late 1920's. Maps published by the government indicated all lost territories by notes telling how and when they were taken from China.

There was a catch to the last question and answer: Feng decided what was good and bad for the *lao-pai-hsing*.

Ousting President Li Yüan-hung

After the Chihli clique defeated Chang Tso-lin in 1922, the victors decided to reinstate Li Yüan-hung as President of China, and also to restore the parliament that Chang Hsün had forced Li to dissolve as a prelude to the Manchu restoration in 1917. These moves reflected, first of all, the desire of the Chihli warlords to expel President Hsü Shih-ch'ang, who had supported both the Anfu and Fengtien cliques. Second, the Chihli leaders, and Wu P'ei-fu in particular, hoped that the return to "legitimacy" would deprive the South of the banner under which it had set up a separate regime, and would thus lead to the reunification of the country under Chihli leadership. Before accepting reinstatement, Li Yüan-hung demanded the abolition of military governorships and the reduction of the armed forces. Wu P'ei-fu and Ts'ao K'un agreed to these conditions—which were never to be fulfilled—and on June 11, 1922, Li Yüan-hung assumed the presidency for the second time.

Li could be reinstated as President only because he had the support of the Chihli clique, which controlled the central government. That support, however, was not unanimous. Wu P'ei-fu was the Chihli leader primarily responsible for Li's reinstatement.[22] During the following months other elements in the Chihli clique worked against Wu and Li, and they succeeded in driving Li out of office and out of the capital just one year and two days after he had resumed the presidency. In the events preceding Li's removal from office, Feng Yü-hsiang and his troops played a leading role.

After the First Chih-Feng War, the Chihli clique began to split into factions. One of these was the Tientsin faction, which included the supporters of Ts'ao Jui, brother of Ts'ao K'un and former Civil Governor of Chihli. Ts'ao Jui recognized that Wu P'ei-fu had become the chief military figure in the Chihli clique, but that Wu's personal loyalty to Ts'ao K'un restrained him from acting arbitrarily. Ts'ao Jui and his followers wanted to create a rift between Wu and Ts'ao K'un, thereby eliminating Wu's influence on the central government. Ts'ao K'un's immediate followers constituted another faction, which was called the Paoting faction after the location of Ts'ao's headquarters. This group also resented Wu P'ei-fu's ascendancy, and aspired to raise their leader, Ts'ao K'un, to the presidency. The Paoting and Tientsin factions cooperated to undermine Wu in every possible way.

Wu P'ei-fu himself headed the third major group, sometimes referred to as the Loyang faction.[23] Wu's faction was not weak, but his reluctance to move against Ts'ao K'un limited his ability to counter the maneuvers of the Tientsin and Paoting factions.

The anti-Wu factions had their first major success near the end of 1922. In September of that year, a cabinet had been formed with Wang Ch'ung-hui as Premier. Wu P'ei-fu supported this cabinet, and, in fact, two of the cabinet ministers were Wu's confidants. However, in November the Tientsin faction succeeded in having the Minister of Finance, Lo Wen-kan, arrested for bribery. Wu P'ei-fu promptly wired the President that the arrest was illegal, and vigorously supported Wang Ch'ung-hui's cabinet. The extent to which Wu's enemies had succeeded in dividing Wu and Ts'ao K'un was demonstrated three days later when Ts'ao sent telegrams attacking Lo Wen-kan. Open clashes between Wu's and Ts'ao's factions followed, but Wu was unwilling to force the issue with his patron and superior, and therefore withdrew his support from Lo Wen-kan and Wang Ch'ung-hui. Wang's cabinet was dissolved on November 25, and in December Chang Shao-tseng, the nominee of the Tientsin faction, became Premier. Wu P'ei-fu was defeated, and he assumed what he called a "spectator's" role with regard to Peking politics. Both the Tientsin and Paoting factions became even more active in preparing for Ts'ao K'un to become President.[24]

Although Wu P'ei-fu had virtually abandoned the Peking political arena, he was very active on the military scene in the early months of 1923. His hopes for peaceful reunification had not been realized, and therefore he turned to a policy of reunification by military force. He made various alliances with militarists in Kwangtung, Szechwan, Fukien, and elsewhere, and initiated military campaigns to wipe out all anti-Chihli military power. By mid-1923 none of these campaigns had been markedly successful.[25] In view of Wu's political and military setbacks, his enemies were quite optimistic by the spring of 1923, and they began to move directly against Li Yüan-hung.

The financial straits of the Peking government provided the ammunition to attack President Li. By the spring of 1923, the government was unable to meet many of its normal obligations. Unpaid Chinese ministers and consuls abroad threatened to return home if funds were not forthcoming. Salaries for many government employees were also in arrears. In April the teachers of eight government colleges went to the Ministry of Education to demand their salaries. The musicians of the Presidential Band and the coolies who tended the presidential mansion were also demanding their back pay.[26] Most important from the standpoint of the government's survival, the Peking police and garrison troops were unpaid, as were government troops in the area of the capital, including Feng Yü-hsiang's army.

At the time Feng was ordered to leave Honan in the fall of 1922, he had been promised a continued remittance of $200,000 per month from Honan revenues. According to Feng, the total amount he received from this source during the following ten months was $160,000, and the pay of his troops was consequently far in arrears.[27] Feng, together with Wang Huai-ch'ing, commander of the garrison troops, continually pressed the government for money.* Late in April they succeeded in obtaining a check that they hoped could be cashed the following month.[28] This was probably the check that one source says could not be cashed in May "owing to lack of funds." Shortly afterward the police and garrison troops were paid 70 per cent of one month's salary, and Feng also received a portion of his arrears.[29] This pittance, however, did not silence the demands of Feng and Wang for more money.

In the meantime, Feng was attempting to gain control of the Peking octroi so that he would no longer be at the mercy of the government in financial matters.† The man who held the octroi directorship at that time was a Wu P'ei-fu appointee, and the anti-Wu factions in the capital gladly cooperated with Feng as a means of striking at Wu. This cooperation was also inimical to Li Yüan-hung's interests, for the octroi revenues had traditionally been used for the upkeep of the President's palace, the payment of his salary, and various municipal expenses in the capital. As early as April the question of changing the director of the octroi was put before the cabinet, which consisted mostly of Ts'ao K'un's supporters. Feng Yü-hsiang's nominee, Hsüeh Tu-pi, was selected.[30] President Li Yüan-hung, however, refused to sign the mandate that would legalize the change. At about the same

---

* The vicissitudes of warlordism created constantly shifting sets of bedfellows. Wang Huai-ch'ing had led the troops that defeated the Luanchow rebels.

† The octroi, a levy on merchandise coming into Peking, was similar to the likin taxes collected elsewhere in China. It originated in the Sung dynasty as the National Gate Tax, and when the capital shifted in subsequent centuries, the tax followed. During the Ming dynasty, both Peking and Nanking had octroi taxes. Although the tax was abolished a number of times, it was always reestablished. At times the nine gates of Peking were organized into several collectorates, but at the very beginning of the warlord period all stations were organized under one collectorate, the Ts'ung-wen-men Octroi Administration, often called the Hatamen. During 1923, the octroi revenues averaged something over $200,000 per month. (CYB, 1925–26, pp. 871–72.)

time, and without consulting the cabinet, Li allotted funds to parliament for the drafting of the constitution. Ts'ao K'un's adherents thought Li did this to gain favor with parliament in order to win the next presidential election. On the basis of these two acts—refusing to sign the octroi mandate and allotting funds without cabinet approval —the entire cabinet resigned on June 6.[31]

On June 7 Li Yüan-hung repeated his refusal to sign the mandate that would make Hsüeh Tu-pi director of the octroi, and Feng Yü-hsiang issued a circular telegram declaring that the President was interfering with the legal functions of the cabinet.[32] Feng's wire was considered tantamount to a demand that Li Yüan-hung resign; but Li refused to do so, and continued his attempts to organize a new cabinet. On the following day, June 8, the Tientsin faction organized demonstrations by "citizens' corps," and there was some danger that Li Yüan-hung might be the object of violence. As if to stress this danger, at 6 A.M. the next morning the Peking police and garrison troops went on strike, alleging their lack of pay as the reason. However, Feng and Wang Huai-ch'ing sent letters to parliament and to the foreign diplomatic corps stating that they would assume responsibility for maintaining order in the capital, and throughout the day police and security forces in mufti roamed the city.[33]

On June 10 there were further demonstrations. About 1,000 people bearing signs urging Li Yüan-hung to resign surrounded Li's home. Li sent urgent requests for police protection, but no assistance came. On the 12th a number of police, soldiers, and "citizens' groups" again gathered in front of Li's home, and at about noon word came that Feng Yü-hsiang and Wang Huai-ch'ing had resigned, giving as their reason the nonpayment of their troops. Li urged Feng and Wang to reconsider, but they were adamant. Faced with this situation, and with the possibility that he might be removed from office by force, Li Yüan-hung fled to Tientsin on June 13.

With Li Yüan-hung out of the way, the Tientsin and Paoting factions worked assiduously to promote the election of Ts'ao K'un to the presidency. Although Wu P'ei-fu was opposed to such a move, he stepped into the background and did not attempt to obstruct his chief's ambitions. After almost four months of maneuvering, and after bribes to parliamentarians said to total 15 million silver dollars, Ts'ao K'un was elected President of China on October 5.

Although several factions combined to force Li Yüan-hung out of office, the support of Feng Yü-hsiang was essential for the plot's success. Feng's army dominated the capital militarily, and if Feng had supported the President, his enemies would have been stymied. When Feng actively intervened against the President, Li was virtually helpless. This is why some general histories of the period state simply that Li's downfall was brought about by Feng Yü-hsiang. Feng's stand also altered the balance of power within the Chihli clique, strengthening Ts'ao K'un vis-à-vis Wu P'ei-fu.[34]

The ouster of Li Yüan-hung caused Chinese public opinion to turn against Ts'ao K'un and those who had participated in the incident.[35] Feng Yü-hsiang, hitherto highly esteemed by the public, was widely censured. A group of Chinese Christians in Anch'ing (present-day Hwaining), Anhwei, expressed their displeasure by writing Feng; they accused him of exhibiting a character quite the opposite of that generally ascribed to him, and admonished him to keep to the straight and narrow.[36]

Feng appeared very disturbed by this shift in public opinion, and almost immediately began denying his involvement in Li's ouster.[37] Most later writings by Feng and his supporters either gloss over the incident or omit mention of it altogether.[38] Other pro-Feng writers assert that Wang Huai-ch'ing told Li Yüan-hung that Feng's demands for funds masked his real intention, which was to drive Li from office, and that consequently Li interpreted Feng's basically innocent acts as part of a hostile scheme.[39] But such apologies assume that Feng was both naïve and ignorant of political currents in the capital, a completely unwarranted assumption. There is no doubt that Feng participated in Li's downfall, and very little doubt that he foresaw the consequences of his participation. Only one question remains: what were Feng's motives?

As with so many questions about warlord politics, a definitive answer would require access to messages and other documents that either do not exist or are not available, as well as knowledge of unrecorded conversations. Nevertheless, an answer may be inferred from the known facts and from the logic of the situation.

First of all, whatever other factors may have entered into Feng's calculations, there seems no reason to doubt that his ostensible reason —his need of money—was a very real one. Feng did not find his stint as tuchün of Shensi financially rewarding, and he declared that in this respect his stay in Honan, a richer and more populous province, was a welcome respite for his army.[40] After having been cut off from the revenues of that province, he was naturally eager to obtain control of a reliable source of funds, and the octroi was such a source.

Feng knew, of course, that Wu P'ei-fu would resent his seeking control of the octroi. But under the circumstances, Wu's opposition was much less important than Ts'ao K'un's approval. Feng's relations with Wu were already cool. His relations with Ts'ao, however, were good. Indeed, during the two or three months preceding the demonstrations against Li, Feng visited Ts'ao frequently, though the content of their discussions is not known.[41] In any event, by mid-1923 Wu P'ei-fu seemed to be isolated politically and not very successful militarily. Moreover, Wu had made it clear that he would bow to Ts'ao K'un's desires as far as Peking politics was concerned.

The Paoting and Tientsin factions were apparently dominant, and Feng could hope to acquire a source of revenue by cooperating with them. Indeed, he could look forward to a general improvement in his fortunes under a Ts'ao K'un government, and this was clearly a powerful motivation. But he joined the winning factions not only because they were winning, but because their enemies—Wu P'ei-fu and Li Yüan-hung—were, if not his own enemies, at least not his friends.

Ts'ao K'un's accession to the presidency could not solve the government's financial problems. The revenues of the central government were simply insufficient to meet all the demands made upon them. The pay of government employees continued to be in arrears, and in March 1924 even the cook for the Cabinet Office in Peking refused to work because he had not been paid.[42] However, Feng Yü-hsiang's financial situation seems to have improved at the end of 1923 and during early 1924, doubtless as a result of gaining control of the octroi.[43] In November 1923, Feng was also promoted to marshal, the highest military rank in the country. This was not quite the distinction it might seem, since Ts'ao K'un awarded this rank to practically "everyone in the army above the rank of Brigade Commander."[44]

Shortly after this, an important change occurred in Feng's personal life that influenced his later career. On December 17, 1923, Feng's wife died in Peking. Mrs. Feng, a simple and uneducated woman, had taken no part in her husband's career.[45] Two months after her death, on February 19, 1924, Feng married a woman completely different in background and character from his first wife.[46]

Her name was Li Te-ch'üan.* At the time of their marriage, Feng

* Chin (No. 14, p. 10) says that Feng's marriage to Li had a sort of John Alden twist. According to Chin, shortly after Feng's first wife died, Feng asked a friend, Ch'iu Pin, to help him find a new wife. Ch'iu asked Li Te-ch'üan for assistance. Li introduced Feng to several women, and during this process Feng became inter-

was forty-two years old, and Li Te-ch'üan was twenty-eight. Li's uncle had been "in charge" of a rural Christian church at the time of the Boxer uprising, and he and most of his family were killed at that time. Li was raised a Christian and was educated in schools administered by the American Board of Commissioners for Foreign Missions. She later studied at Bridgman Academy and the Union Women's College, after which she taught at Bridgman for a year or two, and then worked as a pastor's assistant in a large Congregational Church in Peking. For the year and a half before marrying Feng, Li Te-ch'üan worked in the Peking YWCA. She was said to be an effective speaker and organizer.[47] As soon as she became Mrs. Feng, she began to assist her husband in his educational program and other projects.*

The Second Chih-Feng War

Although Chang Tso-lin's Fengtien armies were defeated in the war in 1922, his base in Manchuria was not invaded. When the Chihli-controlled government stripped Chang of his ranks and titles after his defeat, Chang simply declared himself independent of the government and proceeded to reorganize and strengthen his armed forces. Instructors of all sorts were employed, both foreign and Chinese, and huge quantities of equipment and munitions-making machinery were purchased. In northern China it was generally believed that Chang planned to invade Chihli by the summer of 1923, and Wu P'ei-fu made military preparations to counter such a move. However, at the beginning of May bandits attacked a train at Linch'eng, in Shantung province, and kidnapped over three hundred passengers, including many foreigners. Foreign powers reacted so strongly that there seemed

---

ested in Li herself. Mrs. Elizabeth Stelle wrote a memo for me (with the cooperation of two other missionaries who knew something about Li) in which she said that Feng had stipulated that his next wife must be Christian, educated, and thrifty. According to her version, Feng heard about Li's work at the YWCA, arranged to meet her at the home of a mutual friend, and proposed shortly afterward. Louella Miner (Journal, Mar. 26, 1924) wrote that Feng and Li married so quickly after the first Mrs. Feng's death because Ts'ao K'un was pressuring Feng to marry one of his daughters.

* It has been asserted that Li Te-ch'üan very early showed strong leftist political tendencies, and that she influenced Feng in that direction; this may be true, although it is difficult to determine. After Feng Yü-hsiang's death, which occurred on the eve of the establishment of the People's Republic of China, Li Te-ch'üan became an important member of the new government. She served as Minister of Health, as head of the Chinese Red Cross, and in many other important posts. She has been a member of many diplomatic missions to foreign countries.

a real possibility of foreign intervention in China, and the renewal of civil war was consequently postponed.

In the meantime, as mentioned above, Wu P'ei-fu had abandoned hope of unifying China by political means, and had turned to a policy of unification by military force. Leaving politics mainly to his patron, Ts'ao K'un, Wu initiated, sponsored, or supported military campaigns in many areas of China. Although these campaigns had not shown much promise at the outset, they became increasingly successful, and by mid-1924 Wu controlled most of China proper.* By this time, too, the uproar over the Linch'eng train affair had subsided, and an incident was all that was needed to spark the delayed civil war.

The incident occurred at the beginning of September 1924, when war broke out between the tuchüns of Kiangsu and Chekiang for the possession of Shanghai.†⁴⁸ The tuchün of Kiangsu, Ch'i Hsieh-yüan,

---

* The alignment of provinces in the fall of 1924 was as follows. The Chihli clique, or Wu P'ei-fu, controlled or strongly influenced Chihli, Shantung, Kiangsu, Honan, Anhwei, Shensi, Hupeh, Kiangsi, Fukien, and Szechwan. Hunan and Kansu, while not controlled by Chihli militarists, were pro-Chihli. Anti-Chihli areas were Manchuria, Chekiang, and Kwangtung. Yunnan, Kweichow, Kwangsi, and Shensi were essentially neutral.

† Shanghai is, of course, in Kiangsu, but Lu Yung-hsiang acquired a foothold there in the following fashion. Early in 1917, Lu was appointed Defense Commissioner of Shanghai and the surrounding area by the Anfu government. At the same time, he was Co-Director of Military Affairs of Kiangsu. In the fall of 1919 he was appointed tuchün of Chekiang, but he retained his post in Shanghai until July 1920, when one of his trusted followers, Ho Feng-lin, succeeded him as Defense Commissioner. Thus, the Shanghai area was actually within the jurisdiction of Chekiang instead of Kiangsu. One reason Lu was so eager to retain control of Shanghai was the presence of an arsenal there. Perhaps more important, the revenues derived from the Shanghai opium trade were reportedly about $20,000,000 per year. (Lynn, p. 136.) Lu was the only Anfu militarist of importance who managed to retain his position after the defeat by the Chihli faction in the summer of 1920. Ho Feng-lin also kept his post at Shanghai. Immediately after the defeat of Chang Tso-lin in 1922, Lu Yung-hsiang stepped down as tuchün and declared himself Director of Military Affairs of Chekiang, in effect asserting his independence from the Chihli-dominated central government. Chang Tso-lin, seeking to retain some influence in northern China, found a natural ally in Lu and established ties with him. Ch'i Hsieh-yüan, who became tuchün of Kiangsu in 1921, resented Lu's influence in Shanghai and tried to counter it. Friction between the two men increased in 1923, when the chief of police in Shanghai was assassinated. Ch'i Hsieh-yüan appointed a replacement, but Lu Yung-hsiang and Ho Feng-lin backed a different man, whose seizure of the post almost precipitated war between Kiangsu and Chekiang. However, Wu P'ei-fu was at that time trying to get control of the neighboring province of Fukien, and did not want Ch'i to risk a war until that had been achieved. In the summer of 1924, Sun Ch'uan-fang, under orders from Wu, drove the Anfu forces out of Fukien. These defeated troops made their way to Chekiang, where Lu Yung-hsiang welcomed and assisted them, in direct defiance of Wu P'ei-fu. This angered Wu, and, with Fukien now in his camp, he was ready to oust Lu Yung-hsiang from

was an ally of Wu P'ei-fu, whereas the ruler of Chekiang, Lu Yung-hsiang, was allied with Chang Tso-lin.[49] In the early days of the fighting, Ch'i Hsieh-yüan seemed to be losing, and he appealed to Wu P'ei-fu for assistance. Wu ordered General Sun Ch'uan-fang to go to Ch'i's aid from Fukien, and other forces were also sent. In response to these moves Chang Tso-lin invaded Chihli, but not in time to save Lu Yung-hsiang, who fled to Japan on October 13. It was the end of Lu but the beginning of the Second Chih-Feng War.

Many believed that Wu P'ei-fu had chosen this time to begin the war because Chang Tso-lin's military reorganization was not yet complete, and some of his new troops had not been thoroughly trained.[50] If that was true, it made all the more remarkable the surprising fact that the Chihli side seemed ill-prepared for the war when it came, despite the fact that it had been expected for so long.[51] Wu began seizing "men, carts, animals, and everything else he needed," according to one observer.* In traveling over four different railroads during September and October, the same observer passed "train after train loaded with poor men snatched from the fields or streets."[52]

Wu's strategy called for the advance of three separate armies, and he appointed Feng commander of the Third Route Army, which was to invade western Jehol. The bulk of the Chihli forces were organized as the First Route Army, under P'eng Shou-hsin; this army was ordered to the front at Shanhaikuan, the main gateway to Manchuria from northern China. The Second Route Army, commanded by Wang Huai-ch'ing, was ordered to the vicinity of Hsifengk'ou, near the Chihli-Jehol boundary. Wu P'ei-fu, of course, was commander-in-chief of the Chihli armies.[53]

Early in September, Wu gave Feng at least $100,000 for military expenses.[54] However, Feng complained bitterly that he was given inadequate funds and insufficient arms and ammunition.[55] Feng claimed that Wu's orders called for the army to forage in the localities through which it passed, an expedient to which Feng strenuously objected.[56] These complaints may have made Wu P'ei-fu suspicious of Feng. In

---

Chekiang as part of his general policy of unification by force. Thus began the so-called Kiang-Che War. It was, in short, a local war fought over the possession of Shanghai and the surrounding area. However, since Wu supported Ch'i Hsieh-yüan, and Chang Tso-lin supported Lu Yung-hsiang, it marked the beginning of the Second Chih-Feng War.

* A report in the NCH, Oct. 18, 1924, p. 107, said that in Peking "practically all motor cars owned by Chinese companies are being taken, and things have reached the stage when the mechanics are fast dismantling all the vehicles they have in stock to avoid having them commandeered by military authorities."

any event, from the time it became clear that the Chihli and Fengtien armies were really going to war, there were rumors that Feng would not participate. Reports that Feng would declare his neutrality reached Mukden in early October. More general rumors to the effect that "several influential military leaders of the Chihli troops" would "declare their independence immediately after Marshal Wu's departure for the front" circulated widely.[57] It is not surprising, in view of these rumors, that Wu P'ei-fu began to doubt Feng's reliability. Thus, according to Feng, Wu sent a "supervisor" along with the Third Route Army, and also ordered Hu Ching-i, who commanded a unit of the Second Route Army, to keep an eye on Feng and to kill him if he made a wrong move.[58] Unfortunately for Wu, Hu Ching-i was the wrong man for such an assignment: he was already a party to Feng's plan to betray Wu. Moreover, the "supervisor," Wang Ch'eng-pin, was also in on the plot, as was Sun Yo, vice-commander of the Peking garrison.

On September 10, 1924, Sun Yo visited Feng at Nanyüan, apparently in connection with commemorative services for Feng's fallen soldiers. Feng took Sun to an isolated arbor for private discussion. After some preliminary conversation in which they both agreed that they were little more than "running dogs of the warlords," Feng allegedly remarked to Sun, "Today Wu and Ts'ao are dictating to the government, the nation is in chaos, and the people are troubled. For a long time I have been determined to act on behalf of the nation to eliminate these evils, but I have not yet dared to move because I am alone." Sun Yo replied that he not only would be willing to cooperate with Feng, but would approach Hu Ching-i, who was also dissatisfied with the present state of affairs, and get his assistance.[59] About a week later a representative came to Feng from Hu Ching-i to discuss plans for revolt. This conference was followed by several others between Feng and Hu or the latter's representatives after Feng's army had left the capital, ostensibly to take part in the anti-Fengtien campaign.[60] By mid-October their plans were ready, and they awaited only a favorable opportunity to put them into effect.

The Seizure of Peking

On September 21, the first of Feng's units began moving northward. On the 23rd Feng and his chief officers took leave of Wu P'ei-fu, and on the following day Feng departed from the capital with the last of his troops.

Feng's army moved northward slowly, and units were left at several points en route. About 10,000 men were stationed at Peiyüan, just north of Peking, on the pretext that they needed further training. By mid-October Feng had other troops of his at Miyün, about fifty miles north of Peking; at Kupeik'ou, just at the Great Wall; at Luanp'ing, about twenty miles north of the Jehol border; and probably at other spots in between.[61] The largest contingent was apparently at Kupeik'ou.

In the meantime, the First Route Army had suffered a series of defeats. Feng had kept constantly informed of the situation on the Shanhaikuan front, and when it seemed clear to him that the position of the First Route Army was critical, he decided this was the opportunity he had been waiting for. On the evening of October 20, he issued orders to most of his army to return to Peking at top speed. He commanded one brigade to go directly to Changhsintien, south of the capital, to cut the Peking-Hankow Railway. He had Hu Ching-i's representative sign a written statement supporting the revolution against Wu, and then wired Hu Ching-i to march quickly to the Luanchow area in northern Chihli to sever the Peking-Fengtien Railway behind Wu P'ei-fu's armies.[62]

By October 22 Feng and all of his men were at Peiyüan, and at 8 P.M. they headed for the capital. By midnight they had reached the An Ting Men, a northern gate to the city. Sun Yo was ready, and his men opened the gate for Feng's troops. The occupation of the city had been well planned, and was executed quickly and efficiently. Postal, telephone, and telegraph offices were occupied; railway workers were replaced by Feng's soldiers. The President's mansion was surrounded, government offices were taken over, and approaches to the legation quarter—the refuge of the defeated—were blocked off. Soldiers were stationed at all other key points in the city, including all major intersections. Each of these soldiers wore an arm band on which was printed: "[We are] sworn to die to save the country, to love the people, and not to harm the people."[63] On the morning of October 23, the citizens of Peking awoke to find the city sealed off from the outside world, and firmly in the hands of Feng Yü-hsiang.

On October 23 and 24, Feng issued proclamations addressed respectively to the people of Peking, to the northern provinces, and to the entire nation. Each proclamation pointed out that the country had for many years been rent by civil wars, from which all classes of society had suffered. Moreover, these wars had been fought for personal gain, not for national interests. In 1924 various areas of China had been hit by drought and flood, which had imposed additional hardships on the people. The nation must have peace, Feng said, and militarists must no longer rule the land. It was in order to achieve peace, he asserted, that he and his associates had returned to Peking. But he admitted that more than military power was necessary to effect the reforms the nation needed. Therefore a peace conference should be convened to settled the problems facing the country and to bring a new order into being.[64]

On October 25, a statement was issued announcing that the armies that had taken part in the coup d'etat were now formally organized as the Chung-hua Min-kuo Kuo-min-chün, the National People's Army of the Chinese Republic. Feng Yü-hsiang was named commander-in-chief of the Kuominchün, and commander of the First Army of the Kuominchün. Hu Ching-i was made a vice-commander-in-chief, and commander of the Second Army. Sun Yo also became a vice-commander-in-chief, and commander of the Third Army. The Kuominchün, the announcement declared, would be completely at the service of the people.[65]

On October 24, President Ts'ao K'un was forced to issue mandates calling for an immediate cessation of hostilities, and dismissing Wu P'ei-fu from his several posts; Wu was appointed Tupan of Land Development in Tsinghai. This position, of course, was simply a euphemism for exile, and nobody really expected Wu to accept it.

When Wu P'ei-fu learned of Feng's betrayal, he hurried back to Tientsin with a small contingent of picked troops. He hoped that his armies in the north would hold the Fengtien forces at bay until he could obtain assistance from his allies in central China with which to defeat Feng Yü-hsiang. Then he would return north and continue the fight against Chang Tso-lin. However, the tuchüns of Shansi and Shantung cut off reinforcements from the south, and the Fengtien army broke through the Great Wall, cutting Wu's communications with his troops near Shanhaikuan. After a few engagements with Kuominchün troops near Tientsin, Wu and a few thousand soldiers fled to their ships and sailed to the Yangtze. In the course of a few weeks, Wu had been toppled from his position as the leading militarist in China to the status of a fugitive with a price on his head.* It was a catastrophe from which Wu never fully recovered.[66]

---

* The seizure of Peking by itself did not account for Wu's downfall. The basic factor was the defeat of Wu's armies at Shanhaikuan, but the Peking coup had an important bearing on this, too. The fact that Feng did not engage the Fengtien army in Jehol forced Wu to divert three divisions from Shanhaikuan to the west, but they did not achieve their positions until after the coup, when they were forced to surrender to the Fengtien army. Moreover, the Fengtien general in west-

136 PLOTS IN PEKING

On November 2 Feng forced Wu's chief, Ts'ao K'un, to resign the presidency that had cost him so much in money and prestige. However, Ts'ao did not gain his freedom by his resignation; he remained a prisoner in Peking for many months. Under Feng's sponsorship, a regency government was set up under Huang Fu, one-time Minister of Education and Foreign Minister. This government managed affairs while Feng, Chang Tso-lin, and other leaders discussed the future of northern China.

Three days after the formal establishment of the regency government, Feng Yü-hsiang executed another coup that was in some ways more dramatic and created more of a furor than his original seizure of the capital. On the morning of November 5, one of Feng's brigade commanders, Lu Chung-lin, led a body of soldiers to the Forbidden City, where he demanded an interview with "Mr. P'u-i." P'ui was the personal name of the Emperor Hsüan-t'ung, the Manchu ruler who had presided over a shadow court in Peking since the Revolution of 1911. Although Lu wanted to see the emperor himself, he was finally persuaded to explain his mission to the comptroller of the Manchu house. Lu stated that P'u-i, his wife, and the two surviving dowager consorts had to leave the Forbidden City within three hours. Moreover, he presented a revised Favorable Treatment Agreement and demanded that P'u-i sign it.

Early in 1912, when the Manchu emperor had been forced to abdicate, the Republic of China had concluded with the Manchu royal house an agreement providing, among other things, that the emperor retain his title, that he receive from the Republic a sum of $4,000,000 per year, that he continue the ceremonies at the Ch'ing ancestral temple required by tradition, and that he receive from the Republic of China all the respect due a foreign sovereign.[67] The revised articles presented by Lu Chung-lin abolished the imperial title and allowed the emperor only those privileges accorded by law to any other citizen of the Republic. It cut the emperor's annual allowance to $500,000, but promised that $2,000,000 would be provided to set up industrial establishments to provide work for the poor, and that poor Manchus would have preferential rights of employment in these institutions. Furthermore, the emperor and his family were to leave the palace immediately and take up residence wherever they wished; the govern-

ern Jehol, Li Ching-lin, knew that Feng did not intend to fight, and therefore sent large bodies of his troops eastward, where they were the decisive factor in the last great battle of the war. Finally, news of the Peking coup had a disastrous effect on the morale of Wu's troops at the front.

ment of the Republic was to assume the responsibility of protecting them. The government also promised to protect the Ch'ing tombs and temples, and guaranteed that the Ch'ing family's personal property, as distinct from property they held that was regarded as public, would not be confiscated.[68]

P'u-i did not sign the revised articles, but he did have to leave the palace. He went to his father's house, where Feng's troops guarded him as a virtual prisoner. Toward the end of November the regency government came to an end, and Tuan Ch'i-jui became provisional chief executive. One of Tuan's first acts was to remove the restrictions on P'u-i's movement, and on November 29 the ex-emperor fled to the Japanese legation. The monarchy in China was definitely ended.*

Motives Behind Feng's Coup

Feng's coup d'etat was a spectacular event, which naturally elicited widespread comment from both contemporaries and later writers. The motives behind Feng's act have been variously ascribed to his personal antagonism for Wu P'ei-fu, to his having been bribed by Chang Tso-lin, to his having been allied with Kuomintang revolutionists, to his desire for power, and to less credible factors such as his obedience to the will of God. Actually, the coup was a complex affair, and though many aspects of it are not yet clear, it is evident that all previous interpretations of it have been oversimplified.

First of all, Feng's explanation of the coup as a cooperative effort of Sun Yo, Hu Ching-i, and himself is undoubtedly correct as far as it goes. That this trio carefully planned the coup was evident in their smooth execution of it, and, indeed, their collusion was common knowledge among informed observers at the time.[69] But on the really important question of what motivated their actions, Feng's account cannot be trusted. Writing long after the event, Feng would have his readers believe that the coup was executed in behalf of Sun Yat-sen. According to their plans, Feng wrote, Sun Yat-sen eventually was to

---

* For P'u-i this flight marked the beginning of a long period during which his freedom was limited and he was used as a pawn in the political maneuvers of others. He remained a guest at the Japanese legation until February 1925. Then he went to the Japanese concession in Tientsin, where he stayed for almost seven years, until November 1931. He was then taken to Manchuria, where in March 1932 the Japanese inaugurated the state of Manchukuo. Four days later, P'u-i became chief executive, or regent, of that state, a move which, he later explained, was forced on him by the threat of "drastic action" if he refused. Two years later an imperial system was established in Manchukuo, and P'u-i became emperor of that state. He was in Russian hands for a time after World War II, and most recently has been writing his autobiography in Communist China.

be invited "to administer everything." Sun was "China's only revolutionary leader," and had the plotters not supported him, they would have been "simply opportunists seeking power, not true revolutionaries."[70] There is little doubt that this explanation, written long after Sun Yat-sen had become the symbol of the Chinese revolution, bears little relation to the facts. Most writers who have accepted it have done so to bolster Feng's later revolutionary pretensions, or to build a case against him as a radical, depending on their point of view.[71]

The main evidence adduced to prove Feng's sympathy with the Kuomintang before the coup (and thereby to substantiate his account of its motivation) is the Kuomintang membership of both Hu Ching-i and Sun Yo, and Feng's contacts in 1924 with Hsü Ch'ien, Sun Yat-sen's representative in Peking. However, by 1924 both Hu Ching-i and Sun Yo were militarists first and Kuomintang members second. Hsü's relations with Feng were close, and he doubtless urged Feng to join the Kuomintang. But there is no reason to think Feng was won over in 1924. On the contrary, the evidence shows that Feng was not committed to Sun Yat-sen's program at this time, and that he did not have Sun in mind when planning the coup. Feng's diary entries prior to the seizure of the capital summarize many speeches given to his men, and none include praise of Sun or the Kuomintang. The books Feng read during this period, and the reading material he recommended to his officers and men, did not include Kuomintang writings.[72] Even more important, the statements Feng made immediately after the coup in an attempt to justify it contain no reference to Sun or the Kuomintang.[73] Most important, his actions after the coup were not in support of Sun Yat-sen.

Although Sun Yat-sen does not appear to have figured in the coup, as Feng alleged, it is possible that Kuomintang agents knew of Feng's plans, and were even involved to some extent. The reason for suspecting this is that the anti-Chihli groups at that time consisted of the Fengtien, Anfu, and Kuomintang factions, and since Feng definitely negotiated with the first two groups, it is probable that the last group was also involved.[74]

Although observers were mistaken in attributing the coup to Kuomintang influence, they were correct in pointing to the poor relations between Feng and Wu P'ei-fu as playing an important part in determining Feng's course of action. As mentioned earlier, Feng was never really one of "Wu's men." Ever since 1914, Feng had been formally under the command of the central government, and his relationship with Wu came about as a result of his accepting Ts'ao K'un's protection in 1918.[75] The two men first began to have close and continuous contact in 1922, at the time of the First Chih-Feng War. Shortly afterward, when Feng was tuchün of Honan, the rift between them first apeared, and a series of incidents steadily widened it. From the outset, Feng took no pains to treat Wu tactfully. On Wu's birthday in 1922, Feng sent him a bottle of distilled water as a sign that he disapproved of Wu's drinking wine.[76] Not long afterward, he sent Wu a list of suggestions about how Wu might improve his administration.[77] Neither of these acts sat well with Wu.

Some of the more serious incidents that estranged Feng and Wu have already been mentioned. Wu never forgave Feng for the murder of Pao Te-ch'üan in Kaifeng in 1922.[78] Feng, on the other hand, attributed his dismissal from the tuchünship of Honan to Wu's machinations, and always held it against him.[79] In 1923, Feng had openly joined with Wu's enemies to force Li Yüan-hung from office. In short, by 1924 their personal relations had deteriorated, and they stood on opposite sides of the division within the Chihli clique. Obviously, therefore, Feng could hope to gain nothing from a major increase in Wu's power. A victory over Chang Tso-lin would provide Wu P'ei-fu with the wherewithal to crush all his enemies and rivals, and Feng could see himself among them. In such circumstances, it was natural that Feng should become receptive to the suggestion of revolt—even if the suggestion came from the Japanese.

Feng Yü-hsiang's coup was remarkable in many ways. Not the least remarkable feature about it was that whereas Peking residents learned of the coup when they awoke on the morning of October 23, readers of Japanese newspapers in Manchuria read an account of it on October 22.[80] Moreover, at a lunch at the Japanese legation on October 22, Ts'ao K'un's secretary was told by his hosts that if Ts'ao wanted shelter at the legation that night, it would be prepared for him; the secretary unaccountably did not tell Ts'ao of this remarkable invitation.[81] It also happened that among the people roaming the streets of Peking on the morning of October 23 was a Japanese journalist who was there because he had received information two days earlier that Feng would attempt to seize the capital on that day.[82] Indeed, the population of China outside Peking first heard of the coup from Japanese radio broadcasts, although these, at least, were actually after the event.[83]

These strange facts were hardly noticed in the excitement of the coup; few commentators, for instance, saw any significance in the fact that the early editions of the Japanese newspapers in Manchuria that reported the coup appeared before the coup was under way. These facts have also gone unmentioned in the standard histories of the period, and yet they are important clues to one of the least-known stories in modern Chinese history. In a word, the coup by Feng Yü-hsiang—long reputed to have been bitterly anti-Japanese—was actively supported, probably financed, and perhaps even conceived by Japanese army and diplomatic personnel in China.

Because of the secrecy surrounding the operation, and the natural reluctance of Chinese to admit any connection with a Japanese-sponsored plot, many details are still unclear. However, there is enough evidence to warrant a tentative reconstruction of the plot's main lines. Such a reconstruction demands some imagination, and by its nature will contain some error. But it will be closer to the truth than the usual explanation that the plot was primarily the creation of Feng, Sun, and Hu.

It is, of course, well known that the Japanese were interested in China and active there in the warlord period and even earlier. The Twenty-One Demands, the Nishihara Loans, and the appropriation of German interests in Shantung were only the most conspicuous manifestations of ceaseless Japanese efforts to extend Japan's interests in China. Japanese interests received a severe setback in 1920, when Tuan Ch'i-jui and the pro-Japanese Anfu clique were defeated and ousted from positions of power. They were further threatened in 1922, when the Chihli faction defeated Chang Tso-lin, who had long been supported by Japan. After 1922 the power and the attitude of the Chihli faction ruling in Peking were of great importance to Japan. By mid-1924, although Japan had begun the Shidehara policy of conciliating China, there were Japanese military men, businessmen, and others who preferred to rely on force, and who were particularly sensitive about the possibility of changes in northern China and Manchuria. Baron Okura Kihachiro, for example, was one of the most important Japanese capitalists involved in Manchuria, and on the eve of the Peking coup the American chargé in Tokyo reported to his government that

Okura interests in Manchuria . . . have prospered magnificently at the hands of Chang [Tso-lin], and it is known that Mr. Okura regards with true apprehension the possibility of any change in the status quo. Smaller Japanese merchants operating in Manchuria . . . have been endeavoring to elicit the sympathy of the government on behalf of the Mukden faction.[84]

Moreover, in September 1924 Chang Tso-lin signed a contract with Japan permitting that country to build a railroad from Taonan to

Anganghsi (Taonan-Tsitsihar), a road of potentially great strategic and economic importance to Japan.[85]

The Japanese recognized that the real power in the Chihli faction was Wu P'ei-fu. Wu favored friendly relations between China and Japan so the two countries could cooperate to preserve the purity of Oriental culture from Western contamination; it was perhaps this attitude that led Japanese officers in China to believe that they could use Wu. In February 1924, Hayashi Yasakichi, the Japanese military attaché in Peking, submitted a report to his superiors stating that although Wu had hitherto opposed Japanese interests in China, he could probably be brought around to support Japan. Hayashi strongly recommended that a Japanese officer who had known Wu for many years be assigned the task of winning him to the Japanese point of view.[86]

It is not known what efforts, if any, the Japanese made in this regard, but whatever they did apparently failed. In any event, there was little time, for by the spring of 1924 it was generally accepted in northern China that another Chihli-Fengtien war was in the offing. Such a war had ominous implications for Japan. Wu had defeated the superior military power of Chang Tso-lin once already. He was now bent on unifying China by force, and this meant ousting Chang Tso-lin from Manchuria. The Japanese could not view this prospect with equanimity, and began seeking other means to handle Wu. In the report mentioned above, Hayashi also noted that Feng Yü-hsiang was one of those within the Chihli faction who was envious of Wu's power and would like to reduce it. Moreover, Feng's army was the most formidable military force in the Chihli group, with the exception of those troops directly under Wu P'ei-fu. It was therefore natural for the Japanese to think of an anti-Wu revolt led by Feng Yü-hsiang as a means to their end.

Feng was reputedly anti-Japanese. Accordingly, in order to persuade him to overthrow Wu and to ensure that the distribution of power in northern China after the revolt would not be inimical to Japanese interests, other Chinese factions had to be brought into the plot to influence both Feng and subsequent political events. From the Japanese point of view, an alliance between the pro-Japanese Anfu politicians, led by Tuan Ch'i-jui, and Feng's army was the ideal arrangement. The Japanese could then remain in the background and work through Tuan Ch'i-jui. If their plans were successful, Feng, Tuan, and Chang Tso-lin would emerge as the three leading figures in northern China, and at least the last two were friendly toward

Japan. If he could be induced to join the plot, the chances were that Feng himself would become more amenable to Japanese intentions in China.

To persuade Feng to revolt, and to bring him into alliance with the Anfu group, an intermediary was needed. For this purpose Huang Fu was perfect. Huang Fu had studied in Japan, spoke Japanese, and had many Japanese connections.[87] He also had connections with the Anfu clique, and from 1916 to 1924 he acted as Peking representative for Lu Yung-hsiang, the only Anfu tuchün to retain his position after the An-Chih War. Finally, Huang Fu was well acquainted with Feng Yü-hsiang, and frequently addressed Feng's troops at Nanyüan.[88] Huang Fu became the middleman.[89]

Unfortunately, one of the facts that is still unclear is the date, even the approximate date, when Huang Fu first approached Feng with plans for the coup. However, it was probably several months before the coup occurred, and thus well before Feng made arrangements with Sun Yo and Hu Ching-i.[90]

But what arguments could Huang Fu use to persuade Feng to revolt against Wu P'ei-fu? There were several arguments that could have appealed to Feng as being plausible enough, or possibly as a convenient façade behind which he could serve his own power interests. Huang could have pointed to the unpopularity and inefficiency of Ts'ao K'un's government; to the detrimental aspects of Wu's policy of unification by force; to the disastrous possibility of Chang Tso-lin's occupying northern China in the event of a Chihli defeat; and so on. But in addition to these arguments, about which we can only speculate, Huang Fu was authorized to offer Feng ¥1,500,000. Feng may have been offered much more, with the remainder to be paid after Wu was eliminated as a factor in Chinese politics.[91] As a clinching argument, Huang reportedly showed Feng a document proving that Ts'ao K'un was involved with American agents in some undesirable scheme.[92]

These considerations, especially the financial inducement, must have influenced Feng's decision to revolt. But without the background of strained relations between him and Wu, they probably would not have been sufficient. Feng was shrewd enough to realize that as things stood he would have been in jeopardy had Wu been victorious. A successful revolt not only would remove this threat, but would also make Feng the leading militarist in northern China. With the assistance of the Anfu clique and the Japanese, who would in turn make arrangements with Chang Tso-lin, there was every reason to believe that such a revolt would succeed.

It was understood from the outset that Tuan Ch'i-jui would head the government to be established after Wu's overthrow.[93] Tuan was the natural, almost the only, choice. He was acceptable to the Japanese because of his pro-Japanese orientation. And he was acceptable to both Feng Yü-hsiang and Chang Tso-lin for two reasons. First, he had no independent military power, and thus did not threaten the future of either man. Probably a more important consideration was the tuchüns of the Yangtze valley. These militarists were supporting Wu P'ei-fu in the war against Chang Tso-lin. Their reaction to any revolt against Wu was clearly of great importance, for they might come to his aid. Second, even if Wu were overthrown, the Yangtze tuchüns could refuse to recognize the new leaders in Peking. The choice of Tuan Ch'i-jui as head of state minimized both dangers. The immediate military danger was lessened because Tuan had sufficient influence with the tuchün of Shantung to persuade him to obstruct any reinforcements coming to Wu P'ei-fu from the south.[94] As for the long-range problem, Tuan Ch'i-jui, as a senior Peiyang militarist who was not identified with either the Kuominchün or the Fengtien faction, would be much more acceptable to the tuchüns of the Yangtze valley than any nominee of Feng's or Chang's.

Tuan had withdrawn from national politics after his defeat in 1920, and was presumably devoting his time to the study of Buddhism. He had to be brought back into the political spotlight. This was achieved on September 15, 1924, when he issued a circular telegram condemning Wu P'ei-fu and Ts'ao K'un, and announcing his support of Chang Tso-lin.[95] On October 19, Feng's personal emissary returned from a conference with Tuan.[96] Two days later, Tuan declared he would be willing to accept the leadership of the nation if he were requested to do so.[97] Two days after that Feng seized Peking, and in the conferences that followed, Tuan received precisely such a request.

It was doubtless through Tuan or the Japanese that arrangements were made between Feng and Chang Tso-lin to avoid hostilities on the Jehol front.[98] In any event, it is certain that such arrangements were made.[99] While Feng was marching north on the way to the Jehol front, he worked out the final details with a representative of Chang Tso-lin.[100] As mentioned above, these arrangements allowed Fengtien troops to be transferred from the Jehol front to fight Wu P'ei-fu's armies, and thus contributed to Wu's defeat.

Besides their involvement in Feng's plot to overthrow Wu, the Japanese also rendered what can only be called military assistance to Chang Tso-lin. That is, the Japanese intelligence system in China collected military information of value to Wu's enemies and broadcasted it.[101] The Japanese spread both anti-Wu propaganda and false news throughout southern China. These false reports helped dissuade the Yangtze tuchüns from aiding Wu.[102]

Whereas it seems certain that Huang Fu, Feng, and Tuan Ch'i-jui —with the Japanese in the background—made an agreement to move against Wu P'ei-fu, it is not so certain that Feng's seizure of Peking was in accord with that agreement. It is possible that Feng's sudden return to the capital was his own idea, and that the original plan called for him to hurry his forces from Jehol to Luanchow and attack the rear of Wu's army in cooperation with Hu Ching-i. This is a persuasive possibility, for neither the Japanese, Chang Tso-lin, nor Tuan Ch'i-jui were eager to see Peking dominated by Feng's troops.

In view of the fact that Huang Fu acted as liaison between Feng and Tuan rather than between Feng and the Japanese, and the fact that Feng communicated directly with Tuan, one might wonder if Feng actually knew that the Japanese were involved in the coup. There is no question that Feng knew of the Japanese involvement. Circumstantial evidence is provided by the fact that from July 1924 into the spring of 1925 Feng received a series of visits from Japanese army officers, government personnel, journalists, and others.[103] Add to this that Feng later expressed surprise at Japanese press criticism of the coup, which he said the Japanese had proposed in the first place.[104] Finally, and most significant, a Japanese army officer, Matsumuro Takayoshi, accompanied Feng from Kupeik'ou to Peking at the time of the coup.

Matsumuro was a young officer in the process of becoming a China "expert." While in Peking, he attended two diplomatic functions at which he was seated next to Feng. On the basis of these meetings, Feng invited him to Nanyüan to inspect his troops. He therefore was acquainted with Feng by the time the Second Chih-Feng War began. When the hostilities started, Matsumuro proceeded with other foreigners to the Shanhaikuan front as a military observer. But shortly before October 23, Hayashi Yasakichi suddenly summoned Matsumuro to Peking. When he reached the capital, Hayashi told him that Feng was going to turn against Wu P'ei-fu, and that he, Matsumuro, should proceed immediately to Kupeik'ou, meet Feng, and return with him "to direct the execution of the coup."[105] Matsumuro promptly departed.

Matsumuro insists that his only function was to plan the military details of the coup. However, this must be viewed skeptically.[106] Feng clearly had already made his plans. It seems more probable that Ma-

tsumuro was sent—perhaps in the guise of a military observer—to keep
an eye on Feng for the Japanese in Peking. His friendly acquaintance
with Feng would have made him a more desirable agent than most
other Japanese in the capital.

Under whatever pretext Matsumuro accompanied Feng, his appearance at Kupeik'ou at that time implied at the very least Japanese
knowledge of the coup. But more than that, Matsumuro asserts that
as soon as he arrived at Kupeik'ou, Feng "confided everything to me
in order to get my opinion." Besides, Feng also asked Matsumuro not
to speak of the matter with any of Feng's officers, which suggests that
Feng was accepting Japanese support without their knowledge.[107]

It is also significant that within four months after the coup, in February 1925, Hayashi Yasakichi reported to his government that "in
recent times significant changes have occurred in Feng's attitude toward Japan. Now he seems to be aware of the important place it
occupies in the international complexities of the Orient, and is therefore able to understand the merits of entering into an alliance with
our empire."[108] Hayashi was not mistaken; immediately after the
coup, Matsumuro became a personal adviser to Feng, and there is
documentary evidence that on several occasions he acted as intermediary between Feng and Japanese authorities in China and Tokyo.

None of these points is conclusive. However, in the absence of evidence to the contrary, they add up to a convincing case that Feng was
well aware that the Japanese were, in some measure, the "sponsors"
of the revolt.

Although the Japanese wanted to eliminate Wu P'ei-fu as a power
in China, an aim that accorded with the desires of the Anfu and Fengtien factions, none of these groups approved of P'u-i's ouster. It was
for this act that Feng was criticized by the Japanese press, and by Japanese generally.[109]

Feng's evicting P'u-i from the palace served several ends. First, Feng
had always favored eliminating the vestiges of the monarchy. After
the unsuccessful attempt by Chang Hsün to restore the monarchy in
1917, Feng had advocated that P'u-i be made an ordinary citizen, and
that the Treaty of Favorable Treatment be abrogated; in essence, the
proposals he supported then were those he put into effect in November 1924.

Moreover, as long as P'u-i retained the imperial trappings there
would be encouragement for plotters interested in restoring the monarchy. Indeed, rumors periodically swept the country that a restoration was imminent. In the spring of 1921, for example, such rumors

were very widespread, and in April it was reported that "all government departments are agitated by the prospects of a monarchy-res-
toration movement within the next few days."[110] In 1923 there was a
conspiracy to take P'u-i to Manchuria, where he was apparently to be
proclaimed emperor (with Chang Tso-lin the power behind the
throne) as a prelude to an attempt to unify China under the aegis of
the monarchy.[111] In the spring of 1924, there was a resurgence of rumors about an impending restoration, and they may have had some
basis in fact.[112] Thus it is quite possible that Feng was partly motivated by a desire to eliminate the threat of a restoration, as he asserted,
particularly since he knew that in a restored monarchy Chang Tso-lin
would possess great influence in Peking. And Feng's fears about Chang
were not groundless; indeed, shortly after Chang arrived in Peking,
he began making plans to restore P'u-i to at least the status he had
held before November.[113]

In addition, by the dramatic act of expelling the Manchu emperor,
Feng may have hoped to distract public attention from his treachery
against Wu P'ei-fu. P'u-i's expulsion suggested that Feng was motivated by a deep commitment to the Republic. Thus presumably both
the nation and Feng's soldiers would see that his betrayal of his commander-in-chief was prompted by high principles, not the self-seeking
that he so frequently deplored in other warlords. Feng may even have
foreseen the possibility of using the ousting of the emperor as evidence
to counter allegations of subservience to Japan in case the Japanese
role in the coup should become known.

The day after P'u-i was forced from the palace, the American
chargé in Peking wrote that his eviction was inspired by Bolsheviks
"working through the Kuomintang for the purpose of finally eliminating monarchical restoration and further inciting anti-imperialist
feeling and so anti-foreign feeling."[114] It is true that Feng was in close
contact with some Kuomintang leaders; he knew their attitudes, and
perhaps they encouraged him. In any event, faced with the prospect
of sharing power in northern China with Chang Tso-lin, Feng could
not have been unaware of the advantages of establishing more cordial
relations with the Kuomintang. But there is no evidence that Feng's
act was "inspired" by the Russians or the Kuomintang; it simply happened that Feng's aims coincided with theirs.

Feng has frequently been charged with seizing and selling valuable
art objects from the palace collection after he forced P'u-i out. Shortly
after P'u-i departed, a Commission for the Readjustment of the Ch'ing
Household Affairs was established, with Li Shih-tseng at its head.[115]

One of its duties was to inventory and determine the disposition of all property in the palace, which was now considered the property of the nation. Li reportedly worked in great secrecy, with Feng's troops preventing even high officials from visiting the palace. In the meantime, curio and art experts were claiming that objects from the Ch'ing collection were appearing on the market.[116] It was doubtless to discredit such rumors that the palace was opened for inspection by the foreign community late in 1925, a year after the commission had begun its duties. According to one foreign observer, "There was evidence that there had been no looting, but that on the contrary great care had been taken to prevent the removal of historic pieces."[117] It is certainly true that in the early 1930's, when Japan threatened Peking, thousands of cases of palace valuables were shipped to safer regions. So if Feng did take any art objects, it must have been a small number only.[118]

Aftermath

It was clear to everyone that the regency government set up under Huang Fu was meant to serve only until the organization of a new government was decided upon. On November 10, Feng Yü-hsiang, Chang Tso-lin, and Lu Yung-hsiang arrived at Tientsin for a series of conferences with Tuan Ch'i-jui to settle upon the form of the new government.[119]

If, as suggested above, one of the factors figuring in the selection of Tuan as head of state was the anticipated reaction of the Yangtze tuchüns, it was an astute calculation. These tuchüns were in a delicate situation. They disapproved of Feng's revolt against their leader, Wu P'ei-fu. But with Wu's military power shattered, they had to consider their own provincial positions. If they defied Feng and Chang, they might be attacked and defeated. Yet if they accepted the leadership of Feng or Chang, they would at the very least lose a great deal of face, and be criticized as disloyal. To avoid either of these alternatives, as soon as the Tientsin conference began they wired that they would not recognize the authority of Peking unless Tuan Ch'i-jui were made head of state.[120]

On November 24, Tuan assumed the title of Provisional Chief Executive, and in that capacity promulgated the "Articles on the Organization of the Government of the Provisional Chief Executive." For the time being, everybody was satisfied: Tuan, Feng, Chang, the Yangtze tuchüns, and, incidentally, the Japanese.

On the day Tuan took office, he also announced his cabinet. Not a single portfolio was assigned to supporters of Feng Yü-hsiang.[121] This was significant, but not as significant as it seemed to many people at that time. Feng, like everyone else, knew that the government rested, in the final analysis, on his own Kuominchün and the armies of Chang Tso-lin. The influence he could exert on the Peking government would be determined in the long run by how rapidly he could catch up with Chang's superiority in arms and men. Therefore Feng adopted the grand manner. On November 25, he issued a telegram stating that since peace prevailed and he considered his purpose achieved, he would now resign and travel abroad. He even invited Wu P'ei-fu to go with him.[122] But Feng did not go abroad. He went to the northwest and began to strengthen his army for the test he knew would come.

7. Tupan of the Northwest

When Feng resigned in late November 1924, he went into isolation in the hills west of Peking, presumably to study and prepare himself to go abroad. Tuan Ch'i-jui, however, refused to accept Feng's resignation, as Feng certainly knew he would. Feng submitted a second and a third resignation, and others after that, but they were likewise rejected by the government. This was simply a shadow play designed to demonstrate Feng's sincerity and lack of personal ambition, and the government—whose capital was garrisoned by Kuominchün soldiers—played its appointed role by attesting to Feng's indispensability. Early in January, however, as part of the change in terminology that substituted for the abolition of warlordism, the position of Inspector General of the Army was eliminated.

This change did not leave Feng without a formal position. Almost two years earlier, in May 1923, Feng had been appointed Tupan of Northwestern Defense.*[1] He had virtually ignored this appointment, and had made no attempt to exercise the prerogatives of the office. Now, at the beginning of 1925, Feng set up headquarters in Kalgan and proceeded to give substance to this title, all the while affirming his intention to resign. In the meantime, during December and January, Feng's chief subordinates were given formal positions of authority in the Northwest. Chang Chih-chiang and Li Ming-chung were appointed military governors of Chahar and Suiyuan respectively.†

Lu Chung-lin, who had been in charge of ousting P'u-i, was garri-

---

* The practical meaning of the titles tuchün and tupan was identical, but the "tuchün system" or "tuchünate" had fallen into such general disrepute that even the tuchüns paid lip service to the need to abolish it. Since it was impossible to abolish it in fact, its "abolition" was achieved by the simple expedient of eliminating the title and substituting what the *China Year Book* called "the virgin title of Tupan."

† Suiyuan and Chahar (and Jehol as well) were Special Administrative Areas, somewhat analogous to territories in American history. They became provinces when the Kuomintang reorganized the government in 1928. Military governors of these areas were called *tut'ung*.

son commander of the troops in Peking, thus assuring Feng's continued military domination of the capital. But despite this domination, Feng did not have complete control over the Peking government, for he had to contend with the powerful influence of Chang Tso-lin. During most of 1925 Feng and Chang vied for political supremacy in the capital. Tuan Ch'i-jui was in the uncomfortable position of being pressured by both these antagonistic warlords.

Although Feng was very much concerned with the vicissitudes of Peking politics, most of his energies were spent on administrative and military affairs in his own vast domains. The total area of Suiyuan and Chahar was larger than that of France, Belgium, and Holland combined. In August 1925, Feng also acquired jurisdiction over Kansu, and thereby added an area larger than Italy and Denmark put together.

Most of these areas were in the transition zone of northern China, where the peasant farmer gives way to the nomadic herdsman. Nevertheless, there were large cultivable areas where wheat, barley, potatoes, oats, and other crops could be grown. Moreover, the livestock industry could be expanded far beyond its existing scope, and there were also various natural resources awaiting exploitation. The country was not poor, but was underdeveloped and underpopulated. Though the area of Suiyuan and Chahar was larger than that of France, their combined population was probably not much larger than that of Paris. As soon as Feng arrived in Kalgan, he embarked upon a grand program to develop and populate his domain.

It was also during 1925 that Feng had his first close and extended contact with the organization that was soon to dominate a new Chinese revolutionary movement—the Kuomintang. This contact was promoted primarily by the Russians, who gave Feng material aid in an attempt to bring him and his army into the Kuomintang camp. But Feng did not move into the party's orbit, for to have done so would have meant sacrificing his personal ambition and discarding the principles of warlord power that he had learned during the preceding fifteen years. Feng welcomed Russian military assistance, of course, and he accepted enough generalizations from the political ideology of the Kuomintang to encourage the Russians to continue their aid. But Feng saw this military buildup as serving his own ends, not those of the Kuomintang or any other group. Feng still thought of national power as a prize that his army might win for him, and not until his personal military might proved inadequate in the spring of 1926 would he turn seriously to the Kuomintang.

Colonization

Feng's general plans for the Northwest called for the development of agriculture and industry to make the region self-supporting and capable of producing large revenues. Perhaps the most striking feature of his plans was his colonization scheme. Feng outlined a five-year project designed to lure millions of poor peasants to the Northwest from the overcrowded areas of Chihli, Shantung, Anhwei, and other provinces. As a start, fifty villages were to be built, each one accommodating two hundred families. Sufficient land was to be allotted around each village for each family to have a farm. An agricultural bank was to be established to furnish the newcomers with the necessary capital. Loans on favorable terms would be provided for building the villages, and for buying land, tools, and livestock.[2]

The pilot project was set up in west-central Suiyuan, in the vicinity of Wuyüan. This area was located between the old and new beds of the Yellow River, and in earlier days had been served by an excellent irrigation system. Many of the irrigation canals had dried up, and Feng requested assistance from the China International Famine Relief Commission in developing a plan for reconstructing them. The area had great agricultural potential; indeed, despite the deteriorated irrigation facilities, some fine crops were still being produced there.[3]

In an attempt to entice settlers from more congested regions, Feng sent agents to Shantung and Honan to inform the people there of the great opportunities awaiting them in the Northwest.[4] He urged his soldiers to write their friends and families about the advantages of pioneering this undeveloped region. To advertise the richness and fertility of the area, Feng proposed that photographs be taken of attractive sites and distributed among potential colonizers. When he discovered an ex-soldier who had amassed several thousand head of livestock and many acres of land, Feng wanted to make a movie of his life and have it shown in the provinces of the Chihli plain. Moreover, he arranged for settlers to travel from their homes to the Northwest at reduced train rates.[5]

Although the land that Feng was so eager to colonize was not cultivated, it was the traditional property of the Mongolian tribes that still roamed Inner Mongolia with their herds. Feng came to an agreement with some Mongolian princes whereby he could acquire as much land as he could use for about a dollar an acre.[6] Many Mongols, however, were very disturbed by the prospect of wholesale Chinese immigration, which threatened to transform the region into strictly Chinese provinces. Among the steps Feng took to reassure them was the publication of a bilingual newspaper, in Chinese and Mongolian, to publicize the advantages to Inner Mongolia of development and colonization.*[7]

Feng also had his own troops open land to cultivation, and recruited men who would serve as soldier-colonists.[8] Apparently the men were not given title to the land while they were still in uniform, but soldiers discharged because of age were given their own plots. A retired officer received about 45 acres and an enlisted man about 25 acres. Much more was promised for the future, which Feng painted in rosy terms. "According to my plans," he told one of his regiments, "in the future every man in my army will be able to obtain 275 acres of land; each man will be able to bring his parents, marry a girl student, till his own fields, and provide for his own. How happy it will be."[9]

Feng hoped to create a group of model villages composed of houses built by the colonists themselves. To show what could be done by using inexpensive local building materials, Feng had his troops build a "New Village" or "Model Village" outside of Kalgan. It was completed by August, and became a showpiece that perhaps influenced foreign visitors more than Chinese peasants. The New Village was designed to be a self-contained community, not unlike contemporary American housing developments. Identical brick cottages surrounded a large hall that was to be the center of community life. Schools, churches, recreation areas, and a library were all provided; wells were dug and fitted with mechanical pumps, and flowers were planted throughout the village.[10]

The outbreak of war at the end of 1925 terminated Feng's colonization program before it could achieve substantial results. A report in September said that 1,000 families had emigrated to Feng's domain

---

* Before Feng's arrival in the Northwest, newspapers had existed in that area only in "an intermittent and sporadic manner." Feng's administration, however, used officially controlled newspapers to spread news concerning its activities. By mid-1925, two newspapers were published in Kalgan: the *Chahar Daily News* and the *Chahar Official Gazette*. The *Daily News* was the Mongol-Chinese bilingual paper, normally consisting of four sheets. It was sold primarily in Kalgan, and had a circulation of about 600 copies per day. The *Chahar Official Gazette* was a seven-page publication devoted exclusively to official reports and other government news. It was published only in Chinese, and its circulation was limited largely to officials. In Suiyuan there were also two newspapers, the *Suiyuan Daily News* and the *Suiyuan Official Gazette*, which were almost identical with the two papers published in Chahar. The circulation of the *Suiyuan Daily News* was 450 copies per day, and that of the *Official Gazette* about 100 copies per day. (Despatch from E. F. Stanton, U.S. vice-consul at Kalgan, to the Secretary of State, June 12, 1925, 893.911/210.)

from Shantung, and even earlier there were stories of immigrants carving out new lives in the Northwest.[11] In the end, however, the program effected no significant change in the population or economy of the region.

Development Projects

Economic development of the Northwest required the creation of transportation facilities whereby settlers could reach virgin lands and their products could be brought out. Feng immediately attacked this problem by building a 400-mile motor road from Paotow, the western terminus of the Peking-Suiyuan Railway, to Ninghsia, where the Great Wall meets the western side of the Yellow River's great loop.* The road was formally opened on September 30, 1925, only five months after Feng's troops began work on it. Feng later extended it to Lanchow, in Kansu province.[12] The road had a military as well as an economic importance, for it was used to bring Russian supplies from Outer Mongolia.

Feng also had ambitious plans for railroad construction in the Northwest; indeed, Feng's hopes for economic development centered mainly on railroad building and his colonization scheme. As Tupan of the Northwest, he controlled the Peking-Suiyuan Railway, and he wanted to extend this line from Paotow to Ninghsia, paralleling the motor road constructed by his men, and then push it forward into Sinkiang. Feng's troops actually began work on the roadbed for this extension. He also proposed to build two branch lines, one going north from Kalgan into central Chahar and thence to Urga, and another, also going to Urga, from P'ingtich'uan, in eastern Suiyuan. However, these plans required more funds than Feng could raise. He asked the government to supply a million dollars in order to start work on the first of these projects, the extension of the Peking-Suiyuan line to Ninghsia. Feng did not really expect to get this money; his real hope was to interest foreign capitalists in his plans. As early as December 1924, Feng requested American Minister Jacob Gould Schurman to persuade American businessmen of the great profits to be made from investing in the development of the Northwest. In the following six months Feng's agents several times approached the American vice-consul at Kalgan with similar requests, and late in the summer of 1925 one of Feng's men talked to a representative of the Ford Motor Company along the same lines.[13]

* The Ninghsia mentioned here is a city. The province of Ninghsia did not exist in 1925, but was created in 1928 from a portion of Kansu. When the province came into existence, the city became the provincial capital. It is today called Yinch'uan.

At the same time that he was soliciting foreign funds, Feng did something that deterred most foreign investors: he took steps to block a foreign loan that would have consolidated all of the outstanding debts of the Peking-Suiyuan Railway and secured them by the Maritime Customs.* Such a move would have taken the regular revenues of the railway out of Feng's hands, and put them in the hands of a committee designated by foreigners and Chinese. (Feng was to have no say in selecting the committee.) Without such a provision, potential investors had to rely not only on Feng's good faith, but on his remaining in control of the railway for a long time. Few people were willing to invest in the circumstances.

Of course, after the May 30th Incident, Feng would have been hard put to find a Western capitalist who was willing to cooperate with him in anything, for he issued some very harsh denunciations of Western activity in China. But his hostility toward foreigners was very selective: he was neither anti-Russian nor anti-Japanese. Hayashi Yasakichi reported in February that Feng's attitude toward Japan was changing, and this was confirmed by Feng's statements and actions in mid-1925. On July 20, Feng told interviewers that he had contemplated opening the Northwest to all foreign capital, but that recent events had forced him to reconsider. "I have decided," he said, "to accept only the offers of those who have the same color and ideas as we Chinese, namely my friends the Japanese." He declared that he would accept Japanese money and advisers, and that he hoped to send 10,000 students from the Northwest to study in Japan. Moreover, he hoped to engage about a hundred Japanese educators to organize public education in the provinces under his control.[14]

On June 19 Feng met Baron Okura Kihachiro, director of the South Manchurian Railway and a famous Japanese capitalist. According to Feng's diary, their talk centered on the need for Sino-Japanese cooperation in resisting the white race.[15] This meeting was brought about

* Under the terms of an agreement signed in Peking on May 30, 1925, a new loan was to be made that would have consolidated all the indebtedness of the Peking-Suiyuan Railway. The agreement stipulated that in the almost certain event that the upcoming Tariff Conference decided to secure China's unsecured foreign obligations by the Maritime Customs, the Peking-Suiyuan loan was to be considered an unsecured loan and placed in the control of the Director General of the Customs. In addition, the agreement forbade the execution of any other first lien on the railway based on the earnings of the line. This section of the agreement precluded the exploitation of the railway by the controlling warlord, who of course was Feng. There was also a provision that the revenues of the railway were to be deposited in Chinese banks, making it impossible for Feng to appropriate them. Consequently Feng arranged to have the loan blocked. (Dailey, "Feng Yü-hsiang and the Peking-Suiyuan Railroad Debts," p. 159.)

by Feng's Japanese adviser, Matsumuro, who supports Feng's assertion that he and Okura did not discuss economic questions. Matsumuro admits that he himself asked Okura about the possibility of investing in the development of the Northwest, and, according to Matsumuro, Okura said that he would be willing to help "when the proper time came."[16]

It is probable, despite Feng's denial, that he and Okura discussed economic questions. In a report written a few months before the Feng-Okura meeting, the Japanese military attaché in Peking stressed the economic and strategic importance to Japan of the areas along the Peking-Suiyuan Railway, and noted that the Americans were already active there.[17] Japan also must have been concerned about countering the influence of the Russians, who had recently established relations with Feng. Baron Okura's trip doubtless was undertaken with such considerations in mind; indeed, one writer who was then serving with Feng's army says the Japanese offered Feng a large loan to finance reclamation and development projects. If such a loan was proposed, it was probably conditioned on Feng's rejecting Soviet aid. In any event, Feng received no such loan.[18]

Feng's plan to send 10,000 students to Japan—an idea that originated with Matsumuro—did not materialize. Only about thirty-six students were sent; most of them studied in Japanese military academies.[19]

Throughout the autumn of 1925, Feng continued to maintain friendly contacts with Japan. Matsumuro, of course, remained at Feng's headquarters. In August Feng sent a representative to visit leading businessmen, officials, and others in Japan. The visit was said to have the purpose of "clearing up misunderstandings," but nobody knew just what this meant.[20] Two months later, in October, Feng sent one of his leading officers, Han Fu-chü, to observe military maneuvers in Japan. Feng told Han that there were three groups in Japan: one devoted to the destruction of China, another that saw no future for China, and a third that envisaged a great future for China after she achieved unification. He instructed Han to make contacts with the third group particularly, and in general to convey Feng's desire for amity and cooperation between the two countries.[21]

By the time Han Fu-chü returned to China, Feng was at war with Chang Tso-lin, and the connection Feng had maintained with Japan was broken shortly afterward. Feng's diplomatic overtures to Japan were very revealing of his attitudes, but did nothing to accomplish their intended purpose, the development of the Northwest.

Feng also hoped to exploit the mineral resources of the Northwest. In February an American named Manning told Feng that he would be willing to help develop new mines, but he evidently proposed unsatisfactory terms; at least there is no evidence that he had any further association with Feng. A few weeks later Feng sent a message to Peking asking for a qualified person to supervise the development of mining, but, again, little seems to have been achieved.[22]

In sum, Feng's grand plans produced few results. In the words of a Chinese proverb, he "dreamed a thousand new paths, but woke and walked the old one." There were several reasons for this, but certainly a major one was a lack of funds.

Revenues

Financial difficulties had beset Feng throughout his career, and his stay in the Northwest presented the customary problems. Feng needed large sums to support his expanded army and to promote his various schemes for regional development. To obtain them he drained every possible source of revenue.

One lucrative source was the Peking-Suiyuan Railway, and Feng exploited it for all it was worth. Before he took over the line, many government officials and military officers enjoyed free transportation. Under Feng's administration nobody rode free; even high officials purchased tickets. He also raised the price of shipping grain by rail. Chinese and foreign merchants alike had to pay squeeze of four to twelve dollars a ton before freight cars would become "available."[23] Feng also appropriated the salt revenues, which were supposed to go to the central government.[24]

Feng's administration devised a remarkable variety of taxes. For example, a monthly billboard tax was collected, with assessments based on the size of the advertisement. Feng took steps to ensure that this tax brought in revenue: in one town signboards carrying moralistic admonitions were distributed to shops, which were compelled to display them and to pay the tax on them. A 3 per cent levy was decreed on all important commodities coming into Kalgan, but this caused such widespread opposition that it was reduced. Special taxes were levied on grain and wool. A load tax was levied on all shipments leaving Kalgan, regardless of whether they were going five or five hundred miles. A 20 per cent surtax was imposed on cigarettes, virtually all of which were British- or American-made. When foreign producers retaliated by ordering their agents to halt cigarette sales, Feng's men threatened to close down any shop that refused to sell cigarettes. Businesses were taxed on their total capital, as well as on their profits. There were many other taxes; indeed, as an American official put it, they were "so numerous and in some instances . . . so absurd as to appear almost incredible when it is considered that they bear the endorsement of supposedly responsible, benevolent and intelligent officials."[25]

Feng employed an extraordinary variety of methods to raise funds. He established the Northwest Automobile Transportation Company, which was simply a monopoly of automobiles in the Northwest.[26] In the absence of other facilities in that undeveloped region, many businesses relied heavily on automobile and truck transport. Feng's monopoly thus gave him both a source of revenue and a means of indirect control over many enterprises, and also facilitated his arranging the transport of Russian supplies from Urga to Kalgan. Feng's troops collected entrance fees at all tourist attractions in Peking.[27] He even opened a hotel in Kalgan, the Honest and Clean Hotel, ostensibly because the rates at the other hotels were too high, though perhaps the profit motive was not entirely lacking.[28] Feng took advantage of the anti-British feeling fostered by the May 30th Incident to confiscate about 27,000 British-owned sheep, which he used to feed and clothe his men.[29]

Another moneymaking measure was the establishment of the Northwestern Bank, which received formal permission from the government to issue bank notes at the end of March, 1925. The bank had no capital, but other banks, money changers, and merchants were compelled to accept its currency, much to their distress and indignation. Several branch banks were also set up.[30]

Feng's vigorous search for funds resulted in an appreciable rise in revenue, at least initially. As early as March 1925, Feng declared with satisfaction that the tax revenues of Suiyuan had doubled.[31] It is possible, however, that Feng's multifarious taxes so depressed business activity in the Northwest that the end result was to lessen his revenues. In any event, in the sparsely populated Northwest there were simply not enough people to tax. As a consequence, Feng compromised his reform measures more than usual in order to obtain money.

Reforms

By 1925 Feng's reputation as a reformer was well known, and it was expected that he would repeat the usual pattern of reforms in the Northwest. By and large he did; however, there were some changes. Feng customarily forbade the cultivation and sale of opium, and during his stay in the Northwest he was reputed to have taken drastic measures to suppress this drug. Even a journalist who was critical of Feng's "excessive preoccupation with the question of funds" gave him credit for attempting to eradicate opium when he knew that he was thereby depriving himself of the "best source of revenue in the country." However, Feng was not nearly so selfless: in the spring of 1925 opium was being sold openly in Kalgan, and since its sale was illegal, a fine that amounted to a tax was imposed. It was paid at the time of purchase for the convenience of all concerned. Even a Kuominchün source admits that fines against opium offenders brought in quite a bit of revenue.[32]

Although Feng seems to have profited from the sale of opium, it is nevertheless true that he established an "opium refuge" for men and a similar institution for women. Evidently most of the patients came voluntarily out of a concern to break their addiction, although some may have been brought by force.* A doctor visited each refuge daily. The course of treatment lasted one month, and was free to the poor; those who could pay were charged low rates.[33]

Kuominchün sources claim that Feng closed all the brothels when he went to the Northwest, but this is not true.[34] Feng almost surely used the brothels as a source of revenue. However, as with opium, Feng's taxation of prostitution did not keep him from opening a school designed to teach prostitutes more constructive ways of earning a living.[35]

Feng established various other welfare institutions in Kalgan. A nursery was organized to care for unwanted—often illegitimate—children. When they reached the age of five, these children were sent to an orphanage that cared for orphans from five to fifteen years of age. Here they were given an academic education and were also taught some trade or skill. Care for the blind and crippled was provided at another home, which also housed impoverished old people. A clubhouse for laborers was built in Kalgan, and rooms were set up all over the city where ricksha coolies—many of whom were homeless and spent the night in the open—could sleep in warmth. Feng also had a bathhouse erected for poor workers where they could bathe and have their clothes washed, dried, and deloused.[36]

In Kalgan, Feng's medical corps ran a clinic that was open to civilians. Moreover, he invited an American missionary doctor, Dr. Charles Lewis, to establish a hospital in the Northwest. Dr. Lewis was

* A similar ambivalence characterized Feng's policy toward cigarettes. Although he increased the cigarette tax, train travelers to Kalgan were met by vendors selling anti-cigarette tracts. (Strong, p. 600.)

to set it up and direct it, and Feng was to finance it. It was to be a civilian hospital, and Feng thought it would contribute greatly to the Christianization and civilization of the Northwest.[37] This project evidently did not progress very far before the outbreak of the war that was to end all of Feng's projects.

As usual, Feng took pains to promote literacy. Many young people —probably students—were sent into the streets, where they gathered groups around them for instruction in elementary reading. Such groups could be seen in the streets "here, there, and everywhere."[38] "Schools for the Masses" were set up in which government officials served as teachers. Teachers were employed to teach people in their homes, although, considering the paucity of available teachers and the large number of illiterates, this could hardly have been a very comprehensive program. A schedule of punishment, including fines and imprisonment, was posted for those who refused to study.[39]

Although Feng's Kalgan projects received the most attention from observers, similar welfare measures were instituted in Suiyuan. Later, when Kansu came under Feng's rule, many of the same measures were announced.* However, the natural appreciation the people of the Northwest would have felt for Feng's welfare measures was dissipated by Feng's relentless search for money. Merchants had suffered greatly under Feng's predecessor in Kalgan, but the American vice-consul in that city wrote that they "groaned even louder—in private—over the multitude of taxes imposed by Marshal Feng in the name of education, public improvements, and good works."[40] A merchant in a town twenty miles north of Kalgan said that he had done business in that district all of his life, and that business conditions had never been worse than they were under Feng. Indeed, by the time Feng had been in control for about three months, this merchant decided to close his business and move to Tientsin.[41]

The Kuominchün

The name "Kuominchün," applied by Feng and his associates to their armies at the time of the Peking coup d'etat, had a very short official life. After the organization of the government under Tuan Ch'i-jui, the various armies presumably became instruments of the government, and the name "Kuominchün" implied an autonomy in-

---

* In August the government issued a mandate, doubtless instigated by Feng himself, appointing him Tupan of Kansu. This enormously increased the area under Feng's jurisdiction. Feng sent one of his division commanders, Liu Yü-fen, to substitute for him as administrator of the province. See below, pp. 193ff.

compatible with such an arrangement. Therefore on December 10, 1924, the name was officially abolished, and Feng's army was officially designated the Northwest Army, since Feng was at that time Tupan of Northwestern Defense. Notwithstanding this order, the name "Kuominchün" stuck to Feng's troops. In 1925, especially, the name was still applied to all three armies—Hu's, Sun's, and Feng's—although Northwest Army and First Kuominchün were used interchangeably to denote Feng's units.*

Feng left Honan at the end of 1922 with approximately 20,000 men. By the eve of the Second Chih-Feng War, his army had grown to about 35,000, although it was still organized as one division and three mixed brigades.[42] During and immediately after the war, Feng's army expanded rapidly as a result of vigorous recruiting and the absorption of well over 10,000 men from Wu P'ei-fu's shattered units.[43] Feng continued recruiting through November 1924, and by early December it was estimated that he had 60,000 men under his command in and around Peking.[44] At the beginning of 1925, when Feng's men took over Chahar and Suiyuan, at least three brigades already in Chahar were absorbed by the First Kuominchün, and new recruits were also added. Therefore, by April 1925 Feng had seventy to eighty thousand men under his command. Continued recruiting, together with absorption of defeated bandits, constantly swelled Feng's army, so that by the late summer of 1925 it apparently numbered over 100,000 men. At this time they were temporarily organized into twelve divisions, a form they retained until the spring of 1926. This change was not official, and is not mentioned in standard military histories.[45]

This extremely rapid expansion of his army created many problems for Feng. The wholesale absorption of bandits and of troops from Wu's defeated units threatened to attenuate or destroy the spirit of discipline and loyalty that Feng had worked so long to inculcate. Moreover, Feng could not maintain the same personal contact with the rank and file now that he had four or five times as many soldiers scattered throughout the Northwest. It is understandable that indoctrination now became the mainstay of his training program.

---

* Ultimately, four additional armies of the Kuominchün came into existence, all but one dating from 1926 or later. However, they are little-known, and the name "Kuominchün" calls to mind the three armies mentioned above, especially Feng's. For the Fourth Kuominchün, see Li T'ai-fen, p. 253; *KMCKMS*, chap. 9, pp. 67–68; *NCS*, May 19, 1925, p. 5, and May 22, 1925, p. 5. For the Fifth Kuominchün, see Li T'ai-fen, pp. 277–81; *KMCKMS*, chap. 9, p. 88; *WSH*, p. 625. For the Sixth Kuominchün, see Li T'ai-fen, pp. 285–86, 294, 310. For the Seventh Kuominchün, see Li T'ai-fen, pp. 140–41.

After Feng absorbed former enemy units into his Kuominchün, he replaced their officers with officers from the units he had led before the Second Chih-Feng War.[46] There was a weakness implicit in this policy, for the large numbers of men recruited made it necessary for Feng to appoint young and relatively inexperienced officers to positions of high command. Of course, the highest positions were reserved for those who had been with him longest, and who shared the same regional and military background. That this was Feng's policy is seen in a survey of the backgrounds of thirty officers who held leading positions in his army in 1925. Twenty-five of the thirty were from the same geographical area—the plain of the Yellow and Hwai Rivers, which is divided into Chihli (Hopei), Honan, Shantung, and Anhwei provinces. Four of the remaining five were staff members who did not actively command troops. Those four were graduates of colleges or military academies in China or Japan. Of the other 25, only two graduated from military academies, and the rest began their careers in the ranks.[47]

Feng paid particular attention to the continued indoctrination of his officers, to maintaining his personal contacts with them, and to shaping their attitudes toward the men they commanded. Although Feng could not maintain close ties with the rank and file, he insisted that his officers do so. The principle of leadership that Feng repeated to his commanders most frequently was that they must "share the bitter and the sweet with their men," with the emphasis on the bitter. This, he said, was the "way of leadership."[48]

In the months following the Peking coup d'etat, the Second and Third Kuominchüns also expanded rapidly. By the summer of 1925, the Second Kuominchün numbered upwards of 250,000 men. This increase was attained by absorbing troops from Wu P'ei-fu's defeated units and from other groups—including bandit gangs—defeated in local wars in Honan and Shensi. The army, however, was neither unified nor disciplined; an inordinately large number of the troops were opium addicts; and its fighting strength did not approach what the large number of troops suggests.[49] Not without good reason were the men in the army called "rabble," and the army itself referred to as a "bandit army."* Indeed, the undisciplined rapacity of the Second

---

* A memorandum by Mr. Willys Peck, member of the American legation in Peking, was enclosed in a letter from Minister J. V. A. MacMurray to the Secretary of State, Jan. 16, 1926, 893.00/7125. This memorandum describes in some detail the brutality, the looting, and the utter lack of discipline that characterized the Second Kuominchün. Among other things, Mr. Peck wrote: "A strange thing about the soldiers

Kuominchün in 1925 was a major factor in stimulating the growth of the Red Spear Society, the White Spear Society, and other self-protective peasant societies.[50]

At the time of the seizure of Peking, Sun Yo's troops numbered only about 5,000. As head of the Third Kuominchün, Sun also expanded his army, largely by absorbing defeated troops. By the summer of 1925, he controlled something over 30,000 men.[51] Sun's army, like the Second Kuominchün, was poorly trained.

These armies, of course, were not in the Northwest with Feng. Their participation on the winning side in 1924 had to be rewarded in the only coin that had genuine value for a warlord—regional authority. Early in November 1924, Hu Ching-i was ordered to Honan to manage military affairs, and Sun Yo was made civil governor of the same province. Shortly afterward, Hu was made military governor of Honan.

The presence of two Kuominchün leaders in a single province was an extremely unsatisfactory arrangement, and it was necessary to line up a post in another province for Sun Yo. The situation was further complicated by armed resistance to Kuominchün armies in Honan by military units under the warlord of Shensi. In early 1925, there was an extremely complex series of military struggles in Honan and Shensi. After the first phase of this war, which established fairly well the authority of the Second Kuominchün in Honan, Hu Ching-i died. After Hu's death (on April 10, 1925), he was succeeded as head of the Second Kuominchün by Yüeh Wei-chün, one of his brigade commanders. Yüeh was even more reluctant than Hu had been to permit Sun Yo to remain in Honan. A second phase of the war then began during which Sun invaded Shensi and finally achieved control of that province. He was formally appointed Tupan of Shensi in August 1925. There was still latent opposition to Sun in Shensi, and much opposition to Yüeh in Honan.

By the autumn of 1925, therefore, the three Kuominchün armies together numbered somewhere in the neighborhood of 300,000 men;

---

of the 2nd Kuominchün is that when they commit robberies, which may happen in the case of anyone they meet, they are generally very polite. The procedure is as follows: 'I see you have a very nice coat. Will you kindly loan it to me?' If the loan is effected without demur, well and good. If there is the slightest objection on the part of the owner, the soldier will draw his revolver and shoot him on the spot, although in a manner which betrays no anger. In fact the soldiers of this army appear to consider the taking of life as a very trivial circumstance."

they controlled all of northwestern China, plus Honan and Shensi. But only Feng's personal army, the First Kuominchün, could be considered an efficient military organization capable of waging sustained war, and only the regions occupied by that army were relatively free of organized military units potentially inimical to the Kuominchün. In any major war, Feng would have to rely primarily on his own resources.

A shortage of armaments was a major deficiency in Feng's resources, for there was no arsenal in the regions under his control. At Kalgan there was a mint, and Feng used its machinery for the production of weapons. However, this machinery could produce and repair only small weapons such as bayonets, sabers, hand grenades, and perhaps a few rifles and machine guns. The mint's production of rifle bullets seldom exceeded 5,000 cartridges per 24-hour period.[52] In the sparsely populated and underdeveloped Northwest, there were no other factories that could be adapted to the production of arms. Nor did Feng have control of any seaport, so that he was unable to import by sea either arms or the machinery to make them. The only boundary that Feng controlled was to the west, and it was therefore natural for him to turn to the Soviet Union.

Russian Aid

The Russian Revolution had an enormous impact on China. Until about 1920, that impact was felt largely in the realm of ideas; Chinese intellectuals were attracted to Marxist-Leninist thought for several reasons, but above all they admired its anti-imperialist orientation. From 1920 on, Russian influence entered China not only in the form of ideas, but also in the form of agents from the Soviet Union and from the Communist International, or Comintern. The first Comintern agents helped to establish the Chinese Communist Party, and also sought other Chinese groups that they might sponsor. After one or two false starts they selected the Kuomintang, and in 1922 the Soviet Union decided to throw its full support behind that party.[53] At that time Sun Yat-sen's fortunes were at a low ebb, and he therefore accepted the hand extended by the Russians.

In the autumn of 1923 a Russian agent, Mikhail Borodin, arrived in China, and not long afterward he was officially appointed adviser to the Kuomintang. Borodin promptly and energetically began to work toward transforming the Kuomintang into a strong, disciplined party at the head of a mass movement. In January 1924, under Borodin's guidance, the Kuomintang was reorganized into a centralized organization similar to the Russian Bolshevik Party. Members of the recently formed Chinese Communist Party were permitted to enter the Kuomintang. During the following three and a half years, Borodin and other Russians worked closely with Kuomintang and Communist leaders to make their alliance under the Kuomintang's aegis the dominant political, ideological, and military force in the nationalist revolution.

In pursuit of this goal, the Russians attempted to strengthen the Kuomintang in all spheres of activity, and to bring other military-political groups under the influence of party principles and personnel. In this latter endeavor the Russians played a most important part: they had the material aid and technical assistance to offer militarists in exchange for their admitting Kuomintang political workers into their organizations. Not long after the Peking coup, Feng Yü-hsiang was approached along these lines.

It is not clear exactly when Feng first came to an understanding with the Russians. China formally recognized the Soviet Union at the end of May 1924, and in July the first Russian ambassador, Leo Karakhan, presented his credentials. During the following months, Feng and Karakhan had social contacts in Peking, and conceivably more businesslike discussions also.[54] In any event, there were rumors at least as early as December 1924 that Feng had come to an agreement with the Russians.[55] These rumors may have been groundless, but it was probably not long after this that some sort of arrangements were made.

Documents captured from the Russian embassy in Peking imply that the Russians made their first serious overtures to Feng on April 21, 1925.*[56] There are good reasons to question this; it seems likely that some kind of arrangements were made as early as February.[57] However, it was not until April that final agreement was reached between Feng and the Russians, and Russian instructors began working in his army.[58]

The understanding that Feng and the Russians arrived at provided that the latter would supply Feng with instructors and material aid, and Feng, in return, would oppose imperialism and allow Kuomin-

---

* On April 6, 1927, Chinese police and soldiers, under orders from Chang Tso-lin, raided several buildings in the compound of the Soviet embassy in Peking. They seized large quantities of documents as well as a number of Chinese leftists who were hiding there. Many of the documents have been published, and it is these that are referred to here.

tang political workers into his army.[59] But there was a contradiction built into this agreement. If the Russians were to achieve their ultimate and most serious goal, the political indoctrination of Feng's troops, Feng would lose the one thing that he had most consistently and jealously guarded throughout his career—absolute and independent control over his army.

From the very beginning, Feng showed himself reluctant to permit Kuomintang or Russian political activity in his army. He gladly accepted Russian assistance, but when it came to anything that threatened to loosen his own tight control over his troops, the Russians found Feng frustratingly obdurate. He treated the Russians as instructors in his army rather than as personal political-military advisers.[60] In June, a report to Ambassador Karakhan from a Russian in Feng's army stated that Feng openly refused to allow the Kuomintang to carry on political work in the army.[61] Almost a year later, Russian officers in the First Kuominchün were still complaining that "Feng sets severe restrictions on political work in the army. It is allowed only when necessary and in the interests of Feng."[62] It is therefore not surprising that a progress report written by a team of Russian inspectors early in 1926 lamented that there was "indeed a wide margin between the influence we had expected to wield and the actual results." "In short," the report said, "our hopes have vanished like bubbles."[63]

Of course, the Russians working in Kalgan did not need an inspection team to tell them they were not making the headway they had hoped for. From the outset they were disturbed by Feng's determination to confine their teaching efforts to military, nonideological subject matter. They knew that a reassessment of their relations with Feng was in order, and that such a reassessment should proceed from a decision about where Feng stood in the Chinese political scheme. Was he a warlord or a revolutionary?[64]

In June 1925, a Russian, probably the head of the advisory group, had offered two possible answers to this question in a letter to Karakhan:[65]

(1) Feng is a man of definite principle, allied with the various movements in China and a symbol of the anti-imperialist national revolutionary movement in North China.

(2) Feng is an ordinary militarist who is forced by circumstances and geographical location to act temporarily in the interests of Soviet Russia, since Russia is a nation which wishes to see the weakening of all imperialist countries (particularly Japan).

If the first estimate was accepted, the writer continued, the correct policy would be to strengthen Feng's military force at every opportunity without fearing possible danger. Russia's primary objective would then be to strengthen Feng's fighting capacity and his capacity for independent action. But acting on the second estimate would call for a policy whereby

we would carry on our work through other means. On the one hand, we would assist Feng in order that he might carry out the tasks we assign him. On the other hand, we would ensure against the possibility of his contradicting our interests. Material aid would then be of primary importance. [We would plan our aid] in such a manner that should we refuse it Feng would be reduced to a secondary position if not completely defeated. We would therefore direct our assistance so that once our support is withdrawn, his army would revert to its original state.[66]

The letter then summarized evidence that supported only the second estimate, and suggested that the corresponding policy should be followed.

The work of the Russians within the First Kuominchün fell into four general categories: inspecting and evaluating the army in terms of military knowledge and efficiency; supplying weapons and other material aid; attempting to develop elements in Feng's army amenable to Russian or Kuomintang leadership; and, connected with this last, instructing the men in various newly established schools.

Feng had confidence in the military competence of the Russians. He asked them to write frequent reports on the administration of the army and on basic military problems.[67] He also requested them to inspect the various units of the army, noting deficiencies and recommending improvements. A comprehensive inspection of most of Feng's units was carried out during the summer of 1925.*[68]

* The inspecting officers noted that parade-ground drill was in general executed superbly, and that the physical condition of the men was excellent. The rifles carried by the rank and file were well-maintained, but were unsatisfactory because of their age. Some had been manufactured as early as 1901; many had pitted barrels and could not shoot straight. Both officers and men were ignorant of the theoretical principles of shooting. None of the soldiers or officers questioned by the inspector could draw the trajectory of a bullet, nor could they explain the principle on which a rifle sight operates. Some of the men thought that a bullet went straight from the gun, continued straight for a certain time until it was spent, and then fell to earth. Notwithstanding this theoretical ignorance, however, their marksmanship was of a fairly high order, even with their worn and rickety rifles. The troops also used poor tactics, in the opinion of the inspector. In maneuvers the men moved across a field in close, even ranks, without attempting to take advantage of the terrain. Machine guns were moved with the men, instead of being used to cover their advance. Moreover, machine gunners were very slow in assembling and dismantling their weapons. Cavalry troops were not trained to exploit the potentialities of their mounts; they were essentially a mounted infantry. (Allen, pp. 64–96.)

One of the deficiencies noted by the inspecting officers was that large numbers of troops had very old, worn rifles. This shortcoming was partially remedied by shipments from the Soviet Union. During the summer of 1925, Feng reportedly received about 15,000 infantry rifles, 9,000 pistols, and 30,000 hand grenades; transportation difficulties prohibited the sending of heavy weapons.[69] In addition to the importation of small arms, Russian advisers supervised the construction of several armored cars and armored trains at Kalgan.[70] These were a novelty in China at that time; they had first been used, with great success, by the Fengtien army during the Second Chih-Feng War.

By the end of 1925, the Russians had helped organize schools for training artillerymen, advanced infantrymen, cavalrymen, machine gunners, engineers, and intelligence experts. Another school evidently trained officers for guard units.[71] Running these schools occupied most of the time and attention of the Russian mission to Feng's army; a majority of the mission's members served as instructors.[72]

The various schools were apparently effective centers of military instruction. But the Russians wanted them to be more than this, as the aforementioned Soviet inspection team reported:

We often think that, lacking means to control Feng's entire army, we should begin our work in the schools, that we should first inject propaganda into Feng's army and then surround it ideologically. We think that by using officers graduated from the schools to control Feng's army we are executing a compromise method of infiltration of Feng's army, and that we should consider this task a prerequisite of all military work.[73]

However, the report continued, there were many difficulties involved in carrying out such a plan. The heavy work load exhausted the limited number of Russian instructors; and there were not enough interpreters for the instructors who were available.* More-

---

* The total number of Russians working in the First Kuominchün is difficult to ascertain. There were at least 36 Russians, though the number may have been appreciably larger. See Wilbur and How, p. 321. In WSH, p. 526, Feng says that he asked the Russians for "30 or 40 advisers." In an interview in the spring of 1959, one of Feng's former officers informed me that in 1925 he had about 70 Russians in his units alone, and estimated the total in the army as a whole at about 200. There were also other nationalities represented in Feng's army. Matsumuro Takayoshi was an adviser through 1925, but he did not engage in teaching troops; indeed, he does not seem to have done anything, except, of course, observe. There was also one Italian officer and one German. See also p. 191.

In view of the language problem, communication between the Russian instructors and the Chinese students was inevitably slow and difficult. Some of the interpreters were Chinese students who had majored in Russian in Chinese universities. Their work was extremely tedious and exhausting. One describes the experience thus: "The work in Kalgan was hard and tiresome. Russian instructors would de-

over, it had begun to seem as if the entire premise of the plan was false. The Russians were finding that low-ranking officers were so subservient to high-ranking officers that they were not open to any ideas except those of their superiors. The conclusion seemed obvious: the Russian effort to gain influence in the Kuominchün must concentrate on Feng Yü-hsiang and his top subordinates.[74]

The difficulties outlined in this report were real enough, but the main obstacle to Russian success was not mentioned: Feng Yü-hsiang's vigilance in the matter of his army's indoctrination. This vigilance was most clearly illustrated in the fate of a military school established especially for university students. After the incident of May 30th, 1925, when the Shanghai police under an English officer fired on a crowd of demonstrators, there was a great resurgence of anti-foreignism, particularly among students. One result was to stimulate many students to seek military training, which, presumably, they would ultimately use against the foreign powers in China. In line with this feeling, Feng Yü-hsiang opened a special military school in Kalgan for students. Between 600 and 1,000 students enrolled.[75]

The curriculum of the school was patterned after the Whampoa Academy, a school established by the Kuomintang under Russian guidance in southern China. The Russians hoped to make the Kalgan school the Whampoa of the North. About a third of the students were political activists from the left wing of the Kuomintang. They met together several times a week, put out a weekly handwritten newspaper, and generally attempted to spread their influence among other students. Feng expelled several students who seemed to him too far to the left.[76] Then, only a few months after it had been established, the school was suddenly closed because it threatened to become a center for Kuomintang propaganda.[77]

From the Russians' point of view, the results of their work were disappointing in that activity to which all others were subordinate—political indoctrination. In fact, had Feng shown absolutely no receptivity to the ideas espoused by the Russians, they might have discontinued their aid. However, some of their ideas—considered as

---

liver their lectures. We would listen, write them down, and then translate them into Chinese. Our translations were printed and distributed among the students. We worked all day long, our fingers grew numb, cramps tightened the muscles of our right arms. We did not know Russian very well, but our knowledge seemed superb in comparison with that of other translators. After a day's work, with our eyes and fingers tired, we would fall into a heavy slumber. We had no time to go to a bathhouse. We grew filthier and filthier every day." (Tretiakov, p. 307.)

ideas and not as instruments of Russian subversion—were not fundamentally incompatible with Feng's own. In addition, the overall situation in China in 1925 exerted its own logic on Feng's outlook. As a result of these factors, there was a shift of emphasis in Feng's thought and in his indoctrination programs that marked the beginning of a change.

Political Orientation

Feng's oft-repeated claim that he had sympathized with the ideas of Sun Yat-sen from the earliest years of the Republic was unquestionably an attempt to link himself with the man who had become the symbol of the Chinese nationalist revolution. The most that can be said is that some of Feng's ideas before 1924 were compatible with some of Sun's ideas; but even if Feng recognized that compatibility, he attributed no significance to it at the time. Before the end of 1924, it is true, Feng's social and religious attitudes were different from those of the ordinary warlord. Nevertheless—his periodic denunciations of warlordism notwithstanding—Feng for the most part accepted the political-military framework of the time. He thought that government officials should be moral and should "love the people," but he never espoused—indeed, he seemed hardly aware of—any comprehensive and developed political ideology. It was not until 1925, when Feng became associated with the Kuomintang, that his political thinking acquired some sophistication.

Most foreign observers in China viewed Feng's sudden concern with political ideology as an outward sign of his conversion to Communism; indeed, by mid-1925 the foreign press in the country had generally abandoned the label "Christian General" in favor of "Red General." Rumors that Feng had converted from Christianity to Bolshevism arose shortly after the Russian assistance began, and were doubtless inspired by that assistance. Feng's own troops inevitably heard these rumors, and of course there was the visible evidence of Russians and Russian supplies in their camps. Therefore, in mid-July Feng issued a statement to his troops to clarify his position.

Feng's statement advised his men to ignore "wild talk" about the spread of Communism in his army; Bolshevist propaganda was absolutely prohibited among his troops. Russia and China were geographically close, the statement continued, and there naturally was some intercourse between them. But the customs and spirit of the two nations were different; and there was certainly no reason to put aside the wisdom of Chinese sages like Confucius and Mencius in favor of foreign ideas. Newfangled ideas were not required to tend to the business at hand: caring for the needs of the *lao-pai-hsing*. The statement admonished all officers to bear this in mind.[78]

This statement was doubtless written with one eye on public opinion. Nevertheless, Feng's other eye was on his army, and he meant what he said. Nobody knew this better than the Russians. Feng was not a Communist in 1925. However, at that time most observers saw little, if any, difference between the Kuomintang and the Communists; if Feng was committed to the Kuomintang's cause, or espoused "Sun Yat-sen-ism," he was a "Red General." And since Feng's pronouncements increasingly reflected Kuomintang influence, his reputation as a radical grew, particularly among foreigners.

From the spring of 1925 on, Feng studied the ideas of Sun Yat-sen, his main source being Sun's lectures on the "Three Principles of the People." Feng occasionally used Sun's ideas in talks to his officers, some of whom were given copies of these lectures.[79] Feng's use of Sun's lectures might seem to contradict the earlier statement that he was unwilling to expose his army to any ideas other than his own. But the contradiction is more apparent than real, for Sun's ideas—to the extent that Feng accepted and disseminated them—did not threaten his control over his army. There were two reasons for this: first, Sun's ideas tended to bolster rather than undermine the indoctrination that Feng had given his men; and second, Sun's death precluded any possibility that the men of the Kuominchün might look to him rather than Feng for political guidance.

Virtually the only Kuomintang propaganda used by Feng in his army was Sun Yat-sen's lectures on the Three Principles of the People. These lectures discuss the need to develop Chinese nationalism, and in this connection stress the importance of throwing off all foreign control. They argue for popular sovereignty and social and economic reforms. However, the lectures do not link the realization of these goals to the policies or the leadership of the Kuomintang. That was not the purpose of the lectures; the role of the party is assumed, but not specifically developed. In fact, there are only four or five allusions to the Kuomintang in the entire sixteen lectures.

As ideas, these three principles were perfectly acceptable to Feng. They did not contradict what he taught his troops; they only complemented his own reiterations of the need to resist foreign encroachments, to make China strong, and to love and save the people. Feng's men could find in Sun's lectures only confirmation of what their commander had been telling them for years, albeit in a treatment more scholarly, comprehensive, and sophisticated than Feng's. In view of this, and because the lectures did not emphasize the role of the Kuomintang, they could be distributed to Feng's men with little fear that they would undermine his own teachings.

The basic reason why Feng concerned himself with Sun's ideas at this time was to help fulfill his bargain with the Russians. But his interest also was related to Sun's death, which occurred on March 12, 1925. With Sun gone, the acceptance of his ideas did not entail the acceptance of his leadership, nor that of anyone else in the Kuomintang, for Sun as yet had no successor. In fact, as unlikely as it seems from our vantage point today, at the time it seemed possible that Feng himself might replace Sun as party leader.

As Feng surveyed the political scene in mid-1925, how did his prospects look in light of the distribution of power? In the Northeast was Chang Tso-lin, who directly or indirectly controlled eastern China from Manchuria to Shanghai. Opposite Chang was Feng himself, who controlled the vast areas of the Northwest and, through his allied armies, the provinces of Honan and Shensi. In central and southern China were various other militarists, and in Kwangtung was the Kuomintang. The ultimate struggle in northern China clearly would be between Feng and Chang, and the victor could dominate the militarists of the South, at least as long as they were disunited. That domination would be facilitated, and have a more progressive political cast, if the victor was supported by the Kuomintang. Moreover, the Kuomintang offered Russian aid. Therefore Feng's drawing closer to the Kuomintang offered immediate military advantages and the promise of long-range political gain.

The Kuomintang and the Russians wanted to subject Feng's military power to party leadership. But there is no reason to think that Feng had any notion of subordinating himself to the Kuomintang. The Kuomintang had not yet shown the military potential that it was to demonstrate a year or two later; indeed, through all of 1925 Kuomintang armies were struggling just to gain control of Kwangtung, and the province was not securely in their hands until the spring of 1926. Feng had every reason to believe that a victory over Chang Tso-lin, though it might be facilitated by Russian-Kuomintang assistance, would leave him the dominant power in the country, with the Kuomintang as a sort of junior partner. It would also end his dependence on the Russians for supplies because it would give him access to the sea. In such circumstances, Feng could well have anticipated that the Kuomintang would be subordinate to the Kuominchün, rather than vice versa.

None of Feng's writings mention such ambitions, yet it is hard to believe he did not entertain them. For one thing it would have been out of character: Feng never missed an opportunity to advance his power, and surely he must have realized that the existing situation was propitious for doing so. Indeed, the possibility of succeeding Sun Yat-sen was specifically called to his attention. About two and a half months after the death of Sun Yat-sen, a Kuomintang leader, Li Lieh-chün, traveled to Kalgan and "launched a boom for Feng Yü-hsiang as the logical successor of Sun Yat-sen as head of the Kuomintang."[80] Of course, as the situation turned out, the boom was somewhat premature.

Although Sun Yat-sen's writings did little to alter Feng's ideas in 1925, there was a noticeable shift in his political attitudes brought about by events in China. In 1925 the whole issue of imperialism in China was coming to a boil. Although there is no reason to doubt that Feng sincerely opposed Western political and economic domination of China, it is nevertheless true that he seized upon the issue as a means of getting the support of the Chinese people and of retaining the support of the Russians and the Kuomintang. Feng did not accept the entire political program of the Kuomintang, but he accepted with a vengeance the anti-imperialist, anti-foreign aspects of it. After May 30, 1925, that was enough.

The incident in Shanghai on May 30, when Chinese were shot by foreign-led policemen, had tremendous repercussions throughout China. Feng joined in the chorus of indignation. A week after the incident, he wrote in his diary that the Shanghai killings showed that foreigners looked on Chinese as worse than "cattle or horses." He resolved to "wipe out this humiliation," and thought the incident would provide an instructive example to his men of the evils of imperialism.[81] During the following months, a recurring theme in Feng's lectures to his officers and men was British brutality toward Chinese in general, and, in particular, the gross culpability of the British in the Shanghai affair.[82]

One of the devices Feng had always used to teach his men was the didactic drama, and shortly after the May 30th Incident he ordered one of his officers to write a play about it, which was subsequently performed for the troops. The message of "The Shanghai Tragedy" could be summarized in a sentence, but the following lengthy description is included here as an illustration of Feng's indoctrination procedures.[83]

The theater was filled with soldiers and officers of the People's Army [the First Kuominchün]. The main topic of conversation was the shooting at Shanghai.

The author of the play came onto the stage in parade uniform. He explained to the audience that the play, written by him in obedience to Feng's orders, represented the Shanghai shooting and the events of recent days. Soldiers of his company would perform the play. He hoped that the spectators would be tolerant of the literary quality of the play, for he was not a writer. He was only a patriot, and he said he would be glad if the play stimulated their feelings of patriotism and their readiness to fight for China. He finished his speech with the words, uttered in the typical fashion of Chinese agitators:

"Foreigners are shooting our brothers and plundering our country. Can it be that you do not think that we should arm ourselves?"

This appeal called forth a storm of applause and approving voices. [The author] saluted and went into the wings.

The play began. Onto the stage came workers dressed in blue serge. They crowded into the corner of the stage, near the door of an imaginary factory. (On the stage, as usual, there was no scenery.) One after another, they made short speeches.

"We work sixteen hours a day. We receive only thirty cents."

"We are poorly fed. On that amount of money we can not buy food for ourselves."

Then from the wings came a group of street merchants, who joined the workers and supported them with cries:

"The foreigners are ruining our trade!"

"The foreigners are taking our bread from us!"

Then came a Japanese policeman, who was dragging and beating a woman factory worker. She tore away from him and ran to the workers with a cry that the boss had made advances to her, and when she refused him she was chased from the factory and was not paid for her work. A new crowd of people joined the group, and the workers began to shout that the boss be brought to them. In answer to this, from the wings came a group of Japanese policemen and a group of Europeans. They opened fire on the crowd, and many fell to the ground. The crowd ran from the stage and came out of other doors, representing a demonstration. A white flag was carried in front of the crowd. On the flag was written: "We demand justice"; "We demand that we not be beaten."

Again a detachment of police and foreigners came out and opened fire. The demonstration was broken up and the demonstrators ran from the stage. Onto the empty stage were brought stretchers on which the wounded lay. A doctor came from the wings and bound their wounds; and then, while the wounded moaned and groaned, the doctor made a long speech, directed to the audience, about the violence caused by the foreigners, and about how they outrage the dignity of the nation and shoot the Chinese people. He also ended his speech with the appeal: "Do you not really think that we must take up arms?"

When the stormy applause died down, one of the wounded raised himself on his stretcher and cried out:

"They have knocked out one of my eyes, but it is better to lose both eyes than to see China's shame!"

Onto the stage came the relatives of the wounded men, and amidst stormy cries, tears, and lamentations, a soldier, representing an old woman, dressed in a gown under which his soldier's trousers were visible, turned to the audience and cried out:

"Two of my sons have been killed and a third wounded, and I am left alone in my old age. Yet if I could still bear children, I would again give birth to a son in order that he might fight for the freedom of China."

Stormy applause followed the old lady, whose words ended the play.

The acting of the soldiers was rude and simple, and the whole play consisted of the speeches at the meetings and the calls to struggle for the liberation of the country, but the play had an enormous success.

Besides arousing his troops against foreign misdeeds, Feng also spoke out before the nation on behalf of the strikers and students. He contributed $20,000 to the Shanghai strikers and at the same time denounced the "slaughter" of Chinese by the British.[84] Feng singled out the British in his denunciations of foreigners. They had always been the chief culprits, he said, and the aim of China must be to "break the economic backbone of England in China." If this could not be achieved peacefully, Feng declared, China would have to take up arms.[85]

Early in July, Feng issued an open letter to the Christians of the world in which he deplored their failure to protest the massacre of innocent Chinese. Many foreigners had demonstrated their sympathy, Feng wrote, but organized Christianity had taken no stand. Were Christians afraid? Did they support imperialism? Did they endorse the brutalities of the British? Feng called on Christians to redeem themselves by immediately lodging a protest against the Shanghai massacre. He believed that the fate of Christianity hung in the balance.[86]

It may have seemed to some observers, in view of this statement and his relations with the Russians, that Feng's own Christianity hung in the balance. Indeed, as far as his personal beliefs were concerned, such a conjecture was far from groundless: after this time Feng was much cooler toward organized Christianity. However, this did not affect his use of Christianity as a means of troop indoctrination. Feng's swollen army contained thousands of men who had been under his flag for only a few months. In order to indoctrinate these men, and to create on a larger scale the same kind of cohesive, loyal force that he had molded before 1924, Feng reorganized and greatly expanded the program of Christian proselytizing in his army.

In the spring of 1925, Feng prevailed upon a Chinese minister, Marcus Ch'eng, to accept the position of Chaplain General in the First Kuominchün, and urged him to set up a more systematic program of Christian study than had heretofore existed. A so-called Christian Council was organized at Kalgan, with Ch'eng acting as general secretary and aided by a staff of seven assistant secretaries. They planned to assign a chaplain to every 1,000 soldiers, with a secretary for every 10,000, the secretaries being directly responsible to the Christian Council. The Council secretaries also undertook to compile textbooks for Bible study, hymn books, and other Christian literature. At the same time, Madame Feng established schools for officers' wives in several centers of the Northwest. The Kalgan school required officers' wives to attend a three-month course, and presumably the same requirement existed in the other centers. In these schools the wives were instructed in Christianity, in the "hope that in this way the Christian influence may reach all the homes of the officers."[87]

In July, the same month in which he issued his statement to the Christians of the world, Feng told Marcus Ch'eng that Christianity needed to be integrated with Chinese life and civilization, and lamented that some Chinese tended to become "foreignized" when they became Christians. To combat this in his army, at least, Feng required prospective chaplains to study Chinese literature thoroughly.[88]

By the late fall of 1925, some fifty chaplains were at work among Feng's troops, and they expected to double that number very quickly. To assure that the "right kind of men" were engaged, the army set up a school for training chaplains. The school opened with 46 students on October 1, 1925, just a few weeks before Feng closed the special military school for students. The entrance requirements included an ability to read English and to write Chinese. The course of study was two years, and included study of the Confucian classics as well as of the Bible.[89]

To sum up, 1925 witnessed a shift in Feng's political orientation in the direction of a greatly increased emphasis on anti-imperialism. This shift may well have reflected Feng's increased awareness and resentment of the dominant position of the Western powers in China. But it also was undoubtedly motivated by pragmatic considerations:

it coincided with the line taken by the Russians and the Kuomintang, and thus assured their support; it also accorded with the feelings of most politically articulate Chinese, especially students, and therefore allowed Feng to stand as a spokesman for this influential group;[90] and it tended to elevate him from the status of regional warlord to that of national leader. But Feng's increased anti-imperialism was not accompanied by any other changes in his outlook. In particular, his view of troop training and indoctrination was unchanged. Loyalty and military ability were what he wanted of his troops. Feng called on the Russians to help him build up his men's military abilities. To build up their loyalty he called, as he always had, primarily on himself and God.

8. Defeat

Late in 1925 Feng's inevitable war with Chang Tso-lin finally began. It started auspiciously for Feng, but the tide soon turned against him, and he removed himself from the scene in an attempt to placate his enemies and thus bring the war to an end. He and his family traveled to the Soviet Union, where they remained for about six months. However, the anti-Kuominchün coalition would not settle for Feng's personal withdrawal, and they relentlessly pressed the war against his army until it was forced into a long and bitter westward retreat. Armed with some new ideas and with Russian promises of more military aid, Feng returned to China in the autumn of 1926 to find his exhausted and demoralized army dispersed throughout Suiyuan and Kansu.

Outbreak of War

The Second Chih-Feng War left Feng sharing control of northern China with Chang Tso-lin. In the following months, the Manchurian warlord organized a northeastern bloc of seven provinces, made up of the coastal provinces as far south as Kiangsu, plus the Special Administrative Area of Jehol. Feng tried to counter this move by creating a northwestern bloc, consisting of his own districts and the provinces controlled by the Second and Third Kuominchüns. This bloc-building—a manifestation of the competition for territory and strategic position—was a direct cause of the war that broke out near the end of 1925.* Moreover, the formation of the two blocs involved

---

* The process of creating the two blocs went on for about a year after the conclusion of the Second Chih-Feng War. Briefly, this process was formalized and reflected by the following events and appointments.

In December 1924 Chang Tso-lin was appointed Tupan of Northeastern Defense; that is, he was formally confirmed as military head of those provinces that formed the solid base of his power: Fengtien, Kirin, and Heilungkiang. On December 11 a Chang Tso-lin man, K'an Chao-hsi, was made Tut'ung of the Special Administra-

two foreign powers—Japan and the Soviet Union. Thus the enmity
between Feng and Chang was intensified by that which existed between these two rival nations. Chang's control of the coast cut Feng
off from Chinese arsenals and foreign arms merchants, and thus drove
him to seek Russian support. Chang, on the other hand, was supported by Japan, which considered the Soviet Union its chief adver-
sary in northern China, and especially in Manchuria. Therefore
Japan had a vested interest in Chang's thwarting Feng, just as the

---

tive Area of Jehol. Li Ching-lin, another of Chang's generals, was appointed Tupan
of Chihli on the same date. However, a portion of western Chihli remained under
Feng Yü-hsiang's control, and Feng's troops occupied the capital, although there
were also some Fengtien troops there during the second half of 1925.

The Second Chih-Feng War was touched off by a clash between Ch'i Hsieh-yüan
and Lu Yung-hsiang; ironically, this conflict broke out again after the war had
ended elsewhere. Fengtien troops under Chang Tsung-ch'ang intervened to clear
the way for the return to Kiangsu of Lu Yung-hsiang, who was appointed Tupan
of that province in January. Lu did not formally assume office until April, although
he controlled the province in the interim. On August 3 Lu resigned, and Yang Yü-
t'ing, Chang Tso-lin's chief of staff, was appointed Tupan on August 29.

Chang Tso-lin was extremely eager to have a reliable man as Tupan of Shantung, to secure the entire Tientsin-Pukow Railway in case he should launch a
campaign to the south. Therefore in April the Tupan of Shantung, Cheng Shih-
ch'i, was ordered to become Tupan of Anhwei, and Chang Tsung-ch'ang became
Tupan of Shantung. Cheng Shih-ch'i, however, could not take over the Anhwei
post, so Chang Tso-lin endeavored to get his own man in that position also. He
succeeded when, on August 29, Chiang Teng-hsüan was made Tupan of Anhwei. By
the end of August 1925 Chang Tso-lin's bloc consisted of Fengtien, Kirin, Heilungkiang, Jehol, Chihli, Shantung, Anhwei, and Kiangsu.

Feng Yü-hsiang was less successful in building his bloc. As Tupan of Northwestern Defense, Feng had under his control the Special Administrative Areas of
Suiyuan and Chahar. In August he also acquired Kansu.

The head of the Second Kuominchün, Hu Ching-i, was made Tupan of Honan
immediately after the Second Chih-Feng War. He promptly took up that position,
although military opposition to his rule was not eliminated by the time of his
death on April 10. Yüeh Wei-chün inherited Hu's command of the Second Kuominchün and also his position as Tupan of Honan.

Sun Yo, head of the Third Kuominchün, was appointed civil governor of Honan
at the same time that Hu Ching-i was made Tupan. This, however, was most unsatisfactory; under the conditions of warlordism, a civil governor and a military
governor could hope to get along only if one of them had no army. Sun Yo therefore did not take up his post, but remained at Paoting, which he had occupied
in the last phase of the Second Chih-Feng War. Li Ching-lin objected strenuously
to this, for Paoting was an important railroad town in Chihli. Sun finally had to
give up Paoting, and in late July he successfully invaded Shensi. He was appointed
Tupan of Shensi on August 29.

There are two noteworthy features about this series of appointments. (1) Feng's
bloc was not as strong as Chang's; Chang's men acquired more provinces, and
provinces that were richer and more favorably located. (2) Chang's supporters in
Kiangsu, Anhwei, and Shantung were more reliable than Feng's backers in Honan
and Shensi. Sun Yo and Yüeh Wei-chün ignored Feng's wishes and plans whenever
it was in their interest to do so.

Russians looked upon Feng as, among other things, an obstacle to the extension of Japanese influence in northern China. Moreover, Russian aid to Feng may have hastened the onset of the war by threatening to eliminate Chang Tso-lin's chief advantage, superiority in arms and equipment. The longer Chang waited, the better his enemy would be equipped.

As early as March 1925 Chang Tso-lin told foreign diplomats of his determination to attack the Kuominchün in the near future.[1] In May it seemed the time had come. Chang decided to send troops to Peking "for the protection of the capital," a task that Feng's men had monopolized up to that time. A Fengtien army marched south, and Chang himself went to Tientsin to direct operations. But the inevitable showdown was postponed when Feng Yü-hsiang withdrew peacefully from the positions Chang wanted to occupy. At the same time, the Russians took several measures to temper Chang's aggressiveness: veiled threats appeared in the Russian press; army maneuvers began on the Manchurian frontier; and diplomatic notes were sent to the Peking government expressing complaints about the Chinese Eastern Railway. Moreover, at the end of the month the crisis in China's relations with the powers caused by the May 30th Incident resulted in a temporary détente between Feng and Chang. It was not until October that war broke out, and then it was started not by Feng or Chang directly, but by Sun Ch'uan-fang.*

Sun Ch'uan-fang, intent upon carving a warlord empire for himself in east-central China, was particularly concerned over the extension of Fengtien power into Kiangsu, where he controlled several districts that he feared he might be forced to relinquish. Beyond this, there was the natural anxiety arising from the prospect of having a powerful rival in the neighborhood. Sun's concern was intensified by a series of ominous events. After the May 30th Incident, Fengtien

* Sun Ch'uan-fang was a native of Shantung. He graduated from the Peiyang Military School at Paoting in 1906, after which he went to Japan for further military education. After his return to China he served under Wu P'ei-fu, and was promoted to brigade commander for his work in the An-Chih War. In 1923 Wu appointed Sun military governor of Fukien as part of his policy of unification by force. Specifically, Wu hoped Sun would be a barrier against Kwangtung, on the one side, and threaten Lu Yung-hsiang, the independent Anfu militarist in Chekiang, on the other. In the fall of 1924, when the Chekiang-Kiangsu war broke out as a prelude to the Second Chih-Feng War, Sun cooperated in the attack against Lu Yung-hsiang. After Lu's defeat Sun was made governor of Chekiang, and one of his subordinates became governor of Fukien. After Wu fled from northern China, he hoped for the military support of Sun Ch'uan-fang. Although Wu still had great prestige and was respected by Sun as his former leader, Sun had the army, and therefore determined the conditions of such support.

troops occupied Shanghai. Moreover, Fengtien authorities attempted to open the Kiangnan arsenal, which had been dismantled after the Second Chih-Feng War. The appointment of Yang Yu-t'ing, Chang Tso-lin's own chief of staff, as Tupan of Kiangsu seemed to be another indication of a more forceful Fengtien policy in that area, and thus a threat to Sun Ch'uan-fang. Still another factor in Sun's mind—and in the minds of all warlords at this time—was the Special Conference on the Chinese Customs Tariff, which was to open on October 26. As the situation stood, it seemed that any increase in revenues that China might gain from this conference would accrue to Chang Tso-lin, a windfall that none of his enemies wanted him to have.

The Kuominchün leaders agreed to cooperate with Sun Ch'uan-fang against Fengtien. They apparently hoped that an attack by Sun would draw the main Fengtien forces south, permitting the Kuominchün to sweep in from the west and cut the enemy off from its Manchurian base. Sun launched his offensive in mid-October. The Fengtien troops in Kiangsu and Anhwei, fighting in unfamiliar territory and at the end of a long supply line, retreated rapidly. Although Chang Tso-lin moved about 70,000 troops into Chihli in early November, they took up positions facing the First Kuominchün instead of proceeding south as it was hoped they would. Chang Tso-lin had no wish to engage Feng while Fengtien troops were under attack in Kiangsu and Anhwei, yet he had to be prepared for an assault by the Kuominchün. But Feng did not fight. Instead, he deployed his troops in defensive positions, withdrew from the points that Fengtien troops wanted to occupy, emphatically proclaimed his desire for peace and his intention to be neutral, and then sent representatives to Mukden to see what he could exact in return for that neutrality.

By the middle of November, Sun Ch'uan-fang had halted his advance after conquering Kiangsu and Anhwei. The Second Kuominchün had already started an offensive against Shantung. But still Feng Yü-hsiang did not move. In fact, his representatives met with those of Chang Tso-lin to negotiate a formal peace agreement that provided for complete Kuominchün control of the Peking-Hankow Railway.* Thus although Feng called for peace, he exploited the war situation, and all the time kept his own army out of action. Some

* In practical terms, Kuominchün control of the Peking-Hankow Railway meant Fengtien evacuation of Paoting and Taming, two important towns on the railway, which Sun Yo had finally yielded to Li Ching-lin at the end of April. In November troops of the Second Kuominchün took over these towns, even before the Fengtien men had completely evacuated them. It is possible that Feng wanted his own units to occupy these towns, and that Yüeh's move surprised him.

observers concluded that Feng was trying to avoid committing his troops in the hope that Sun Ch'uan-fang and Yüeh Wei-chün would win the war for him. Others thought that Feng genuinely wanted peace. But there was also a third possibility—that Feng was simply waiting for something to happen. And on November 22 it happened: one of Chang Tso-lin's leading generals turned against him.

Kuo Sung-ling's Revolt

After Chang Tso-lin's defeat in the 1922 war with Chihli, he had reorganized his army and embarked on a program to strengthen and modernize it. This process had gradually brought a number of new men into influential positions in the Fengtien army, men who had not participated in Chang Tso-lin's rise to power. They were products of a new kind of military education, and considered the techniques of military administration and warfare employed by the old-timers to be somewhat outmoded. Consequently, Chang's chief subordinates began to divide into cliques of "new" officers and "old" officers.

One of these new officers was Kuo Sung-ling. Kuo was on intimate terms with Chang Tso-lin's son, Chang Hsüeh-liang, the so-called "Young Marshal." Indeed, Kuo was the actual leader of the troops nominally under Chang Hsüeh-liang's command. Kuo was unpopular with some Fengtien officers, partly because of clique rivalry, partly because of resentment over his influence with the "Young Marshal," and perhaps also partly because of personal characteristics. This unpopularity may have played a part in blocking Kuo's appointment to provincial leadership after the Second Chih-Feng War. However, although Kuo did not become a military governor, his force was expanded, and by the autumn of 1925 he had under his command at least 50,000 of the best-trained and best-equipped men in the entire Fengtien military organization. He was nevertheless dissatisfied, and these two factors—general disapproval of Chang Tso-lin's "old-fashioned" administration, and resentment over being bypassed in the distribution of territorial rewards—led Kuo to rebel against Chang Tso-lin in November 1925.[2]

Kuo Sung-ling planned his revolt in cooperation with Feng Yü-hsiang. It is not clear how Feng and Kuo first made contact, but it was widely believed that their liaison was initiated by their wives, who had been schoolmates and remained close friends.[3] In autumn of 1925 Kuo went to Japan to observe military maneuvers. Feng's subordinate Han Fu-chü also went, and it is probable that a prelim-

inary understanding was reached there.[4] Later, on the eve of the revolt, Feng and Kuo concluded a formal agreement. Sources differ on
its details, but the following major points seem clear.

(1) Feng and Kuo would call upon Chang Tso-lin to retire. Of
course, they did not really expect the Manchurian warlord to heed
their appeal. But good form demanded that they make it, although
such a request was considered tantamount to a declaration of war.

(2) If necessary, Feng would give Kuo military support. Kuo was
confident that he could overthrow Chang Tso-lin, and Feng's troops
therefore might never see action. However, if Kuo met unexpected
difficulties or was attacked from the rear, Feng's army was to join in
the struggle.

(3) If the revolt was successful, Kuo Sung-ling would have a free
hand in Manchuria.

(4) Li Ching-lin would be rewarded for cooperating in the revolt.
Li, the Tupan of Chihli and one of Chang's chief supporters, had a
strong army in his province, and his attitude was thus critical. The
plotters therefore brought him into the conspiracy. As a reward he
was to receive Jehol, in addition to retaining Chihli. Feng was to have
the right to station troops along the railroad in southern Chihli, but
all revenues from the province were to go to Li.[5]

The revolt began as almost all warlord operations began—with a
circular telegram. On November 22, Kuo Sung-ling, who was then in
northern Chihli, issued a wire demanding that Chang Tso-lin turn
his administration over to his son and retire. Three days later, Feng
Yü-hsiang and Li Ching-lin sent similar telegrams.[6]

Kuo Sung-ling marched northward, winning victory after victory,
and on December 1 he entered Manchuria.* The following day, Li
Ching-lin turned against the conspirators and announced his continued loyalty to Chang Tso-lin. Li's sudden turnabout may have
been caused by fear that Chang Tso-lin would take reprisals against
Li's mother, who was then in Manchuria.† It is also possible that Li
was never genuinely in accord with Feng and Kuo, and simply waiting

* When Kuo entered Manchuria, he found proclamations posted throughout the
country announcing that the government would pay: (1) $800,000 for the capture
of Kuo Sung-ling alive; (2) $80,000 for Kuo's head; (3) $50,000 to anyone who could
prove that he had killed Kuo; (4) $40,000 for the destruction of Kuo's quarters; and
(5) $10,000 each for any of Kuo's subordinate commanders. (Weale, p. 272.)
† There were reports, as in NCS, Dec. 3, 1925, p. 1, that Kuo Sung-ling's father was
executed by Chang Tso-lin, and Li's mother taken into custody. NCS, Feb. 4, 1926,
p. 5, reported that a letter was published in Mukden from Kuo Sung-ling's parents
expressing thanks to Chang Tso-lin for exempting them from punishment and for
treating them with compassion.

for the best time to make his stand known. If Li's agreement with Feng and Kuo was made in good faith, his change of heart may well have been prompted by a reconsideration of the rewards promised him. It was evident that the defeat of Chang Tso-lin would be followed by an expansion of Feng's influence in northern China, and the most obvious area for that expansion was the province of Chihli. Moreover, when the plot was first elaborated, the conspirators had assumed that the Second Kuominchün would have successfully invaded Shantung before the revolt against Chang Tso-lin began. That invasion was launched early in November, but it had conspicuously bogged down by the end of the month. Therefore it looked as if Li need fear not Kuominchün troops, but a Fengtien army, at his rear in Shantung. Thus a campaign against Chang Tso-lin would be far more risky than it had originally seemed.

Although Li's defection from the plot brought Feng's army into action to prevent an attack on Kuo's rear, it did not have any immediate effect on Kuo's campaign in Manchuria. Kuo was brilliantly successful on his own, and within a week after his troops passed the Great Wall, the American consul at Mukden soberly reported that Chang Tso-lin had suffered a complete debacle, and that his position was "absolutely hopeless."[7]

The Japanese, of course, were vitally concerned over any change in the power structure of Manchuria. However, a number of Japanese felt that Chang Tso-lin had asserted too much independence, and that Kuo might be a more amenable ruler of Manchuria; indeed, it is doubtful that Kuo would have moved against Chang in the first place without some assurance that Japan would consider him an acceptable replacement. But the Japanese military insisted upon maintaining Chang Tso-lin in power, particularly in view of Kuo's affiliation with the Russian-sponsored Feng Yü-hsiang. Therefore, in mid-December, Japanese "neutrality" shifted in favor of Chang Tso-lin. Whereas reinforcements for Chang were brought from Kirin on the South Manchurian Railway, use of the railroad was denied to Kuo Sung-ling. More important, the commander of Japanese forces in Manchuria declared that belligerents could not enter the South Manchurian Railway Zone. Since Mukden was in the zone, Kuo Sung-ling was effectively denied the chief prize he sought, the capital. Kuo nevertheless continued his offensive, and there were rumors that if he defeated Chang in the field, the Japanese would arrange for the old Manchurian warlord to retire, and let Kuo enter Mukden to take the spoils of victory.

The decisive battle began on December 23 in the vicinity of Hsin-minfu, about 30 miles west of Mukden. The Fengtien troops fell back, as they had in all the earlier battles, but suddenly cavalry from Kirin and Heilungkiang attacked Kuo's rear. This unexpected assault utterly confounded Kuo's troops, who were already somewhat demoralized by the belief that Japan was determined to block their victory. Indeed, it has been alleged that the attacking troops were Japanese in Chinese uniforms.[8] Whoever they were, Kuo's officers and men promptly surrendered to them, while Kuo and his wife fled in disguise. They were captured and shot the next day. On Christmas morning their bodies were displayed in a Mukden public square.[9]

Meanwhile, things were not going well for Feng Yü-hsiang. Feng's promise of military support to Kuo was meant for just such a contingency as that of December 2, when Li Ching-lin turned against the Feng-Kuo alliance. Feng finally had to commit his army to battle. Under the command of Chang Chih-chiang, about 80,000 troops of the First Kuominchün advanced to the vicinity of Tientsin, where the first clash occurred on December 9. What followed during the next two weeks amazed many foreign observers, for the struggle between Li Ching-lin and the Kuominchün was one of the bitterest that had occurred during the Republican period. As one diplomat put it, Li's defense was "not what is expected from the usual Chinese military officer," especially when hampered by wintertime conditions.[10] Although the Kuominchün outnumbered the Fengtien force, Li conducted his campaign with great skill and stubbornness. Moreover, Feng's men were not aided by the ineffectual attempts of the Second and Third Kuominchüns to break through Li's left flank near Machang. It was not until December 23, the same day that Kuo Sung-ling's revolt collapsed in Manchuria, that Li Ching-lin finally yielded Tientsin to Feng's army. And Li had reason to be quite satisfied as he retreated to the haven of Shantung: the Kuominchün had suffered heavy casualties;* the Second and Third Kuominchüns had been unable to cut the Tientsin-Pukow Railway, thus allowing Li to retire

---

* State Department document 893.00/7065 contains a report on the care of Feng's wounded after the battle of Tientsin. The report, dated Dec. 29, 1925, was written by Commander Charles M. Oman of the U.S. Navy Medical Corps. It offers an interesting illustration of one aspect of warlordism in general and of conditions in the Kuominchün in particular. Commander Oman wrote as follows (I have modified his punctuation):

"About two weeks ago, when actual fighting began between General Li's and Marshal Feng's armies near Tientsin, wounded began to arrive in Peking. At first they were taken to the Peking Union Medical College Hospital, but the number soon was so great that they were taken to the Nan Yuan barracks about 6 miles south of the city.

with all of his remaining men and equipment in good order; and Feng had been delayed so long in Tientsin that he had been unable to aid Kuo Sung-ling.[11]

Defeat

The bald fact facing Feng Yü-hsiang on Christmas 1925 was that although he had won a battle, he stood a good chance of losing the war. Long-range prospects for the Kuominchün were ominous. Chang

---

"These are large, one-storied, . . . brick barrack buildings. One section had been used as a hospital, but about four or five months ago all the equipment and medical personnel had been removed to Kalgan. No provision had been made to reestablish a hospital here when hostilities began. There were about 150 beds, but no other equipment, such as tables, lights, instruments, dressings, or drugs, had been provided.

"The wounded came in so rapidly that the authorities of the Peking Union Medical College on their own accord went down and took charge, their doctors, nurses, and some foreign and a few Chinese civilians responding.

. . .

"One thousand cases came in in about three days, and then 1,500 more in the next three days. Marshal Feng's own medical department showed no signs or indication of any preparation beforehand for the care of the wounded behind the lines, nor did they demonstrate any signs of any idea what to do when the emergency arose, nor any skill—based on western ideas—in the care of the wounded when they did arrive.

"The wounded were received from two to five days after injury, and the wounds were [typical] of armies using machine guns, rifles, high explosives, and shrapnel. The wounds were, as a rule, bandaged; some had iodine painted on and iodoform dusted in . . . , [which] showed some form of first aid at the front. A great many wounds were of a very severe nature. From the nature of the wounds I formed the opinion that the mortality on the field of battle must have been high, and it also was very evident that, with the proper provision for evacuation and care of the wounded at the front, many lives could have been saved and much suffering alleviated.

"In Nan Yuan hospital the barracks are well heated, but beds are scarce and a great many men lie on straw. The men are well and warmly clothed, appear well fed, and average about 19 years of age, although there are a great many boys 14 to 16 years old.

"The Chinese civilians have not responded in any degree to help care for the wounded, and the Army Medical Corps seems to me wholly inadequate in number and poorly trained.

"The foreign doctors and nurses and some civilians, assisted by civilian Chinese doctors and nurses from the Peking Union Medical College, Methodist Hospital, and Salvation Army, have practically organized, operated, and carried on the care of the wounded. At present there are some 2,500 wounded at Nan Yuan and 1,000 at some barracks about one mile beyond.

"From a survey of the whole situation, it appears that Marshal Feng made absolutely no preparation for the care of the wounded behind the lines and very little on the battle front. They are depending on foreign aid for the care of their soldiers, and seem perfectly satisfied that we should go ahead and do it all. It is even difficult to get the members of his medical corps to help us when we tell them what to do, and the civilians do not respond, probably because they do not wish to be associated with any particular military party."

Tso-lin was back in business at the old stand; Kuo Sung-ling's soldiers had now returned to their former allegiance, and the Fengtien army was little the worse for Kuo's revolt. Feng therefore faced the formidable Manchurian enemy that he had successfully avoided all year.* In addition, Li Ching-lin and Chang Tsung-ch'ang were in Shantung, preparing an offensive against the Kuominchün. This would have been bad enough, for it put Feng between two enemies. But there was worse to come. Chang Tso-lin and Wu P'ei-fu put aside their mutual enmity out of a common hatred for Feng, and at the beginning of 1926 they united against him.

Realizing the serious threat posed by this hostile coalition, Feng took steps to avoid or mitigate a defeat that seemed distinctly possible. One corollary of the individualistic nature of warlordism was that the removal of either of two warring warlords often would terminate the conflict. Feng therefore thought his resignation might save the day; if he personally left the scene, his enemies might end their war against the Kuominchün. Moreover, Chang and Wu might even

---

* Just before the year's end, Feng was involved in one of those acts of personal violence that occasionally punctuated the monotonously impersonal violence of warlordism. On December 29, soldiers of the First Kuominchün forced Hsü Shu-cheng from the train on which he was traveling, and shot him to death. Although Feng denied responsibility, it was generally believed that Hsü was murdered on his orders; given Feng's firm control over the Kuominchün, no other conclusion can be drawn. Hsü was a close associate of Tuan Ch'i-jui, and was one of the outstanding leaders of the Anfu clique before that group was dissolved in 1920. Hsü had continued to play a conspicuous role in Chinese politics, and had acquired the image of a warlord wheeler-dealer who had his fingers in many pies, not all of them savory. In October 1924 he was seized by police of the Shanghai foreign settlement, and was forced to leave the country. Hsü went on a tour "to investigate political and military conditions in Europe," and was received with cordial ceremony in many cities of the western world. He finally returned to China December 10, 1925. He had just concluded consultations with Tuan Ch'i-jui in Peking when he was killed.

The most obvious motive for Hsü's murder was revenge; in 1918 Hsü had murdered Lu Chien-chang, Feng's patron and relative. In fact, the story was circulated that it was Lu's son Lu Ch'eng-wu who killed Hsü, and that Kuominchün soldiers simply helped him find the opportunity. However, skeptics pointed out that Lu Ch'eng-wu was a mild man; moreover, others asserted that Lu was in Shanghai on the day of the shooting. In any event, the ultimate responsibility was clearly Feng's, and revenge was evidently the chief motive. It has been alleged that Feng also had political motives, and this is certainly possible. However, no substantial evidence for this has been revealed. See Fuse, pp. 131–32. NCH, Jan. 16, 1926, p. 91, has a long account of the murder told by one of Hsü's companions on the fatal trip. American Minister J. V. A. MacMurray discussed the incident in two wires to the Secretary of State, one on Jan. 5, 1926, 893.00/6906, and the other on Jan. 18, 1926, 893.00/7122. J. C. Huston, American consul at Hankow, discussed Feng's possible motives in a report to Minister MacMurray, Jan. 13, 1926, 893.00/7110. Also see Hsieh Kuan-lan, no. 41.

begin fighting each other. By way of justifying this hope, Feng told the story of a hunter who set two tigers against each other until one was dead and the other so exhausted that the hunter could kill him with ease. "The militarists," Feng said, "are similar to those tigers," and the spoils that might set them to quarreling were "Peking and the President's chair."[12] On New Year's Day 1926 Feng resigned all of his offices. About a week later Chang Chih-chiang was formally appointed to Feng's former position as Tupan of Northwestern Defense.[13]

At the time of Feng's resignation, there were reports that his decision was the result of rivalry among his subordinates, although it is not completely clear why such rivalry should have such an effect. However, there may have been some disagreement in the top echelons of the Kuominchün. An American diplomat in Kalgan, with good sources of local information, reported a "protracted and stormy interview" between Feng and Chang Chih-chiang shortly after the Tientsin battle.[14] A few days later, the same observer asserted that Feng had departed from Kalgan in haste and secrecy because he could no longer rely on the loyalty of his subordinates, especially Chang Chih-chiang.[15] In retrospect, it seems unlikely that there was any such serious friction among the army leaders; certainly the subsequent history of the Kuominchün does not confirm such a hypothesis.* Of course, it is possible that the Kuominchün leaders themselves started rumors about discord in their ranks. If Feng's departure was intended to convince his enemies that the army was no longer under his command, it had to appear genuine. On the other hand, it is also possible that there was some disagreement over the appropriate military tactics and strategy to use in dealing with the difficult situation that confronted the Kuominchün at the beginning of 1926.[16]

The announcement of Feng's resignation did nothing to deter an offensive by the anti-Kuominchün forces. It began with an attack by Wu P'ei-fu against Honan. Honan was still occupied by the Second Kuominchün, which had become infamous in that province for the

---

* The distribution of power after the Tientsin victory is among the reasons given for friction among Kuominchün leaders. It has been alleged that Feng's chief subordinates resented Sun Yo's appointment as Tupan of Chihli, a post he received in December at Feng's recommendation. However, it seems much more likely that the post was given to Sun so that the First Kuominchün would not be the formal authority in the province, over which the anti-Kuominchün allies would first seek to establish control. Inexplicably, Sun evidently wanted the position. He never exercised authority over any portion of the province except Tientsin and its immediate environs. For an account of Sun's transfer from Shensi to Chihli, see Li T'ai-fen, pp. 254–57.

inefficiency of its administration and the variety of its corruption and misrule. As soon as Wu launched his attack on Honan, the Red Spears in the province rose up against Yüeh Wei-chün's bandit-soldiers, facilitating Wu's invasion. By late February his troops had taken the capital city, Kaifeng, and by the beginning of March Yüeh Wei-chün's power in Honan was completely destroyed.[17]

It was fortunate for Wu that the Red Spears hated the Second Kuominchün so much, for Wu commanded a fairly weak force at the outset of his campaign. After his wanderings following Feng's 1924 coup, Wu had settled in Hankow, under the protection of his former subordinate Hsiao Yao-nan. Hsiao kept tight political and financial control over Hupeh, and Wu could not obtain the wherewithal to create a powerful new force. However, Hsiao died on February 14, 1926, and Wu promptly made himself heir to Hsiao's resources, appointing his own lieutenants as civil and military governors of Hupeh. In this fashion, Wu once again came to the fore among the military powers to be reckoned with; his alliance with Chang Tso-lin and his anti-Kuominchün offensive suddenly became very ominous for Feng's army.

Wu's Honan campaign was supposed to be coordinated with a Fengtien attack on Chihli, but this did not begin until the fighting in Honan was almost over. On February 20, Li Ching-lin, supported by Chang Tsung-ch'ang, crossed the Chihli border and launched the struggle to reclaim the province. Sun Yo, as Tupan of Chihli, had taken over Tientsin, and his Third Kuominchün met the Fengtien troops just south of the city. Sun's units immediately crumpled before Li's army, which could easily have taken Tientsin if units of the First Kuominchün had not hurried south to take over the city's defense.

Early in March, the Fengtien army initiated a sustained offensive against the Tientsin front. Flustered by the assault and fearing for the worst, the Kuominchün tried everything. On the one hand, Feng's men stubbornly resisted the attackers. On the other hand, they put out peace feelers to Chang Tso-lin.[18] At the same time, they probably sought an alliance with Sun Ch'uan-fang against Wu P'ei-fu.[19] But neither of these ventures succeeded, and the fighting continued. Kuominchün supplies dwindled; replenishment of ammunition was imperative. Early in February a Russian ship, the *Oleg*, had attempted to deliver a large load of war supplies into Tientsin harbor for the Kuominchün, but the ship drew so much water that it could not cross the sandbar outside of Taku and had to depart. In the middle of

March the *Oleg* returned, having been sufficiently lightened to allow it to reach Tientsin. However, Fengtien authorities had been warned of its arrival, and the ship was captured before its cargo could be discharged.*[20] This was a stunning blow to the Kuominchün. Low on ammunition, with Chang Tso-lin's troops to the north, Li Ching-lin threatening from Shantung, and Wu P'ei-fu to the south, the Kuominchün had to shorten its lines. On March 20 Lu Chung-lin issued a circular telegram lamenting the horrors that the war was imposing on the Chinese people and stressing the Kuominchün's determination to pursue the peaceful development of the Northwest. The following day, the Kuominchün evacuated Tientsin and withdrew to the vicinity of Peking. The withdrawal, involving about 100,000 men, was superbly executed, "with less confusion than would result from the average Chinese commander's efforts to evacuate a brigade."[21]

Feng Yü-hsiang had been watching events from his semi-retirement in Suiyuan. Now, faced with the determined opposition exemplified in the Tientsin battle, Feng left China for an extended stay in the Soviet Union. Despite Feng's move, the anti-Kuominchün armies relentlessly pursued their quarry to Peking, where Feng's men prepared to retreat even farther. Still attempting to divide his enemies, Lu Chung-lin on April 9 ordered the arrest of Tuan Ch'i-jui, released Ts'ao K'un, and declared his willingness to hand over Peking peacefully to Wu P'ei-fu. This transparent maneuver failed to set anti-Kuominchün leaders to fighting over Peking, as Lu had hoped. Ts'ao K'un promptly showed that he was weary of high-level Chinese politics; he disappeared into the French Hospital.† Wu P'ei-fu refused to be enticed from his alliance with Chang Tso-lin.[22] The assault on Peking continued. Finally, during the early morning hours of April 16, the Kuominchün evacuated the capital. Again it was a beautifully

---

* The American Consul General at Mukden was told that the French consul at Vladivostok had informed the French embassy in Peking of the *Oleg*'s cargo and destination. The French embassy, in turn, allegedly informed the French consul at Mukden, who told the Fengtien authorities, thus enabling them to seize the *Oleg* when it arrived.

† Neither Ts'ao K'un nor Tuan Ch'i-jui ever assumed a position of importance in Chinese political life after this. Ts'ao K'un formally resigned the presidency, and remained in quiet retirement the rest of his life. Tuan Ch'i-jui managed to elude the soldiers Lu sent to arrest him, and returned to his residence and position as chief executive immediately after the Kuominchün abandoned Peking. However, he had no significant support from any quarter; indeed, he was pretty much ignored. Therefore, on April 19 Tuan, his son, and various followers took refuge in the Legation Quarter, and on the following day went to Tientsin, which brought to at least 26 the number of ex-tuchüns living there.

executed retreat, swift and without disorder or unnecessary losses. The troops moved directly to the famous Nankow Pass, about 30 miles northwest of Peking, where they dug in behind formidable natural and man-made fortifications.

Normally in a struggle between warlords, defeats such as those suffered by the Kuominchün might have been enough to satisfy the victors and terminate the war. However, as early as March, a few days after the Kuominchün evacuation of Tientsin, the anti-Kuominchün coalition had resolved to continue the campaign until Feng's army was disbanded and thus eliminated as a potential power in China. There were several reasons for this unusual determination. First, both Wu P'ei-fu and Chang Tso-lin had powerful reasons to dislike Feng personally: his treachery had toppled Wu in 1924; and he had cooperated in Kuo Sung-ling's revolt, which had come within a hair's breadth of ending Chang Tso-lin's rule in Manchuria. Second, Chang and Wu were opposed to the radicalism that Feng presumably represented; the war against Feng became a struggle against the possible Bolshevization of northern China. The Japanese military in Manchuria was much concerned with the possible extension of Russian influence in northern China, and very likely encouraged Chang in his determined opposition to Feng. Finally, the allies feared the Kuominchün's potential ability to make a comeback. They saw that continued Russian sponsorship would be inevitable if the Kuominchün were merely sealed off in the Northwest. On the one hand, this would mean a continued danger of radical influences in northern China; and on the other hand, it would virtually guarantee that the Kuominchün, with Russian assistance, would eventually make another attempt to dominate northern China.[23]

The Kuominchün was already demonstrating its military prowess by its defense of Nankow. This was not to be a temporary stopover like Peking; the army dug in. The topography around the Nankow Pass made it nearly impregnable, and the Kuominchün did its best to make it even more so. They dug an excellent system of trenches, and constructed shrapnel-proof dugouts and other fortifications that fanned out for 12 miles in front of the entrance to the pass.

In addition, Lu Chung-lin tried hard to replenish the ranks and the purse of his army. Vigorous efforts were made to recruit Mongols from Inner Mongolia for a cavalry force that was needed to protect the lines of communication with Urga. In order to raise funds, so-called "public credit short-term notes" were issued that were presumably redeemable after one year. The Kalgan Chamber of Commerce was forced to accept $800,000 worth of these notes, a transaction that understandably made the president of the Chamber a "nervous wreck." Suiyuan had to take half that amount. Attempts were even made to force foreign firms in the Northwest to subscribe to this loan, but that approach was finally abandoned. On July 1 railroad-freight rates were hiked by 40 per cent, but this added little revenue since not much freight was being shipped at the time.[24]

The anti-Kuominchün allies failed in every attempt to dislodge Feng's men from the Nankow Pass. The months wore on and the stubborn battle continued. The Russians sent arms and ammunition to the Kuominchün, but it was never enough to allow Feng's men to feel that their supply was adequate; on several occasions ammunition ran low. Russian soldiers also fought side by side with Kuominchün soldiers. There were endless rumors about the participation of Russians and Russian-trained Mongols in Kuominchün military operations, and they were sometimes said to number in the thousands. Actually, by the summer of 1926 there may have been as many as 400 Russians fighting with the Kuominchün, most of them involved in the technical aspects of combat, such as directing gun batteries.[25]

Unfortunately, the Kuominchün acquired another enemy shortly after its retreat to Nankow: on May 18 Kuominchün troops clashed with soldiers of Yen Hsi-shan in northern Shansi. Yen was a notorious "fence-sitter"; as one means of maintaining his uncontested control of Shansi, he seldom took sides in the warlord struggles that swirled around him. But Yen had little chance when the anti-Kuominchün allies demanded that he attack the Kuominchün rear. If he refused and the allies won—as seemed likely—they might make things difficult for him. In addition, Yen was worried that the Kuominchün might retreat from Nankow into Shansi. Therefore he mobilized his troops in northern Shansi to try to cut the Peking-Suiyuan Railway. At that time Shansi's border extended farther north than it does at present, and the province embraced a large section of that railroad, which the Kuominchün leaders deemed it essential to control. It was both an artery of supplies and communications, and an obvious avenue of rapid retreat should it prove impossible to hold Nankow. In the face of Yen's apparently hostile attitude, the Kuominchün moved quickly to establish firm control over the railroad; however, control could be maintained only at the cost of continued fighting.[26]

In the meantime, the defense of Nankow went on. About 90,000 Kuominchün troops held out against about 450,000 allied soldiers. Barrage after barrage of heavy artillery fire rained down on the Nan-

kow defenders as spring gave way to summer, and summer to fall.
Finally the end came. The Kuominchün did not have the troops or
the resources to hold out against such great odds. Moreover, Kuominchün leaders did not want to expend their remaining strength in the
defense of Nankow; they wanted their army to be able to fight again
another day. There was also the constant fear that Yen Hsi-shan
might succeed in expelling the Kuominchün from the Peking-Suiyuan
Railway, and thus cut off the retreat route. With these considerations
in mind, the Kuominchün once again withdrew.

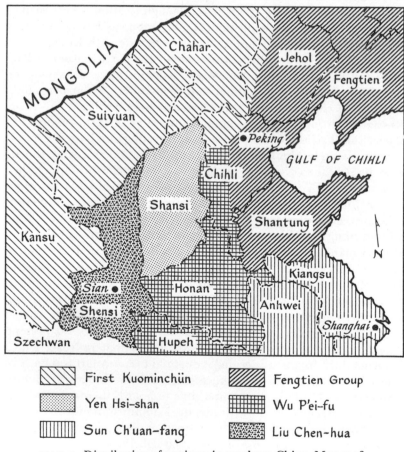

MAP 2. Distribution of territory in northern China, May 1926.

On August 16 the main body of the Kuominchün began the flight westward. Although Lu Chung-lin's arrangements seem to have been well-made, the operation was not as successful as the earlier Kuominchün retreats. A supply of gasoline caught fire. There was a train wreck in which a large sum of money was lost. There were not enough railroad cars available to transport all the troops; and even those fortunate enough to ride found that the end of the line was at Paotow, after which they had to march. The retreating men were harassed by bandits, who took this occasion to exact revenge for the Kuominchün's earlier anti-bandit campaigns, as well as to seize whatever guns and supplies they could find. As discipline broke down, many soldiers themselves turned to banditry. Feng's fine army was on the verge of disintegration.[27]

The men of the Kuominchün have taken great pride in the stubborn courage their army displayed in the defense of Nankow. In addition, they have attributed great historical significance to this struggle on the grounds that it tied up troops of the northern warlords so that the Kuomintang's Northern Expedition could advance with little opposition. There is truth in this claim, but the retrospective attempt of Kuominchün leaders to represent their defense of Nankow as a purposeful part of the Kuomintang's revolutionary war is not true. The defenders of Nankow were fighting for themselves and for their generals. That they fought so well was not due to revolutionary zeal as much as to the endurance and bravery of Feng's peasant troops, and the discipline and training he had given them.

The Kuominchün in Kansu

During late 1925 and 1926, while the bulk of the Kuominchün was fighting the allied anti-Kuominchün armies in eastern China, Feng Yü-hsiang's men in Kansu were undergoing similarly hazardous experiences. Kansu was a large, distant, and undeveloped region, the most sparsely settled province in China proper. Despite Kansu's remoteness and backwardness, it held several attractions for Feng in 1925. As a frontier region, it could serve as another testing ground for his experiments in colonization and economic development. The Kansu opium tax was a lucrative source of revenue, an important consideration for Feng, who was in perennial financial difficulty.[28] Moreover, Kansu was a corridor through which Feng might ultimately spread his influence into Chinese Turkestan, and the trade route linking China proper with Central Asia offered another source of revenue. Control of Kansu further guaranteed the security of Feng's lines of communication with the Soviet Union. And perhaps of most immediate importance, in view of the fact that Feng was expecting war with Chang Tso-lin, Kansu could serve as a haven should the fortunes of war require that the Kuominchün retreat westward.

The events that had given Feng his opportunity to penetrate Kansu began when the Tupan, Lu Hung-t'ao, fell ill in the summer of 1925. Two of Lu's subordinates took advantage of his illness to force him from office. One of the conspirators, Li Ch'ang-ch'ing, was a brigade commander in Lu Hung-t'ao's division. After the expulsion of Lu, Li appointed himself division commander, took over Lu's former troops, and began to recruit others. Pao Yü-hsiang was the other conspirator. He had been a subordinate of Li Ch'ang-ch'ing's, and now he claimed Li's former position as brigade commander. Feng Yü-hsiang, ever alert to the main chance, seized the opportunity presented by all this confusion to have himself appointed Tupan of Kansu on August 29. Of course, Feng did not want to go that far from the center of his interests, and so he sent a leading subordinate, Liu Yü-fen, to be acting governor of the province. When Liu Yü-fen and his troops arrived in Kansu early in October, Li Ch'ang-ch'ing and Pao Yü-hsiang dominated Lanchow.

Liu Yü-fen promptly moved into the headquarters of the former Tupan, while Li Ch'ang-ch'ing and his troops camped just outside the city. The situation was very unstable and dangerous; Li would not obey Liu's orders, and Liu feared that Li was preparing to attack him. Liu's Kuominchün units were superior to Li Ch'ang-ch'ing's troops, but Liu hesitated to start a conflict that could easily spread to involve other Kansu troops, none of whom looked favorably upon the Kuominchün interlopers. Therefore, with the approval of Feng Yü-hsiang, Liu resorted to guile.

Kuominchün headquarters in Lanchow first announced that the central government had confirmed Li and Pao in their newly acquired positions as division commander and brigade commander, respectively. Shortly thereafter, Liu Yü-fen gave a banquet for Li and Pao. The feast was held in a building where a large number of Liu Yü-fen's troops were hiding. At a signal, these troops moved in to seize Li and Pao. Bodyguards who tried to resist were shot down on the spot. Li and Pao may also have been murdered immediately, or they may have been sent to Paotow and shot there. Shortly afterward, their troops were assimilated into the Kuominchün.[29]

During the warlord period, it was by no means unusual for the officially appointed military governor to be unable to exercise effective authority over his entire province. In Kansu, however, this was *always* the case. The province was divided into about eight areas, each controlled by an independent militarist, although the warlord at Lanchow was customarily the military governor and to all appearances in charge of provincial affairs. The situation was further complicated by the fact that some of the regional militarists in the province were Muslims, whereas others were Chinese.[30] When Liu Yü-fen deposed Li Ch'ang-ch'ing, he acquired more or less uncontested control of Lanchow and the surrounding area, but his authority over the rest of the province was weak or nonexistent. Such a limited realm would not have satisfied Feng Yü-hsiang under any circumstances, but it was especially unsatisfactory when the war with Fengtien began to go badly and the security of the Kuominchün rear became a matter of vital concern. Liu Yü-fen therefore began to take steps to achieve complete control over Kansu.

In December Liu convened a conference in Lanchow attended by representatives of each of the leading warlords in the province. These representatives must certainly have been both amazed and appalled at the bold proposals made by Liu Yü-fen. Liu asserted that the Tupan of the province was, after all, in charge of provincial matters, and he listed a series of specific rules that all local militarists were expected to follow in order to make the Tupan's authority a reality. For the most part these regulations limited the independence of the warlords in recruiting, organizing, and training troops.[31] The conference participants all agreed with Liu's proposals. This, of course, was normal warlord procedure: everyone was always in favor of unity, peace, and obedience to constituted authority. In any event, the fighting ability of the Kuominchün was well-known, and there was also the memory of what had happened to Li Ch'ang-ch'ing. However, it was not in the warlord nature to relinquish independence so easily. The local militarists were willing to accept the form but not the reality of subordination, and some of them resolved to move against the Kuominchün at the first opportunity.

The steady retreat of the Kuominchün in Chihli provided that opportunity. The time seemed propitious for an uprising by the Kansu warlords not only because of the military troubles of the Kuominchün, but also because Wu P'ei-fu was urging several of them to revolt, an indication that they would have his support if it were needed. In May 1926 Chang Chao-chia and Han Yü-lu began a drive toward Lanchow from their headquarters in eastern Kansu. Not long afterward, K'ung Fan-chin and other Kansu warlords attacked the Kuo-minchün from the south. Western Kansu was largely in the hands of Muslim warlords, who stayed aloof from the war raging in the other sections.* The fighting was severe and prolonged. It was not until the end of August that the rebels were finally put down and Kuominchün authority extended over the regions south and east of Lanchow. To achieve this, Chang Chih-chiang had been forced to send large numbers of reinforcements to Liu Yü-fen. That he should do so in the midst of the Chihli struggle showed how much importance was attached to holding Kansu.[32]

The Kansu rebellion presented an additional difficulty for the Kuominchün at what was already a particularly trying time. But it was a catastrophe with far-reaching implications for the people of Kansu. To begin with, the province was not wealthy and had few agricultural resources. The burden of supporting thousands of additional troops and sustaining the hardships of weeks of war was therefore a very heavy one. In those areas where fighting took place, animals and carts were requisitioned in large numbers, and peasants were often forced to leave their homes to carry supplies or care for the animals. Even if a peasant had a draft animal, he was afraid to use it openly, and it therefore lost much of its utility.† But it was not the war alone that caused suffering in Kansu; nature also struck hard. There was drought in some parts of the province during the spring, and famine conditions appeared in several areas. Hailstorms destroyed a large portion of the crop in the most important grain-producing district of the province. (Much of the land elsewhere was taken up by poppy cultivation.) And on top of all this, the Kuominchün demonstrated its customary efficiency in collecting taxes.[33]

---

* An American botanist traveling in the Northwest reported that the Kuominchün authorities ordered Muslim generals in western Kansu to march against anti-Kuominchün troops in the southeastern portion of the province. If such orders were issued, the Muslims avoided any meaningful compliance. Such orders would have been extremely shortsighted, for bringing Muslim and Chinese units into armed conflict could have sparked a conflagration; it had happened before, and Kansu still showed the scars. It would happen again in 1928. (Despatches from C. E. Gauss, Consul General at Tientsin, to Frederick Mayer, chargé d'affaires ad interim: Jan. 27, 1927, 893.00/8388, and Jan. 29, 1927, 893.00/8389.)
† Warlord exploitation of the peasantry was so harsh and so various that one tends to forget that the peasant had a surprising capacity to resist through dissimulation. In July, for example, a Western writer in the NCH, July 26, 1926, p. 151, reported on the heartless requisitioning of animals in Kansu, but also told how the peasants often outwitted the soldiers: "There are a hundred mules hidden not far from where I write, and their hiding places are known to most everyone except the soldiers."

At the end of 1926, a foreign observer tried to sum up the chief results of the first year of Kuominchün rule in Kansu. First, he said, firm tactics have brought the entire province thoroughly under Kuominchün control; scarcely a dog dared bark against the Kuominchün. Second, Kuominchün rule brought heavy taxation, high living costs, and general dissatisfaction. Third, the bright expectations engendered by initial Kuominchün reforms remained largely unfulfilled. Schools were without funds; teachers had not been paid for months; most eleemosynary institutions were forced to close their doors, and those that remained open provided poor care.[34] Naturally this writer was unimpressed by what the Kuominchün leaders regarded as the most important achievement of their stay in Kansu: they had retained a regional base to which they could retreat when catastrophe, which seemed imminent, struck in the East.

Feng Yü-hsiang in the Soviet Union

Feng announced his resignation on January 1, 1926, and three days later departed for P'ingtich'uan, about 100 miles west of Kalgan.* He divided his time between that town and Paotow until March 16, when his motorcade started across the steppe to Urga, the Mongolian capital.[35] In Urga Feng regularly received reports of the military situation in northern China, and perhaps one reason why he remained there for over a month was the hope that the war might swing in his favor. But there was more than that hope involved. Feng's sojourn in Mongolia and his subsequent stay in the Soviet Union illustrate an aspect of the man that was of immense importance in shaping his attitude toward membership in the Kuomintang. Feng had become proficient in the ways of warlordism, but the Kuomintang that presented itself to him at the beginning of 1926 was not a warlord organization. If Feng was to operate effectively within it, he had to learn its organizational characteristics and processes, as well as its ideological features. Feng needed an education.

In 1926 Feng was in some ways still an unsophisticated peasant. His experience had been narrow and his education limited. He was 44 years old, and his entire life had been spent within the confines of the Chinese military system. Of course he had never left the country. Although it later turned out that the Kuomintang under Chiang Kaishek had some of the characteristics of a warlord organization, this similarity was not evident in 1926. A disciplined party interlocked

* On many maps P'ingtich'uan is now called Tsining or Chining.

with mass organizations, government by committees, apparent civilian domination over the military, emphasis on ideological questions, highly developed educational and propaganda sections—all of these things were alien to Feng. With defeat facing his army, Feng had to consider more seriously than ever before the advantages of joining the Kuomintang, but he also had to acknowledge the dangers. These lay in the possibility that Kuomintang workers might acquire influence over his troops, and in his own unfamiliarity with party politics. He was going to join the party near the top; that would obviously be the price for his participation. But he ran the risk of looking foolish, of losing all potential influence in the party by default, unless he mastered the concepts, vocabulary, and formalities of party operations. Therefore, in both Mongolia and the Soviet Union Feng not only sought cultural broadening like a dutiful tourist, but also tried to familiarize himself with the principles and processes required to operate effectively within the Kuomintang.

In Urga Feng was the typical tourist. He roamed through the city, and even beyond its outskirts, enchanted by the exotic sights. He was slightly shocked by the strange burial customs of the Mongols, and he shook his head at the nomad's propensity to relieve himself whenever and wherever nature called. Feng's observations about the computation of Mongol wealth in terms of livestock, the widespread consumption of fermented mare's milk, and other Mongol customs were in the best tradition of the wide-eyed tourist far from the comfortable normalities of home.

But the more serious side of his education also began in Urga. For Feng, Urga was the threshold of the Soviet Union, and much of his time he spent learning about that country. From Mongol leaders and Russian officials he heard the details of the Russian Revolution, the Bolshevik-Menshevik split, and the Soviet system of government. Feng studied the principles of Communist Party organization, and observed at first hand the operation of political institutions in Mongolia. A Mongol explained to him the history of the successive Communist Internationals. He also learned of the organization of the Kuomintang, its shortcomings, and the methods of the party's Central Executive Committee. Feng heard frequent lectures on Mongol revolutionary history, a subject on which both the Russians and the Mongols were eager to see Feng—the warlord of Inner Mongolia—acquire a "correct" view.

Feng's most frequent mentor was his chief Russian adviser, whom Feng habitually referred to as "Adviser Lin." Lin talked with Feng almost every day on some political topic, ranging from the world situation in general to various questions of revolutionary politics. Lin spent much time describing Lenin's role in Russian history, both as a theoretician and as a practitioner of revolution. In addition to these political subjects, Feng also spent some time studying the Russian language.[36]

In Mongolia, too, the advantages of Kuomintang membership continued to be impressed upon Feng. Hsü Ch'ien joined Feng's party in the Mongol capital, and did his best to impress the warlord with the discipline and dedication of the Kwangtung party.* Borodin and Yü Yu-jen also visited Feng in Urga, and added their persuasive voices to the chorus. Feng had been hearing their arguments for almost a year, although not in such a concerted fashion. But Feng's situation now was substantially different from the one he had enjoyed a year before, and this lent great cogency to the argument that he should be in the Kuomintang. So cogent was it that he finally decided to join, and to lead his army in the Northern Expedition in cooperation with the National Revolutionary Army.[31] A few weeks later, he sent two subordinates from Moscow to Canton to manage the details of his admission into the Kuomintang, and to arrange for cooperation between the Kuominchün and the National Revolutionary Army.

On April 27, Feng and his companions left Urga and motored north to what is today called Ulan Ude, where they boarded a train for the long journey to Moscow.† They arrived in the Russian capital

---

* Hsü Ch'ien was born in 1871 in Kiangsi. He obtained the highest degree in the old civil service system during the late Ch'ing, and during the last four years of the dynasty he did varied work in the field of law. He joined the Kuomintang in 1912, and served as Minister or Vice-Minister of Justice in some early Republican cabinets. In 1916 he became a Christian, and he often used the Christian name George. In 1920 Hsü visited Feng Yü-hsiang with a message from Sun Yat-sen. Feng thought highly of Hsü, and there was frequent contact between the two men after the Second Chih-Feng War, when Hsü was in Peking as head of the Russian Language School of Law and Government. Hsü had to leave Peking early in 1926; he went to Urga, met Feng, and accompanied him to the USSR. Subsequently, Hsü held some of the highest positions in the Kuomintang, but his career was destroyed in the Wuhan-Nanking split of 1927. (Some of this information about Hsü Ch'ien was taken from a rough biographical sketch of Hsü kindly loaned to me by Howard Boorman of the Research Project on Men and Politics in Modern China.)

† Among those who accompanied Feng to Moscow were: Hsü Ch'ien; Liu Chi, one of Feng's leading generals; Ho Ch'i-kung, confidential secretary to Feng and later mayor of Peking; Jen Yu-min, Feng's English-language secretary; and several officers. Yü Yu-jen went to Moscow while Feng was there and spent much time with him. Li Te-ch'üan was in the late stages of pregnancy, and remained in Urga. She gave birth to a son on May 8, and shortly after continued on to join her husband in Moscow.

on May 9. Soviet troops gave Feng a rousing welcome at the station, and in the following weeks he was received by many of the highest Russian leaders. Feng discussed the Chinese situation with Georgi Chicherin, Soviet Commissar of Foreign Affairs. To Mikhail Kalinin, President of the Central Executive Committee of the Soviet Union, Feng described his 1924 Peking coup d'etat, and heard in return about some of the difficulties encountered in setting up the Soviet government. When he was received by Kliment Voroshilov, Commissar of Defense, Feng was impressed by the simplicity of Voroshilov's surroundings and dress, which he naturally compared favorably with his own austere mode of life. Feng also visited the Commissar of Education, A. V. Lunacharsky, and Lenin's wife and co-worker, Nadyezhda Krupskaya. He visited Trotsky, who spoke to him about methods of revolution; Feng remained silent in order not to show his ignorance. Upon the invitation of Karl Radek, head of Sun Yat-sen University in Moscow, Feng delivered a speech to the students in which he compared several aspects of Chinese and Russian society to the advantage of the Russians. Feng visited other officials in both Moscow and Leningrad. Stalin was vacationing in the South, and therefore could not see Feng; but he sent his regrets.[38]

When Feng was not talking with Soviet leaders, he visited factories, schools, libraries, army and navy installations, recreation facilities, and so on. This again was Feng the conscientious tourist. He went to various museums, visited the zoo, investigated the water system, and complained sadly that he was unable to visit the company that handled garbage disposal. But this was tourism with a purpose. Feng's guides emphasized the progress that had been made since the Revolution. In this way they identified Communism with progress, and at the same time implied an analogy between Tsarist Russia and contemporary China: both were backward, but under Communism both could move rapidly ahead. And Feng was impressed. There was much that he did not understand, or understood only vaguely, in the Soviet Union, but he approved of what he considered a real concern for the workingman, the lack of corruption in government, and the industry of the workers. Feng's last thought on leaving the USSR was that the people he had met from all walks of life had been basically working people. Certainly Feng left the Soviet Union very favorably impressed by Russian society.[39]

More important than Feng's tourism and his courtesy calls on officials was his political education. The instruction that had begun in Urga was not even interrupted by the train journey to Moscow, and in that city "Adviser Lin" continued the regular talks about political problems and principles. In June Lin was replaced by a man whose surname was Sangurskii, who was to return to China with Feng using the pseudonym Wusmanoff. Wusmanoff, like his predecessor, regularly talked to Feng about politics. Or perhaps it would be more accurate to say that he instructed Feng in the Marxist interpretation of contemporary political problems. They ranged over many topics, including the nature of the Far Eastern revolution, current conditions in Western Europe, party organization, economic principles, the writings of Sun Yat-sen, revolutions and revolutionaries, the importance of cooperation between the army and the masses, and the nature of imperialism. Hsü Ch'ien and Yü Yu-jen occasionally spoke to Feng on similar subjects. Feng also read about some of these topics; the writings of Lenin, he asserted, showed him the importance of combining political experience with theoretical knowledge.[40]

There is little doubt that Feng was genuinely influenced by these discussions with his Russian advisers and Chinese friends. The themes of anti-imperialism and popular welfare were neither new nor alien to Feng, and their presentation as part of an ideological complex more comprehensive than any he had employed before greatly stimulated him.* Although he did not master Marxist principles of social analysis, he was impressed by the importance of theory, and he also respected the discipline and effectiveness of party activity that he had

---

* One example of the influence of Marxism on Feng, and of the extent of his understanding, is the plan for Chinese political reform that he drew up on July 23, 1926. The plan envisaged the following:

(1) The mass of the people are too poor. The state must therefore see to it that each family has property worth at least 10,000 yüan, which will enable them to improve their living conditions.

(2) Since rich families tend to become arrogant and dissolute, there must be restrictions on wealth. All those who have in excess of one million yüan must turn it over to the government for educational purposes.

(3) Those families who voluntarily turn over this excess should be rewarded. Those who flee the country or try to put their wealth in foreign banks should be punished according to law, or else lose their Chinese citizenship.

(4) An examination should be made of how each foreign loan has been used before it is repaid.

(5) Countries that abrogate the unequal treaties will be considered our friends. Those that not only abrogate their own unequal treaties, but help us persuade other countries to do likewise, will be considered our very warm friends.

(6) The capitalist educational system should be abolished.

(7) For the creation of a new China, it is necessary to work toward mechanization and electrification, and to develop science. (*Jihchi*, II, Chüan 7, pp. 50–51.)

observed in the Soviet Union. He recognized that each of these aspects of Soviet political activity had its counterpart in the practices and ideology of the Russian-sponsored Kuomintang, and that they would make it difficult indeed for him to attain leadership, or even to maintain his autonomy, within the framework of the party.

Feng kept a close watch on events in China while he was in the Soviet Union; his commanders telegraphed him regularly, and the Russians also kept him informed. Naturally he was concerned about the trend of events in northern China, and by the middle of July he had decided to return. It is not clear why he waited an additional month to depart, although quite possibly he was negotiating to obtain more military supplies.* He had discussed his military situation with Soviet military leaders shortly after his arrival in Moscow. But in the middle of August, Feng agreed to pay over six million rubles for military supples received before June 1, 1926, and another four-and-a-half million rubles for supplies yet to be delivered. Those receipts were signed on August 15, 1926.[41] The next day, Feng's army began its retreat from Nankow. And the day after that, Feng left Moscow to go home.

* It is conceivable that Feng remained in Moscow for medical reasons. He had several medical and dental examinations while in the Russian capital. Mao, *O-Meng*, pp. 78–79, says Feng had heart trouble.

9. The Northern Expedition

As soon as Feng reached China, he plunged into the formidable task of rejuvenating his army. By the end of 1926, he had reorganized his troops and moved them from Suiyuan through Kansu into Shensi, where he prepared to invade Honan to join the Kuomintang's Northern Expedition. In the spring of 1927, he invaded Honan and quickly gained control of the province. By that time the Kuomintang had split into two rival wings, each of which eagerly sought Feng's support. Feng joined Chiang Kai-shek and the Nanking group not only because their position was more powerful, but also because their political ideas were basically more compatible with his than were those of the Wuhan group. In late 1926 and early 1927, the Left Kuomintang and the Russians had pushed Feng farther left than he wanted to be. By siding with Nanking, Feng freed himself from that pressure, and incidentally struck a death blow to Russian aspirations in China. The Wuhan-Nanking split threw party affairs into such turmoil that the Northern Expedition could not be resumed on a large scale until the spring of 1928. Feng at that time commanded the Second Army Group, and his soldiers made a major contribution to the successful completion of the Northern Expedition, which brought at least nominal unity to the long-suffering country.

Army Problems

Feng Yü-hsiang's two emissaries to southern China, Li Ming-chung and Liu Chi, arrived in Canton on August 22, 1926. On the following day, the Kuomintang government publicly announced that Feng had been appointed Kuomintang representative in the Kuominchün, member of the National Military Council, and member of the National Government Council. A few weeks later, Feng returned to China. On September 16 he arrived at Wuyüan, in western Suiyuan, just north of the great bend of the Yellow River. The following day,

he formally accepted his posts in party and government, and swore
what he afterwards called the "Wuyüan Oath." On behalf of himself
and his troops, he vowed to fight to the death to arouse the masses, an-
nihilate the warlords, expel the imperialists, and preserve China's
freedom and independence.[1] With these formalities out of the way,
Feng turned to the pressing work at hand, the reorganization and supply of his army.

During the retreat from Nankow, Kuominchün units had scattered throughout Suiyuan and into Kansu. Han Fu-chü, with perhaps 20,000 men, was in easternmost Suiyuan. Shih Yu-san, with at
least a division, was in Paotow. A division of Kuominchün cavalry
had stopped at Chotzeshan on the Chahar-Suiyuan border, and another at T'aolin in western Chahar. During the Nankow retreat all
these units had formally enrolled under Shang Chen, Yen Hsi-shan's
chief lieutenant. Other units were in Wuch'uan and Kuyang, both
in eastern Suiyuan. Farther west, there were many troops in the vicinity of Wuyüan. Liu Ju-ming's division was at Lin Ho, near the
Kansu border, and Sun Lien-chung and his men were across the border in eastern Kansu. There were also individual stragglers and small
groups scattered over Suiyuan. Some of these turned to banditry;
some joined the Shensi army; others simply disappeared. But many
gradually made their way back to one of the larger Kuominchün
units. In addition to these troops, in Kansu there were the troops
under Liu Yü-fen who had originally been sent to garrison the province, and two other divisions that had been sent under Sun Liang-
ch'eng and Chang Wei-hsi to put down revolts by minor warlords.[2]

In this situation, Feng faced three major tasks. The first was to
reorganize. He had to reestablish the lines of communication and
subordination between himself and the scattered units. He also had
to try to replace the men lost during the Nankow struggle and the
subsequent retreat. The second task was to acquire supplies. Arms
and ammunition were needed, but food and clothing were essential,
particularly with winter imminent. Solving this problem would go
a long way toward solving the third one, which was to revive the
troops' morale. The extended struggle and the long, disorganized retreat had shattered their martial spirit, and Feng had to find means
to restore it. To tackle any of these problems, he had to have peace
for a while, and since most of the troops were still in Suiyuan, now
under Shansi, the attitude of Yen Hsi-shan was critical.

Yen had been fighting the Kuominchün since spring, and he was
still allied with the Fengtien and Shantung warlords. But Yen was

extremely jealous of his province's independence, and he was eager to keep his allies as well as his enemies at a healthy distance. On August 27, after the retreat of the Kuominchün from Nankow, Yen telegraphed Chang Tso-lin that Shansi troops had occupied P'ingtich'uan, that the Shansi army could now handle all military matters in the Northwest independently, and that neither the Fengtien nor the Shantung army need enter the region. On September 4 Chang Hsüeh-liang talked with Yen in Taiyüan, and they agreed that Suiyuan would be under Yen Hsi-shan's control, although Yen could call for Fengtien aid if he needed it. Four days later Shang Chen was appointed Tut'ung of Suiyuan.[3] Yen thus had a free hand in Suiyuan, where most of the Kuominchün troops could be found. However, Yen did not want to fight the Kuominchün for possession of Suiyuan as long as Feng's stay there seemed to be temporary, and as long as the Kuominchün stayed out of Shansi. And although Shang Chen might have liked more independent authority in Suiyuan, his forces were outnumbered by the Kuominchün units that had ostensibly come under his command. The Kuominchün was therefore able to rest and regroup in Suiyuan without harassment from September to November. At the end of the year, Fengtien troops entered Suiyuan to attack the remaining Kuominchün units, but by that time the main body of Feng's army was already gone.[4]

Perhaps the thorniest problem of reorganization that Feng met on his return was the fact that some Kuominchün units had transferred to the Shansi army, apparently in the belief that Feng's army had been destroyed as a military organization. Han Fu-chü and Shih Yu-san were the two most important officers who had ostensibly changed their allegiance; some Kuominchün leaders felt this proved their complete unreliability. However, their troops comprised an important part of the Kuominchün, and Feng was eager that they return to their old allegiance. After a month at Wuyüan, Feng went to Paotow, where he talked with the two men and their subordinate officers. Shih and Han finally agreed to return to the Kuominchün, and neither was condemned for having joined the Shansi army; their defection was interpreted as a tactical move to obtain supplies and security in a period of defeat. Three years later, when the same two officers deserted Feng at a more critical moment, this earlier defection began to be viewed more harshly.[5]

As Feng worked to bring all of his former units back under his control, he also had to face the more demanding task of supplying them. Most of the units were suffering from a lack of food, winter clothing, funds, arms, and miscellaneous equipment.[6] Feng looked in every direction for money and supplies. A local sheep raiser either volunteered or was forced to provide thousands of sheep without charge; these were used for both food and woolen coats. The city of Paotow and the surrounding countryside were squeezed by various taxes until "every possible penny had been extracted."[7] Feng negotiated with Shang Chen for both food and clothing, and may have received some supplies from him.[8] The Kuomintang government in Canton allotted 1,000,000 yüan a month to the Kuominchün, although Feng claims not to have received all of it.[9] Near the end of the year, a shipment of weapons arrived from the Soviet Union.[10] Evidently other supplies also continued to come to Feng through Kulun, although there are few details. Of course Kansu, the one province still under Feng's control, was called upon to send all the money, animals, men, and supplies it could.

From these various sources Feng obtained enough to outfit his troops, unit by unit, and send them westward. He spoke eloquently to as many of the troops as he could, and always briefed their officers very thoroughly. In this fashion he tried to convince his army that it had done well, and that in the future the soldiers would continue to do great things for themselves and their country. However, Feng's major efforts to revive his army's morale had to wait. The Kuominchün was now part of the Kuomintang military force, and it was scheduled to cooperate in the Northern Expedition. Feng's men were to move from Suiyuan westward into Kansu, then south into Shensi, from there eastward through T'ungkuan, the celebrated pass on the Shensi-Honan border, and then down the Yellow River valley to meet the Kuomintang troops. The combined Kuomintang-Kuominchün armies would then continue north against Chang Tso-lin and his allies. Since Kuomintang soldiers had already reached the Yangtze by the time Feng returned from the Soviet Union, time was pressing; Feng could not afford to give his weary men the rest that they needed. Before the Kuominchün could take its part in the Northern Expedition, it not only had to make a long and arduous march to Shensi, but also had to raise the siege of Sian.[11]

The Siege of Sian

Early in 1926 the Second Kuominchün in Honan was defeated by Wu P'ei-fu and the Red Spears. Some units were captured, others were dispersed, but one unit, commanded by Li Yün-lung, retreated

westward to Sian, where it was joined by a section of the Third Kuominchün under Yang Hu-ch'eng. Together the two groups numbered
about 20,000 men. On April 17 Liu Chen-hua, former Tupan of
Shensi, attacked the Kuominchün troops in Sian. Li and Yang resisted
strenuously, and the attacking soldiers gradually surrounded the city,
beginning a siege that was to last for almost eight months.

Liu Chen-hua took pains to seal Sian up tightly. He had a great
trench dug all around the city, and used the earth from the trench
to throw up breastworks six feet high and three feet thick. Moreover,
strategically located surrounding towns were occupied to obstruct
any force intent upon raising the siege. These measures were very
effective, and conditions within the city became more and more acute.
In October foreigners were finally permitted to leave the city, although some missionaries elected to remain at their posts. By the end
of October cannibalism was reported in the city, and during November deaths were reported to average 500 per day. Estimates of the
total who died because of the siege range from 15,000 to 35,000. No
matter what the correct figure, it is clear that the city suffered a terrible ordeal.[12]

Why did such undistinguished units put up such a determined
attack and such a stubborn defense? Because Liu Chen-hua's forces
were supplemented by Red Spear units under an ex-bandit leader
from Honan. The Red Spears were out for blood, particularly Shensi
blood. The normal antagonisms between the two provinces had been
exacerbated by years of civil war, during which each province had
been invaded by troops from the other. The Red Spears were intent
upon avenging not only the Second Kuominchün's misgovernment
in Honan, but past Shensi cruelties as well.* Their leader was reported to have vowed that no person above ten years of age would
leave the city alive. Be that as it may, it is clear the attackers did not
follow usual warlord procedure, which would have been to leave an
avenue of escape, so that the defenders could conveniently lose the
battle, but save their lives. The defending officers knew that either

---

* It was said that in earlier struggles, when Shensi troops entered Honan, they
sometimes gave the "egg test" to people they encountered. They would hold up
an egg and ask the victim to name it. If the answer was "t'an," he was released,
for this was the pronunciation in the Shensi dialect. If, however, he responded
"tan," the Honan pronunciation, he was killed on the spot. Honan troops in
Shensi allegedly followed the same procedure, but used a circle drawn in the dust
instead of an egg (Chang Yün-chia, pp. 98–99).

surrender or defeat would mean their death, and therefore they refused to capitulate.[13]

The Kuominchün troops in the best position to aid Sian were
those that had earlier been sent to Kansu to fight Chang Chao-chia
and the other Kansu rebels. They could move fairly quickly into
Shensi through the river valleys that link it to eastern Kansu. Sun
Liang-ch'eng, in P'ingliang, was named Commander of the Forces to
Aid Shensi, and marched through Pinchow and Tatao toward Sian.
Chang Wei-hsi's division, at Tienshui, was sent through Lunghsien
and P'ingyang to cover Sun Liang-ch'eng's right flank. Still other
units were sent close behind Sun's troops to render help if needed.[14]

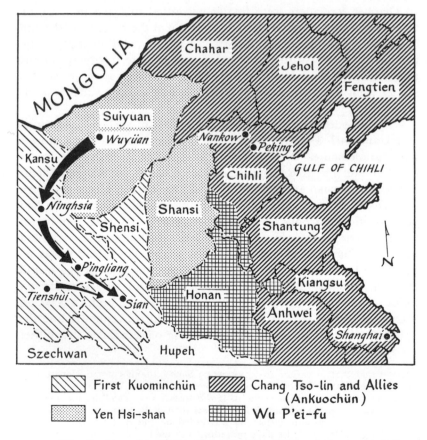

MAP 3. Distribution of territory, Jan. 1, 1927. Arrows show route of Kuominchün retreat from Suiyuan and invasion of Shensi.

After a month of hard fighting, Sun and his fellow commanders drove off the besiegers and ended the siege on November 28.[15] The victories in Shensi yielded booty of "innumerable" rifles and field guns, which helped alleviate Feng's arms shortage.[16] Feng specifically ordered Sun Liang-ch'eng to pursue the enemy forces relentlessly to make sure they did not regroup and resume hostilities. By the end of the year all of Liu Chen-hua's troops had fled eastward into Honan.[17] All during the raising of the siege and the routing of Liu Chen-hua's adherents, the remainder of the Kuominchün was making the long march from Suiyuan through Kansu and into Shensi.

Feng Yü-hsiang himself remained in Suiyuan until November, organizing and inspiring his men, and starting them off. On November 18 he went from Paotow to Wuyüan, where he stayed for six days. He then continued westward, and about a week later he arrived in Ninghsia, where he learned that the siege of Sian had ended. He did not leave Ninghsia until mid-December, when he drove quickly south to P'ingliang. He left there in January, and arrived in Sian late in the month. In each of these places, Feng's work was the same. As his marching units arrived and departed, Feng took roll, checked their equipment, and, most important, talked to them. Day after day he spoke to selected groups of officers and men, always trying to raise their spirits and give them some justification for the hardships of recent months.[18] Certainly the results justified Feng's efforts and hopes. The army, which had been about to disintegrate when he returned to China in September, was again unified physically and spiritually. It effected with remarkable speed and efficiency an arduous march of almost a thousand miles. The Kuominchün was again in a position to vie for national power, but now it would do so under a new political organization and with new political methods and goals.

Political Changes in the Kuominchün

Feng's membership in the Kuomintang naturally meant that Kuominchün political indoctrination had to be brought into line with that of the established Kuomintang armies. A sprinkling of Russian advisers, Chinese Communists, and Left Kuomintang personnel were with Feng to give substance to the new political orientation, and the period between Feng's Wuyüan Oath and May 1927 therefore saw a leftist swing in army indoctrination and in the administration of Feng's territories. Material conditions and Feng Yü-hsiang's vigilance prevented the Kuominchün from going so far left that Feng would lose control of it, although some local civil organs had begun to get out of hand by the spring of 1927.

One of Feng's first moves after his return from the Soviet Union was to establish a Political Department to handle political and propaganda work among the people and in the Kuominchün. Liu Po-chien, a graduate of the Far Eastern University in the Soviet Union and an avowed Communist, was in charge of it. The Political Department was dominated by Communists until the crisis in Wuhan-Nanking relations in the spring of 1927.[19]

Under the general supervision of the Political Department, a political office was set up in each army (*chün*), in each division, and in each brigade; a political officer was appointed to each regiment, battalion, company, and platoon; and a political cell was organized in each platoon (*p'ai*). The overall distribution and number of personnel is not completely clear. On the one hand, each political office was supposed to have between twenty and forty men, presumably including clerical and other staff workers.[20] On the other hand, Feng ordered that twenty propaganda officers be assigned to each division to work full time at political propaganda.[21] Probably these officers were really part of the political office complements or were among the individual officers in units below brigade level.

Rapid creation of this political organization required qualified personnel who were simply not available in Feng's forces. Some political workers were therefore sent to the Kuominchün by the Canton government. Moreover, the Chung Shan Academy was established in Sian to train political workers. University students, many of whom were members of Communist youth organizations, came for training. Most of the teachers also were Communists.[22] The school poured out a stream of political officers, but there is no way of knowing the total number of graduates. Although political activity was most intense and probably most effective in Shensi, where it was under the immediate surveillance of Liu Po-chien, Feng also sent orders to his officers in Kansu to organize political training.[23]

The political officers emphasized the need to overthrow imperialism, to destroy the unequal treaties, to realize Sun Yat-sen's Three Principles, and to save and support the common people, although the last point was formulated with hints of a class antagonism that was never present in Feng's earlier cult of the *lao-pai-hsing*.[24] The Political Department employed several means to get these ideas across to Feng's soldiers. Reading centers, or libraries, were set up for the men, and stocked with books, pamphlets, newspapers, and other materials. This was doubtless the least important method; since most soldiers were illiterate or semiliterate, the primary approach had to be oral. Therefore the political workers were supposed to schedule discussion meetings and political classes, and have propaganda plays acted by a newly established theatrical group. Although all of these techniques were employed to some degree, it is likely that the most widely used and most important methods of indoctrination were lectures and the repetition of slogans.

The reasons why slogans were used intensively are obvious. They could be repeated or chanted in unison while the men marched or worked. They could be posted everywhere—on boards and walls, over doors, in mess halls—and virtually everyone could and would learn the few characters required to read them. Most important, the slogans were easy to understand and memorize, and the meaning and implications could be spelled out in detail by the officers when necessary. The Kuominchün continued to use its time-tested standbys: "Love the people," "Do not molest the people," "Be frugal," and others of similar character. But during this time—September 1926 to May 1927—Feng stressed new slogans: "Politicize the army," "Eliminate corrupt bureaucratic practices," and "Stop giving only lip service to laws and rules." In the spring of 1927 breast patches were distributed bearing the slogan "We are sworn to the death to abolish the unequal treaties."[25]

Songs and catechisms fall into the same general category as slogans. To the repertoire of old songs, which dealt with such things as hygiene and methods of rifle firing, were added new songs that explained the Three Principles of the People, or listed China's humiliations by the imperialists. Feng ordered the use of the following training song in the spring of 1928, and it therefore does not specifically illustrate the indoctrination of the leftist period here under discussion, but it is the kind of training song used throughout the history of the Kuominchün.[26]

> Our nation was founded on agriculture.
> The six grains support the life of the people.
> We depend on it for all our food and clothing.
> This must be clearly recognized.
> In spring the shoots in the field are burgeoning.
> Keep to the center of the road when marching.
> Everyone will avoid trampling the shoots.
> Thus the masses will welcome us everywhere.

New catechisms were created, and old ones modified to accommodate the new political flavor of the Kuominchün. Feng Yü-hsiang considered this method of indoctrination to be very important, and or-

dered officers to conduct catechisms every morning, whether in camp
or on the march. Here is one that was used in the spring of 1927:[27]

Q. Whose troops are you?
A. We are troops of the lao-pai-hsing.
Q. Why do we want to wage war?
A. In order to abolish the unequal treaties.
Q. Whom do you want to fight?
A. We want first to overthrow the traitorous warlords, and second, to over-
   throw imperialism.
Q. Are you well-prepared?
A. We have long been well-prepared.
Q. In what ways are you prepared?
A. First, we understand [revolutionary] doctrine. Second, we have made sac-
   rifices.
Q. Comrades, it is difficult for all of you.
A. We are serving the revolution.

The following illustrates how an old catechism could be amended;
nothing was removed or changed, but something new was added. Indeed, this single addition illustrates quite well the nature and extent
of the changes in the political training of Feng's army after his return from the Soviet Union.* After inspecting a unit Feng took the
role of questioner in this catechism.[28]

Q. Who are our fathers and mothers?
A. The lao-pai-hsing.
Q. Who are our younger brothers and elder brothers?
A. The lao-pai-hsing.
Q. Who are our relatives?
A. The lao-pai-hsing.
Q. Who are our neighbors?
A. The lao-pai-hsing.
Q. When you are no longer soldiering, you will return home and be what
   kind of person?
A. Lao-pai-hsing.

Feng then stopped, praised the men for the facility of their re-
sponses, and spent a few moments emphasizing the message of the
catechism. Then he added another series of questions and answers:

Q. Why do we wage war?
A. In order to overthrow imperialism, the traitorous warlords, grasping and
   corrupt officials, local bullies, and bad gentry.

---

* In the appendix is a translation of a document used in the Kuominchün for
political indoctrination, including a long catechism that reflects in some detail the
character of political teaching in Feng's army at that time.

Q. Why are we working for revolution?
A. In order to establish a clean government.
Q. Do you think this [random] soldier could be a hsien-chang [head of a county]?
A. No.
Q. Why can't he?
A. He is illiterate.
Q. Why is he illiterate?
A. Because he did not go to school.
Q. Why did he not go to school?
A. Because he did not have money.
Q. Why did he not have money?
A. Because he was fleeced by imperialism, the traitorous warlords, the grasping and corrupt officials, the local bullies, and the bad gentry.

In addition to learning verbal formulas, the troops were required to attend lectures or semiformal talks. The political officer, for example, might choose to explain one of Sun's Three Principles in depth, or to elaborate some other Kuomintang tenet. At times he dealt with more immediately practical questions, such as the pernicious consequences of stealing peasants' chickens. A more frequent speaker was the unit commander, whose talks usually dealt with such mundane subjects as personal hygiene or how to plant land mines, but also included analyses of Sun's Will and similar political subjects. And any unit in the vicinity of headquarters could expect occasionally to see Feng Yü-hsiang himself come to talk to the officers, the noncommissioned officers, or the rank and file. To be sure, by this time Feng's army had grown much too large for him to maintain much personal contact with the men in the ranks. But Feng assiduously cultivated his relationship with his officers. Almost every day, and often two, three, or four times a day, Feng addressed a group of officers. In this way, he attempted to maintain the ties that strengthened his officers' loyalty to him personally.[29] Feng's talks dealt, as they always had, with a wide range of practical subjects. However, after September 1926, his political and inspirational topics differed somewhat from those he had talked about before his trip to the Soviet Union.

Feng frequently spoke about some aspect of the Three Principles of the People, or of Sun's Will. And just as he had earlier established himself as the arbiter of what was good Christianity, he quickly became the army's expert on the legacy of Sun Yat-sen's thought and on the history of the revolution. Moreover, he used Sun's thought and the Revolution of 1911 as symbols to cultivate spirit, pride of purpose, and dedication, in much the way he had formerly made use of Christianity. Indeed, from this time Christianity no longer played the central role in Kuominchün indoctrination that it had up to 1926. Feng had been attracted to Christianity by its practical effects: no foot-binding, no opium smoking, and so forth. He thought it could be used "to save the country," or at least give the Kuominchün the moral capacity to save the country. By 1927, however, the politically articulate had decided that more radical ideas were necessary to "save the country," and Feng was greatly influenced by this shift of opinion. Moreover, Feng had been disappointed by the Christian response to the May 30th Incident.[30] Most important, Feng had been forced to accept Kuomintang ideology into his army. This carried with it the danger that his army's loyalty could be transferred to Kuomintang leaders. Because of this, and because Kuomintang ideology was in some ways even better than Christianity for instilling his troops with fervor, Feng met the danger by becoming a spokesman and interpreter for Kuomintang ideology. Sun Yat-sen now assumed the role in Kuominchün indoctrination and in Feng's speeches that had previously been reserved for God. In any event, Feng could not employ Christianity very extensively in his army after late 1926, because he had recruited Muslims in the northwest, particularly in Kansu. They were more sensitive and singleminded about religious matters than the average Chinese, and the administration of the army had to become religiously neutral.,

After Feng's return from the Soviet Union, he also revealed a new view of his own past. Association with Russian revolutionaries, instruction by Russian and Left Kuomintang revolutionaries, and entry into China's pioneer revolutionary party all gave Feng a new revolutionary self-consciousness, and when he looked at his own career in this light, he found it rich in revolutionary history. Feng's discovery that there was such a thing as revolutionary method led directly to the discovery that he had always been acting more or less in accord with it. In other words, Feng discovered what a malleable thing history can be. It was from this time that Feng began to stress his revolutionary background; the chief events of his early career—the Luanchow revolt, participation in the Szechwan struggle in 1916, and so forth—all became chapters in his revolutionary history, even if some of them had to be somewhat modified to fit into it appropriately. Feng even found that he had always admired Sun Yat-sen and his ideas. With such a solidly revolutionary background, it was natural for Feng to assume the role of an authority on revolution in his talks to his officers and men.

Of course, the Kuomintang and Communist political workers in Feng's organization sought to organize the civilian population as well as to indoctrinate Feng's troops, and Feng's Kuomintang status compelled him to cooperate in that undertaking. As his army passed through eastern Kansu on its way to Shensi, every effort was made to indoctrinate the population along the route in the principles and aims of the Kuomintang revolution.* Once settled at Sian, Feng ordered any of his units that went to areas where no district party organizations or peasant unions were established to act quickly to set them up. Military personnel were to render all possible aid and support to workers' organizations. Where party or mass organizations were already in existence, Feng's men were to establish close relations, provide them with material aid such as printing equipment and funds, and generally do everything possible to promote their activity.[31] Under this stimulus, party affairs and the mass movement developed rapidly in Shensi and Kansu, and all regions the Kuominchün controlled were sprinkled with peasant unions, labor organizations, women's societies, and youth groups.[32]

It is hard to say what Feng expected from these various organizations, but it is certain that he soon became irritated and unhappy about their activities. Feng liked order. He wanted to talk about revolution in fiery terms and spur his listeners to provide funds, join his army, unbind the feet of their daughters, stop smoking opium, and spread the word about the patriotic virtues of the Kuominchün. If the public wanted to revolt, that was fine, but they should revolt according to Feng's detailed instructions. Certainly they should not arbitrarily seize land, or kill or expel officials. Yet the mass organizations no sooner became active than they began to agitate for policies more extreme than Feng had anticipated, and they were also involved in several violent incidents. The peasant associations seemed particularly unruly to Feng, but disorder struck even the Chinese household when, according to Feng, women insisted that their husbands share the housework. All of these developments were ominous

---

* Some of the same techniques used to indoctrinate the troops were used to propagandize civilians, including, of course, the extensive use of slogans. One of Feng's political advisers told the story of an old woman who heard someone read a slogan from a wall poster that urged "Down with opportunists!" ("Ta-tao t'ou-chi fen-tzu!") The old woman, interpreting this in terms of her own life, understood "t'ou" to be "to steal" and "chi" to mean "chicken," and she said in a very satisfied manner: "The National Revolutionary Army is really excellent. They are also going to overthrow those who steal chickens." ("T'ou chi-ti fen-tzu yeh yao ta-tao le.") Chien, Hsi-pei, p. 16.

and disturbing to Feng, but he took no major action against mass organizations or excessive leftism before the invasion of Honan.[33]

From the time he arrived in Sian, in the beginning of 1927, Feng busily prepared to launch that invasion. However, he still suffered from very limited financial and material resources. In March he claimed that the Kuomintang government had earlier promised him 1,000,000 yüan per month, but had reduced its commitment to 300,000 on the grounds that Feng also had the resources of Kansu and Shensi. Feng lamented that even this reduced allotment was not received regularly.[34] Feng probably exaggerated the amount by which his allotment was reduced, and also the irregularity of its delivery; he apparently received 600,000 yüan per month.[35] However, he was on firmer ground when he claimed that his two provinces were not rich to begin with, and had been squeezed dry by a succession of rapacious warlords. Shensi in particular had been drained of wealth, and Feng demanded heavy contributions from Kansu, which caused much dissatisfaction among that province's people.[36] He also turned to the printing press, producing 20,000,000 yüan of military scrip that was forced upon the unhappy populace. A few months later, after having acquired the resources of Honan, Feng is said to have redeemed this scrip for more desirable cash.[37]

In such a situation, the Russian contribution was important to Feng. The Russians supplied arms and ammunition, sending them from Kulun to Ninghsia, and then on to Sian and other points.[38] The amount of the supplies was small, and transportation of them costly and difficult, so that Feng could not consider the Russian aid to be a primary source of supply.[39] Nevertheless, Russian help was significant, particularly during the retreat from Suiyuan, when few other sources were available. Feng is reported to have acknowledged that without Russian supplies, especially the ammunition, his army could never have fought its way into Shensi.[40] Moreover, Feng's complaints notwithstanding, some supplies were shipped to him from the Russian-sponsored government at Wuhan after he reached Sian.[41] Of course, Russians also continued to help Feng with their knowledge and experience. Wusmanoff and a few other Russians served as advisers, and Feng frequently consulted Wusmanoff as he prepared for the Honan campaign, the push that would bring him for the first time into contact with Kuomintang armies.

Northern Expedition: Canton to the Yangtze

The Kuomintang was little more than a weak and opportunistic clique before 1923–24, when it was transformed with Russian assistance into a vital, disciplined party that had its own revolutionary army, and was linked with the people through mass organizations. The price for this rejuvenation was to accept Russian advisers in party and military work, and to admit Chinese Communists into the Kuomintang. In this fashion, seeds of rupture were planted in Sun Yat-sen's party; the Kuomintang moderates and conservatives feared that the Russians and Communists might change the character and goals of the Kuomintang, or seize control of it. This potential for conflict in the party was contained as long as Sun Yat-sen lived, but after his death in March 1925 events accelerated toward a crisis.

The Russians, their left-wing Kuomintang protégés, and the Chinese Communists drew their chief support from the mass organizations, labor unions, and peasant associations, which expanded in membership during 1925 and 1926. The only element in the party that could compete effectively with this leftist strength was the military, and the right wing therefore looked to the generals. In March 1926 General Chiang Kai-shek proved that this was not a misplaced hope by carrying out a military coup in Canton that frightened and confused the Left, drove the chief of party and government, Wang Ching-wei, from the country, and prepared the way for a meeting of the Kuomintang Central Executive Committee to "readjust party affairs." The meeting took place in May; it set limits on Communist activity in the Kuomintang, and also named Chiang Kai-shek head of the party and commander-in-chief of the Northern Expedition. But Chiang was not ready for a complete break with the Communists. He needed better financial and political conditions, which, hopefully, would result from the Northern Expedition, and cooperation by the mass organizations was necessary to assure that the Northern Expedition would succeed. He therefore soothed the Russians and Communists by declaring that the whole incident had been a mistake. The Left, in turn, in order to conciliate Chiang, threw its support behind preparations for the Northern Expedition.

The first military act by the Northern Expedition was to dispatch units to support T'ang Sheng-chih. T'ang had been a garrison commander at Hengchow, in southern Hunan, under the Tupan Chao Heng-t'i. Chao was one of Wu P'ei-fu's men. Early in 1926 T'ang succumbed to Kuomintang blandishments, declared himself in favor of the southern cause, and marched against his erstwhile colleagues and superiors. Chao Heng-t'i quickly left the province, but Wu P'ei-fu, then preoccupied in the North with the attack on Nankow, sent reinforcements to Hunan that finally forced T'ang Sheng-chih to retreat and to seek assistance. The units sent by Chiang Kai-shek to support

T'ang marked the beginning of the Northern Expedition; together with T'ang's troops they effectively cleared Hunan of Wu P'ei-fu supporters by the end of July. T'ang was appointed head of the provincial government. In August the Nationalists thrust into Hupeh, and by the middle of the following month the province was conquered; the one exception was Wuchang, which resisted siege until October 10.

After the conquest of Hupeh, the Nationalists had two alternatives. They could continue north through Honan, join Feng's Kuominchün, and together march to Peking, after which an army could be sent back to dispose of Sun Ch'uan-fang in the central coastal provinces. The other possibility was to attack Sun Ch'uan-fang first, and advance toward Peking only after no enemies were left in central China. Chiang Kai-shek favored the second course of action, because the first would allow Sun Ch'uan-fang to attack the rear of the Northern Expedition north of the Yangtze, and also because Chiang wanted to control Nanking and Shanghai before going further.

Chiang Kai-shek's first target was Nanchang, the capital of Kiangsi and a key to the eastern provinces. The battle for Nanchang was long and costly to both sides, but the city finally fell on November 9. Within a few days the entire province was in Chiang's grasp. Sun Ch'uan-fang hurried north to ask for help from Chang Tso-lin; they decided that Shantung troops under Chang Tsung-ch'ang should enter Kiangsu and Anhwei to prevent further Nationalist advances. But the Nationalist offensive was relentless. Fukien was taken with little difficulty by the end of December. The Nationalists had to fight for Chekiang during early February 1927, but the province fell by the middle of the month, and the road to Shanghai beckoned. In March Nanking and Shanghai were captured by the Nationalists. This ended the first military phase of the Northern Expedition, and prepared the stage for a political crisis.

While Chiang Kai-shek was at the front directing the Northern Expedition, the Communists and Left Kuomintang in Canton had been working to regain the ground they had lost during the spring. They had made successful efforts to strengthen the organization of the left wing in the Nationalist government, and, more important, had continued to expand the labor and peasant movements. In December the so-called Joint Council was formed in Wuhan to function as a government until all the party and government organizations could be transferred from Canton to Wuhan. The Joint Council was a left-wing organ, guided by Mikhail Borodin, chief Russian adviser in China. Disagreements promptly broke out between the Council and Chiang Kai-shek over finance, the location of the capital, and military strategy. Thus there ensued a tug of war between Chiang, then at Nanchang, and the left wing at Wuhan.

While Chiang debated long-distance with the Joint Council at Wuhan, he also continued to act. When government and party personnel reached Nanchang on the way to Wuhan, they remained there, allegedly agreeing that the location of the capital should be decided by a plenum of the Central Executive Committee to be convened at Nanchang. During this time Chiang was carrying out his expedition in the eastern provinces. However, the leftists were not idle either. They finally succeeded in having the plenum of the Central Executive Committee meet in Wuhan in March 1927, and its decisions further consolidated the left-wing grip on the government. In effect, they reversed the measures pushed through by Chiang after his coup a year earlier, and thus brought Chiang back under the control of the government. In addition, Wuhan had acquired the military support of T'ang Sheng-chih, who looked upon Chiang as a rival and potential enemy.

By the end of March, political relations between Chiang and Wuhan were extremely tense, and T'ang Sheng-chih was at the center of a military group opposed to Chiang and presumably loyal to Wuhan. On April 12 Chiang launched a bloody attack upon the Communists and labor organizations of Shanghai. The reign of terror was shortly extended to other cities. Communists, Left Kuomintang, and Russians at Wuhan, as well as Russian leaders in Moscow, denounced Chiang as a counterrevolutionary tool of imperialism, and put a price on his head. Chiang responded by setting up a new government on April 18 at Nanking. The split in the party was complete.

The left portion of the split—the Communist–Left Kuomintang coalition at Wuhan—had suffered from several sources of confusion and conflict during the first three months of 1927. For example, some Left Kuomintang leaders questioned the advisability of the close links with the Communists and the Russians. Some Communists, too, felt that their party should act independently of the Kuomintang. There was also disagreement about whether it was necessary or even desirable to sponsor agrarian revolt, or, indeed, whether the peasants could be restrained from bluntly carrying out the slogans that the Communists had used to inspire the peasant movement. And the situation was further confused by the Russian leaders, who, in trying to guide the Chinese revolution from Moscow, paid less attention to Chinese realities than to the effects of the China issue on their domestic power struggles. There was also disagreement about the so-called Second Northern Expedition—the military campaign to conquer China north of the Yangtze. One group, led by Borodin and T'ang Sheng-chih, maintained that the expedition should be launched promptly, so that control of the North would fall to Wuhan rather than to Nanking. The Comintern representative M. N. Roy was the leading spokesman for the contention that the revolution should be consolidated in central China first, and that only then should the conquest of the North be attempted.

T'ang Sheng-chih favored the Second Northern Expedition for several reasons. His most immediate goals were simply territory and troops. The acquisition of Honan would bring not only another province under his sway, but a province somewhat removed from the center of social agitation at Wuhan. Moreover, during his participation in the first phase of the Northern Expedition, T'ang had absorbed so many defeated troops that his army had expanded to nearly ten times its former size; he expected a great increase in Honan also. The long-range gains that would follow the seizure of Peking were almost inestimable. In the middle of April the Wuhan government decided to support the Second Northern Expedition, and T'ang promptly began deploying his forces for an offensive along the Peking-Hankow railroad.

Feng Yü-hsiang had played little part in the fight between Wuhan and Nanking. T'ang Sheng-chih had tried to persuade him to take a stand against Chiang Kai-shek early in 1927, but Feng had refused. Nevertheless, there was no indication that Feng was not loyal to the government at Wuhan, which expected him to participate in the Second Northern Expedition. The Wuhan authorities appointed Feng commander-in-chief of the Second Army Group, and ordered him to move his army eastward along the Lunghai railroad to cooperate with T'ang Sheng-chih in the conquest of Honan. Feng, of course, had been preparing for just such a campaign. He had divided his forces into six armies, and had settled on his battle plans.[42] He had also sent propaganda teams into western Honan to persuade the soldiers and populace to support the Kuominchün, a method that had not previously been used by Feng, but had been used with great success by the National Revolutionary Army during the Northern Expedition to the Yangtze. On May 1 Feng accepted Wuhan's assignment, and a few days later his troops started east. By the 10th, they reached

MAP 4. Battle for Honan, May 7, 1927. Feng Yü-hsiang was just beginning his invasion of Honan from T'ungkuan. Loyang was in the hands of one of Wu P'ei-fu's generals. Fengtien troops, who had entered Honan from Chihli in order to resist the Kuomintang advance, had extended their control south along the railroad to the region of Suip'ing. The Wuhan army, under the overall command of T'ang Sheng-chih, was near Chumatien, preparing to march north.

the outskirts of Loyang, held by Chang Chih-kung, one of Wu P'ei-fu's generals, who resisted the Kuominchün attack. Feng's men surrounded the city without engaging in any pitched battles.

In the meantime, Wuhan troops had taken the offensive in southern Honan. Although T'ang was commander-in-chief of the Wuhan troops in this sector, the main thrust of the attack was carried out by Chang Fa-k'uei and his celebrated "Ironsides" troops, some of the best troops in China. The fighting capacities of these crack units were

MAP 5. Battle for Honan, May 27, 1927. On May 10 the Kuominchün launched an offensive to capture Loyang. One after another, the surrounding towns fell, and Loyang was finally taken on May 26. The road to Chengchow was open. In mid-May Wuhan troops initiated the siege of Suip'ing, but did not capture it until June 24. In the meantime, Wuhan troops went around the city and continued north. After three days of battle, they took Shangtsai on May 17, but suffered cruel casualties. At the same time, Wuhan troops fought a severe battle over Hsip'ing, which they finally captured. After about a week of hard fighting, Wuhan troops captured Yench'eng on May 27.

put to the test by the rugged Manchurian soldiers of the Fengtien army. The Wuhan soldiers moved northward from one victory to another, but at a terrible price in casualties for each advance. The battle for Shangtsai went on for three days, occasionally becoming very fierce, until the Fengtien troops retreated on May 17, having inflicted heavy losses on Wuhan. Hsip'ing also fell on the 17th, after several days of stubborn Fengtien resistance. After five days of hard fighting, Wuhan troops occupied Yench'eng on May 27, and on the

MAP 6. Battle for Honan, June 1, 1927. Wuhan troops captured Linying on May 28, after one of the bloodiest warlord battles to that time, and captured Hsüch'ang on May 29. As the Fengtien army retreated, it destroyed the railway bridges, which so slowed down the Wuhan army that it did not reach Chengchow until June 1, by which time both Chengchow and Kaifeng were firmly in the hands of Feng Yü-hsiang. Feng had moved swiftly eastward, meeting little opposition from the northward-fleeing Fengtien troops, and had occupied Chengchow on May 30.

same day southern units attacked Linying, the Fengtien army's strongest point along the Peking-Hankow Railway. The fight the next morning was said to have been one of the bloodiest of the era. Wuhan units occupied the city that afternoon; the next day the southerners took Hsüch'ang. At this point the Fengtien army decided to give up the region south of the Yellow River. They began a rapid retreat, destroying some railroad bridges in the process, to the north of the river, and made no attempt to defend Chengchow.[43] The Fengtien defeat might have been much more complete, perhaps might even have opened the way to a prompt continuation of the Northern Expedition, if Yen Hsi-shan had cooperated with the anti-Fengtien armies as he had promised. But Yen did not move, despite several wires from Feng urging him to.[44]

The Wuhan losses in the Honan campaign were greater than in any other phase of the Northern Expedition since it had left Canton. As is usual for wars of this period, precise casualty figures are almost impossible to obtain. However, an official of the Rockefeller Foundation who helped provide medical care for wounded soldiers was informed that there were 10,000 wounded men in Wuhan alone. Allegedly, these included only those who were wounded in the arms or legs, and therefore the total number of casualties was presumably much larger. One observer estimated there were 40,000 casualties in all. The most reliable figure is probably 14,000, cited by Wang Ching-wei only two weeks after the end of the campaign. That would be about twenty per cent of the Wuhan forces.[45] Thus by the time the Fengtien army decided to retreat north of the Yellow River, the Wuhan army was battered, bleeding, and appreciably reduced in strength. And although Fengtien soldiers no longer obstructed the road to Chengchow, Feng Yü-hsiang was racing for that city from the west.

While T'ang Sheng-chih's army was clawing its way up the Peking-Hankow Railway, Feng's men had remained near Loyang, which was finally taken on May 26. The road to Chengchow and Kaifeng was clear for the Kuominchün, which hurried eastward to occupy them on May 31 and June 1, respectively. Feng suffered about 400 casualties during the entire campaign.[46] When Wuhan soldiers arrived at Chengchow on June 1, they found the city firmly in Kuominchün hands; there was some disagreement over who reached Kaifeng first, but Feng's men kept the city. In short, after T'ang Sheng-chih's army had made all of the sacrifices, Feng gathered in the spoils. He now bestrode the Peking-Hankow Railway, and anyone who hoped to push a campaign against the northern warlords would first have to deal with Feng. Moreover, in both Loyang and Chengchow Feng's men found large stocks of weapons and ammunition.

Feng and the Party Split

As the Wuhan-Nanking split gradually widened in early 1927, Feng Yü-hsiang scrupulously avoided publicly favoring either party, although it was generally thought that he was in the Wuhan camp.

Indeed, after Chiang's Shanghai coup in April 1927, the Russians in Moscow as well as in Wuhan somewhat pathetically counted upon Feng to replace Chiang Kai-shek as their chief military supporter. Feng to all appearances accepted that role; he took the post of commander-in-chief of the Second Army Group when the Wuhan government offered it, and he took the part in the Honan campaign that Wuhan assigned him. But these actions were based primarily on military considerations. Feng wanted to control Honan if possible, and, like all warlords, preferred to have an official title to make things respectable. He certainly did not denounce Chiang Kai-shek in the uncompromising terms used by the Wuhan leaders. On the contrary, Feng sent telegrams to both sides urging unity, and stressing the evil that a continued split would cause for the revolution and the country.[47] And when the Honan campaign ended with Feng secure in key northern portions of the province, he sent announcements of his victory with grand impartiality both to Wuhan and to Nanking. Then Feng conferred with both sides in rapid succession to see what they had to offer.

Between June 10 and 12 top Wuhan leaders met with Feng at Chengchow. Wang Ching-wei, who had returned to China at the beginning of April and had been restored to his leading position in the government and the party, brought with him other members of the Presidium of the Political Council of the Kuomintang: T'an Yen-k'ai, Sun Fo, Hsü Ch'ien, and Ku Meng-yu. Yü Shu-te, a Communist who was involved in Kuominchün political work, Teng Yen-ta, Chief of the Political Bureau of the Kuomintang, T'ang Sheng-chih, and Yü Yu-jen were also there. Feng was in a very advantageous position at this conference, largely because of his favorable military situation. His army outnumbered T'ang Sheng-chih's, and T'ang's forces had been weakened by the Honan campaign. Active hostility from Feng would therefore have been catastrophic for Wuhan. If Feng were to withdraw from Wuhan and act independently, it would still present the Wuhan government with great difficulties, for Feng controlled the route by which any northern expedition from Hupeh would have to travel. Moreover, Wuhan needed military backing to strengthen its bargaining position with Chiang Kai-shek, and Feng controlled the most formidable army in the area.

The decisions of the Chengchow Conference were therefore little more than formal acceptance of Feng's demands. T'ang Sheng-chih's army was to be sent back to the Wuhan region to put down radical activity there, and Honan was to be given over completely to Feng.

Since autumn 1926 all provinces acquired by the Nationalists had used the committee system of government, and therefore Feng's official position was Chairman of the Honan Provincial Government Commission. The commission consisted of ten men besides Feng, most of whom were Feng's subordinates. The Conference also formalized Feng's rule in Shensi and Kansu by establishing committee governments comprised of the men who were already administering those two provinces. Although Yü Yu-jen was appointed Chairman of the Shensi Provincial Government Commission, he did not take up this post, and was shortly replaced by Feng's appointee. The conference also approved Feng's plans for reorganizing his armies, and apparently gave Feng formal responsibility for military affairs to the north and east of Chengchow, which was tantamount to assigning him the province of Shantung.[48]

One confusing detail about the Chengchow Conference concerns Feng's expression of his attitude toward the growing division within the Wuhan camp. For several months before the conference, Left Kuomintang leaders had become increasingly disturbed over the tendency of the peasantry in Hunan and Hupeh to take up arms and try to carry out the agrarian revolution under whose slogans the Communists had organized them. The Left Kuomintang leaders, disapproving of this radicalism, which frightened them, concluded that they would be better off divorced from the Communists and their Russian mentors. Such a separation might also facilitate reunion with Nanking under favorable conditions for the Left Kuomintang. The last straw came at the beginning of June, when Wang Ching-wei was shown a wire from Stalin demanding immediate agrarian revolt, liquidation of unreliable generals, and organization of a Communist and peasant army. Wang and his associates could not tolerate this, and were therefore thinking about ending the alliance with the Communists when they went to Chengchow to talk to Feng.[49]

Since Feng did not like Communist activity for much the same reasons as the Left Kuomintang, there is no reason to question the evidence to the effect that Feng and the Wuhan leaders agreed at Chengchow on the need for anti-Communist policies.[50] On the other hand, although Communists participated in the Chengchow Conference, the Communist leadership evidently did not know afterward that Feng had taken such a definite stand against them.[51] Therefore one can only conclude that Left Kuomintang leaders, excluding Communists, talked in private with Feng about the need to restrict the Russians and the Chinese Communists.

In any event, Communists and Left Kuomintang alike must have departed from Chengchow with little idea that Feng might arrange a deal with Chiang Kai-shek. Feng denounced Chiang on several occasions, and told Wang Ching-wei personally that Chiang had urged Feng to delay his entry into Honan until T'ang Sheng-chih's troops had been defeated by Fengtien. This, Feng declared, proved that Chiang was a "wolf-hearted, dog-lunged, inhuman thing."[52] It thus appeared that Feng would support Wuhan in any negotiations with Nanking. However, within two weeks after Feng's insulting remarks, he was in friendly conference with Chiang Kai-shek at Hsüchow.

Feng and his 500-man bodyguard arrived in Hsüchow on June 19, and conferred on the 20th and 21st with Chiang and other Nanking leaders.* There was some significance in the fact that the conference could be held in Hsüchow, a town in northern Kiangsu where the Tientsin-Pukow Railway intersects the Lunghai Railway, for Chiang Kai-shek's troops had conquered it only shortly before. While the battle for Honan was in progress, Chiang had conducted his own northern expedition, advancing his armies by three routes through Kiangsu and Anhwei, and without the difficulties T'ang Sheng-chih's forces had met on their northern march. By the first week in June, the Fengtien units had been pushed north of the Lunghai railroad, so that Chiang now held the eastern end of the road that Feng straddled in the west.[53]

Over the conference table in Hsüchow, Feng and Chiang discussed some questions on which no firm decisions were or could be made, such as the future of the Kuomintang, the role of that party in the political life of the country, and the convening of a National Assembly. Feng recommended that great care be exercised to recruit good-quality party members, that they be carefully taught, and that party discipline be severe. This was like approving of motherhood, and Nanking's representatives nodded agreeably and voted to send Feng's recommendations to the party's central organs for discussion.[54] However, more immediately pressing problems were also resolved.

On the key question of military authority, the conference not surprisingly decided that each leader would continue to be commander-in-chief of his armies, and that integrated command would be achieved by making both men subject to the government's Military Affairs Committee. The amount of Feng's monthly financial

* Other participants in the Hsüchow Conference included Hu Han-min, Ts'ai Yüan-p'ei, Chang Ching-chiang, Li Shih-tseng, Li Ming-chung, Ho Chi-kung, Huang Fu, Niu Yung-chien, Li Lieh-chün, Pai Ch'ung-hsi, and Wu Chih-hui.

allotment was settled, of course.[55] They also talked about reforming political units, although it is not clear precisely what they decided. Feng and Chiang agreed that the Northern Expedition had to be continued. Chiang may have argued for a campaign against T'ang Sheng-chih to consolidate the Yangtze before proceeding north, but Feng would not consent to this.[56] They did issue a joint statement on the Northern Expedition; it stressed their devotion to the Three Principles and their determination to wipe out the warlords, tools of the imperialists.[57]

A major question was the fate of the Wuhan government. It was decided that Feng would wire the Wuhan leaders an ultimatum to make peace with the Nanking group, and in the same wire reveal his attitude toward the Communists. Therefore, immediately after the Hsüchow Conference was over, Feng issued a circular telegram addressed to Wang Ching-wei and other Kuomintang leaders at Wuhan. The wire alluded to Feng's discussions with them only a few days earlier in Chengchow, where they had talked of the oppression of factory owners by the workers and the oppression of landowners by the peasants. The people, Feng declared, wanted to suppress such despotism. However, radical elements had wormed their way into the Kuomintang, were refusing to obey orders, and were attempting to gain control of the party and to throw the country into confusion. The only solution had also been discussed at Chengchow: Borodin should return to his own country immediately; those members of the Wuhan government who wished to go abroad for a rest should be allowed to do so, and the others could join the Nanking government. In view of the severe crisis facing the country, Feng's wire concluded, "I feel constrained to insist that the present is a good time to unite the Nationalist factions for the fight against our common enemies. It is my desire that you accept the above solution and reach a conclusion immediately."[58]

This ultimatum was a terrible blow to the Russians, who had counted on Feng's backing ever since Chiang Kai-shek had turned against them. Only two weeks before the Hsüchow Conference, an official publication of the Comintern had rejected as imperialist rumors the suggestion that Feng might collaborate with Chiang Kai-shek. The article asserted that "Feng Yü-hsiang and his army have not trusted Chiang Kai-shek since the latter's action in Canton in March 1926."[59] Feng's defection would be the final confirmation that Stalin's China policy was based on erroneous premises, and therefore it was heresy to suggest that Feng could defect. When Feng took that impossible step, it ended the Russian attempt to guide the Chinese revolution. Of course, the Moscow press excoriated Feng as a deserter, a traitor, and a counterrevolutionary. Borodin, who had talked at length with Feng on several occasions and thought he knew him, was so stunned when he was informed of Feng's statement that he could not believe it. "He is still with us," Borodin insisted. "I am sure—he stays true to Hankow."[60] But not long after, Borodin had to start the long journey home, together with all the other Russian advisers and technicians.

Feng's action also destroyed the hopes of the Left Kuomintang that they might settle the Wuhan-Nanking split on their own terms. Having turned their backs on the peasants and workers, the Wuhan leaders needed the support of strong militarists. Without Feng, they had only T'ang Sheng-chih, who was all but military dictator in Wuhan for a while. But T'ang was pursuing his own interests, and the Wuhan leaders knew that they could order him to do only what he was already willing to do. In any event, Feng now blocked the way against a renewal of the Northern Expedition by Wuhan, which might have brought prestige and legitimacy to their cause.

Although Feng's decision to cast his lot with Nanking shattered many hopes, it really should not have surprised anyone, at least not those who were familiar with warlord politics. That it surprised the Russians showed how seriously they had misread the realities of the Chinese scene. Given the situation of early summer 1927, Feng could hardly have acted otherwise. Military and political considerations alike dictated that he withdraw from Wuhan. Chiang Kai-shek had more to offer as an ally than did T'ang Sheng-chih; his army was stronger, his government was more stable, and he had much more revolutionary respectability. Moreover, Nanking had been conducting negotiations with Chang Tso-lin even before the Hsüchow Conference, and it was expected in many quarters that a deal would be concluded between Chang, Yen Hsi-shan, and Chiang Kai-shek, which would further weaken Wuhan's bargaining position even with Feng's support.[61] The crux of the matter was that Wuhan wanted Feng's support not to fight Chiang Kai-shek, but to give leverage to the Left Kuomintang leaders, so they would not have to go with empty hands to talk to Nanking about party reunification. But Feng was more interested in his own bargaining position, which was better if he negotiated with Chiang on his own account before any serious attempts had been made to reunify the party. In addition, a Yen–Chiang–Chang pact might well include agreements that would be most unfavorable to Feng. Chang Tso-lin particularly disliked Feng, and everyone considered Feng somewhat radical; Feng's best bet was to show his true colors as soon as possible.

Feng's political inclinations drove him in the same direction as the military and strategic considerations. He had never pretended to be a Communist, and his activities in Sian—his most leftist period—had shown that, although he liked to deliver very revolutionary speeches about the needs of the workers and the peasants, he drew the line when the workers and peasants started getting disorderly; Feng wanted an orderly revolution, and he would provide the orders. Moreover, Feng was ready to break off his relationship with the Russians. It was his isolation in the Northwest that had driven Feng to accept Russian aid in the first place. For more than a year after aid began he had stalled on his part of the bargain, to let Russian political organizers into the Kuominchün. It was Russian pressure at a time when Feng's army was in dire extremities that forced Feng to join the Kuomintang and to accept political workers. Although Feng genuinely seemed to believe in the inherent merit and political-military utility of Sun Yat-sen's ideas, he was not pleased by the political activity in his army that followed his entry into the Kuomintang. He could not afford to alienate the Russians as long as he was locked in western China, but once in Honan, in the heart of China, where Russian military aid was no longer essential or even conveniently available, he could do without them. Furthermore, there were rewards for doing so. He could eliminate Communist influence in his army and his provinces, cooperate with Chiang Kai-shek, and be accepted by the Nanking government. He could also eliminate the taint of Bolshevism, which was no longer worth the price for one who, like Feng, was not a true believer.

When Feng returned from Hsüchow, he ordered all Russian advisers and technicians sent home, and all the Communists purged from his army.[62] Probably all the political workers who had been sent to the Kuominchün by the Nationalist government were sent packing.[63] Feng's purge, however, was far gentler than those conducted by Chiang Kai-shek and T'ang Sheng-chih, in which many were killed. Feng executed no Communists at first. Throughout late 1927 and early 1928, Feng occasionally referred to the problem of the Communist threat, and his policy became harsher.[64] He was startled by the Communist attempt to seize Canton in December, and organized a special unit to ferret out Communist conspirators.[65] Shortly afterward, leaders of some obscure disorder in the countryside were labeled Communists and Feng ordered them executed.[66] On the whole, however, Feng's purge was comparatively mild, perhaps because the Communists had made fewer inroads into his authority than Feng had feared. In any event, the suppression of Communist political activity ended the kind of social agitation Feng had found so offensive in Shensi.

Feng wanted only the content of political propaganda among the people changed; he did not want the propaganda discontinued. One of the lessons he learned from the Communist political workers was the importance of political work among the masses. To his propaganda officers, among whom were women, Feng quoted Sun Yat-sen to the effect that one worn-out writing brush could triumph over 100,000 Mausers. He wanted them to be as ardent and earnest as Christian missionaries, making particularly clear to the people how much his army had done for them. However, the people should only be persuaded to support the revolution, not to make one.

The political indoctrination of Feng's troops was also changed, although not very dramatically. At the height of Communist influence, the indoctrination had been primarily nationalistic, and this continued to be the chief orientation. Perhaps some emphasis was shifted onto the abomination of warlordism and away from the evils of imperialism, but both continued to be major themes in Kuominchün training. Feng repeatedly pointed out that the warlord armies fought for the good of only one or two persons, not for the people, and that his army strove only for the welfare of the people, and therefore could not be considered a warlord army. Of course, references to peasant associations and labor unions disappeared from all Kuominchün propaganda, which went back to the tried and true themes, the need to plant trees, to end footbinding, to be frugal, and so on.[67]

Feng also tried to purge any left-over Communist ideas from the minds of his men. For example, he deplored Communist attempts to stir up class warfare, saying that this tended to destroy the nation. He also refuted the idea that the Chinese revolution was part of the world revolution, as the Communists had asserted, because such a concept tended to dull the sharp edge of Chinese nationalism. As usual, Feng was naturally very concerned about the efficiency and discipline of his troops, and he particularly feared how they would be affected by earlier Communist preachings about equality. In a typical speech, he expressed his worries in this way:

Now I want to talk to you all again about Communist propaganda. When we were in T'ungkuan [just before the invasion of Honan in May 1927], some Communists told the troops that it was unequal for soldiers to march by foot while officers ride horses. Therefore, if you want equality, you must do away with ranks. Afterwards, the troops opposed officers' riding horses. I asked the soldiers if, since riding and marching were unequal, it was unequal for cavalry troops to ride horses while infantry troops marched. They replied that it was unequal. Accordingly, the army's cavalry would be eliminated. Now I am much taller than you; this is also unequal. What good method can you propose to make us equal? The soldiers were silent. Moreover, after the Women's Associations were established, women in the T'ungkuan region went to meetings every day, and paid no attention to the children or to cooking meals. When their husbands spoke about this, the women said that the care of children is not the work of the woman alone, but should be evenly divided; only that was equality. Thus disorder was created in the households.[68]

In the second half of 1927, however, Communist influence among his men was not Feng's chief worry about them. Feng's army had expanded so rapidly, and now embraced so many units of diverse origin and character, that the unique spirit he had created in his organization was badly adulterated. Smoking, drinking, visits to prostitutes, all became more frequent than they had been a few years earlier, when Feng could impose his ideas of discipline on every soldier and officer. Therefore Feng took a new step in indoctrination; he launched a New Life Movement on September 17, the anniversary of his Wuyüan Oath. On that day he issued an order urging each man to imagine that he had died the day before, and was now born anew, and to decide that his new life would not be characterized by the vices that had stained the old one. Feng distributed to all of his troops the following admonition, or oath, which was to be their guide to a new life:

> Abstain from smoking and drinking.
> Abstain from prostitutes and gambling.
> Do not be arrogant or lazy.
> Eliminate waste and extravagance.
> Be diligent and frugal.
> Sacrifice for the party.
> Then the national revolution will be able to succeed.[69]

The idea behind this movement is clearly and strikingly similar to that behind the much better known New Life Movement launched by Chiang Kai-shek in the mid-1930's.

Completion of the Northern Expedition

It was absolutely clear after the Chengchow and Hsüchow confer- ences that Feng would not support the Communists or radical ele- ments in the Kuomintang, who therefore had no significant military backing, and the Wuhan government purged them from the Kuo- mintang with remarkable speed. In July Communists were formally excluded from the party, and they were more and more persecuted by T'ang Sheng-chih, who dominated the Wuhan area militarily. Many Communists were killed, although not all of those who were killed were Communists. Thus the Wuhan government quickly be- came respectably moderate. But the Left Kuomintang leaders did not join the Nanking government. On the contrary, while they were purging Communists, they were also trying to remove Chiang Kai- shek from leadership at Nanking. They branded him a counterrevo- lutionary who aspired to military dictatorship, and they demanded he submit to the mandates of the legitimate government at Wuhan. On July 21 Feng Yü-hsiang suggested that the two sides meet in Kai- feng to discuss their differences, but the Wuhan leaders promptly replied that they would not attend such a conference, because rap- prochement with a Nanking dominated by Chiang Kai-shek was un- thinkable.

The Left Kuomintang was not Chiang's only antagonist. Sun Ch'uan-fang launched a new offensive, on July 24 recaptured and reoccupied Hsüchow, and prepared to continue south to Nanking. This military setback intensified the disagreements within the Nan- king group; Li Tsung-jen and Pai Ch'ung-hsi in particular asserted that Chiang's leadership was keeping the two wings of the Kuomin- tang apart. Such profound rifts in the party not only left little chance to continue the Northern Expedition, but seemed to threaten the very existence of the Kuomintang. In the face of this crisis, Chiang Kai-shek declared that he would not obstruct party unity, and re- signed on August 12. Shortly afterwards, he went to Japan.

With Chiang gone, Kuomintang leaders of all factions met in Nan- king in September to reunify the party and integrate the two gov- ernments. Ostensibly, these discussions unified both the party and the government, but in fact the deep fissures were simply papered over, not closed. On the one hand, the civilian leaders were divided by personal and political rivalries and ambitions; on the other hand, the civilians found it difficult to exercise genuine control over the party's military commanders. Furthermore, many nonrevolutionary, non-Kuomintang military leaders had been absorbed by the Northern Expedition on its way to the Yangtze. The next three months were confused for both party and government; cliques and individuals jockeyed for power, and threatened to fragment the Kuomintang into quarreling and ineffective factions.

In this situation, the party leaders turned once again to Chiang Kai-shek. He had returned from Japan in November, and had promptly begun discussing further reorganization of the government with Wang Ching-wei. In December, some of Wang's subordinates were involved in a Communist insurrection at Canton, where Wang had established himself a month or so earlier. This incident discredited Wang and the left, and strengthened Chiang and the right. Chiang also had the continued support of the Shanghai financiers who had originally backed him in the spring of the year, and of Feng Yü-hsiang, who had repeatedly wired Chiang to come out of retirement and lead the revolution.[70] Therefore, in January, Chiang assumed the positions of Commander-in-Chief of the Nationalist Army, Chairman of the Kuomintang Central Executive Committee, and Chairman of the Military Affairs Commission. Thus he again dominated the Nanking government, just as he had at the time of his retirement, but now he was relatively more powerful because there was no longer a competing government at Wuhan. The Nanking government, of course, was still not strong. It was still wracked by internal division and conflict, and it did not even control all of southern China. But presumably things would improve after a successful conclusion to the Northern Expedition.

Although the confusion in the Nationalist camp had suspended the Northern Expedition during the second half of 1927, peace had not broken out as a consequence. On the contrary, during those months a jumble of military actions had convulsed northern China. First there was the July offensive of Sun Ch'uan-fang and Chang Tsung-ch'ang that captured Hsüchow on July 24. By mid-August, the same troops had conquered most of Kiangsu and Anhwei north of the Yangtze. Shortly afterwards, a northern army knifed into eastern Honan along the Lunghai Railway. Before Feng could meet this threat, he had to remove a potential enemy in his rear. Chin Yün-ngo, a former subordinate of Wu P'ei-fu, had joined the Kuominchün when it invaded Honan, and Chin's army became one of the frontal armies comprising Feng's command. But Chin was dissatisfied with his status and authority from the outset, and Feng knew better than to count on any warlord who felt independent in his own right. Feng at first withheld money from Chin, and in September launched a brief campaign that eliminated Chin as a military power in Honan.[71] In the same month, Feng sent an army eastward to expel the northern invaders. After a long, hard battle in the Lanfeng-Kweite region, Feng's men defeated the northerners, and drove on to recapture Hsüchow on December 16. In the meantime, a Nationalist army under Ho Ying-ch'in had fought its way north along the Tientsin-Pukow Railway, and joined Feng in Hsüchow. By the end of the year the line dividing northerners and Nationalists had once again been pretty well stabilized north of the Lunghai Railway.[72]*

The reluctant warlord, Yen Hsi-shan, also went to war in late 1927. Since 1926 Yen had been involved in a web of conversations with representatives from Nanking, Peking, and Feng's headquarters. Yen wanted independence, security, and neutrality, and although he had promised to support the Kuomintang, he did not want to take any irrevocable action until it was absolutely necessary. After Sun Ch'uan-fang had rolled the Nationalist armies back to the Yangtze, northern leaders became more insistent that Yen join the northern coalition, which had taken the name Ankuochün. The northerners wanted to invade Honan along the Peking-Hankow Railway, and Yen's province not only paralleled that line closely, but actually included it between Chengting and Changte. During August and September, the northerners pressed Yen to join the Ankuochün, but he resisted, and relations between the Shansi tuchün and the Ankuochün leaders deteriorated. At the end of September there was a border clash between Ankuochün and Shansi troops, and on October 3 Chang Tso-lin issued a public declaration of war against Yen Hsi-shan.[73] Some fighting continued during the following month, and the Ankuochün conquered most of Suiyuan and parts of Shansi. In the spring of 1928,

---

* The change from 1926 to 1927 gives us a chance to illustrate Feng's personality and behavior with his troops. On New Year's morning 1927, Feng assembled the entire body of his men at Chengchow to extend New Year's congratulations. Feng said: "Today is New Year's Day. According to common custom, we should explode strings of firecrackers. But we do not have enough money in our treasury. Moreover, we also want to economize, so we will not buy strings of firecrackers. So we will make a great noise with our mouths and shoot off the cannon, and let it go at that. Come! Come! Come! After me! P'eng! P'eng! Pang!" The entire army shouted loudly "P'eng! Pang!" for over ten minutes. Feng explained this kind of action by one of his favorite remarks: "Poor boys like us must use poor methods." (Chien, Hsi-pei, pp. 16–17.)

this war was submerged in the bigger one caused by the resumption of the Northern Expedition.

A few weeks after Chiang Kai-shek resumed his posts in the party and the government, the Military Affairs Council formally charged him to complete the Northern Expedition without delay. During February and March Chiang conferred with other leaders, including Feng, whom he visited at Kaifeng on February 16, and completed plans and arrangements for the campaign.[74] On the last day of March, Chiang proceeded to his command headquarters in Hsüchow, on the fringe of enemy territory.

Chang Tso-lin was commander-in-chief of the Ankuochün. The other major northern chieftains were Sun Ch'uan-fang, former leader of his own bloc of provinces in the central coastal region; Chang Tsung-ch'ang, Tupan of Shantung; Ch'u Yü-p'u, Tupan of Chihli; Yang Yü-t'ing, Chang Tso-lin's Chief of Staff; and Chang's son, Chang Hsüeh-liang. Yang and Chang Hsüeh-liang led Fengtien troops, the hard core of Ankuochün strength. The bulk of this force was concentrated along the Peking-Hankow Railway, facing Feng's armies southward in Honan, and Yen Hsi-shan's troops westward in Shansi. Ch'u Yü-p'u's men were in southern Chihli, in the region of Taming. Chang Tsung-ch'ang led some troops in southeastern Shantung, although his star was at that time rapidly declining; not only had his brutality and oppression made him extremely unpopular in Shantung, but he had proved to be incompetent as a military commander. Thus his role was taken over by Sun Ch'uan-fang, with the approval of Chang Tso-lin and his own acquiescence. Sun was a competent leader, and the defense of Shantung's key centers was largely his responsibility. Troops under his command were centered in the area around Tsining, although there were some in other regions of southern and southwestern Shantung. Altogether there were about 400,-000 men fighting under the northern banner.[75]

Chiang Kai-shek commanded over sixty separate armies, a total of about 700,000 troops.* The majority of these units were organized into four army groups. The First Army Group, which included many of the southern units and the Whampoa men who had started the

* The Northern Expedition consisted of eight armies when it began in 1926. Seven of those were organized by the Nationalist Government in Canton, while the eighth was under T'ang Sheng-chih, who joined the Kuomintang at the beginning of the Northern Expedition. By the time the northern advance stopped at the Yangtze to resolve the Nanking-Wuhan split, the number of armies had reached 50 because of the warlords who joined the Nationalists rather than fight

Northern Expedition, was under the command of Chiang himself; it included almost all the troops who were effectively under the direct command of Nanking. Its chief thrust was to be along the Tientsin-Pukow Railway, and into eastern Shantung. The various armies under Feng comprised the Second Army Group, which was poised in northern Honan for a push along the Peking-Hankow Railway, and eastward into western Shantung; other units were to penetrate Shantung from eastern Honan. The Third Army Group consisted of Yen Hsi-shan's Shansi troops. They were to pour into Chihli along three routes: along the Taiyüan-Chengting Railroad, through Lingchow and Kwangling toward Paoting, and over the Peking-Suiyuan Railway to Kalgan and Peking. The Fourth Army Group was under Li Tsung-jen, and was to keep order in the rear and to provide aid to the First and Second Army Groups if needed; units of the Fourth Army Group came north only in the last days of the campaign.[76]

Chiang Kai-shek ordered a general offensive on April 9. Units of the First Army Group pushed rapidly into southeastern Shantung and along the Tientsin-Pukow Railway. Men of the Second Army Group invaded western Shantung. The Nationalist advance was quick, and Sun Ch'uan-fang decided to try a bold move. He launched his own southern expedition, an attempt to seize Hsüchow, and thus cut off the First Army Group from the rear and open the door to Honan by way of the Lunghai Railway. However, Sun's troops were cut off and defeated in northern Kiangsu. This was a double defeat, for Sun had taken troops from Tsining to attempt this venture, and the weakened Tsining defenses fell to Sun Liang-ch'eng on April 16. With hardly a pause, Feng's men swept forward with breakneck speed, spearheaded by swift Kansu cavalry that Feng had organized while in the Northwest. In fact, this cavalry unit, with other Kuominchün units under Sun Liang-ch'eng, seized the outskirts of Tsinan on April 24, but they were so far in advance of all other southern units that they had to withdraw temporarily. They returned to take the capital city on April 30. Early in May, there was a clash between Japanese and Chinese troops in Tsinan—the celebrated Tsinan Incident—that engendered a long series of charges, counter-

them; these armies were accepted into the National Revolutionary Army with little more reorganization than a change in name. A report by J. Hall Paxton, vice-consul at Nanking, on Nationalist military organization, April 10, 1928, 893.-20/80, lists and discusses fifty separate armies under the Nationalists. Those under Feng and Yen raised this total to over sixty.

charges, and tedious negotiations. In the meantime, however, the Nationalists skirted Tsinan and continued to push northward.[77]

While the Nationalist armies raced through Shantung, there was also serious fighting in the west. During April Feng's best troops were locked in stubborn battle with crack Fengtien units near Changte, in the northern tip of Honan; others of Feng's troops fought against Ch'u Yü-p'u in the Taming area. At that point Fan Chunghsiu, one of Feng's recently acquired subordinates, revolted and attacked Loyang with the encouragement of Chang Tso-lin, but his revolt was quickly put down by Kuominchün troops from Shensi.[78] Fan's attack did not slow Feng's advance, and early in May the Ankuochün armies finally gave way and retreated to a defense line in the Paoting-Techow area. The Second Army Group took over the key points in southern Chihli, and marched north to Shihchiachuang, where they joined Yen Hsi-shan's men who had moved in from the west. The southern advance accelerated during the rest of the month. Feng's men occupied Techow on May 12, and Machang on May 15. Fengtien troops were also retreating along the Peking-Suiyuan Railway, and on May 25 units of Yen's army occupied Kalgan. Five days later Chang Tso-lin's troops abandoned Paoting; on June 1 Chang Tso-lin departed from Peking, and for all practical purposes the war was over.

There is little doubt that Feng Yü-hsiang's army could have led the way into Peking. Nationalist authorities, however, had decided otherwise, and Feng bowed to that decision. For months before the Northern Expedition resumed in April 1928, the leaders of the Northern Alliance had looked upon Feng as their major enemy. Until the last minute Chang Tso-lin hoped to negotiate a peace with Yen Hsi-shan and Chiang Kai-shek at Feng's expense.[79] Chang had personal grievances against Feng dating from 1924 and 1925, and from the long war between his army and the Kuominchün in 1925–26. Moreover, Chang felt that Feng was a Bolshevik, his break with the Russians notwithstanding. A number of foreigners in China, particularly the Japanese, held a similar view of Feng, and therefore did not want him to occupy Peking. Other diplomats also felt that since the diplomatic corps was in Peking, it had to be occupied by a most reliable and stable general, a description they felt did not fit Feng. As a result, it was arranged at least as early as May that Yen Hsi-shan, not Feng, would occupy Peking.[80] It seems likely that Chiang Kai-shek was pleased with this arrangement, since Feng was presumably more difficult to handle than Yen. In any event, on June 8 Shansi troops finally entered the old capital city. Although pockets of troops and bandits in northern Chihli held out for some time, the capture of Peking symbolized the victorious end of the Northern Expedition.*

* Those who feared Feng's radicalism, his duplicity, or both seemed to have their worst fears confirmed during the occupation of Peking, when one of Feng's units broke a Nationalist pledge. Chinese and foreigners in the city, fearing outbreaks of disorder in the time between the departure of the Ankuochün and the arrival of the Nationalists, had requested that a reliable Fengtien unit remain in the city until relieved by the southerners. The diplomatic corps participated in a request to the Nationalist government that it permit the designated unit to return to Manchuria unmolested and under arms. The Nanking government agreed, and General Pao Yü-lin was assigned the peace-keeping task by Fengtien authorities. On June 8, when Yen's troops arrived at Peking, Pao Yü-lin and his troops departed. However, they had not gone far when they were stopped by Kuominchün troops under Han Fu-chü, disarmed, and brought back to the city. There were strong protests from the diplomatic corps, and in July the Manchurians were allowed to return home. Apparently Han Fu-chü was simply expressing irritation and frustration at having to permit Yen Hsi-shan's troops to occupy the capital. Feng evidently had no part in ordering the action, although he stood by Han Fu-chü during the storm of criticism it raised. Li T'ai-fen, pp. 483 84. See also despatch from Minister J. V. A. MacMurray to the Secretary of State, July 3, 1928, 893.00/10174; report from Consul General C. E. Gauss, July 7, 1928, 893.00 P. R. Tientsin/1; NCH, July 7, 1928, p. 8.

10. End of the Kuominchün

Some historians have described the achievement of the Northern Expedition in brightly nationalistic colors as the end of warlordism and the inauguration of a new era of national unity under the Kuomintang government. Such a picture is an exaggeration. The Northern Expedition did not eliminate the warlords; it simply brought them into the Kuomintang. Not only were the major militarists, such as Feng Yü-hsiang and Yen Hsi-shan, transformed into ostensible pillars of the Nationalist government, but dozens of lesser warlords were brought into the movement with their armies intact and their attitudes and goals fundamentally unchanged. This strengthened the already powerful tendency within the Kuomintang for the military to dominate the civilian elements. It was then that the party and the nation began to reap the bitter harvest sown by the party rupture in early 1927. As long as the foundations of party power included mass organizations such as labor unions and peasant unions, or even less organized mass support, the civilian politicians could hope to use such popular strength to control the party militarists. However, the mass organizations had been Communist strongholds, and they were destroyed in the anti-Communist purges. Real power in the Kuomintang thus passed to the military just when the military, as the result of the absorption of warlords, was becoming less committed to the original goals and principles of the Kuomintang.

Certainly the Northern Expedition did not create a genuinely unified state. The country was divided into five major groups of provinces. Although the Nanking government claimed authority over the entire nation, it actually controlled only Kiangsu, Kiangsi, Chekiang, Anhwei, and Fukien, and there were doubtful areas within these provinces. The Kwangsi faction, led by Li Tsung-jen, Li Chi-shen, and Pai Ch'ung-hsi, held Kwangtung, Kwangsi, Hunan, and Hupeh. Feng Yü-hsiang still ruled Kansu, Shensi, and Honan, and also supposedly Shantung, although the continued Japanese presence there prevented him from exercising any effective authority. Yen Hsi-shan held Suiyuan and Chihli, which was called Hopei by the new government, and, of course, Yen continued to rule Shansi. The Three Eastern Provinces—Manchuria—not only were dominated by the Fengtien faction, but did not come under even the nominal juris-diction of Nanking until the end of the year. The remaining scat-tered provinces either were clearly outside the major groupings, or were in such flux and confusion that it was unclear who controlled them and what their relations with other provinces were.

These conditions were all but institutionalized by the Kuomin-tang's reorganization of the government in October 1928. On the one hand, the military emerged as the dominant arm of government. On the other hand, the new military administration gave high and rough-ly equal military positions to the chief warlords, with Chiang Kai-shek at the apex of the organization.[1] Feng was named Minister of War and Vice-Chairman of the Executive Yüan, and other warlords received high positions in the government or army. In essence, this continued a warlord practice: naming a man to a central govern-ment office whose importance was proportional to his independent regional power. Moreover, the warlord's regional authority was in-stitutionalized in two ways. First, trusted subordinates of the war-lords were made chairmen of the provincial governments in their leaders' satrapies; thus they were the equivalent of the former tu-chüns. Second, branch political councils were set up at Canton, Han-kow, Kaifeng, Taiyüan, Peiping, and, at the end of the year, Mukden; each was presumably the party organ for regional control, but was in fact regional headquarters for warlord control in the name of the party. In short, warlordism continued unabated, but the warlords had become officials of the Nationalist government.[2]

Their status as officials made the warlords no more willing than ever to give up their independence, and the years following the es-tablishment of the new national government in 1928 were full of conflict as Nanking attempted to impose central authority upon one warlord after another. When faced with such attempts, the warlords resorted to armed force against Nanking, which meant in practice against the armies of Chiang Kai-shek. In the spring of 1929, the Kwangsi clique unsuccessfully moved against Chiang over control of Wuhan revenues. This matter was hardly settled when Feng and Chiang clashed over authority in Shantung. A struggle between the two dragged on for over a year, leading to an alliance between Feng and Yen Hsi-shan against Chiang Kai-shek. In 1930 the allies were defeated in a bloody war, which effectively ended Feng Yü-hsiang's career as a power in China.

Failure to Disband

Everyone recognized that for China to become genuinely unified personal armies had to be eliminated. Moreover, the enormous number of men under arms, generally estimated at not less than two million, was an intolerable drain on an already ravaged economy. Consequently there was talk about disbanding the troops almost as soon as Peking fell to the Nationalists. In July 1928 the leaders of the National Revolutionary Army conferred on this question in Peiping. All agreed that disbandment was necessary, although Yen and Feng disagreed on what principles should guide the process. Yen advocated reducing all armies by the same proportion, whereas Feng proposed that the old or unfit should be weeded out, no matter from what army. It was rather a hollow disagreement, however, since neither Feng nor Yen nor any of the other conferees intended to cut his forces substantially. They all signed a statement recommending troop disbandment, but the question was left to be resolved after the formal reorganization of the government.³ When Feng returned to Kaifeng in August, he announced his army would be reduced and reorganized into twelve divisions, but any diminution in size was almost certainly the result of weeding out untrained or incompetent men; in other words, it was a process of strengthening, not weakening, his forces.⁴

On January 1, 1929, the Disbandment Conference formally convened at Nanking to settle once and for all the question of troop reduction. Most of the leaders of the party and the government were there, as were the outstanding military men of the country.⁵ Each of the major warlords was represented, and the important committee chairmanships were distributed among them. Feng Yü-hsiang was Chairman of the Committee to Investigate Proposals for Military Disbandment. Other committees were on Military Reorganization (Yen Hsi-shan), Military Supplies (Li Tsung-jen), and National Defense (Li Chi-shen); Ho Ying-ch'in chaired the Drafting Committee and the Proposals Committee. At the third general session of the conference, a special commission was formed to draw up plans for disbandment and military reorganization. The chairmen of the above committees were on it, and Feng Yü-hsiang was its chairman. The commission recommended, and it was decreed on January 17, that the country be divided into six disbandment areas, centered at Nanking (Chiang Kai-shek), Loyang (Feng Yü-hsiang), Taiyüan (Yen Hsi-shan), Mukden (Chang Hsüeh-liang), and Wuhan (Li Tsung-jen), with the three provinces of Szechwan, Yunnan, and Kweichow to form the sixth area. The conference further agreed that the nation's armed forces would be limited to 65 divisions, each of 11,000 men, and that the total annual expenses for the military should be limited to 41 per cent of the nation's revenues. A National Military Reorganization and Disbandment Commission, which included the nation's chief military leaders, was created to implement these decisions. Feng was made director of one of the four departments into which the commission was divided. With all of these decisions and recommendations settled, the Disbandment Conference formally closed on January 25, 1929.[6]

A few naïve observers may have had high hopes that the Disbandment Conference would really begin disbanding troops, that the militarists could be patriotic and self-sacrificing enough to abolish the armies that had raised them to power.* Such hopes were idle, for the warlords equated disbandment with yielding power to Chiang Kai-shek, who, in their eyes, deserved it no more than any other warlord. Theoretically the greatest reductions were to take place in Li Tsung-jen's Fourth Army Group and in Feng's Second Army Group.[7] In fact, there were no significant reductions made by any warlord camp; if anything, recruiting and expansion continued. Indeed, a few months after the Disbandment Conference, warlord conflicts again broke out in northern China.

* According to the reports submitted by the various military leaders to the Disbandment Conference, the total number of men under arms was less than generally estimated, although still large. Of course, all of the leaders could be expected to understate in this matter. A report by Ernest B. Price, consul at Nanking, to the American legation, Feb. 6, 1929, 893.00 P.R. Nanking/9, gives approximately the same total number of troops as Lo Chia-lün, XXIV, 24–25, although the two sources differ somewhat on the distribution. The following figures are from the latter source:

First Army Group (loyal to Chiang Kai-shek)	240,000 men
Second Army Group (loyal to Feng Yü-hsiang)	220,000 men
Third Army Group (loyal to Yen Hsi-shan)	200,000 men
Fourth Army Group (loyal to Li Tsung-jen, Li Chi-shen, and Pai Ch'ung-hsi)	230,000 men
Fengtien (loyal to Chang Hsüeh-liang)	120,000 men
Kirin (loyal to Chang Tso-hsiang, but in Fengtien group) and Heilungkiang (loyal to Wan Fu-lin, but in the Fengtien group)	40,000 men
Yunnan (loyal to Lung Yün)	30,000 men
Szechwan (control divided among about 7 warlords) . . .	180,000 men
Kweichow	20,000 men
Miscellaneous units	340,000 men
Approximate total:	1,620,000 men

Feng's Regional Administration

Almost immediately after the conclusion of the Northern Expedition, Feng's reputation and public statements made him something of a symbol of frugality, simplicity, and reform in government, which of course made many Kuomintang officials a little uneasy. For example, when Feng went to Nanking at the beginning of August, city authorities temporarily closed down some vice operations, and enforced rigid working hours on some customarily dilatory government workers. Of course, Feng was not directly responsible for these orders, but they were an attempt to preclude criticism by him. Feng's behavior in Nanking further dramatized his image. He received visitors between five and seven o'clock in the morning, a practice that presumably kept the number of callers at a minimum. In his travels through the city, Feng rode in the front seat of a truck. He wore a plain soldier's uniform, handmade cotton shoes, and a battered straw hat. At that time, when many new officials in Nanking and elsewhere were using their positions to garner wealth and luxury, Feng's message was striking and clear.[8]

Feng was also a self-appointed spokesman for extensive national reconstruction. He gave speeches about it, and it was the only subject he was usually willing to discuss freely with newsmen. By and large, however, Feng's ideas on national reconstruction seldom went beyond generalizations so grandiose that they embarrassed the central government. He recommended that the government spend vast sums to promote emigration from the heavily populated coastal regions to the thinly settled Northwest. He said that China should build 100,000 miles of railroad lines, and create a complete highway system, appropriate sixty million dollars to establish factories, another fifty million for agricultural relief, and still other monies for housing, education, and other public services, set disbanded soldiers to constructing irrigation facilities and similar public works, and so on.[9] Feng sketched a tall order for a government that could command the revenues of only four or five provinces at best, to say nothing of its lack of technical and other facilities.

Although Feng made unrealistic demands in Nanking, his administration of Kansu, Shensi, and Honan was much more practical. On the one hand, Feng promoted several of the reforms he was already known for. On the other hand, he tried to squeeze all the revenue possible from his provinces, and thus intensified the economic difficulties that plagued their populations.

Civic improvements, particularly in the provincial capitals, were Feng's most conspicuous reforms. It was reported that Feng ordered each district in his provinces to plant at least 45 acres (300 mow) of trees. Not every district complied, but some trees were planted, especially in Kaifeng, which was ringed with saplings. Moreover, public flower and recreation gardens were planted in vacant areas throughout the city. The mayor's office attempted a botanical exhibit in which all the continents and seas on earth were represented by flowers. Swings, seesaws, and other playground equipment were set up in vacant lots and in front of public buildings. Feng's troops repaired old roads and built new ones. Posters appeared everywhere extolling personal and party virtues, and denouncing imperialism. A large number of statues in Buddhist and Taoist temples were destroyed, and some of the temples were converted into secular public buildings. Confucian temples were not molested. Feng also ordered that conditions be improved in the prisons, which were traditionally notorious as foul holes.[10]

There was a campaign against foot-binding. The provincial governments of Shensi and Honan established centers for unbinding feet, and sternly ordered all local officials to do their best to end the old custom. Shensi officials were particularly diligent, and advertised their success by hanging discarded foot-binding cloths before the government buildings, where they made a gay sight. A similar campaign was launched for public cleanliness. In Chengchow, for example, the 1st and 15th of the month were designated as sweeping days, and officials went out with everyone else to sweep streets and generally clean up. Each merchant had to keep a water jar in front of his store to water the street with. In Kaifeng, there was a plan to paint all homes and stores in the city, and at least some were actually painted.*[11]

Kuominchün sources claim that Feng prohibited prostitution and

---

* The Republic of 1912 adopted the five-barred (red, yellow, blue, white, black) flag, but in October 1928, the Nationalist government officially adopted the flag with a white sun on a blue sky over a red background, which is still the Nationalist flag. The Kuomintang flag is a white star on a blue field. It was apparently the dominance of blue and white in these two flags that inspired a certain color consciousness in some warlords, including Feng Yü-hsiang. In Kaifeng, he ordered all store fronts to be painted blue, and the walls of the houses white. Liu Chen-nien, a warlord who held Chefoo and the surrounding area in early 1929, "ordered that the exterior of every place of business [in Chefoo] be painted blue, resulting, since no particular shade was specified, in a variety of interpretations of that color." (Report from J. V. A. MacMurray to the Secretary of State, Feb. 18, 1929, 893.00 P.R./15.)

opium smoking. It is possible, but doubtful, that brothels were closed, since Feng was at that time looking everywhere for funds, and could have used the lucrative prostitution tax. In any event, the financial gain of the opium trade was too great for Feng to ignore, and opium was sold freely and openly after taxation.[12] In fact, Feng even tried to use a large quantity of opium to pay a debt to an American firm.[13] Of course, Feng did not allow his own subordinates to use the drug, and he executed at least one district magistrate for using it. He also ordered the authorities in his three provinces to censor plays and movies; he worried about what too much sex and violence might do to public morals.[14]

Feng also promoted educational reforms. Dr. Ling Ping, the Western-trained educator whom Feng had called in to direct educational work in Honan a few years earlier, was made the head of Chung Shan College in Kaifeng, a position whose holder could indirectly control the curriculum and administration of the middle schools throughout the province. The curricula of the primary and middle schools were modified to include material on the principles of the Kuomintang. Military drill was given to students in middle schools and higher, and the T'ung-tze Chün, a boys' group somewhat similar to the Boy Scouts, was organized for the younger ones. In Honan, at least, training classes were organized to ensure that all teachers and administrators had the same goals and the same methods. Church-operated schools were forbidden. In addition to the regular school system, special courses were set up to promote literacy among adults. Similar measures were ordered in all of Feng's provinces, although the most substantial progress was made in Honan, particularly in Kaifeng.[15]

Another of Feng's reform measures was to establish a Rural Training Institute to train peasants for village leadership in Honan, Shensi, and Kansu. The institute was designed to promote, among other things, the improvement of village organization, including the beginnings of self-government, which was conceived of as a way to implement the political tutelage program that Sun Yat-sen had envisioned for the second stage of the revolution. The institute was also supposed to teach the peasants how to develop the economic and cultural life of the village. Students were selected from those peasants who had received an elementary education. The first course, of four months' duration, began in August 1927 with 300 students. This was not as many as Feng wanted, but the peasants were generally reluctant to apply for the school because they feared that somehow they might end up in Feng's army. Moreover, no peasants came from distant Shensi or Kansu, so Feng ordered the governments of those two provinces to send about ten men each for the second class, which started with about 700 students after the graduation of the first. The chief subjects were military drill, cooperative buying and selling, history and principles of the Nationalist government, elementary facts of scientific farming, and village planning. The course of study included practical work in a model village. Of course, if the institute was to have any value, the graduates had to return to village positions where their learning could be put to use. There is no indication that this occurred, and no reason to assume that it did.[16] The structure of authority in a Chinese village could not be stretched arbitrarily to give a position of leadership to a man simply because he had studied for a few months in a rural institute. In any event, one person would find it almost impossible to bring about qualitative changes in village life unless his efforts were supplemented by correlated work, propaganda and education, and so forth.

Some of Feng's other measures were also directed at improving conditions in the countryside. He organized classes in which district (hsien) officials were taught principles of good administration, and he established rules of behavior for officials at all levels. One of Feng's most urgent problems was the anti-government peasant organizations, of which the Red Spear Society was the most important. The Red Spears had been effective in fighting the Second Kuominchün in Honan in 1926, and Feng realized that they could be a formidable enemy. From the time he entered Honan, Feng tried to convince the Red Spears that he was working for their interests. He also sent men to help the peasants organize self-protection societies and to train them in methods of self-defense.[17] This testimony of Feng's sincerity was designed both to render the Red Spears more cooperative, and to bring some of the peasants more or less under Feng's organizational influence.

A few foreign missionaries were effusive about Feng's reforms, and tried to interpret the colorful flower gardens and waving clouds of foot-binding cloths as signs that a new and better era had arrived. But measured against the magnitude of the problems faced by the people of Honan, Shensi, and Kansu, Feng's reforms just before and after the Northern Expedition were not only trivial but actually in-

sulting in their irrelevance. All three of his provinces had been ravaged by the incessant warfare of the previous decade. Neither Kansu
nor Shensi was rich to begin with, and the extensive planting of
opium had been on land formerly used to grow food. What little
food reserves those provinces had were taken by Feng's army during
1926 and 1927. Moreover, Kansu was the scene of a festering, gradually expanding war between Muslims and Chinese. Honan's central
location, and its two important railways, made it an avenue for
armies, and a prize for which warlords repeatedly fought, wreaking
widespread destruction in the process. By late 1928 millions of people
were suffering from famine in the three provinces.* The famines were
caused largely by drought, the depredations of bandits, the damage
wrought by war, and unremitting and ruthless overtaxation. This
last was a most important factor. It must be remembered that famine
in Chinese history has often meant famine primarily for the poor; it
was caused not so much by the utter unavailability of food as by the
peasants' inability to pay for scarce and high-priced local food, let
alone even higher-priced provisions from neighboring regions. Thus
Feng Yü-hsiang contributed to the famine in his provinces by his
merciless taxation.

In Honan, for example, a 100 per cent military surtax was levied
on all freight shipped on the Lunghai Railway, including foodstuffs.
On the section of the Peking-Hankow Railway passing through Honan a 40 per cent tax was collected. This boosted prices in Honan,
and with likin, land taxes collected five years in advance, and various other taxes, placed an almost unbearable burden on the Honanese people.† In December 1928 an American officer was sent to Honan

---

* Many other provinces had similar histories, and they too were suffering from
famine by late 1928. On January 14, 1929, an American committee reported famine
conditions in Hunan, Hupeh, Shantung, Hopei, Shansi, Chahar, Suiyuan, Shensi,
and Kansu. In all cases, the causes were both natural disasters, particularly
drought, and the lack of reserves because of bandit or troop activities and exploita-
tive taxation. This is from a letter to Col. E. F. Bicknell, American Red Cross,
from D. O. Lively, National Director of China Famine Relief, U.S.A., Feb. 23,
1929, in 893.48L/107.

† While these conditions prevailed in Honan, Feng presented the people of Kai-
feng the following slogans to arouse interest in modern science:
   Save the country by studying the sciences.
   Save the country by studying chemistry.
   Save the country by manufacturing our own mechanical appliances.
   Save the country by producing iron.
   Save the country by producing steel.
   Save the country by manufacturing medicine.

to find out how bad the famine conditions were. He was convinced, he reported,

> that Feng and the . . . local authorities are doing practically nothing to alleviate . . . suffering . . . , in fact are adding to it tremendously by causing foodstuffs to be even more expensive than elsewhere. *Everyone* [original emphasis] agrees that if the surtax, likin, etc., on food supplies were cut out, the situation even in the bad parts of the province would be very materially improved.

In several reports, he emphasized that the people everywhere complained of the heavy taxation, and his informants unanimously claimed that "not one cent had been used for relief work of any kind."[18]

As a matter of fact, Feng not only took few if any relief measures, but interfered with relief efforts of other agencies. Feng's men "borrowed" $120,000 deposited in a Kaifeng bank by the China International Famine Relief Commission, which led the commission to restrict its activity in Honan.[19] Early in 1930 the commission brought about 3,000 tons of grain into Shensi for famine relief, but during the same months Feng drew at least that much out of the province. This prompted one of the foreigners in charge of Shensi relief to conclude that the commission was "merely replacing grain seized by the military, and the contributions in America and China were in effect helping underwrite the past and present wars."[20]

In sum, conditions were very bad in Shensi and Honan during 1928 and 1929. But in Kansu they were even worse, for there the ravages of civil war and famine were compounded by the brutalities of religious war.

Revolt in Kansu

In the 1920's, Kansu was part of China's cultural hinterland. Sparsely populated, with a large proportion of Muslims, it was far from the agricultural and business centers of the nation. The nearest railhead was many miles away, and there were no facilities for water transport. Kansu was thus rather cut off from the mainstream of events in China. Conversely, what happened in Kansu was often little known outside of that province, and as a consequence great tragedies went by almost unnoticed. The upheavals caused by the entry of the Kuominchün in late 1926 were followed in 1927 by a violent earthquake in the northwest of the province. Moreover, with the establishment of Kuominchün authority, there came the inexorably efficient tax collectors. The resentments thus created, combined with traditional Muslim-Chinese enmity and the Kansu Muslims' desire to oust the non-Kansu rulers, the Kuominchün, created a tinder-dry situation that finally burst into flame in the spring of 1928.

It is difficult to be precise about the immediate causes of the Kansu rebellion. It is possible that the smoldering resentment against already extortionate taxes was suddenly fanned when Feng's men tried to increase them.[21] Certainly one factor was the ambition of Ma T'ing-hsiang, an important Muslim leader, who resented the dominance of the Kuominchün and hoped to establish his own provincial government. He had no difficulty finding support among Kansu Muslims, who disliked the idea of outsiders holding local authority; such provincialism was common in China, and the Muslim leaders may have anticipated support even from Kansu Chinese. Moreover, Chang Tso-lin encouraged Ma with funds and possibly supplies, hoping that a rebellion in Feng Yü-hsiang's rear would hobble his capacity to cooperate in the Northern Expedition.[22] In any event, Feng's preparation for the Northern Expedition offered Ma T'ing-hsiang one of the best chances he was ever to get. Another factor that may have triggered the revolt was a rumor that the Kuominchün was going to take over some areas in Kansu that were still under Muslim leaders.[23]

Violence first erupted in early April 1928, west of the Tao river in southwest Kansu. Hochow, the largest city in that region, was besieged three times in the following six months. Each time the Kuominchün drove the Muslims back, but it was not strong enough to disperse or destroy the rebels. Indeed, this was the story of the rebellion; as soon as Muslims were defeated in one place, they sprang up elsewhere, and when the Kuominchün pursued, the Muslims returned to the first place. Soon all of southwest Kansu, west of a line running north and south through Lanchow, was in flames. Moreover, although the revolt began specifically against the Kuominchün, and anti-Kuominchün feeling nourished it to the end, the old mutual fear and hostility of Muslims and Chinese quickly transformed it from a rebellion into a religious war. Terrible cruelties were practiced: children were torn apart or thrown onto swords; people were cut to pieces or subjected to the tortures that are so often a feature of holy wars. There were numerous massacres, and even allowing for exaggeration it is clear that many thousands were slaughtered. By the time Kuominchün reinforcements could report the "pacification" of the rebellion in September, well over 100,000 people had died.[24]

But the pacification did not take. Within a few months violence

1 Feng Yü-hsiang, ca. 1904

2 Feng Yü-hsiang, ca. 1913

3 Feng Yü-hsiang with his wife and
two younger children, ca. 1918

4 Feng's troops at a baptismal service, ca. 1920

5 Feng Yü-hsiang, ca. 1923

6 Feng Yü-hsiang and Chiang Kai-shek, ca. 1928

7 Feng Yü-hsiang participating in work with his troops

8 Feng Yü-hsiang, Chiang Kai-shek, and Yen Hsi-shan

9 Feng addressing his troops, Kaifeng, ca. 1928

10 Feng and the People's Anti-Japanese Allied Army, 1933

flared again. In January 1929 much of southern Kansu was again in the hands of the rebels. On February 14 about 20,000 Muslims forced their way into Tangar, a city of some 5,000 families in western Kansu. An American eyewitness described the sack of Tangar:[25]

[The Muslims] forced an entrance [to the city] by ladder over the north wall. Immediately they began to murder the Chinese in a most brutal way, cutting over the head with swords. You can not imagine the awfulness of those that are wounded and yet living.

It seemed as though they were organized into different bodies; while some did the killing others did the looting, . . . carrying it away to safety. At present almost nothing remains in this, once the most wealthy business center north of . . . Szechwan . . . along the Tibetan border. It is difficult to buy cloth for bandages. There is no food nor flour to be had, they cleared it all out. Now the people are suffering hunger.

[The Muslims] were in the city only about two hours. But during that time the official figures show more than 2000 killed, 700 wounded, and $2,000,000 damage. This is for the city only. Since then many more have died from wounds and starvation. The above are official figures and no guessing at all.

There are many villages that have been almost completely destroyed. Tangar is about half burnt out.

Kansu suffered not only bloody violence but also widespread famine during 1928–29. Essentially, famine was caused in Kansu by the same factors that caused it elsewhere in northern China at that time. Weather conditions were adverse; local warlords forced peasants to plant large areas with opium poppy; warlord conflict drove men from the fields, destroyed crops, and generally dislocated normal agricultural activity. Moreover, Feng Yü-hsiang's officers in 1925 and 1926 had squeezed from the people every possible dollar, every available ounce of grain, to take care of the Kuominchün during the struggle with Chang Tso-lin and the subsequent retreat through Kansu into Shensi. By the beginning of 1927, all of Kansu's reserves were exhausted. Drought conditions began in that year, but did not become critical until 1928. At that time, the people faced high and "almost innumerable" taxes; harvests were poor or, in some areas, nonexistent; and there were no reserves to fall back upon. On top of all this came the frightening ravages of the Muslim revolt, which left fields smoking and peasants dead or fleeing. An all-consuming poverty fell over the land: draft animals began to die or were eaten; carts and parts of homes were sold for a pittance or burned for fuel. Death was everywhere, and responsible people insisted that reports of cannibalism were true.[26]

Kansu's agony was intensified and prolonged by the obstacles in the way of getting large-scale relief from outside the province. Relief organizations could not operate effectively in the midst of the Muslim revolt. Most important, the dearth of transportation facilities made it difficult to ship large quantities of supplies under even the best of conditions. More than anything else, Kansu needed a railroad. Mr. G. Finlay Andrew, who toured Kansu early in 1929 for the China International Famine Relief Commission, emphasized the inadequacies of Kansu transport. He even found it difficult and expensive to obtain carts for his inspection tour. He finally acquired three, each with two mules, for the trip from P'ingliang to Lanchow, but three of the mules died from malnutrition before the trip was completed. Mr. Andrew described his journey west of P'ingliang:[27]

Prepared as we were for sad sights..., I do not think we were quite ready for the conditions we found existing from Longteh-hsien to Anting-hsien. Longteh, Chingning, Hweining and Anting furnished conditions increasing in severity in their order of sequence. We had not proceeded far outside P'ingliang when we passed dead bodies lying by the roadside.

All along the road, we were met by increasingly sad sights. Emaciated forms staggered along till they were unable to move another step, whereupon they simply dropped in their tracks. Parents were crawling along..., leaving their starving children, too weary to move another step, crying piteously after them. Whole families were sitting desolately by the roadside, at an end of all their resources and not knowing what to do next.... The dead were better off than the living.

There is no way of knowing exactly how many lives were lost during the Kansu tragedy. Inevitably, estimates vary enormously. In January 1930 one informed speaker put the figure at 2,000,000, but others would certainly put it much lower.[28] Yet there is no doubt that the combined famine-revolt in Kansu was a catastrophe of staggering proportions. Politically and militarily, Kansu became less an asset than a liability for Feng Yü-hsiang. That was one reason why he was eager—indeed, he thought it essential—to acquire richer territory elsewhere in northern China. Specifically, he hoped and expected to get Shantung, and that expectation shaped his policy when the Kwangsi warlords revolted in the spring of 1929.

Revolt of the Kwangsi Clique

The lifeblood of a regional warlord was regional revenue. As long as a warlord could retain the lion's share of the funds collected in his provinces, it mattered little to him that he was nominally an agent of Nanking. But conflict was inevitable when Nanking tried to channel those funds into its own coffers. That is what happened early in 1929, when the Kwangsi clique of warlords clashed with Nanking.

In the autumn of 1927, the Nanking-Wuhan rift had broken briefly into open warfare, during which T'ang Sheng-chih, at the head of the Wuhan armies, was defeated. He left the country, and the Nationalist generals who had ousted him took over Hunan and Hupeh. Those generals were part of the so-called Kwangsi clique, a military faction that originated in a split between Kwangtung and Kwangsi officers in the early days of the development of Kuomintang armed forces in the Canton area.[29] After the reorganization of the Nationalist government in late 1928, the Kwangsi militarists retained control of Hunan and Hupeh through the Wuhan Branch Political Council, of which Li Tsung-jen was Chairman. Li Chi-shen and Pai Ch'ung-hsi were the other two best-known Kwangsi leaders. Although these men considered themselves Nationalists, they were not followers of Chiang Kai-shek, and had become increasingly jealous of their independence as Chiang's domination over the party increased. Chiang, on the other hand, had tried to reduce their independence by appointing Lu Ti-p'ing chairman of the Hunan provincial government. Lu, of course, was loyal to Chiang, obeyed Chiang's orders, and was thus an enemy within the Kwangsi camp.

The inevitable crisis came over the question of funds. The Kwangsi militarists wanted to control all monies collected in Hunan and Hupeh, whereas Lu Ti-p'ing sent government revenues to Nanking. Early in February the Kwangsi leaders formally requested the Nanking government to permit the Wuhan Branch Political Council to supervise the collection and expenditure of national government funds in Hupeh and Hunan, which was tantamount to asking that the funds be given to the Kwangsi warlords. The government refused. This was clearly a far-reaching challenge, for without financial independence, the Kwangsi clique would promptly lose its military independence and its regional autonomy. The Kwangsi leaders responded by dismissing Lu Ti-p'ing from his position on February 19, and two days later sent an army to attack him at Changsha. Lu fled, and the Wuhan Branch Political Council appointed Ho Chien chairman of Hunan.[30] Thus arose the first major test of Nationalist unity. Could the Nationalist government really control the country, or was it only a facade for unbridled regionalism?

Chiang Kai-shek promptly moved to enforce the authority of Nan-

king; in fact, it is possible that he had worked behind the scenes
to bring this test of strength about. He faced a twofold problem,
military and diplomatic. He had to defeat the Kwangsi troops in
the field, but he had to be sure that Feng Yü-hsiang would remain
neutral or support the government. A Kwangsi-Feng alliance might
prove disastrous for Nanking. Chiang sent a personal representative, Shao Li-tzu, to negotiate with Feng.[31] Although the substance
of the talks was not revealed publicly, it was generally believed that
Chiang gave Feng two million dollars and promised him complete
control over Shantung once negotiations with the Japanese had
ended, and possibly even some authority in the mid-Yangtze provinces.[32] There is no way to tell about the financial arrangements,
and although subsequent events confirmed that Feng expected Shantung, that had been settled before the Kwangsi revolt; Sun Liang-
ch'eng had been appointed chairman of Shantung in the last days of
the Northern Expedition. In fact, the rumors about Chiang's concessions to Feng in return for support were probably exaggerated.
Although representatives from Wuhan tried to bring Feng into an
anti-Chiang coalition, Feng had no reason to leap to the side of
Kwangsi, and Chiang Kai-shek knew it. Certainly Feng would not
throw in his lot with the rebels at the very outset of such an uncertain venture. If the Kwangsi-Chiang war had dragged on, Feng would
doubtless have reconsidered his position, but in fact it was soon over.
In any event, after his talks with Shao Li-tzu, Feng declared himself
loyal to Nanking.

Feng ordered Han Fu-chü to Wuhan at the head of a large force.
Chiang Kai-shek, among others, suspected that Feng intended to seize
Wuhan and present the Nanking troops with an accomplished occupation of the area, much as he had done at Chengchow and Kaifeng
in May 1927, when T'ang Sheng-chih expected to get those cities.
Chiang's German military adviser, Colonel Max Bauer, planned a
very efficient campaign. Nanking troops rushed at top speed to Wuhan, and occupied the cities forty-eight hours before Feng's men arrived. In fact, the Kwangsi troops evacuated Wuhan without a struggle. This move was widely attributed to Feng's participation: that
Feng's support of Chiang meant that the anti-Kwangsi forces were
simply too powerful to tackle.

The dust had hardly settled after the Kwangsi affair when Nanking's authority was challenged again. This time the challenger was
Feng himself, and the issue was Shantung.

The Loss of Shantung

Kuominchün soldiers had carried the brunt of the fighting in Shantung during the Northern Expedition. As a reward, Feng was given authority over that province, which was consistent with the warlord methods and values then prevailing. Control of Shantung was extremely important to Feng. Although he already had three provinces, Kansu was remote, undeveloped, and chaotic, and Shensi and Honan were so ravaged by war, brigandage, and drought that they could not be counted on for funds or supplies. Shantung had also been terribly despoiled during its several years under the rapacious Chang Tsung-ch'ang and his undisciplined "army" of riffraff and bandits. However, Shantung had seaports and railroads. The latter were an excellent source of revenue, and the former would give Feng access to foreign arms and military equipment. Feng had always been cut off from the sea and from the infusions of power that could come from it. The acquisition of Shantung, it seemed, would finally correct that deficiency.

The Nanking government legitimized Feng's possession of Shantung by appointing Sun Liang-ch'eng chairman of the provincial government, although Shih Ching-t'ing administered the province until Sun could drop his military duties and take up his post on October 1, 1928. However, the provincial government could not control the key areas of the province as long as Chinese-Japanese relations in Shantung remained unsettled. Since the Tsinan Incident in the middle of May 1928, the Japanese had been occupying Tsinan and the entire railroad zone between Tsinan and Tsingtao. Thus exactly those features of the province Feng found attractive were in Japanese hands: the provincial capital, the east-west railroad, and the chief port. Feng therefore had to wait until negotiations between the Nationalist government and Japan finally cleared the way for him to take over the Japanese-occupied areas.

Feng was apprehensive about the delay, and urged a rapid conclusion to the Sino-Japanese talks. He knew that Chiang Kai-shek did not relish his ruling Shantung, and he knew also that the longer the situation remained unresolved, the greater was the chance that it might turn against him. Feng also worried about the Japanese attitude. The Japanese were jealous of their interests in Shantung, and were certainly not eager to turn over the railroad to Feng, whom they disliked and distrusted. The Japanese remembered his association with the Russians, and they suspected that he had not completely turned his back on radicalism. To combat this attitude, Feng told Sun Liang-ch'eng to be friendly with the Japanese, to yield on differences, and generally to try to mollify them until they had departed and the province was safely in Feng's hands.[33] Moreover, Feng directly tried to convince the Japanese of his cordiality and general reliability.

Early in July 1928 Feng informed the military attaché of the Japanese legation in Peking that he would like to travel to Japan in the near future to attend lectures at the military academy, inspect various facilities, and become better acquainted with the situation in Japan. In other words, he wanted to be friends. Feng also asked that Matsumuro Takayoshi be assigned as his adviser. Matsumuro was the Japanese army officer who had been Feng's adviser for about a year after the Peking coup d'etat. In the autumn of 1928, Matsumuro was working in the office of the chief of staff in Tokyo, and he was sent back to

MAP 7. Shantung, January 1929. The blank areas north and south of the railroad were under no organized control, and were overrun with brigands and remnants of armies. Liu Chen-nien, Ku Chen, and Liu Hei-ch'i were nominally Nationalist, but were actually independent.

China to see if he could be of any help in the Shantung negotiations. However, he was not permitted to be Feng's adviser. Neither his sojourn in China nor Feng's brief flirtation with Japan seem to have had any significant consequences.[34]

The Japanese-garrisoned areas were not the only regions in Shantung that were outside Feng's control. Indeed, the situation in that province was complex and unstable during late 1928 and early 1929. Feng Yü-hsiang controlled the Tientsin-Pukow Railway from Techow to Yenchow, and almost all of the province west of it. Chiang Kai-shek's generals tried to hang on to some portions of the province, but by the end of the year they controlled only the Tientsin-Pukow Railway south of Yenchow. Some small, independent warlords in the southern and eastern parts of the province had declared allegiance to the Nanking government, but their loyalty was more nominal than real. When Chang Tsung-ch'ang and Sun Ch'uan-fang fled precipitously before the Northern Expedition in the spring of 1928, many of their units were left in Shantung, mostly to the east of the Tientsin-Pukow Railway. Some of these were fairly large units, such as brigades, which retained their organization and unity. The leaders of these forces established their control over as many districts as they could, and thus carved out significant chunks of the province. They ruled their satrapies with utter disregard for the Nanking government, although a few of them raised its flag and used its name. Other Chihli-Shantung army units fell apart and became disorganized brigands who, with local bandits nurtured by years of rapacious warlordism, preyed mercilessly on the countryside to the north and south of the Tsinan-Tsingtao Railway. The situation in those regions was extremely chaotic, and there was much looting and indiscriminate bloodshed. The area held by Feng, on the contrary, was completely pacified. The American consul at Tsinan declared in late 1928 that "reports from regions where Feng's troops are stationed are unanimous in stating that never have these regions enjoyed such peace and order; ... reports from other regions are equally unanimous in saying that brigandage was never worse." However, he also stressed that, as usual, Feng's firm order included "unbearable taxation."[35]

Eastern Shantung—the region to the east of Kiaochow Bay, including the port of Chefoo—was seized by Liu Chen-nien in September 1928. Liu, a former commander of Chang Tsung-ch'ang's bodyguards, declared that henceforth he would give his allegiance to the Nationalist government. But when both Nanking and Feng Yü-hsiang sent representatives to Liu to discuss questions of taxation and administration, Liu disposed of these agents by simple, cold-blooded murder. By the end of October more than forty men had been murdered, including some local figures who had objected to Liu's assumption of power. Liu was able to continue his independent rule undisturbed until March 1929, when Chang Tsung-ch'ang drove him out in a comeback try. A month later Liu expelled Chang Tsung-ch'ang from the province for what proved to be the last time. He continued to share the rule of eastern Shantung with some other petty warlords who paid only lip service to the Nationalists.[36]

In the spring of 1929, Feng Yü-hsiang's long wait for Shantung seemed about to bear fruit. On March 28 Chinese and Japanese plenipotentiaries finally agreed on terms for the settlement of the Tsinan Incident and the withdrawal of Japanese troops from Shantung. Japan pledged to move her troops out of the province within two months from the date of signing. The Japanese, however, intended to do so well before that deadline. They arranged with Sun Liang-ch'eng to turn Tsinan over to his troops on April 16, and during the following days they would move eastward along the Tsinan-Tsingtao Railway, permitting Chinese troops to assume authority in their wake. Sun Liang-ch'eng was prepared to occupy Tsinan with the troops he had on hand at his Taian headquarters. Feng Yü-hsiang had troops in Honan that could move swiftly into Shantung to garrison the Tsinan-Tsingtao Railway zone. The Japanese estimated that the entire process would take about two weeks. They planned to be out of Shantung by May 3rd or 4th.

Perhaps everything would have gone according to plan if the Kwangsi revolt had not crumpled so rapidly. But with the threat from central China disposed of, Chiang Kai-shek boldly seized the chance to assert the authority of the central government over Shantung, and to prevent the further expansion of Feng's regional power. Chiang had the Nanking authorities order Sun Liang-ch'eng not to send troops into Tsinan or the railroad zone. Sun received this order on April 15. The next day a Nanking official notified the Japanese that Sun would not provide troops, but that the national government would set the date on which other units, to be designated in due course, would take over from Japan. The Japanese were amazed; the Nationalists had been complaining for almost a year about Japan's troops in Shantung, and now they were asking Japan to delay the withdrawal! Although they were annoyed, they secured their government's permission to postpone their evacuation.[37]

On April 22, Chiang Kai-shek issued further instructions. Sun Liang-ch'eng was told to take over the city of Tsinan, but Chiang had detailed troops to "assist" Sun by garrisoning Tsingtao and the eastern portion of the Tsinan-Tsingtao Railway; in other words, Chiang would control the chief port and communications to it. In the meantime, Chiang had concentrated great military power in Shantung. Fang Chen-wu's troops had poured into the province. A couple of minor Shantung warlords had been persuaded by Chiang to take an open stand against Sun. Moreover, Chiang had bribed one of Sun's division commanders. Thus about 60,000 potentially hostile troops faced Sun, who had only 40,000 men immediately available. Of course, Sun's well-trained soldiers could doubtless have defeated those heterogeneous units, but that would have set off a general campaign against Feng Yü-hsiang in all of his provinces. Feng and Sun knew this, and immediately understood Chiang's move for what it was: an attempt to snatch Shantung from Feng's grasp, and by extension, a demand that Feng bow to the central government or fight. Since Feng was not prepared to bow, this was a declaration of war.[38]

Feng was not ready for a campaign in Shantung. Chiang not only had many troops there already, but could move others in from Kiangsu. More important, Yen Hsi-shan was in Hopei, and if he cooperated with Chiang, Feng would be caught between deadly pincers. Furthermore, the Japanese were still involved, and their negotiations had naturally been primarily with the central government. Even if Feng could drive Chiang out of Shantung, there was little chance that the Japanese would turn it over to the Kuominchün without the sanction of Nanking. Feng was thus caught in a military and political situation that left him no chance to acquire Shantung. He therefore chose to withdraw from the province with his forces intact. On April 25 Sun Liang-ch'eng issued a telegram of resignation, and on the next day all Kuominchün troops in Shantung began to leave the province. Feng's adherents in Nanking also left immediately for Feng's territories. These included Lu Chung-lin, Acting Minister of War, and Y. L. Tong, Vice-Minister of Foreign Affairs.

The Final Struggle

When he plucked Shantung from Feng's grasp, Chiang Kai-shek began a protracted and complex struggle that was not resolved until late in 1930. The main strength of the Kuominchün quickly gathered in Honan, and railroad bridges and facilities were destroyed to obstruct any invasion of that province. However, the invasion did not come, at least not immediately. Feng's soldiers did not meet Chiang's on the battlefield until several months of denunciations, bribery, and political-military maneuvering had passed.

During May, Feng and Chiang exchanged several open telegrams, which were primarily designed to justify their actions to the public. Feng charged that Chiang Kai-shek had packed the Third National Congress of the Kuomintang with his own supporters to keep himself in power, and that Chiang had favored his own First Army Group in the distribution of military funds. Both accusations were true, although Chiang generally ignored the first one in his several wires to Feng. Chiang explained the unequal allotments by saying that soldiers from the south and east were accustomed to a higher standard of living than those from the north and west, and that prolonged arrears of pay would therefore cause worse discipline problems among them than among the northwestern troops, who were not only accustomed to hardship, but also well cared for by Feng's own diligence and efficiency. Chiang also emphasized how important unity and peace were to the nation, and asserted that armies should not be considered the private possessions of their commanders. He deplored the rumors that were circulating about Feng: that he was storing military supplies to be able to defy the central government; that he had shortened his defense lines to prepare for a sudden attack on Peking; that he was plotting with the Kwangsi clique. He knew that these were only rumors, Chiang added, but they would be scotched definitively if Feng came to Nanking. Feng declined the invitation, noting that Li Chi-shen, a leader of the Kwangsi clique, who had gone to the capital under the personal guarantee of five Kuomintang leaders, had been arrested when he arrived.[39]

Chiang also sent a telegram to Feng's troops, urging them to be loyal to the government and the revolution in spite of their long association with Feng.[40] However, twenty-eight of Feng's commanders had already signed a circular telegram denouncing Chiang, demanding his resignation, and urging Feng to lead a punitive army against him.[41] On May 20 Feng notified the various foreign legations in China of his election as commander-in-chief of the Northwestern Route Army of the Party-Safeguarding and National Salvation Forces. He asked the foreign powers to remain neutral in the developing conflict, promised that foreigners would be protected, and asserted that the revolutionary government he intended to create would not honor any new foreign loans to the "illegal" Nanking government.[42] A few days later, the Standing Committee of the Kuomintang Central Executive Committee dismissed Feng from all government and party offices, and authorized a punitive mandate to be issued against him.

But far more important events happened in May than these self-righteous mutual denunciations. For the first time, Feng suffered what had become commonplace for many other warlords: the defection of key subordinates. Han Fu-chü, Shih Yu-san, and several lesser officers went over to Chiang Kai-shek, and took more than 100,000 of Feng's best troops with them. Observers then and since have unanimously ascribed these defections to bribery on an enormous scale, and are doubtless correct.[43] Certainly Shih Yu-san did not join Chiang because of any commitment to Chiang's position, for he soon revolted against him; in fact, Shih shifted allegiances so frequently after this that some wit dubbed him "Shih San-fan," which means, loosely, "Triple-crosser Shih."[44]

These defections stunned Feng Yü-hsiang. Indeed, they might be considered the most important event in Feng's career. It was not just the number of troops lost to him, but also their quality. Although Feng in early 1929 probably had close to 300,000 men under him, many of the units were of doubtful loyalty and poor quality. The hard core of Feng's military strength lay in his old Kuominchün units, and the defectors took much of that core. Moreover, they took most of Honan, Feng's most valuable province economically and strategically. Han Fu-chü was immediately named chairman of Honan by the Nanking government. Feng's loyal troops were in the western end of Honan and in Shensi. The defections also hurt the morale of Feng's army; the first betrayals led the men to expect more.[45] No one can be sure what would have happened if those defections had not occurred, but it is at least possible that the Kuominchün would have won the war with Chiang Kai-shek. Feng's ex-subordinates still think that the defections may have been the critical factor in the following struggle. One commander told me unequivocally that if they had not taken place, "The whole realm definitely would have been ours" ("T'ien-hsia i-ting ch'eng-le wo-men-ti").

After Han and Shih switched sides, Chiang sent still another wire to Feng, urging him to go abroad.[46] However, Feng's cause was not lost, for at that juncture he received the backing of the next most important warlord in northern China, Yen Hsi-shan. The relations between Feng, Yen, and Chiang during the second half of 1929 were somewhat obscure then, and still are now, largely because there is so little information about what went on behind the scenes. However, events tell much of the story. The first public manifestation of an understanding between Feng and Yen came at the end of May, when Yen wired Feng that he would like to go abroad with him. Subsequently, the two men exchanged several wires whose ostensibly serious discussion of the joys of foreign travel amused knowledgeable political observers. Yen wrote that henceforth he and Feng would "be inseparable ... and ... wander about in foreign countries in a carefree and lighthearted manner."[47] Feng replied that this was just what he had always wanted, that he was preparing to leave, and that if Yen started early he should wait for Feng in Berlin.[48] Chiang Kai-shek recognized Yen's sudden interest in traveling for what it was: a statement of support for Feng Yü-hsiang that altered the entire political situation in northern China.

Representatives of Yen, Chiang, and Feng immediately met to seek some means short of war to resolve the differences between Feng and Chiang. By early July agreement had been reached. Although there was no official announcement of terms, Chinese and Westerners alike understood that the punitive measures against Feng and his men would be canceled; that Chiang would pay the Kuominchün arrears, with a first installment of $3,000,000; that the government would keep the Kuominchün intact under Lu Chung-lin, a commander named by Feng; that the heads of the provincial governments of Shensi, Kansu, and Ninghsia would be retained;* and that Feng's trip abroad, for which he would receive $200,000 traveling expenses, would be postponed for several months.[49]

Subsequent events confirmed most of these points. On July 5 the Nanking government canceled the order for Feng's arrest. Feng went to Shansi, where he remained so secluded and apparently inactive during the following weeks that it was rumored Yen had placed him under arrest. Lu Chung-lin and other loyal commanders remained in charge of the Kuominchün. During August Y. L. Tong, a relative and supporter of Feng, was reinstated as Vice-Minister of Foreign Affairs; Lu Chung-lin as Acting Minister of Military Affairs; and Hsüeh Tu-pi, Feng's chief civilian associate, as Minister of Public Health. In short, Feng and his men seemed to be in good odor again since Feng would presumably soon "wander about in foreign countries."

It is possible that during July and August Feng actually toyed with the idea of going abroad.[50] However, it is more likely that his representatives busily conferred with other anti-Chiang groups about ways to force Chiang Kai-shek to resign. Chiang's chief enemies were the

---

* Among the changes made by the Nationalist government after the Northern Expedition was the creation of a new province, Ninghsia, from part of Kansu. Since Kansu was one of Feng's provinces, one of his subordinates, Men Chih-chung, was appointed head of the new province.

members of the former left wing of the Kuomintang, who had come to be called the Reorganizationists. The name expressed their aim: to reorganize the national government. They claimed that Chiang Kai-shek had packed the Third Congress of the Kuomintang, and that party and government leaders therefore held their positions illegally. Furthermore, they denounced the government for not carrying out the political and social tasks of the revolution. In August and September, it was generally believed that Feng and Yen had representatives meeting secretly with Reorganizationists and others to plan moves against Chiang Kai-shek.[51]

But in the fall of 1929 the Reorganizationists had no reason to hurry into a coalition with northern warlords. The chief aims of the Reorganizationists were to expel Chiang Kai-shek from his dominant position in the government and the party, to give Wang Ching-wei the authority to be taken from Chiang, and to alter the policies of the party to make it a better instrument for what the Left Kuomintang considered the true ends of the revolution. Alliance with the warlords might help them achieve the first goal, but would not help with the others. The warlords wanted independence, not subordination to another wing of the party, and the Reorganizationists knew it. They saw little to be gained by exchanging the domination of Chiang for that of Feng. Therefore, although the Reorganizationists sympathized with the northern attitude insofar as it was anti-Chiang, they were not prepared to enter an alliance with the warlords as long as their own military men seemed able to capture enough territory to create a viable anti-Chiang base.

On September 17 Wang Ching-wei's chief military supporter, Chang Fa-k'uei, denounced Chiang Kai-shek and opened a military campaign against him. Shortly afterward the Reorganizationists issued a lengthy manifesto condemning Chiang and his government as dictatorial, corrupt, abusive of people, and illegal.[52] The Nanking government responded by ordering the arrest of the Reorganizationist leaders, and, of course, mobilizing its military to meet the new challenge. The Kuominchün seized the opportunity, and on October 10 twenty-seven of its leading officers issued a joint denunciation of Chiang, and asked Feng and Yen to lead a punitive campaign against Nanking.[53] This technique, having subordinates ask their leader to do what he wanted to do, was frequently used by Yüan Shih-k'ai, and had become common during the warlord period. Chiang Kai-shek promptly ordered an offensive against the Kuominchün.

In the war that followed, Yen Hsi-shan played a curious role. Both Feng and Chiang claimed his support, and both with reason. On the one hand, Yen accepted appointment by Chiang as Deputy Commander-in-Chief of the National Land, Sea, and Air Forces; thus Yen was second only to Chiang himself in conducting the anti-Kuominchün campaign. On the other hand, Yen did not want to fight Feng. Basically, Yen sympathized with Feng's attitude toward Chiang and the Nanking government. He knew that if Feng were eliminated, Nanking would become so powerful that he would lose almost all his independence.[54] Yen had also expressed his great friendship for Feng, and invited him to go abroad; it would not look good for him to turn around and attack his prospective traveling companion. Furthermore, Yen was a northerner, like Feng. Northern leaders and people alike looked suspiciously at the Kuomintang government, which was dominated by southerners.[55] In any event, for all these reasons, Yen did not fight on either side.

Most of the war took place in western Honan, in a great semicircle to the south and east of Loyang. During the second half of October and in early November, there was much fighting in that region, but the front remained stationary. At times things looked ominous for the government forces, and Chiang Kai-shek himself went to the front to sustain them. Suddenly, in the second half of November, the Kuominchün withdrew from Honan. There was some speculation that this was not a purely military decision, but, rather, a product of behind-the-scenes negotiations between Chiang and the Kuominchün commanders.[56] At that time, there was an undeclared war between Russian and Chinese forces in Manchuria, and Chang Fa-k'uei was advancing on Kwangtung.[57] The Nanking leaders could ill afford to be tied up in Honan, and it is very likely that they resorted to soft words and hard cash. On the other hand, the Kuominchün would not have benefited from easing the pressure on Nanking unless it also badly needed respite. Thus, at bottom, military necessity certainly dictated the Kuominchün retreat in late November.

Chang Fa-k'uei proved no more successful in his campaign against Canton than Feng Yü-hsiang had been in Honan, and early in 1930 the Reorganizationists in the South and the warlords in the North finally began to come together in their opposition to Chiang Kai-shek. Even more important, Yen Hsi-shan finally abandoned his ambiguous neutrality; a Peiping poster announced "Yen Hsi-shan is off the fence and is now astride the tiger."[58]

Yen opened the next phase of the struggle on February 10, 1930, with a wire to Chiang that stressed the futility of a policy of unification by force, and advised him to retire. This initiated an extraordinary flurry of telegrams during February. Chiang and other Nanking leaders fired off one wire after another stressing the importance of national unity, deploring the personal character of warlord armies, urging Yen to place public good before private interests, and exhorting obedience to the central government. Yen replied with a series of telegrams that accused Chiang of dominating the government and the party by military power, and condemned his suppression of dissidence by force and his expulsion of revolutionaries from the Kuomintang. Yen volunteered to resign with Chiang, an offer Chiang dismissed as insincere. On February 21 Wang Ching-wei, who had been expelled from the Kuomintang in December, joined the war of telegrams with a manifesto that scathingly denounced the Nanking government for bribery, corruption, dictatorship, and the use of "unspeakable tactics" to silence adverse criticism.[59]

During March some final telegrams were fired off, but the northerners also took more concrete steps. In the middle of the month Yen seized all the organs of the Nanking government in his provinces. Nanking military units were disarmed; Peiping's telegraph and telephone administration was taken over; and Kuomintang newspapers were closed. Yen also threatened to seize the Tientsin Customs office, a threat he carried out in June.*[60] Kuominchün and Shansi commanders issued wires asking Feng and Yen to lead a punitive expedition against Nanking, and almost immediately afterward Kuominchün troops under Sun Liang-ch'eng pushed into Honan toward Kaifeng.

At the beginning of April Yen formally took office as commander-in-chief of the anti-Chiang forces, with Feng acting as vice-commander; the positions reflected the relative power of the two warlords. The northerners also worked to bring the Reorganizationists to Peiping to help form a "legal government." But the prospects of such a coalition did not frighten Nanking very much. Indeed, 'although the government had authorized a punitive expedition on April 5, Chiang followed a defensive policy only, evidently in the belief that the heterogeneous anti-Chiang coalition must surely fall apart quickly.[61]

Chiang had good reason to expect his enemies to quarrel, for the

* Yen Hsi-shan appointed B. Lenox Simpson Commissioner of Tientsin Customs. Simpson wrote several books about China under the pseudonym Putnam Weale. In October 1930, after Yen Hsi-shan had already resigned as head of the northern government and Fengtien authorities were in control, Simpson was shot in his home by unidentified gunmen, and he died a few days later.

protracted negotiations in the North finally produced a so-called "Enlarged Conference of the Kuomintang"; it was "enlarged" because it had to accommodate so many viewpoints. It included the northern warlords, the Left Kuomintang or Reorganizationists, and the so-called Western Hills group from the right wing. All shades of the political spectrum were thus represented, held together primarily by their enmity toward Chiang Kai-shek.[62] The conference opened in Peiping in mid-July, and agreed on government organization by the end of August. On September 9, 1930, the leaders formally took the oaths of their new offices in a simple ceremony that included a bow before the portrait of Sun Yat-sen, and a reading of his will. Yen Hsishan was sworn in as Chairman of the State Council. Feng, who was at that time on the battlefront, was made a member of the Council, as was Wang Ching-wei.

But while the politicians were organizing the government in Peiping, their fates were already being decided on the battlefields of Shantung and Honan, and in conference halls in Mukden. In early July the Nanking forces gave up their defensive posture and launched an offensive north along the Tientsin-Pukow Railway against Shansi troops in Shantung, and west against the Kuominchün in Honan. Fighting was intense during July and August, and casualties on both sides were heavy. Against fierce resistance, the Nanking troops made slow but steady progress. By the beginning of September Shantung was lost to the northerners, and the main Nationalist thrust turned against Chengchow. A major government offensive was launched at almost the same time that the northern government was formally organized in Peiping. But the death blow did not come from Nanking. It came from Manchuria.

From the beginning of their quarrel, both Nanking and the northern warlords had sought the support of Chang Hsüeh-liang, who had inherited Chang Tso-lin's position as warlord of Manchuria. Both sides had appointed Chang to an official position, for it was clear that the Fengtien army might decide the issue if it were thrown to the right side at the right time. Chang Hsüeh-liang, however, had remained neutral and uncommitted. It was generally known that he, like many others, disapproved of many features of the Nanking government, but he was also for national unity. Moreover, he was deterred from joining the northern coalition by the presence of Feng Yü-hsiang, his father's old enemy. In fact, as early as May 1929 Chang had joined other Manchurian officers in a denunciation of Feng's policies.[63] Since then, except for occasional telegrams about the need for peace, Chang still had not become involved. But on September 18, Chang issued another wire pointing out that national issues must be solved through proper channels by the central government.[64] This telegram was understood to be directed against the northern coalition, and this interpretation was promptly confirmed when Manchurian troops entered Hopei and occupied Peiping, Tientsin, and the rest of the province. Yen Hsi-shan resigned his recently assumed post even before the arrival of the Fengtien troops. On September 22 the Shansi soldiers, who had taken Peiping from Fengtien soldiers two years earlier in the name of the Nationalist government, turned the city over to Fengtien troops, who took it in the name of the same Nationalist government. In the meantime, Chiang Kai-shek's troops rapidly occupied the key centers of Honan. By early October the war was over.

Yen Hsi-shan left Shansi after the defeat, although he later returned to head the province as one of the Chiang's stable of tamed warlords. But in Chiang's eyes, Feng was too independent, unpredictable, and dangerous, and had too great a potential for national leadership, to be allowed to control either territory or an army. Some of Feng's units had defected to Chiang in the closing days of the war, when defeat was imminent, and the remainder were to be "reorganized." This did not necessarily mean dispersion; some of Feng's units were kept together and used their great fighting capacities against the Japanese invaders in the 1930's. They also played a large part in the civil war between the Kuomintang and the Chinese Communists. But none of this was done under the leadership of Feng Yü-hsiang. Chiang forced Feng to relinquish control of his troops, and thus for most practical purposes terminated Feng's career as a warlord.

11. The Last Years

Feng Yü-hsiang lived for eighteen years after the collapse of the Yen-Feng coalition, a period exactly as long as his warlord career before the defeat. But in terms of his role in the history of modern China, the years after 1930 were anticlimactic, because Feng, cut off from the command of troops, could exercise no real influence on national affairs. For some of those years Feng remained in seclusion, refusing to lend his reputation to Chiang Kai-shek or anyone else by serving quietly in a government post, and attempting to retain the capacity for independent action should the opportunity arise. During that time Feng spent his days painting, writing poetry, and studying to acquire some of the advanced learning that had been denied him by the pressures of his active career. Feng abandoned this quiet life during the war with Japan, and devoted his energies to helping build up Chinese patriotism, unity, and resistance. The end of the war, however, also ended Feng's commitment to unity at any price; as the bitter conflict between the Kuomintang and the Communists flared up again, Feng increasingly used his influence against Chiang Kai-shek. He did not go over to the Communists, although he was moving in that direction when he died in 1948. Since then, the Communists have honored him as a progressive militarist.

Seclusion

After the close of hostilities in 1930, Feng withdrew to the vicinity of Fenchow, some 75 miles or so southwest of Taiyüan, in Shansi. Here he remained pretty much in seclusion. He may have participated in a few minor educational projects, sponsoring a local school or two, but most of his energies were spent studying and writing. He wrote much poetry, all in the vernacular and all concerned with the themes that had been his stock-in-trade during his public life: the hardships of the common people, the need to eliminate vice and backwardness, the exploitation of bad officials, the virtue of frugality, the vice of ostentation, and so on.[1] In his dress and conduct, too, Feng continued to emphasize utter simplicity. For example, he customarily wore coolie garb.

At the end of 1931, Feng went to Nanking to demonstrate his support for the government in the crisis engendered by the Manchurian Incident. Early in 1932, the government appointed him Minister of Home Affairs. However, Feng knew that as a minister he would be essentially a rubber stamp for the ruling Kuomintang faction. Therefore he did not take up the duties of his new office, and formally resigned after two months.

In the summer of 1932, Feng and his family moved to T'ai Shan, the sacred mountain not far from the city of Taian, in Shantung. Here he continued his life of study. He devised a plan to acquire a college education by engaging a series of professors to teach him for a few months at a time. In mid-1932, for example, the head of the economics department of a Peiping university lectured daily to Feng and his wife, Li Te-ch'üan. Moreover, an American missionary friend of the family regularly provided Feng with English books, of which aides gave him rough interpretations. Some, although not all, of these books were about Christianity; Feng at that time still described himself as a follower of Christ, though one with no interest in organized Christianity, of which he expressed some disapproval.[2] In October Feng suddenly left his mountain retreat and moved to Kalgan, a first step toward reentering political life. As soon as he arrived in Kalgan, he began issuing statements denouncing the government for not being able to devise constructive policies for national development, and particularly for its ineffective response to the Japanese seizure of Chinese territory.[3]

Shortly after Feng settled down in Kalgan, the Japanese army in Manchuria began encroaching on the territory of Jehol. After several weeks of alleging Chinese provocation in Jehol, the Japanese army invaded the province in February 1933 and completed the takeover in early March. This rapid conquest had important political repercussions in northern China. Chang Hsüeh-liang had lost much of his power when the Japanese seized Manchuria, but he had managed to retain enough troops to make him the single most important military leader in the North. However, the rapid and easy Japanese conquest of Jehol further weakened his position and reputation. In March 1933 Chang publicly accepted responsibility for the loss of Jehol, resigned his posts, and prepared to go abroad. The Nanking government took over Chang's position in the North, but there was much doubt that it could deal effectively with northern hostility and suspicion. Moreover, politically conscious Chinese were indignant over the Japanese seizure of Jehol on the heels of the conquest of Manchuria, and over the weak Chinese reaction. They became even more indignant when the Japanese penetrated eastern Chahar.

Feng had been urging armed resistance to Japan for some time. He told Chiang Kai-shek that Chinese troops should attack Japanese forces in northern China and Manchuria, and that he would support Chiang completely and enthusiastically if only Chiang would lead an anti-Japanese campaign.[4] It was this declaration, and others like it, that caused some organizations to look to Feng as a possible anti-Japanese leader. In the middle of April, over sixty civil organizations joined together to wire Feng at Kalgan, urging him to lead troops against the Japanese.[5] The Nanking government was understandably disturbed by the position Feng was beginning to assume in the eyes of anti-Japanese and anti-Chiang groups, and urged him to go immediately to the capital for consultation. But Feng was much too wary to walk into the city where Chiang's power was greatest, and where other anti-Chiang leaders had been forcibly detained. Early in May concern over Japanese activity intensified when Japanese troops occupied Dolonnor in Chahar, and then moved into a strip of the Chahar-Jehol border region, including Kuyüan, Paochang, and Kangpao. Shortly after this the government concluded the Tangku Truce with Japan; it called for Chinese demilitarization of part of northern China. All these developments combined to outrage Chinese nationalism, and also seemed to offer Feng a chance for a comeback.

The People's Anti-Japanese Allied Army

On May 28 Feng announced that he had organized a new force—the People's Anti-Japanese Allied Army—and that he had formally assumed the position of commander-in-chief two days earlier. He condemned the government for failing to make any sincere attempt to resist the Japanese aggressors, and for having refused reinforcements and supplies to those troops who did resist the invaders.[6]

Whereas some of Feng's supporters saw only self-sacrificing patriotism in this undertaking, many other observers tended to discount such selfless motives, and saw the venture as directed against Chiang Kai-shek. There was truth in both views, for Feng's personal and national aspirations coincided. Like many of his compatriots, Feng genuinely feared Japanese activity in northern China and wanted the nation to resist it. That was impossible as long as Chiang Kai-shek dominated the government and persisted in a policy of nonresistance. But since Chiang's policy was unpopular among nationalistic groups, Feng's proposals further undermined Chiang's political prestige; Feng's support of resistance was, by definition, anti-Chiang. And if Feng could gain enough backing for opposition to Japan, he might be able to reestablish himself in a position of regional power.

According to the official account of the Anti-Japanese Army, over 100,000 men were organized within a month; other estimates put the figure at 60,000 or 70,000.[7] Feng evidently hoped that students and other incensed nationalists would flock to his banner, but the army was primarily made up of various military units. Many were former Jehol troops who had been expelled by the Japanese and had not yet found a place to settle. Manchurian soldiers also joined in order to fight against the invaders of their homeland. Scattered Chahar units participated, and Feng evidently attempted rapid recruiting—one report says conscription—in Chahar. Fang Chen-wu, who became one of the leaders of the army, brought about 10,000 of his former troops from Shansi. There may have been some participation by the Chinese Communists, although the extent and nature of it are obscure; in the final analysis, it seems not to have been significant.* Few, if any, of the units that made up the Anti-Japanese Army had as many rifles as men; no more than three-quarters, perhaps only two-thirds, of the men had weapons.[8]

The chairman of Chahar province was Sung Che-yüan, one of Feng's former generals, who commanded former Kuominchün troops reorganized as the 29th Army of the central government. This excellent fighting force could have transformed the Anti-Japanese Army from a motley and unimpressive group into a formidable military organization. However, Sung Che-yüan wired the government that he was not a part of Feng's movement. At the same time he refused

---

* Meng Po-ch'ien, a former Communist who had personal connections with Feng Yü-hsiang, wrote about Chinese Communist activities in the People's Anti-Japanese Allied Army, but some of his dates are wrong and his facts unclear. Presumably the Communists welcomed a crisis in the North to divert Chiang Kai-shek from his Fourth Extermination Campaign. Meng also stressed that the Russians had an interest in Feng's army, and reported Feng's alleged admission that the Russians, through a couple of Chinese Communist intermediaries, had encouraged the formation of the Anti-Japanese Army and had promised to supply it. (Meng Po-ch'ien, pp. 8, 88–92, 96–97.) In response to charges that he was in some way linked with Communism, Feng requested newspapers to send qualified reporters to Chahar who could see for themselves whether the charges were true or false. (Feng, Ch'a-ha-erh, Pien II, pp. 16–18.)

to come into conflict with his old commander, and would not even go to Kalgan to take up his post as long as Feng was thére. But anti-Chiang leaders elsewhere in the country hastened to support Feng. The Southwest Political Council, with headquarters at Canton, publicly declared it backed Feng, and sent a storm of telegrams to individuals and groups urging them to do likewise. With much fanfare, troops were also sent from Canton, but they did not get very far; at least they never reached Chahar. It is possible that Canton also sent funds to Feng.[9]

Feng quickly appointed men to take over as many official posts in Chahar as possible. Many of the government's appointees relinquished their positions readily, probably because Sung Che-yüan and his troops were not there to support them. Feng's chief aim in placing his own men in local offices was to facilitate recruitment of troops and, especially, collection of taxes, although it is doubtful that Feng obtained much revenue before the entire venture came to an end. The Nationalist government, of course, completely opposed Feng's moves to establish himself in regional power. At the same time, Nanking also disapproved of Feng's aims toward Japan. Not only was the existence of the Anti-Japanese Allied Army contrary to the policy of the government, but it could trigger a Japanese counterattack that might result in the loss of even more territory.

The Anti-Japanese Army in late June initiated an attempt to retake the areas in Chahar that had been seized by the Japanese. By that time Japanese troops had already departed from Chahar, leaving the captured regions in the hands of Manchukuo troops. Feng's men succeeded in chasing those units out of the border region. In mid-July Feng's men also reconquered Dolonnor, and the entire province of Chahar was thus back in Chinese hands.[10] Although this achievement elicited an enthusiastic response from the anti-Chiang groups that supported Feng's activities, it further alarmed both Nanking and the Japanese. The Kuomintang government ordered Feng to disband his troops and leave the province, and government units moved into position for operations against the Anti-Japanese Army. At the same time, Japanese troops returned to the attack in Chahar. In the face of this combined opposition, Feng knew that the Anti-Japanese Army could not hold out. Moreover, by late July it was obvious that the undertaking was not going to become the focal point of nationalist patriotism to the extent necessary to alter the internal balance of power. Thus neither of Feng's chief aims—the expulsion of the Japanese and the weakening of Chiang Kai-shek—was attainable. In addition, although Feng was commander-in-chief of the Anti-Japanese Army, he had no genuine ties with the disparate, basically independent units that made up the army. Therefore it was clearly best for him to retire from the scene and assume the role of a fettered hero. On August 6 Feng handed control of Chahar affairs over to Sung Che-yüan, and he departed from Kalgan a week later. Fang Chen-wu and Chi Hung-chang, the other two chief figures in the Anti-Japanese Army, continued the struggle for some weeks, but were soon routed by their combined enemies.*

The Sino-Japanese War

Feng returned to T'ai Shan, where he lived in a famous temple on a scenic slope of the celebrated mountain. Here he resumed his studying and writing, occasionally leaving his mountain retreat to speak before some group or organization. He continued his improvised college education, studying political economy, psychology, and presumably other subjects. There is evidence that at this time Feng had very close ties with Communists, or, at any rate, with extreme leftists; indeed, it is possible that he belonged to a Communist-sponsored secret society.[11] Books published at that time, with the clear aim of promoting Feng's political career, had a flavor of Communist collaboration not apparent in his other writings.[12] However, if Feng did have such leftist connections, nothing seems to have come of them.

Feng also continued to write poetry, including at least two volumes of poems that accompanied drawings of rural life published by a Chinese artist, Chao Wang-yün.[13] Although the chief theme of these poems, as of his earlier poems, was the harshness and backwardness of Chinese life, they also expressed Feng's sorrow and indignation that much of the country had fallen into the hands of foreigners. He had in mind the encroachments on Chinese territory by foreign na-

---

* On November 10, 1934, Chi Hung-chang was shot by a Kuomintang gunman in a room of the Chinese Grand National Hotel in the French concession at Tientsin. Chi was not killed, but the French police turned him over to the Chinese authorities, with those accused of the attack. Chi was executed on December 1 by order of Chiang Kai-shek. Chi had been moving steadily left, and allegedly was involved in the Fukien revolt of 1933, which set up a short-lived "People's Republic." This incident is described in a report of the Political Branch of the French Police of the International Settlement at Shanghai, titled "Discovery of the Shanghai Central Bureau of the Chinese Communist Party." It is dated April 8, 1925, which is evidently a typing error for 1935. The report was originally obtained by Harley F. MacNair in China, and was left with his papers when he died. The present writer obtained the papers by the kind aid of Donald Lach and Earl Pritchard. See also Chin, No. 14, p. 11.

tions since the mid-nineteenth century, but particularly the more recent incursions of the Japanese. For example, a drawing of villagers
exchanging New Year's greetings inspired this poem by Feng:[14]

> On New Year's Day,
> New Year's greetings are exchanged;
> Everyone gathers to kowtow, heads bobbing
>   as if pounding garlic.
> Time speeds by like a flying arrow:
> One year passes, and then another,
> And the nation grows weaker day by day.
> Last year we lost Manchuria.
> This year we lost a province and a half.
> Vast and beautiful rivers and mountains:
>   where are they now?
> It is unbearable to think about! Unbearable to see!
> Let men of spirit arise and act!
> Recover our lost lands!

Feng had good reason to be concerned. Japanese penetration of
northern China had gone on steadily ever since the creation of Manchukuo. First Jehol was lost and then came the encroachments on
Chahar that produced the Anti-Japanese Army. During 1934 and
1935, Japanese pressure on northern China never let up, and caused
important setbacks for China. By the middle of 1935, Japanese civil
and military advisers were entrenched in Kalgan, and their influence
was felt throughout Inner Mongolia. The Ho-Umetsu Agreement of
July 1935 forced the Chinese to withdraw those men and Kuomintang organizations in Hopei that the Japanese considered objection-
able. In sum, the Japanese eliminated or significantly reduced Nationalist control over large areas of northern China.

This persistent Japanese encroachment finally brought Feng out of
his study and back into the center of public life, where he became a
spokesman for the growing number of Chinese who demanded vigorous resistance to Japan. He left T'ai Shan in late 1935, and formally
accepted office as Vice-Chairman of the Military Affairs Commission
on January 6, 1936. Thereafter he lived in Nanking, where he became
a conspicuous figure as a sort of talkative young elder statesman.

Shortly after his arrival in Nanking, Feng gave a series of talks to
the Central Political Council that described China's situation in compelling terms. In a speech given in December 1935, Feng listed in detail each actual or attempted Japanese encroachment on Chinese territory or sovereignty, and by the length of his list he emphasized the
enormity of the Japanese invasion and the ominous evils it por-

tended. Feng urged the government to formulate a comprehensive plan of resistance in which all elements of the nation—government, party, army, people—would cooperate to oppose further Japanese outrages. However, Feng admitted, no plan could succeed without the cultivation of a widespread spirit of resistance in China, and that spirit had been stultified by the prevalence of so many vices among the people—drinking, smoking, whoring, laziness, and so forth. The best way to eliminate these vices, Feng declared, was by means of the New Life Movement Chiang Kai-shek had inaugurated the year before. Feng stressed that the New Life Movement should first make its influence felt on the highest officials in the country.[15]

In a later speech before the same body, Feng literally took the offensive against Japan. He declared that if the Chinese were to develop their will to resist Japan they would have to reevaluate the nature of the Japanese threat. The Chinese should not believe the Japanese propaganda that the invaders were invincible. On the contrary, Feng said, the Japanese suffered from many deficiencies and weaknesses that were not shared by the Chinese. For example, he said, Japanese agricultural communities were so impoverished—so debilitated by hardship and want—that the entire nation was weakened economically. Moreover, Feng declared, Chinese troops had shown themselves to be braver than Japanese troops. He urged his countrymen to take stock of their own strong points, and to recognize the weak points of the enemy.[16]

During 1933 and 1936, such speeches as these were contrary to the government's policy of nonresistance. Indeed, on at least one occasion, when Feng expressed similar ideas in a newspaper interview, the government disavowed his remarks. Nevertheless, Feng did not attempt to separate himself from the government because of these differences; instead, he tried to become the spokesman in the government for a policy that, rejected by the men in power, was supported by many nationalistic Chinese. Feng was motivated by both national and personal considerations, just as he had been in the organization of the Anti-Japanese Army a few years earlier. On the one hand, there is no reason to believe that he did not sincerely and earnestly believe in the necessity of resisting the Japanese. On the other hand, there is little doubt that Feng still had hopes of assuming a position of genuine power and leadership. He seems to have envisaged a concatenation of events something like this: he would become a spokesman for a strongly nationalistic, anti-Japanese policy; ultimately the pressures from people with similar views would become so great that the government would be forced to adopt a policy of resistance to Japan; at that time, strong nationalist groups would become more influential, and he, as a leading exponent of the new policy, would find various opportunities open to him. To assure that his attitude was widely known, during the late 1930's Feng published several volumes of his speeches, letters, telegrams, and other miscellaneous material, all designed to show him in a nationalistic and patriotic light. It is very doubtful that Feng at that time had any hope of ousting Chiang Kai-shek. He was too practical to have any illusions about his political strength as compared with that of Chiang. He simply wanted to promote an anti-Japanese policy and, at the same time, be prepared to take advantage of whatever opportunities such a policy might bring. Indeed, the very nationalism that Feng extolled required him to support national unity, and that entailed support of Chiang Kai-shek. Therefore when Chang Hsüeh-liang seized Chiang Kai-shek in the celebrated incident at Sian in December 1936, Feng promptly wired the Young Marshal, urging that Chiang be immediately returned to the capital and offering to go to Sian to serve as a guarantor of Chang Hsüeh-liang's safety.[17]

Feng was much in demand as a speaker, and he addressed a great number and wide variety of audiences.[18] He frequently spoke to students, his engagements ranging from elementary schools to universities, from military academies to medical schools. Wherever he spoke, the preservation of China in the face of the Japanese threat was his main theme. When the war with Japan broke out in 1937, Feng threw all of his support to the government. He urged one of his former commanders to fight enthusiastically for the government, explaining that "Chiang's victory is our victory."[19] Feng used his rhetorical abilities to raise funds and to stimulate general support for the war effort, tasks in which he was reportedly quite successful. His words, which had once elicited tears and enthusiasm from his troops, drew money and jewelry from his civilian audiences.[20] Of course Feng moved with the government to Chungking. During the last two or three years of the war, he cut down on his public activities and lived quietly in the wartime capital.

Visit to the United States

When the Japanese threat to China disappeared in 1945, the pressure for Chinese national unity disappeared with it. The fragile united front that had bound the Kuomintang and the Communist Party somewhat reluctantly together during the war could no longer be maintained, and soon the flames of civil war roared once again over the already ravaged land. On a smaller scale, the forced unity of the Kuomintang itself began to dissolve. Groups and persons who disapproved of Chiang Kai-shek's policies tried to find ways to translate their attitudes into action. Feng Yü-hsiang was just such a person. The features of Chiang's rule to which Feng had always objected still existed: Chiang's dictatorial position, the corruption of Kuomintang officials, and the absence of effective reform measures. However, it was dangerous and difficult to criticize Chiang Kai-shek in 1945–46. Moreover, the trend of the developing Kuomintang-Communist struggle was not yet clear, and Feng, like many others, was caught up in a whirlpool of events that he could not influence. He decided to get out of the country until the situation became clearer and then decide on the best course of action. Feng asked the government to appoint him head of a commission to investigate irrigation and water conservation facilities in the United States.[21] In the spring of 1946, the appointment was officially announced. On the eve of his departure, Feng sent a letter to Chiang Kai-shek in which he pleaded for the preservation of peace, for more efforts at social reform, for more meaningful attempts to initiate genuinely democratic practices such as freedom of the press, and for elimination of bureaucratic corruption and administrative laxity.[22] The tone of the letter was critical but not denunciatory; and on that note Feng and his wife sailed from China in early September 1946.*

The United States government had requested Walter Clay Lowdermilk to arrange an itinerary for Feng and his group, and to guide the Chinese visitors throughout the tour.[23] Dr. Lowdermilk, who had met Feng on an earlier occasion in China, was then Assistant Chief of the United States Soil Conservation Service. In 1946 he was living in

---

* Relations between Feng and his wife were very strained at that time; they were hardly speaking to each other when they arrived in America. Rumor had it that Feng had become intimate with a young woman in Chungking during the war, and this explanation is supported by the fact that Li Te-ch'üan discussed the possibility of a divorce while they were in California; indeed, according to Mrs. Walter Lowdermilk, whom I interviewed in Berkeley, California, in June 1961, she even mentioned Feng's dalliance. Lo Chia-lun, in an interview with me on Taiwan in October 1958, said that Feng had such an affair, and that Feng's wife and some of Feng's staff had the girl carried off to another part of the country. The rumor of Feng's affair is also mentioned in Mao, O-Meng, p. 5. It has been suggested that the story of Feng's affair was fabricated by him and his wife for political purposes. However, it is not clear what they might have hoped to gain from such a tale, unless it was an element in their obtaining government permission to leave the country.

Berkeley, California. After Feng and his wife arrived in San Francisco in mid-September, they stayed for a while as guests in the Lowdermilk home, and then Feng began the tour that had been planned for him.* The commission visited various dams and power plants in California, and several soil-conservation projects. The investigators then moved eastward to Boulder Dam and the Grand Canyon, which concluded about the first third of the itinerary. An engineer in the group customarily informed the commission's hosts at each installation they visited that Feng was "an army general, and so he only wants to know about things in general."[24] He was right. As Dr. Lowdermilk later recalled, "during the tour, I soon came to feel that Feng was not much interested in the irrigation works and so on. What he was interested in was having his picture taken by motion picture cameras in the localities he visited. But he was not particularly interested in the technical aspects."[25]

As the trip continued, Feng did not even bother to feign interest. More and more of his time was spent conferring with aides, dictating letters and articles, and generally attending to matters of Chinese politics. When Feng insisted on remaining at the Grand Canyon despite the arrangements that had been made for him in many other localities, Dr. Lowdermilk left the party, and the inspection tour for all practical purposes came to an end.

After Feng abandoned the activities for which he ostensibly came to this country, he continued to travel eastward. He stopped at some missionary headquarters and looked up a few old missionary friends. But mainly he talked about Chinese politics, denouncing Chiang Kai-shek, and American support of him, in unequivocal terms. Ultimately Feng set up headquarters in New York City, where he distributed press releases, gave press conferences, and wrote articles on Chinese affairs for the American press. Feng's accusations against Chiang were

---

* Feng originally registered at a San Francisco hotel, but he was so distressed by the sight of youngsters dancing cheek to cheek in the hotel ballroom that he asked Mrs. Lowdermilk if she knew of any available rooms in her neighborhood. The Lowdermilks, realizing that Feng was disturbed by the view of American society he was getting at the hotel, invited him and his wife to stay in their home, and found neighbors who were willing to accommodate the rest of Feng's party. Mrs. Lowdermilk had no servants, and Feng was greatly impressed by the efficiency that she and the other American housewives displayed in the management of their suddenly crowded homes. Soon afterward, Feng purchased a home in Berkeley not far from the Lowdermilk house. (Interview with Dr. and Mrs. Lowdermilk.) Two of Feng's children were then students in California: a son at the University of California, and a daughter at the College of the Pacific (*New York Times*, Sept. 6, 1948, p. 6).

generally those that have since become very familiar, and, indeed, were already common at that time. Chiang was a dictator, Feng averred, who allowed no criticism or dissent, and who might well be compared with Adolf Hitler. Moreover, Feng claimed, Chiang tolerated an appalling degree of corruption; he would excuse any sort of malfeasance by a loyal subordinate. Chiang's policies tended to perpetuate the civil war, Feng said, and therefore the United States should withhold all aid from him. Indeed, full-fledged civil war might have been prevented

if the United States, instead of pouring billions of dollars into China, had ... used its good offices to bring about a new agreement; if the United States had stayed out entirely—maintained absolute neutrality—the war would have petered out for lack of means. Weapons supplied to Chiang Kai-shek usually fell into the hands of the Communists. In effect, the United States armed both sides.[26]

Feng compared the U.S. loans to Chiang to the Nishihara loans Japan made to warlord governments in China after the First World War.[27] Moreover, he said, American aid to Chiang Kai-shek was directly related to the number of Chinese casualties; when America gave much aid, many Chinese died, whereas few died when American aid was small.[28]

Feng recommended that the United States government support moderate groups in China, like the Democratic League and the anti-Chiang elements in the Kuomintang. Feng's avowed attitude toward the Chinese Communists was somewhat ambiguous. Although he was reported to have said that Chinese Communists were not true Communists, but were in fact simply carrying out the principles of Sun Yat-sen, that position did not seem to jibe with his expressed support for moderate groups, the so-called "Third Force."[29] The Chinese Communists interpreted Feng's remarks as hostile to the cause of Communist revolution in China. The editor of a Chinese Communist periodical took Feng to task for backing moderate elements, and for not seeking fundamental social and political changes.[30]

On November 9, 1947, Feng and his associates in the United States formed the "Overseas Chinese Association for Peace and Democracy in China." The organization's goals were exclusively concerned with changing America's China policy. The Association wanted the United States government to do the following: (1) discontinue military and financial aid to "reactionaries" in China; (2) withdraw all American military personnel from China; (3) refuse to grant any political loans to China; (4) suspend all relief funds and supplies until such time when they would no longer be used for military and political purposes; (5) adopt a policy of noninterference in China's internal affairs; (6) give aid to China as soon as peace and democracy were achieved.[31] Feng never commented publicly on the contradiction inherent in his call for aid to moderate groups, on the one hand, and his demand for noninterference in China's domestic affairs, on the other.

Nanking authorities could not tolerate Feng's denunciations, and on December 20 the government announced that he had been ordered home. Feng refused to comply with the order, and told the American public that he would be killed if he returned to China. He said that he, like many others, had supported Chiang Kai-shek during the war against Japan only for the sake of maintaining Chinese unity. Now, however, Feng stated, "any loyalty to Chiang's dictatorship would be a betrayal of the Chinese people and the principles of Dr. Sun Yat-sen." Feng also announced that a Revolutionary Committee of the Kuomintang had been formed in Hong Kong at the beginning of 1948, and that its members had resolved

to dissociate themselves from the reactionary Central Committee of the Kuomintang, which has been seized and controlled by Chiang Kai-shek; to rally all Kuomintang members who are loyal to, and willing to fight for, the realization of Dr. Sun Yat-sen's Principles; and to cooperate with all democratic parties and groups in China to overthrow Chiang's reactionary and dictatorial regime, which is the obstacle to an independent, democratic, and peaceful China.[32]

Feng announced that he was honored to have been elected to the Central Board of the Revolutionary Committee of the Kuomintang.

Death

Feng remained in the United States during the spring and summer of 1948, acting as the representative of the Revolutionary Committee of the Kuomintang. He used every opportunity to try to convince the American public that support for Chiang Kai-shek was a tragic error that would result in the loss of Chinese lives and the alienation of China from the United States. By summer, however, there was no longer much need for Feng's admonitions to the American public; the Chinese Communists had already seized the initiative in the civil war, and even the most sanguine Nationalists recognized that a military victory over the Communists was virtually impossible. It required but little more realism to see that the Nationalist cause was lost. It was time for Feng to go home and start mending—or, perhaps, building—political fences there.

On the last day of July 1948, Feng boarded a Russian ship, the *Pobeda,* to return home by way of the Soviet Union. After crossing the Atlantic and the Mediterranean, the ship entered the Black Sea at the end of August. Then, suddenly and unexpectedly, on September 5 the Russian press announced that a few days earlier Feng Yü-hsiang and one of his daughters had died aboard ship, both as a result of a fire.[33] Because Feng was such a colorful and controversial figure, his strange death has aroused much speculation. Many who knew him have toyed with the idea that he was the victim of foul play, and some say unequivocally that he was murdered. Possibly he was; political murder was certainly not uncommon in China at that time. But on whose orders was he killed? Those who accuse Chiang Kai-shek, the most logical suspect, must assume that his gunmen were members of the *Pobeda*'s crew, not an inconceivable but certainly a far-fetched assumption. On the other hand, those who suspect Communist machinations behind Feng's death can offer as possible motives only speculations that are as unconvincing as they are ingenious. Thus, in the absence of evidence to the contrary, there seems no alternative but to accept the official account of his death: on the afternoon of September 1 a movie projector caught fire, and in the ensuing emergency Feng died either of a heart attack or of asphyxiation.[34]

Feng's remains were returned to China. By the time they arrived, the People's Republic of China had come into existence. In the tumult of founding the new government, little attention was paid to Feng. In any event, warlords were clearly out of fashion. However, Feng's widow, Li Te-ch'üan, promptly became Minister of Public Health in the new regime, and subsequently held many other important administrative positions.* As peace settled over China and the

---

* During the war Li Te-ch'üan had been active in various women's organizations and church activities in Chungking. She was President of the China Women's Association and of the Chinese Women's Christian Temperance Union, and Executive Director of the Chungking Sino-Soviet Cultural Association. After the war she was active in child-welfare work and was on several government committees dealing with political and military problems until she left the country in 1946. Although some commentators have alleged that Li always had leftist connections and inclinations, she evidently had no known tie with the Communist movement before 1948. However, Mao Tse-tung was one of the first people she notified of Feng's death, and she held positions of influence in the Communist government from the outset. The wire from Li Te-ch'üan to Mao Tse-tung is in Chung-kuo Kuo-min-tang, p. 18. Mr. Howard Boorman kindly allowed me to see a preliminary draft of the biographical sketch of Li Te-ch'üan that will appear in the biographical dictionary he is editing.

new government could begin to think about writing history as well as making it, Feng Yü-hsiang emerged as a "good" warlord. In 1954 the Communists even published a book of Feng's selected poems.[35] Feng had never been a Communist, but his consistent expressions of sympathy for the masses and his open opposition to Chiang Kai-shek in the postwar years gave him a respectability in Communist society that the government formally acknowledged. On October 15, 1953, five years after his death, Feng's ashes were buried with full honors in a graveyard on T'ai Shan, the sacred mountain where he had spent so many years since 1930. Chairman Mao Tse-tung and Vice-Chairman Chu Teh sent funeral scrolls, and many dignitaries attended in person. Li Chi-shen, himself an old warlord and Feng's colleague in the Revolutionary Committee of the Kuomintang, officiated at the burial ceremony. After the ritual, two of Feng's sons laid the casket of ashes in a tomb.[36]

12. The Moral Warlord

Feng Yü-hsiang was a controversial figure during his lifetime, and has remained controversial since his death. Feng's detractors have maintained that he was brutal, rapacious, scheming, and treacherous —the very model of cunning duplicity. His supporters have asserted that Feng promoted the welfare of the common man, and did his best to foster morality among officials and to eliminate corruption in government. As a matter of fact, there is abundant evidence to support either view. With some oversimplification, it can be said that Feng's critics saw only his warlord methods, whereas his advocates saw only his reformist aims, and neither recognized that to Feng these two aspects of his activity were not at all incompatible.

Feng's attempts at social reform manifested a genuine concern for the common people of China, a concern that was fostered by several elements in his background. In 1912, when his career as an independent warlord really began, Feng was a mature man of thirty. He had already acquired a fairly stable pattern of assumptions, attitudes, and values, absorbed unconsciously from the ideological milieu in which he had grown up. Although by that time Western ideas and values had made inroads in China, they had not yet acquired much currency among the common people, from whom Feng came. Basic Confucian premises were still taken for granted by the uneducated masses in the years around the turn of the century. How completely and naturally Feng accepted them is indirectly shown by his weeping over the death of the Ch'ing monarch in 1908, when Feng was 26 years old. Although his attitude toward the Manchus changed drastically shortly thereafter, the change did not fundamentally alter the overall pattern of his assumptions. Most important for Feng's career as a warlord was that he conceived of government largely in Confucian terms: he believed that good government depended on the

morality of the political leaders and civil servants, and that the prime
duty of a government official was to work for the welfare of the *lao-
pai-hsing*. This belief was confirmed and strengthened by the popular novels that constituted the major portion of his literary diet during his young and formative years, for they frequently exalted the
official who exerted himself on behalf of the common people.[1]

This generalized Confucian concern for the common good was
doubtless given some specific direction by the example of conscientious officials of the nineteenth and early twentieth centuries, for
most of Feng's reform measures were not new to China. Opium
smoking, for example, had long been condemned by scrupulous
Confucian officials. And the Empress Dowager herself issued an edict
in 1902 urging that foot-binding be discontinued. Good government
had always been exalted by Confucian scholars. Feng's various social-
welfare measures—orphanages, poorhouses, public sanitation facilities, and the like—were all similar to programs undertaken during
the T'ung Chih Restoration. This similarity, coupled with Feng's
great admiration for Tseng Kuo-fan, makes it likely that Feng's administrative ideas derived in some measure from the experience of
the great Restoration leader and his associates.

Feng's background also influenced the formation of his social and
political ideas. He came from an impoverished family, and he remembered with sympathy the hard lives of his parents and grandparents.
Most of his friends and his soldiers were of peasant origin, and his
own experience made him appreciate the difficulties of their lives.
Although Feng was sensitive to their economic problems, he was
even more concerned about the distortions imposed on their lives
by ignorance, superstition, and irrational customs. For example, he
lamented the use of acupuncture in lieu of modern medicine, the
cruelty of foot-binding, and the reliance on idols and magic for relief
from life's burdens.

This intimate knowledge of the hardships endured by the Chinese
masses was not only another stimulus to reform, but one that gave
a certain pragmatic and innovative quality to Feng's measures. His
desire to free the poorer classes from oppressions and restrictions
rooted in tradition necessarily implied an acceptance of nontradi-
tional or even anti-traditional methods. In any event, Feng felt no
vested interest in tradition. He had absorbed many traditional attitudes from his environment, and some of them played crucial roles
in determining the course of his career, but he was not traditionalistic. He did not share the view of many late-nineteenth-century

officials that innovation was a threat to Chinese civilization and to their own ruling positions. Rather, Feng was ready to accept innovation where it promised to realize those Confucian values that tradition had taught him were good, particularly the welfare of the *lao-pai-hsing*.

Christianity also influenced Feng's reform ideas, and his acceptance of the foreign faith illustrated the lengths to which his willingness to innovate could go. Christianity had an emotional appeal for Feng, but its most specific attraction was that Christians practiced the virtues he valued and eschewed the vices he abhorred. Moreover, the Christians with whom Feng had the most contact were missionaries, who naturally thought in terms of eliminating deleterious practices and introducing presumably beneficial ones. Feng had something of the missionary zeal himself, and the Christian preoccupation with "good works" contributed to Feng's reform tendencies.

Feng's concern about China's reputation among the nations of the world was also a source of his interest in social reform. Like so many of his contemporaries, he deplored China's relative weakness, and he wanted to eliminate those features of Chinese life that seemed backward in comparison with other nations. This concern became an increasingly conscious nationalism after the May Fourth Incident and the recurrent clashes during the 1920's between Chinese and foreigners in China.

Finally, Feng probably saw a connection between his reformism and his desire for power. He felt that officials should be men of virtue, and his administrative measures were designed, among other things, to show him as a virtuous man worthy of the high position he aspired to.

Despite the diversity of the sources that shaped Feng's reform ideas, the central and most important source was the traditional Confucian concern for the welfare of the *lao-pai-hsing*. Christianity, Feng's class background, the Western influences that were current in the early Republic—all these only confirmed this traditional concern. They were variations on a theme, but the theme itself remained strong and clear.

Feng's Confucian premises not only inspired his dreams of reform and popular welfare, but also determined his concept of the kind of government that could realize such dreams. According to the premises that underlay traditional Chinese society, good government and social harmony required officials who adhered to proper moral principles. The rule of the emperor himself was justified only by his good conduct. Feng accepted and exemplified these assumptions. He seldom thought in terms of political institutions, but always in terms of morally good officials and morally bad officials. He believed his own governing ability was related to his moral development, and his diary is replete with expressions of concern about his growing lazy or arrogant, and of his determination to become a better man, which in turn would make his administration better. To Feng, good government depended primarily on virtuous officials, and whenever he saw bad government he concluded that the officials were evil men.

Feng administered his provinces according to these premises. He thought of himself as a virtuous official, or at least as an official aspiring to virtue, and he also exhorted his subordinates to act in accord with high moral principles. His administration was also extremely paternalistic. He assumed, as the Confucian official of earlier times had assumed, that he knew what was best for the people, whose function was simply to obey orders. Feng never offered the public a clear political program; he was his political program. Feng talked a great deal about his devotion to the Republic, but he did little to encourage the development of republican institutions. From 1926 on, Feng always called himself a "revolutionary," but he gave the word his own meaning: "Revolutionary military men differ from warlords," he wrote in 1927, "in that their greatest determination is to save the country and save the people; they are willing to sacrifice everything to reach their sworn goals."[2] It was all a matter of resolution and character.

In sum, both Chinese and foreign values inspired Feng with a desire to ameliorate the lives of the common people. His Confucian assumptions about government led him to believe that his goals could be achieved by having the right man in power. And his powerful ambition made him think of himself as that man.

Feng's ambition was enormous. Not only is this clear from the facts of his career, but it is unanimously confirmed by those in the best position to know—his subordinates. One of them expressed the consensus when he raised his thumb to symbolize a single individual at the apex of power and remarked: "Feng wanted to be number one."[3] The Russian team that inspected the work of the Kuominchün's Russian advisers in 1925 reported that Feng wanted to be the "big star." In Feng's mind, this was not a selfish ambition, for he identified his desire for personal power with the welfare of his country.

His chief Russian adviser understood Feng perfectly when he said: "He [Feng] considers himself a great star for the good of China."[4]

As a young soldier in his twenties, Feng may not have considered himself such a potential luminary, but he was ambitious even then. He braved the scorn of his comrades to call commands to an empty drill field, and he transferred to Yüan Shih-k'ai's army largely because he saw a greater opportunity for advancement there. Of course, it never occurred to Feng to pursue his ambitions elsewhere than in the military. For one thing, he was virtually born into the army; moreover, when he was a young man the military offered almost the only practicable avenue for personal advancement to one who, like Feng, was both economically and educationally impoverished. But to get ahead in the army, one had to play the game according to certain rules. After 1912, when Feng's career began in earnest, those rules were nothing more or less than the characteristics of Chinese warlordism: one had to have connections; one had to develop independent military power; one had to make temporary alliances, and be ready to shift sides to maintain independence; and so forth. It was thus by mastering the ground rules of military advancement that Feng Yü-hsiang became a warlord.

The nature of warlord competition confirmed Feng's conception of government. Many warlords were clearly immoral, caring nothing for the people they ruled, and conditions in their areas were accordingly very bad. However, the warlord system allowed for a high degree of individualism in regional administrative policies; each warlord was a law unto himself in his own provinces. Therefore Feng could aspire to be a moral leader, and the very immorality of so many of his competitors strengthened his conviction of the righteousness and superiority of his own values. In other words, the same assumptions that led Feng to view good government as the work of a moral man in authority also made the warlord system seem a practicable route for such a man to achieve authority, and thus Feng felt no compulsion to abandon the warlord system to become a revolutionary.

In short, Feng's conception of government by moral men proved to be the perfect rationalization for his warlord career. He felt that his own motives were pure, his ideals high, and his concern for the *lao-pai-hsing* genuine. He was sure that he opposed immoral men, and from that position he slipped easily into believing that all men he opposed were immoral. As a result, Feng could and did compete vigorously for power, secure in the conviction that he was serving not only his own interests, but the interests of the people as well. It was the people, after all, who would ultimately benefit from government by a moral ruler. The struggle for power was, of course, anything but beneficial to the people; they paid, suffered, and died. Feng felt no guilt about that; since he identified his own aspirations with the welfare of the people, the pursuit of the former was simply a way of serving the latter. The hardships suffered by the *lao-pai-hsing* were regrettable, of course, but that was simply the price that had to be paid to extirpate evil and reward virtue. Feng stood adamantly on principle: he was prepared to do anything to save the country and the people, even if it killed them.

Feng was thought to be unique among the warlords; but, except for his Christianity, he has no great claim to uniqueness. Much of what has been said about his background and basic assumptions could be said about various other warlords. A number of them started life in humble surroundings, and investigation would doubtless show that they shared Feng's Confucian attitudes. They also had firsthand experience with hardship and poverty, and they sought advancement along the same military route as Feng. Nor was Feng alone in his concern for social reform and good administration. Other warlords initiated more fundamental, farseeing, and drastic reforms than Feng, and administered their domains with equally conscientious efficiency. Yen Hsi-shan and Ch'en Chiung-ming are the best-documented examples, although Wu P'ei-fu, Chang Tso-lin, and probably several others would also find a place in this category.

Feng's ambitions and attitudes remained remarkably consistent throughout his life as an active warlord, and even afterward. The changes that ostensibly mark his career were caused not so much by shifts in his goals and views as by the kaleidoscopic pattern of evolving Chinese history, which showed Feng in several different lights.

During the five or six years following the death of Yüan Shih-k'ai, most people considered Feng a "good warlord," and some even considered him a unique, independent revolutionary. Those were the years when the most progressive force in Chinese society was the New Culture Movement, which was devoted, among other things, to the uprooting of obsolete or deleterious customs such as foot-binding, opium smoking, nepotism, and arranged marriages. The New Culture Movement centered among students, teachers, writers, and the like, and drew heavily from Western social thought. Although Feng had no connection with the intellectual sources of the New Culture Movement, his administrative policies accorded with many of its aims, and he was therefore viewed as a most progressive leader by supporters of the movement.

During the early 1920's, however, the New Culture intellectuals moved into a new phase:

The new intelligentsia soon became aware that they must awaken the masses of the people to the national crisis and to the people's own interests, and then organize and lead them if the nation were to be saved and strengthened. Mass movement, propaganda, organization, and revolutionary discipline were consequently regarded by the young intellectuals as significant and justifiable techniques for their struggle against world power politics and warlordism.[5]

In short, the trend was toward mass political organization, and Feng Yü-hsiang was not part of that trend.

Feng had never attempted to organize popular support in his provinces. He ruled by fiat; to the people he offered only speeches and slogans extolling virtue, decrying vice, and urging confidence in the Kuominchün. His reform programs were initiated and maintained by his army personnel or, in special cases, by professionals employed by his army; the public participated only as passive objects of Feng's concern. As long as Feng conceived of good government as a product of moral leadership—his own leadership in particular— mass organization was simply superfluous.

In fact, Feng was adverse to the new trend, because it was moving toward more fundamental social changes than he had envisaged. Feng had never thought in terms of a thoroughgoing social revolution. Of course the warlord period was a time of turmoil and change, creating a fluid situation in which many persons found opportunities to move up from the lower classes. Feng himself had risen high from low beginnings, and he was not opposed to others' doing the same; indeed, Feng's rise exemplified the kind of social shuffling that was common in China during periods of disorder, and that had produced men of low estate who had founded dynasties. But Feng saw this as a shuffling of individuals; he did not aspire to transform class relationships. In his provincial administration, he stressed the need to improve conditions for the lower economic classes, but in practice he did not ignore the interests of the upper classes. His occasional cavalier treatment of local gentry simply manifested the autocratic independence inherent in warlord status, not antagonism to such classes per se. Feng was interested in improving the behavior of people in society, not in altering the basic framework of society.

Finally, the shift toward mass organization threatened Feng's

ambitions, for his route to power had been plotted within the warlord system. The uncompromising anti-imperialism of the Russian-
sponsored Kuomintang-Communist alliance also repelled Feng. As
a Chinese, he was anti-imperialist and perhaps a bit anti-foreign,
but as a warlord he could not afford to express such principles or
prejudices freely, for the conditions of warlord power made it necessary to have foreign supporters, whether they were imperialists or
not. As long as foreigners were ready to support one or another
warlord, no warlord could afford to be an uncompromising anti-
imperialist. Feng Yü-hsiang's most vehement anti-imperialism, like
that of other warlords, was usually directed only against those nations from which he could expect enmity in any event. The best
example of this was Feng's reaction to the May 30th Incident in
1925. His anti-imperialist statements at that time were extremely
violent, and were capped by a suggestion of open war with England.
But only with England. Though the chain of events that culminated
in the May 30th Incident originated in Japanese-owned mills, Feng
did not include the Japanese in his denunciation. On the contrary,
in July 1925 he announced that he was going to permit the Japanese
to develop the Northwest, that he was going to send students to
Japan, and that he intended to engage Japanese advisers.

For all of these reasons, Feng resisted strenuously when Russians
and Chinese pressured him to join the Kuomintang in 1925. At the
same time, by dangling the possibility of his cooperation before the
Russians, he tried to exact as much material aid as possible to improve his power position. Thus, in the early years of the Republic, in
a predominantly warlord context, Feng's reforms gave him a revolutionary aura; but when juxtaposed with genuine revolutionaries,
Feng stood out as very much a warlord.

A year later, after his trip to the Soviet Union and his entry into
the Kuomintang, Feng suddenly appeared as a radical; the "Christian
General" became the "Red General." However, Feng's leftist orientation was superficial and temporary. It is true that his public statements, particularly during the first few months after his return to
China, were studded with leftist phrases, but there was more froth
than substance to those, as indeed there was to most of his comments
about his relationship to revolution. Feng responded readily and
sympathetically to the Marxist emphasis on the masses, for it seemed
fundamentally the same as his own stress on the virtues and needs
of the *lao-pai-hsing*. But Feng's reaction to the organizational and in-

stitutional aspects of Communism was ambivalent. On the one hand, he discovered that there was more to revolution, at least Russian-style revolution, than he had dreamed of, and he was impressed by the apparent efficiency of Russian methods. But on the other hand, he recognized that the manipulation and leadership of such a revolution required talents he did not have, and that he should accordingly be wary about getting involved. Moreover, although Feng was impressed by the social reforms that he thought benefited the laboring man in the Soviet Union, he was repelled by the disorder and uncertainty of the kind of social revolution from which they derived. Orderly change dictated by himself was much simpler. Feng wanted revolution by the numbers.

Although the exigencies of warlord conflict drove Feng into the Kuomintang despite the threat that party membership posed to his independence, the Wuhan-Nanking split occurred before the contradiction between Feng's basic warlord views and those of the Kuomintang-Communist alliance could come to a head. Siding with Nanking offered Feng the best of all possible worlds: he could continue under the banner of the Kuomintang, with all of its nationalist-revolutionary symbolism and significance, yet reject the social revolution fostered by Wuhan. At the same time he could remain essentially independent, for his relationship with Nanking was fundamentally a military alliance and did not involve the creation of organs in his provinces that would compete with him for control. Indeed, Chiang Kai-shek, the leader at Nanking, seemed to operate on premises similar to those that guided Feng himself.

It is sometimes asked whether Chiang was a warlord. A simple affirmative reply would be as misleading as a simple negative reply, but it is certainly true that Chiang's rule of the party and the government resembled warlord rule in many respects. Chiang's power was based on regional control, just like that of the warlords. He headed an armed force that was loyal to him personally, largely through the officers of the Whampoa clique. He maintained his rule more through warfare and the manipulation of factions than through the normal operation of republican institutions, and thus he afforded warlords opportunities for their own maneuvers and intrigues. As a matter of fact, Chiang's view of himself was remarkably similar to Feng's. Chiang, like Feng, saw himself as the moral leader destined to unite and lead China. Like Feng, Chiang thought that social problems could be solved by moral example and exhortation once military supremacy had been achieved. It is not surprising that both men were fond of the writings of Tseng Kuo-fan.

Feng and Chiang were allies in 1927 and 1928, but with the defeat of their common enemies their alliance turned into a rivalry resembling the kind of warlord competition in which Feng had been involved before 1926. However, the situation was somewhat different after 1928, for the Kuomintang, having ostensibly unified the country, more than ever represented Chinese nationalism. This, in fact, was one of the differences between the warlords and Chiang Kai-shek; Chiang's position in the nationalist movement was not that of a warlord. Feng Yü-hsiang had always excelled in making his maneuvers for greater personal power seem to be in the national interest, and he recognized that if he flouted Chinese nationalism he would alienate important groups. Therefore he had to justify his actions in different terms. Whereas Feng had earlier denounced his enemies as moral degenerates, tools of the imperialists, and, particularly, oppressors of the *lao-pai-hsing*, after 1928 he accused Chiang of subverting Sun Yat-sen's principles, of violating the rules of the Kuomintang, and of aspiring to be a dictator. Feng's motives acquired an aura of purity because Chiang actually did pursue policies inconsistent with republicanism, with the rules of the Kuomintang, and with the quest of nationalistic Chinese for reform and progress. Nevertheless, Feng had no real chance to seize leadership of the Kuomintang; he was a latecomer to the party, a northerner, a warlord, an outsider in every respect. In any event, Feng never represented a genuine alternative to Chiang's kind of government, but only a different manipulator of it.

On the other hand, Chiang Kai-shek's dictatorial tendencies were strengthened and somewhat justified by the activities of Feng and warlords like him. Feng, for example, refused to yield effective control of his provinces to Nanking, but he demanded for himself and his domain all the benefits a central government normally provides. There was no doubt in Chiang Kai-shek's mind that Feng's goal was to gain control of the government without appearing to violate any revolutionary principles, and Chiang was prepared to ignore republican procedures to block him. Indeed, one of the facets of modern Chinese history that is illuminated by the career of a man like Feng is the inadequacy of the measures taken by the Nationalist regime after 1928 to assure the loyalty and cooperation of the warlords who had joined the Kuomintang. There was, for example, no meaningful attempt to create popular institutions that might have limited the arbitrary independence of regional warlords. Nanking in effect told a man to be loyal, and threatened to attack him if he was not. That was not particularly persuasive to men whose entire careers had been spent under the threat of attack from one quarter or another. Of course, by 1928 it was already very late; the time to have fettered the warlords was during the Northern Expedition.

From 1927 to 1930, the exigencies of the struggle for power made constructive government increasingly difficult in Feng's provinces. His swollen armies voraciously consumed money and supplies, and these had to be provided by people who had been impoverished by earlier wars. Feng's reforms—which had never dealt with fundamentals—became increasingly superficial and nominal, and even a little farcical, in the context of spreading famine and unrest. A few observers thought Feng had abandoned his earlier concern for the *lao-pai-hsing*, but that conclusion reflected a mistaken view of Feng's attitude. Since he equated his own power with the welfare of the *lao-pai-hsing*, Feng saw his efforts to strengthen his army as necessary to the long-range interests of the people, even though they caused temporary hardship.

For several years after his defeat in 1930, Feng continued to hope that he might once again play a leading role in Chinese national politics. That he could harbor such a hope tells as much about China under Chiang Kai-shek as it does about Feng. Politics under Chiang retained so many characteristics of warlordism that defeated but unreconstructed warlords like Feng could believe that a sudden change in the internal balance of power might provide an opportunity for a comeback. On the other hand, the fact that Feng could not make a comeback also says something about Chiang Kai-shek's China. Chiang maintained an internal distribution of power that warlords found it hard to tamper with; moreover, the nationalistic tenor of opinion in the country made it increasingly difficult for a warlord to challenge the central government. Nationalism demanded national unity, and warlord activities were inevitably disruptive. During the war with Japan, the pressure for unity became so irresistible that even the abyss between the Kuomintang and the Communist Party had to be temporarily bridged.

At the end of the war Feng was 63 years old, and had been cut off from the sources of genuine power for fifteen years. Certainly it is doubtful—indeed, inconceivable—that he still believed in the possibility of becoming "number one." In fact, it is very difficult to be specific about Feng's personal ambitions at that time. The speed with which his wife assumed high position in the Communist government suggests at least the possibility that Feng, too, had reason to believe that the Communists would find a place for him. In any event, the pertinence of his criticism of Chiang Kai-shek's rule obscured any opportunism in his motives. Against the background of Kuomintang corruption and ineptitude, Feng once again began to look like a revolutionary in the last years of his life.

Politically, Feng was an anachronism. His political premises and goals were suited to a society that no longer existed. Acculturation by contact with the West had started China moving in a direction that made Feng's political ideas obsolete and restrictive. At the same time, Feng was partly a product of that Western contact. He dreamed of building modern highways, producing automobiles, setting up steel plants, and doing other things necessary to bring China into the mainstream of modern technological civilization. But he never recognized the incompatibility of those dreams with his political assumptions. In this respect Feng was no different from Chiang Kai-shek, Wang Ching-wei, and other leaders of the time, each of whom sought in his own way to graft a new technology onto the old politics. It was a historical coincidence that Feng should die in 1948, just when the establishment of a Communist state resolved that contradiction for China.

Appendix

Appendix

The document below, identified as the "Kuominchün Political Catechism," first published in Lanchow, Kansu, was printed in the *NCH*, Feb. 18, 1928, p. 247. Although it was not dated, internal evidence indicates that it was issued in late 1926. Certainly it was written during the period of strong leftist influence on the Kuominchün, and it illustrates in more detail than the catechisms quoted in chapter 9 the character of the Kuominchün political indoctrination at that time.

The document consists of three parts: Sun Yat-sen's Will, Feng Yü-hsiang's Wuyüan Oath, and a long catechism. I have substituted my own translation of Feng's Oath for the *NCH* version; the original is in *KMCKMS*, chap. 10, p. 131. Note that Feng patterned the phraseology of the Oath after the latter part of the first paragraph of Sun's Will. The catechism is printed as it appeared in the *NCH*, including editorial interpolations in parentheses.

KUOMINCHÜN POLITICAL CATECHISM

Sun Yat-sen's Will

For forty years I have devoted myself to the cause of the people's revolution with but one end in view, the elevation of China to a position of freedom and equality among the nations. My experiences during these forty years have firmly convinced me that to attain this goal we must bring about a thorough awakening of our own people and ally ourselves in a common struggle with those peoples of the world who treat us on the basis of equality.

The work of the revolution is not yet done. Let all our comrades follow my "Plan for National Reconstruction," "Fundamentals of National Reconstruction," "Three Principles of the People," and the "Manifesto" issued by the First National Convention of our Party, and strive on earnestly for their consummation. Above all, our recent declarations in favour of the convocation of a National Convention and the abolition of unequal treaties should be carried into effect with the least possible delay. This is my heartfelt charge to you.

(signed) SUN WEN
March 11, 1925

Written on February 20, 1925.

Wuyüan Oath

The oath of the Commander-in-Chief of the Kuominchün Allies on taking up office was as follows:

The goals of the Kuominchün are, by using the principles of the Kuomintang, to arouse the masses, to extirpate the traitorous warlords, to overthrow imperialism, and to seek freedom and independence for China. We will also ally ourselves in common struggle with those peoples of the world who treat us with equality. We will live and die together, and never stop until we reach these goals. We swear it.

The Catechism

(1) Remember

Question 1—The continuous battling of our army is to destroy the imperialism which is encroaching on our country, and also traitorous militarism. Do you understand this or not?

Answer—We understand.

Question 2—The encroaching imperialism and traitorous militarism which we object to are the Twenty-one Demands which Japan forced our country to accede to in 1915, and the groundless massacre of our students and workmen by the British on May 30, 1925. Things like these our army is eternally opposed to. Japan has seduced Chang Tso-lin and Britain has seduced Wu P'ei-fu to act as their servile dependents and attack us. We risk our lives in battle against them for the sake of saving the government and people, not for the sake of one or two persons. Do you all understand this?

Answer—We do.

Question 3—Our brothers who died to save the government and the people are not yet buried; the wounded have no healing medicines; those who are neither dead nor wounded have neither clothing nor food; have you forgotten this?

Answer—We cannot forget.

Question 4—The whole populace of Chihli, Shantung, Honan and Peking are oppressed beyond endurance by bandits and soldiers who ravish and plunder. Ought we to save them or not?

Answer—We ought to save them.

Question 5—Since this is so, what method should we employ?

Answer—We should, in fearlessness of death, indifference to money, patient endurance of misery and hardship, and understanding of principles, come and save the government and people, swearing to wipe out this disgrace.

(2) Duty

Question 6—What army are you?

Answer—We are the People's Army.

Question 7—What kind of soldiers are you?

Answer—We are soldiers who plan happiness for the masses, not soldiers who fight for advantage to one or two persons.

Question 8—Where do your food, clothing and shelter come from?

Answer—They come from the hands of the masses.

Question 9—What is the relation of the masses to you?

Answer—They are our masters. They are also our fathers, brothers and sisters.

Question 10—Since this is so, ought you to protect them, and risk your lives for them, or not?

Answer—We ought.

Question 11—When you are hungry and cold, how should you conduct yourselves toward the populace?

Answer—We are resolved that even if we starve to death we will not take away anything from the people; if we freeze to death we will not enter their houses.

(3) Justice

Question 12—That our brothers the farmers, builders and weavers should toil ceaselessly and yet be without food, clothing and shelter, while those who have never learned to farm and build and weave should have good food, fine clothing and comfortable houses and do absolutely no work of any kind. Say, all of you, is this just or not?

Answer—It is not just.

Question 13—If those who love idleness but, on the other hand, enjoy good food, fine clothing and comfortable houses are, in addition, given to wild profligacy, reckless gambling, pride, extravagance, and excesses. Say, you men, is it just?

Answer—It is not just.

Question 14—Since this is so, what should you do?

Answer—We shall advocate justice.

Question 15—How will you advocate justice?

Answer—We shall cause everybody to have food, clothing, dwellings and money.

Question 16—Where will you begin in order to carry out this programme?

Answer—Our first step will be to not harass the common people in the slightest degree, nor to allow others to do so. The second step will be to secure land for cultivators and employment for labourers.

Question 17—And what more should be done?

Answer—Workers should eat, and toilers should eat, but those who do nothing at all will meet with our intervention.

(4) National Shame

Question 18—From what time did the browbeating of us Chinese by foreigners begin?

Answer—It began from the Opium War.

Question 19—The Opium War was the forcible introduction by the English of opium into our country. When the war began our country was defeated, and from this time forward continually contracted many one-sided treaties. Do you detest them or not?

Answer—We thoroughly detest them.

Question 20—In the year 1900 the united forces of eight nations entered Peking, ravishing and plundering, burning and killing everywhere, and compelling us to give up territory and pay indemnities. They occupied

Peking and Tientsin with military forces. Up to the present moment there is no hope that the occupied territories will ever be returned. The indemnities were so very heavy that they never can be paid off. The foreign troops which occupy Peking and Tientsin make display of their martial spirit and give themselves airs, oppressing us constantly. Say, all of you, whether it is detestable or not?

Answer—It is most detestable.

Question 21—Britain, Japan, France, America and other such imperialistic governments compel us to acknowledge their consular authority to judge cases in our country. So they commit murder and incendiarism in our land and we cannot interfere. But the minute we Chinese reach a foreign land we everywhere come under the control of foreign laws. Say, all of you, if there is equality under this rule or not?

Answer—There is no equality.

Question 22—Britain, Japan, France, America and other such imperialistic governments grasp our customs' revenues and allow us no liberty in the levying of taxes. They love to import great quantities of goods for sale in China, but when our Chinese goods go to their countries they impose customs duties as they please. Say, all of you, is this economic equality or not?

Answer—It is not equality.

Question 23—Also Britain, Japan, France, America and other such imperialistic governments force us to lease to them numerous foreign concessions. This just means that foreigners have set up many little independent nations inside China's territories, causing us to be wholly deprived of our rights and privileges. Say, is this shameful or not?

Answer—It is shameful.

Question 24—In addition, our country's railways and mines have all been forcibly usurped by them, depriving us of freedom of transportation and liberty to export for coal and iron, so that neither industries nor commerce can thrive. The people are becoming poorer and poorer every day and have no means of livelihood. Say, you men, is it heart-rending or not?

Answer—It is heart-rending.

Question 25—On May 30 of last year the British in Shanghai killed many of our students and workmen, and supplemented it by barbarously killing people in Canton, Hankow, Nanking, Chungking, etc. The most recent case is Britain's gunboat, at Wanhsien, in Szechuan, using her big guns to kill over 2,000 of our countrymen, and burn two large streets. Why do they thus dare to insult us?

Answer—Because we cannot make ourselves strong.

Question 26—Brothers, according to what has been said above, our government will soon be ruined. Our race will soon be destroyed. Only the beating down of imperialism and traitorous militarists and giving China freedom and independence can open a way of safety. Whose responsibility is this?

Answer—This is our responsibility.

(5) Revolution

Question 27—How should we bear this responsibility? We see Mr. Sun Chung-shan (Sun Yat-sen) working over 40 years for revolution for the purpose of saving China. His Three Principles are a formula for the saving of China. The Nationalist Party is a Party for the saving of China. We ought, in obedience to Mr. Sun Chung-shan's spirit of revolution, to extend the Nationalist Party and put the Three Principles into practice. Is this a very important matter or not?

Answer—This is a very important matter. We will ceaselessly press forward National Revolution, and put into practice the Three Principles, not stopping until we have attained our object.

Question 28—Chung-shan's dying injunctions declared that he wished to draw together in a united struggle all peoples in the world who will treat our race as their equals. At present what nations are they which treat us as equals?

Answer—One nation only, the United Soviet; for it, of its own accord, entirely abrogated all unequal treaties which concerned China.

Question 29—At present what nations are they which do not accord equal treatment to us?

Answer—They are Britain, Japan, France and the United States—those imperialistic governments.

Question 30—If we want to put into operation the People's Revolution we must make the masses thoroughly understand the evils of imperialism and traitorous militarism, and also that our troops are for the saving of our government and people. We must unite soldiers, workmen and farmers for a concerted thrust forward. What is the significance of this?

Answer—This means the arousing of the people.

Question 31—What is the "Struggle" (that Mr. Sun Chung-shan exhorts us to engage in)?

Answer—Shedding one's blood for the Revolution; sacrificing one's self for a principle; holding on to the very end; unyielding effort which must attain ultimate success; this is what is meant by "struggling."

Notes

Notes

Complete authors' names, titles, and publication data will be found in the Annotated Bibliography, pp. 357–72. The following abbreviations are used in the notes:

CWR: *The China Weekly Review*
CYB: *The China Year Book*
IIHKM: *Hsin-hai ko-ming*
Jihchi: Feng Yü-hsiang *jih-chi*
KMCKMS: Feng Yü-hsiang, *Kuo min-chün ko-ming shih*

NCH: *North China Herald*
NCS: *North China Standard*
WSH: Feng Yü-hsiang, *Wo-ti sheng-huo*
WTTSSH: Feng Yü-hsiang, *Wo-ti tu-shu sheng-huo*

Chapter One

1. The various geographic and cultural features favorable to regionalism in China are well known. Many are summarized in Northrop, pp. 421–22. Fitzgerald, pp. 30–31, comments on the absence of national patriotism, as does Pratt, p. 65. Provincial differences and provincial patriotism are noted by Vinacke, p. 377. Williams, I, 462, fn. 1, comments on the Chinese view that regions other than one's own are virtually alien territory. Hsieh, pp. 245–46, discusses the degree of provincial autonomy in the Ch'ing. Most standard histories of China mention one or more characteristics of latent regionalism, although not by that name.

2. For the weakness and decentralization of Ch'ing forces at that time, see Powell, "Yüan Shih-k'ai," p. 227, and *Chinese Military Power*, pp. 13–14; Bales, pp. 40–41; Hsieh, pp. 258–59; and Waley, p. 65.

3. Michael, pp. 473–78. The identity of interests between the Manchus and the Chinese gentry is discussed in Wright, p. 52, and Spector, pp. vii–viii.

4. For the regional character of the Hunan Army, see Powell, *Chinese Military Power, passim,* and Spector, *passim.*

5. Spector, *passim.*

6. Powell, *Chinese Military Power,* pp. 24–25; Spector, pp. 20–22, 27, 44, 191–99, 210; Feuerwerker, pp. 12–16; Michael and Taylor, p. 191.

7. For recruitment of the Hunan Army, see Powell, *Chinese Military Power,* p. 24, and Bales, pp. 46–47. Spector gives many examples of the personal nature of the Anhwei Army.

8. Wright, p. 206. Powell, *Chinese Military Power,* p. 26.

9. Feuerwerker, pp. 41–42.

10. Wright, p. 58 and *passim*.

11. Li Chien-nung, *Political History*, p. 142. On pp. 141–42 Li discusses the role of decentralization in China's defeat by Japan.

12. Of the various studies of the Boxer Rebellion, the activities of the provincial leaders are covered most thoroughly in Tan, *Boxer Catastrophe*. For other indications of regionalism's extraordinary development in the late Ch'ing, see Powell, *Chinese Military Power*, pp. 41–42, 135, 167–68, 172–75, 249, 268; Feuerwerker, p. 43; Hsieh, p. 297.

13. Jerome Ch'en, *Yüan Shih-k'ai*, is a full-length biography of Yüan. T'ao, *Pei-yang*, I, 7, comments on Yüan's reputation as a military expert.

14. *NCH*, Oct. 21, 1911, pp. 133–34. See also T'ao, *Pei-yang*, I, 14, and Powell, *Chinese Military Power*, p. 227.

15. T'ao, *Pei-yang*, I, 14.

16. *Ibid.*, p. 13; Powell, *Chinese Military Power*, pp. 212–13.

17. T'ao, *Pei-yang*, I, 16.

18. Powell, *Chinese Military Power*, pp. 41–42.

19. Michael, pp. 482–83.

20. Powell, *Chinese Military Power*, p. 156.

21. *Ibid.*, pp. 191–92.

22. Holcombe, pp. 92–93.

23. Although the facts in this and the following two subsections dealing with phases of warlordism can be found in most accounts of the period, there are no good scholarly accounts of those years that focus on warlord politics. The nearest thing to an exception is MacNair, *China in Revolution*, which has much material on warlord politics. Li Chien-nung's *Political History* also has much information, but the work has been poorly translated and has many errors. The original Chinese work by Li, *Chung-kuo chin-pai-nien cheng-chih shih*, is an excellent standard source of information. Lynn, *Political Parties*, relates the complex struggles and interrelationships of the period in some detail. Lynn was an adviser to several of the important warlords of the period at different times, and his book contains much information on the warlords. Ch'ien, "Role of the Military," emphasizes later years, but treats early warlordism in passing. Houn, *Central Government*, treats the period from the standpoint of the formal political structure with clarity. T'ao, *Pei-yang*, covers the warlord period in detail to 1923. The same author's earlier work, *Tu-chün t'uan-chuan*, is one of the few works that focuses exclusively on the early years, covering the period from Yüan's death to the Anhwei-Chihli War. There are, of course, many other books treating specific aspects of the period that have relevance to warlordism.

24. Houn, pp. 134–39, 179–83. See also *NCS*, May 5, 1926, p. 8.

25. Houn, pp. 126–27.

26. Lo Chia-lun, VII, 75–76; T'ao, *Tu-chün*, pp. 1, 46–50, 69.

27. Brandt, p. 89.

28. Mif, p. 37, says the National Revolutionary Army grew from 60,000 in July 1926 to 170,000 at the beginning of 1927. Wilbur and How, pp. 381–82, say the increase during this period was from 100,000 to 260,000.

29. A report on the "Military Organization of the Nationalist Regime" by vice-consul J. Hall Paxton at Nanking, April 10, 1928, to the Secretary of State, 893.20/80.

30. Quoted in MacNair, p. 160. See *NCH*, Nov. 17, 1928, p. 289, for a breakdown of China into warlord domains of that time.

31. Although a few works cover the political history of the warlord period, there have been no published attempts to analyze the nature and workings of warlordism. An unpublished study by Lucian Pye, "The Politics of Tu-chünism in North China, 1920–1927," was presented in 1951 as a Ph.D. dissertation at Yale University. A Chinese writer, Wang Chi-shan, has written *Chün-fa wen-t'i chih yen-chiu.* I have been unable to locate this work, but its main points are summarized in "Ts'a-p'ing," p. 4. From this summary it seems that Wang's work is more descriptive than analytical, which is also true of the more recent work by T'ao Chü-yin, *Pei-yang chün-fa t'ung-chih shih-ch'i shih-hua,* as well as the present discussion. More spadework is necessary before a thorough analysis of warlordism can be attempted, although Pye's work contains some fruitful ideas.

Several studies of individual warlords are now in progress, but regional studies are developing more slowly. There are a number of sketch histories of Chinese provinces in the State Department's "Records Relating to Internal Affairs of China, 1910–1929." Written by foreign service officers stationed in the regions described, they vary in quality, but some are quite detailed and helpful.

32. Kotenev, *Soldier,* p. 98; *CYB, 1926–27,* p. 1046.

33. Baker, pp. 66–67.

34. *Ibid.,* p. 68; Kotenev, *Soldier,* p. 100; Misselwitz, p. 14. Feng Yü-hsiang was more particular about recruits than some warlords, but he was always able to recruit men quickly and easily.

35. Mao, *O-Meng,* p. 12, gives one example; many others could be cited. Indeed, it was not uncommon for bandits to offer to cease their depredations in return for acceptance into the army.

36. Misselwitz, p. 71.

37. Strong, p. 599, expresses this view.

38. T'ao, *Pei-yang,* I, 19; Favre, pp. 194–95.

39. Gillin, pp. 289–306. 40. T'ao, *Wu P'ei-fu,* pp. 1–105.

41. F. F. Liu, p. 150. 42. Hewlett, p. 189.

43. Pearl Buck, p. 77. 44. *Ibid.,* p. 5.

45. Pye, pp. 78–79; pp. 69–83 discuss the problem of loyalty.

46. Personal interview with a former officer in Feng Yü-hsiang's army, Taiwan, 1959.

47. Impey, "Stalemate," p. 238.

48. For examples, see *WSH,* p. 735; Li T'ai-fen, p. 158.

49. Pye, pp. 121–27, 173–77, 180, 208–11.

50. *Ibid.,* pp. 232–68, discusses the warlords' relations with cabinet government.

51. See, for example, Northrop, pp. 392–93; Gale, pp. 110–11; Kotenev, *Soldier,* p. 100; Close, p. 57; T'ao, *Tu-chün,* p. 128.

52. "Lion," p. 148.

53. Auxion de Ruffe, p. 153.

54. Dr. Paul Hodges, of the Peking Union Medical College, in an interview with this writer in San Francisco in August 1960, said he had helped treat about 1,000 casualties of this war; he declared that the most seriously

308 NOTES TO PAGES 23–26

wounded had not lived to receive treatment because they had not promptly received competent care.

55. *NCS,* Jan. 15, 1926, p. 4.

56. Speer, pp. 157–58, contains a graphic eyewitness description of the conditions endured by some of the wounded in the 1925–26 war in northern China.

57. *NCH,* Oct. 26, 1929, p. 151, contains a copy of the report in which the American Red Cross made this attribution.

58. Woodhead, pp. 129–30.

59. Chang Yu-i, II, 565.

60. *Ibid.,* p. 567.

61. *Ibid.,* pp. 575, 577. Finch, p. 76, makes the extremely questionable assertion that in some areas the land tax was collected for a century in advance.

62. Pearl Buck, p. 76. 63. Chang Yu-i, II, 601–2.

64. *Ibid.,* pp. 580–83. 65. *Ibid.,* p. 584.

66. *NCS,* Aug. 6, 1925, p. 1. 67. *NCS,* May 28, 1926, p. 8.

68. Chang Yu-i, II, 568. 69. *Ibid.*

70. *Ibid.,* p. 571.

71. Despatch from U.S. consul at Amoy, A. E. Carleton, to the Department of State, Jan. 23, 1924, 893.512/232. Clubb, p. 187, has a striking list of taxes collected in Kansu.

72. Altree, pp. 95–96; "Silas Strawn Describes China Conditions," *CWR,* Dec. 4, 1926, p. 4. J. E. Baker was adviser to the Chinese Ministry of Communications from 1916 to 1926, and in his book *Explaining China* he discusses the effects of warlordism on railroad operations. John K. Davis, U.S. consul at Nanking, reported on April 10, 1925, about special military taxes on the Tientsin-Pukow Railway, 893.00/6203.

73. Jowe, "Military Taxes," p. 391; Baker, pp. 77–78.

74. This was described in a news article in the *Hankow Herald* on April 10, 1929. The article was included in the monthly report from the Chungking consulate on military and political conditions in the consular district, 893.00 P.R. Chungking/10.

75. Gillin, p. 303.

76. "Fengtien Opens Attack," p. 166; "Week in the Far East," p. 23; *NCS,* Nov. 21, 1925, p. 8.

77. Gale, p. 161; Jowe, "Chinese Militarism," p. 171; report from Edwin S. Cunningham, U.S. Consul General at Shanghai, Sept. 20, 1924, 893.00/5643.

78. Despatch from Howard Bucknell, Jr., vice-consul in charge at Changsha, to the Secretary of State, Oct. 12, 1922, on the subject of opium in Hunan, 893.114/419; despatch to the Secretary of State from M. S. Myers, consul at Yunnanfu, on the subject of opium, July 12, 1923, 893.114/454.

79. "To Be Paid 'When the War Is Over.'" Chang Yu-i, II, 589–98, gives details on the warlord practice of issuing paper money, and the resulting loss of confidence in this depreciated currency.

80. T'ao, *Tu-chün,* p. 25.

81. Chang Yu-i, II, 599–600.

82. Report from the U.S. consul at Foochow, Ernest B. Price, Nov. 1, 1924,

to the Department of State, reviewing commerce and industry for the quarter ending Sept. 30, 1924, 893.00/5835.

83. Chang Yu-i, II, 598–600. Animals and equipment belonging to foreigners were not exempt from confiscation during a war; see Andrews, *New Conquest*, p. 329.

84. Despatch from U.S. consul at Chungking, C. J. Spiker, to the Secretary of State, April 5, 1924, 893.20/62.

85. Pearl Buck, p. 4.

86. The description appeared in a letter to *The Shanghai Times* on Sept. 26, 1924. It was included in a report from Edwin S. Cunningham, U.S. Consul General at Shanghai, to the Secretary of State, Sept. 26, 1924, 893.00/5647. I have corrected misspelled words and added some punctuation.

87. Chang Yu-i, II, 610–12; see also Finch, p. 126.

88. Isaacs, p. 29.

89. Reports quoted by T'ang, *China in Revolt*, p. 110.

90. *CYB, 1924–25*, p. 957.

91. See, for example, Finch, pp. 68–71, 74–75, and Jowe, "Who Sells the Guns?" Microfilm Roll No. 110 of the State Department's "Records Relating to Internal Affairs of China, 1910–29" contains much material on the arms embargo and arms importation into China.

92. Chien, *Hsi-pei*, pp. 44–45.

Chapter Two

1. Hummel, I, 526–28, has a biography of Liu Ming-ch'uan.

2. For the poverty of Feng Yu-mou's childhood, see *WSH*, pp. 1–4; pp. 4–8 describe his entering the Ming army, p. 8 tells of his marriage, and p. 9 tells of the birth of Feng Yü-hsiang. Some accounts say that Feng was from Anhwei, because the Chinese customarily designate the home of one's father as one's "native village." Feng's "native village" was thus Chuk'o in Chaohsien, Anhwei. He was, however, born in Hsingchichen. Chung-kuo Kuo-min-tang ko-ming wei-yüan-hui, p. 1, gives the date of Feng's birth as the 6th year of Kuang-hsü, or 1880–81. Various other sources give dates ranging from 1880 to 1882. I have followed Feng's own date of 1882, *WSH*, p. 9. On p. 29 he indirectly confirms this date when he says that in 1892 he was 11 sui, or 10 years old.

3. Feng's life at K'angkechuang is described in *WSH*, pp. 10–24.

4. *WSH*, pp. 27–28. Ch'ang, p. 58, says that in the years up to the Revolution of 1911 the two characters in Feng's given name, Yü-hsiang, were different from those now generally considered to be his name. Until then, according to Ch'ang, the characters used were 御香. See also note 83 below.

5. *WSH*, p. 35.

6. *WSH*, p. 37.

7. *WSH*, pp. 63–64.

8. *WSH*, pp. 35–36.

9. Mao, "T'an Feng Yü-hsiang," says that Feng rose from the position of army cook. This is not confirmed by any other source, including Feng himself.

10. *WSH*, p. 48.

11. *WSH*, p. 69.

12. *WSH*, pp. 48–49. Feng had a chop made with the four characters *wai-kuo tien-hsin,* which he retained for many years.

13. *WSH*, pp. 51–62, gives Feng's comments on the Boxer Rebellion, and an account of his actions at the time.

14. *WSH*, pp. 70–71.   15. *WTTSSH*, p. 89.

16. *WSH*, p. 72.   17. *WSH*, p. 73.

18. *WSH*, p. 72.   19. *WSH*, p. 77.

20. *WSH*, pp. 83, 126–27; *WTTSSH*, p. 155.

21. *WSH*, p. 82.   22. Fuse, p. 25; Ch'eng, p. 12.

23. *WSH*, p. 97.   24. *WSH*, pp. 103–6.

25. *WSH*, p. 98.   26. *WSH*, p. 106.

27. *WSH*, p. 99.   28. *WSH*, pp. 99, 108.

29. *WTTSSH*, p. 10; *WSH*, pp. 25–26.

30. *WTTSSH*, p. 12; *WSH*, p. 26; the schoolroom is described in *WTTSSH*, pp. 15–18.

31. *WTTSSH*, pp. 16–17; *WSH*, p. 26.

32. *WTTSSH*, pp. 43–44; *WSH*, p. 28.

33. *WSH*, p. 29, says this second period of schooling was in 1893, which jibes with Feng's description of activities he pursued after leaving the first school. *WTTSSH*, p. 21, says he studied in the first school for three months and then continued in another school for the next year, 1892. I have followed *WSH*.

34. *WTTSSH*, p. 22; *WSH*, p. 29.

35. For Feng's discussion of the difficulties he had reading these two novels, see *WTTSSH*, pp. 30–31, 39–41, 45, 67. For his comments on each of them, see *WTTSSH*, pp. 29–37 and 45–49. It is of some interest to read the passages in K. C. Wu's novel, *The Lane of Eternal Stability,* pp. 178–85, that describe the influence these old Chinese novels had on the education of warlords.

36. *WTTSSH*, pp. 55–56.

37. For Feng's comments on these three novels, see *WTTSSH*, pp. 56, 66, 68, 72–79.

38. *WTTSSH*, p. 139.   39. *WTTSSH*, pp. 80–81.

40. *WTTSSH*, pp. 83–85.   41. *WTTSSH*, p. 87.

42. *WTTSSH*, p. 95.   43. *WTTSSH*, pp. 102–8.

44. *WTTSSH*, p. 136.   45. *WTTSSH*, pp. 163–71.

46. *WSH*, p. 100; *WTTSSH*, pp. 174–76.

47. *WTTSSH*, pp. 110, 157.

48. *WTTSSH*, p. 113.

49. For Feng's comments, mainly a summary of the book's contents, see *WTTSSH*, pp. 113–35.

50. For Feng's comments on Tseng's work, see *WTTSSH*, pp. 145–54.

51. *WTTSSH*, p. 99. It has been impossible to identify this book beyond this title.

52. *WTTSSH*, pp. 99–101. Written in 1904 or 1905, this book discusses women of various areas of the world, stressing their intrinsic equality and their civilizing mission in the family and society.

53. *WTTSSH*, p. 177.

54. *WTTSSH*, pp. 157–58.

55. Li T'ai-fen, p. 3.

56. *WSH*, p. 120.

57. Chung-kuo li-shih yen-chiu hui, p. 885, notes the estimate of the deaths at Yangchow, and on p. 888 indicates the estimates for Chiating. Both of the original texts are in *Liu-yün-chü-shih*, 10th ts'e and 16th ts'e.

58. Wang Hsiu-ch'u, pp. 521–22.

59. *WSH*, p. 121.

60. *WSH*, pp. 121–22; Sonoda, p. 27. T'ao, *Pei-yang*, I, 19, says that Hsü Shih-ch'ang was transferred early in 1911. This date is evidently wrong. *NCH*, Feb. 13, 1909, prints the imperial decree, dated Feb. 9, appointing Hsü head of the Ministry of Posts and Communications, and directing Hsi-liang to assume Hsü's former position. A few weeks later, in *NCH*, Feb. 27, 1909, p. 503, a foreign writer expressed doubts that the "old Boxer and reactionary Hsi Liang" would continue the reforms begun by Hsü.

61. *WSH*, p. 120; MacMurray, I, 787.

62. *WSH*, p. 121.

63. *WSH*, pp. 122–23.

64. *WTTSSH*, p. 185.

65. *WSH*, p. 123.

66. *WSH*, p. 121. Feng says that Wang Chin-ming was the commander of the 1st Battalion, and Shih Ts'ung-yün the commander of the 2nd Battalion; all other sources say the opposite. The positions of the various officers listed in the text are not those they held at the time of the formation of the study group, but those they held in mid-1911.

67. Li T'ai-fen, p. 6, lists 13 men besides Feng. *KMCKMS*, p. 19, lists the same 13 men. It is interesting that both these sources omit Yüeh Jui-chou, who is included in Feng's own list of the original six.

68. *WSH*, p. 124.

69. A good example of attributing membership in the study group to other participants in the revolt is Fuse, p. 27, where it is stated that Pai Ya-yü was a member of the group. Pai was one of the T'ung Meng Hui agitators who attempted to encourage the Luanchow rebels as a means of extending the revolution in the North. He evidently never met Feng.

70. *WSH*, p. 136.

71. *KMCKMS*, p. 19. T'ao, *Pei-yang*, I, 82, also discusses this. *WSH*, p. 143, says there were three factions, the third of which wanted to see whether the revolutionaries won or lost before deciding on their policy. On p. 143, too, Feng lists the leaders of each faction.

72. These 12 requests are listed in Li Chien-nung, *Political History*, pp. 251–52.

73. T'ao, *Pei-yang*, I, 81.

74. *NCH*, Nov. 11, 1911, p. 361.

75. Ling Yüeh, "Luan-chou kuang-fu chi-shih." This is a handwritten manuscript in the Kuomintang Historical Archives in Taiwan. I have a handwritten copy on which the pagination of the original manuscript is not indicated. Future references to this work, therefore, will not include page numbers.

76. Ling discusses the establishment of the Northern Republican Society in Tientsin, and its concern with Luanchow. Hu Ngo-kung's essay in *HHKM* contains several accounts of meetings in Tientsin where the Luanchow ques-

tion was discussed. The revolutionaries were also interested in plans for revolt in Tientsin, Paoting, Peking, and T'ungchow.

77. T'ao, *Pei-yang*, I, 115, mentions the departure of Sun Chien-sheng from Luanchow, but the last character of Sun's ming-tzu is given as 生 instead of the more usual 聲. Hu, p. 276, tells of the group's decision to send two men. Ling gives a different account, and asserts that by Nov. 22 he had already led a group to Luanchow. Although he did lead a "dare-to-die" unit to Luanchow, it is doubtful that he went that early.

78. Hu, p. 276.

79. *WSH*, p. 142.

80. Hu, p. 291.

81. *KMCKMS*, Pien I, chap. 2, pp. 20–21; *WSH*, p. 147.

82. *KMCKMS*, Pien I, chap. 2, p. 21.

83. The telegram is quoted in *WSH*, p. 148, and also in Kuo, pp. 268–69. Feng says that the wire was signed by himself, Wang Chin-ming, and Shih Ts'ung-yün. The names listed after the telegram in Kuo's account include these along with others. The characters used for Feng's given name in this wire are 御香.

84. *WSH*, p. 149.

85. *KMCKMS*, Pien I, chap. 2, pp. 22–23, quotes the telegram in its entirety. The wire is briefly reported in *NCH*, Jan. 6, 1912, p. 28. The government attempted to maintain a cloak of secrecy around the Luanchow affair.

86. T'ao, *Pei-yang*, I, 115; *NCH*, Jan. 6, 1912, p. 30.

87. Li T'ai-fen, p. 8.

88. "Hsin-hai Luan-chou," p. 332.

89. T'ao, *Pei-yang*, I, 116, says Wang and Shih were killed in the fighting. Feng, in *WSH*, p. 150, says the two men were tricked into meeting with the leaders of the government troops for peace talks, whereupon they were seized and executed. "Hsin-hai Luan-chou," p. 332, also says they were executed, but there is no mention of treachery. Ling says they were killed in the fighting.

90. *WSH*, pp. 142–43, 151. On the face of it, Feng's account of the circumstances that prevented him from participating in the revolt is reasonable and probably true. It contains, however, a strange error in dating. The telegraphic declaration that marked the beginning of the Luanchow revolt was issued on Jan. 2, 1912. This is confirmed by T'ao, *Pei-yang*, I, 115, and by an article datelined Jan. 2 in *NCH*, Jan. 6, 1912, p. 28. T'ao says, on p. 116, that government troops began fighting the rebels on Jan. 5 and defeated them on Jan. 8. This, too, is confirmed by articles in *NCH*, Jan. 13, 1912, pp. 95, 97. It is impossible to reconcile these dates with Feng's chronology. Feng wrote, in *WSH*, p. 151, that his comrades at Luanchow were captured on the third day of his incarceration. Since the revolt did not begin until Jan. 2, their capture had to be after that date, presumably sometime between Jan. 5 and 8. Moreover, by Feng's account it was after the execution of Wang and Shih that he was given his very light sentence. He says he then proceeded to Peking, where he met Lu Chien-chang. Lu sent him to Paoting, where he stayed a short while and then boarded a train to return to Peking on Jan. 3! The possibility that Feng may have been reckoning by the lunar calendar, on the basis of which Jan. 3 could be understood to

mean Feb. 20, is precluded by his specific reference to the "3rd day of the first month of 1912."

Chapter Three

1. As mentioned in the preceding chapter, Feng employed different characters for his ming-tzu from 1912 on. It is interesting to speculate whether this change was due to his assuming a position in an important Peiyang unit after having just been involved in revolutionary activity.

2. There is some confusion about the name of Lu's force. Kuo-shih hsin-wen pien-chi pu, p. 61, states that shortly after the riots and mutinies in Peking in early 1912, Lu Chien-chang was ordered to recruit 3,000 men for the Ching-wei-chün (京衛軍). This work was written in 1912, so Lu's force must have been called the Ching-wei-chün that early. Yet WSH, p. 196, says that the Reserve Army, of which Lu commanded the Left Route, was renamed the Ching-wei-chün in 1914, at the time that Lu was put in charge of catching the White Wolf. KMCKMS, Appendix, p. 2, says that the Left Route Reserve Army was renamed the Ching-wei-chün in August 1913.

3. KMCKMS, Appendix, p. 2. Ch'eng, p. 9, says that Feng went to Honan to recruit.

4. WSH, p. 168.

5. KMCKMS, chap. 1, p. 2; Ch'eng, p. 12.

6. WSH, p. 168, says that Feng recruited a battalion in that time. Ch'eng, p. 9, says that Feng commanded about 500 men in 1912. Actually, at that time a full-strength battalion should have numbered over 600 men. Wen, Pien I, pp. 61–65, says that in the army organization of the Republic one battalion was supposed to consist of four companies of 157 men each, or 628 men. CYB, 1914, p. 322, states that an infantry battalion consisted of four companies, each comprising 5 officers and 142 men, plus 12 noncombatants. This would make a total of 588 combatants, plus 48 noncombatants, or 636 men in all.

7. For a summary of Feng's movements at this time, see KMCKMS, Appendix, pp. 2–3.

8. Li T'ai-fen, pp. 9–10.

9. Feng's writings hardly mention the Second Revolution. Even if he had wanted to support the revolution, it would have been difficult for him to do anything. Two of Feng's former officers with whom I discussed this question on Taiwan in 1959 stated flatly that Feng's policy at the time of the revolution was completely determined by Lu.

10. KMCKMS, Appendix, p. 2, describes this reorganization as the transformation of the Left Route Reserve Army into the Capital Defense Army. This may be incorrect; see note 2 above. However, all sources agree that at about this time Feng's unit was expanded to a regiment.

11. WSH, p. 182. According to Feng, they recruited a complete regiment, approximately 1,600 men. Such a statement, however, does not take into consideration the men already under his command. Presumably he means that he recruited enough additional men to bring the total number of his troops up to regiment strength.

12. KMCKMS, Appendix, pp. 2–3.

13. NCH, Nov. 1, 1913, p. 364, reported that the number of the White Wolf's outlaws involved in one incident was 2,500, and other reports in the

NCH mention similar figures. However, *NCH*, Nov. 29, 1913, p. 684, stated that 30,000 outlaws belonging to various bands were always ready to assist the White Wolf. This may be an exaggeration, but there are several other reports that the White Wolf had connections with other bands of brigands.

14. *NCH*, Nov. 8, 1913, pp. 411–12, carried a missionary's account of his experiences while a captive of the White Wolf. He reported that the bandits had been very interested in the progress of the Second Revolution, and that "they appeared to hold Huang Hsing [a revolutionary leader] in the very highest respect."

15. In *Chin-tai-shih-tzu-liao*, No. 3, 1956, there are two items relative to the White Wolf that might shed some light on his political motives if any. For some reason, however, no copies of this periodical issued in 1956 are available in the United States, although issues both before and after that year are in many American libraries. Therefore it has not been possible to examine these two items. The *NCH* reports on the activities of the White Wolf contain several allusions to possible political aims, but these seem to have derived from the reports of the bandits' interest in the revolutionary leader Huang Hsing. Few of the White Wolf's acts were of a political nature. However, in Apr. 1914, the *NCH* carried reports from the Chinese press that the White Wolf had posted proclamations in prominent places in the capital of Shensi. The proclamation is translated in *NCH*, Apr. 25, 1914, p. 268. In it the White Wolf calls himself the Great Tutu of the Army for the Support of Han [people] in China. The proclamation mentions the suffering of the people under the Manchus, their vain expectations of liberty under the Republic, their distress that Yüan Shih-k'ai became a dictator, and concludes with an expression of the White Wolf's determination to "save the lives of our people." He calls upon the people of Shensi to support him, and promises that there will be no slaughter or pillage after he takes the capital. This approach was continued in the following month, when the White Wolf circulated a song to induce people to come to his banner:

> White Wolf, cunning and bold,
> The will of heaven will uphold.
> He calls the hungry to his door
> Friend of the friendless and the poor—
> Two years hence the world shall see
> For rich and poor equality.

This is from the *NCH*, May 23, 1914, p. 590. However, there are no subsequent reports that indicate a continuation of this approach.

16. *NCH*, Jan. 24, 1914, p. 268.

17. *NCH*, Apr. 25, 1914, p. 301.

18. *KMCKMS*, Appendix, p. 3. Most sources do not mention that Feng's regiment was changed into a brigade before it became part of the 7th Division. Feng himself does, however, in *WSH*, p. 196, and so does Yu Tinn-hugh, p. 492; Yu may have taken his information from Feng's autobiography.

19. Fuse, p. 28.

20. *NCH*, May 16, 1914, p. 520.

21. *WSH*, pp. 209–10; *KMCKMS*, Appendix, p. 3.

22. *KMCKMS*, Appendix, p. 3. *CYB, 1914*, p. 323, says that this was about the normal number of men in a mixed brigade.

23. *WSH*, p. 217.

24. *WSH*, p. 366. Feng says the incident occurred when he was "12 sui, right after joining the army." Yet in his earlier account of joining the army he says that his enlistment at that age was only nominal. Therefore this incident probably occurred shortly after he became a regular soldier in 1896. See also Ch'eng, pp. 7–9.

25. *WSH*, p. 366–67.

26. *WSH*, p. 367; Broomhall, pp. 9–10.

27. *WSH*, p. 367.

28. Broomhall, pp. 10–11; Ch'eng, p. 9.

29. *WSH*, pp. 367–68. Feng says that he attended Mott's classes in 1912, but Mott apparently did not arrive in China until early 1913. See Boorman, p. 38, and Broomhall, p. 11.

30. Broomhall, p. 12, implies that Feng was baptized in 1913. Feng himself does not give the date, but indicates that some time elapsed between Mott's sermons and his own baptism. *KMCKMS*, Appendix, p. 3, says it was early in 1914. Jonathan and Rosalind Goforth, p. 14, say that Feng's "final decision" came at the end of 1911, but this seems to be incorrect. Most of the Christian missionaries who have written about Feng have personal knowledge only from about 1918 or later.

31. *WSH*, pp. 367–68.

32. Ch'ang, p. 61.

33. *Jihohi*, II, Ch'üan 8, p. 114.

34. Mao, "T'an Feng Yü-hsiang," p. 8.

35. Verbrugge, pp. 209–22.

36. Kao, p. 28. T'ao, *Pei-yang*, II, 83, says that Ch'en was given control of military affairs in Szechwan on Feb. 20, 1915.

37. T'ao, *Pei-yang*, II, 83, says that Feng was ordered to Szechwan at the same time that Ch'en Huan was sent, in Feb. 1915. Li T'ai-fen, p. 12, says that Feng was ordered to Szechwan in mid-May.

38. *WSH*, pp. 259–60; *KMCKMS*, Appendix, p. 4.

39. For Feng's assertion that he refused to sign, see *WSH*, p. 245. Fuse, p. 29, also says that Feng refused to sign the wire, but Fuse, who is often wrong, apparently took much of his information uncritically from Feng's accounts. My conclusion is based not only on the fact that it would have been difficult for Feng to have refused Lu Chien-chang's request, but on the statement of one of Feng's former officers whom I interviewed on Taiwan in May 1959. He said that although Feng disapproved of Yüan's plans, he reluctantly sent the wire supporting Yüan.

40. *WSH*, pp. 259–61. On p. 262 Feng specifically states that all this was done on Jan. 1, 1916.

41. Included in this generalization are all the sources relative to the National Protection Army mentioned in the following notes.

42. Ts'ai, 4th ts'u, Chün-cheng wen-tien, chung, pp. 24b–25. Li Lieh-chün, in his autobiography, said that Feng's 16th Mixed Brigade established secret connections with Ts'ai Ao, but he gives no date or other details; see Lo Chia-lun, VI, 91.

43. Teng, p. 5. Feng's own account also supports this inference.

44. The unit sent to Hsüchow was a t'i-t'uan. Yu Yun-lung, p. 42, indicates that a t'i-t'uan was equal to a brigade.

45. For Yüan's military plans, see Yu Hui-yüan, p. 42. Liu Kuang-yen, p. 101, indicates a somewhat different disposition of troops.

46. Yu Hui-yüan, p. 27.

47. Ch'en Huan entrusted the defense of Hsüchow to Wu Hsiang-chen, leader of the 4th Brigade of the Szechwan army. Wu's first contact with the Yunnanese was south of the city, where he evidently went to meet them. See Yu Hui-yüan, p. 55. On p. 55 Yu also says that Wu Hsiang-chen had long before shown his sympathy for the Yunnan forces, and only pretended to put up a resistance. Teng, p. 5, says that Wu was defeated by the Yunnanese, although one of his units, at least, put up a spirited resistance. *NCH*, Mar. 11, 1916, p. 672, reported that the government forces stationed in Hsüchow fired great quantities of ammunition while the revolutionaries were still 30 miles away, and then fled in panic on the morning of Jan. 20.

48. Lo Chia-lun, VI, 95; *NCH*, Mar. 11, 1916, p. 673.

49. *WSH*, p. 262. T'ao, *Pei-yang*, II, 159, also states that Feng's forces were at Neichiang, but gives the impression that they remained there until the beginning of March. This is an error; T'ao is mistaken on several facts concerning the fighting in southern Szechwan.

50. *WSH*, p. 264. *KMCKMS*, Appendix, p. 4; Teng, p. 5.

51. *NCH*, Feb. 12, 1916, p. 409, reported that the government officially announced the receipt of a telegram from Feng Yü-hsiang reporting his victory over the rebels at Yangliuchiao, in the mountains about 50 li northeast of Hsüchow. The same issue of the *NCH*, p. 411, reported a wire from Ch'en Huan giving the same information. Since our concern here is to ascertain Feng's position relative to the contending factions, the fact that he reported the victory is significant, even if the victory or the battle never occurred.

52. Teng, p. 5.   53. *WSH*, pp. 264–65.

54. *WSH*, p. 266.   55. *WSH*, p. 269.

56. *WSH*, pp. 269–70.   57. *WSH*, p. 272.

58. *WSH*, p. 272. Feng's account is very vague as to dates, but these remarks can only relate to the battle at the beginning of February. Feng reported to the government after this battle that over 300 of the enemy were killed or wounded; see *NCH*, Feb. 12, 1916, p. 409.

59. Feng admitted as much in a talk to his men seven years later; see *Jihchi*, I, Chüan 3, p. 76.

60. Teng, p. 6, says that one regiment of Feng's troops attacked Hsüchow four times, and each time was repulsed.

61. Lo Chia-lun, VI, 133; *NCH*, Mar. 11, 1916, p. 673.

62. *WSH*, p. 274. Feng asserts that this plan was originally formulated by Liu I-ch'ing, and that he, Feng, accepted it because it was reasonable.

63. *WSH*, pp. 276–77.

64. Teng, p. 6. Also *NCH*, Mar. 11, 1916, p. 671. *KMCKMS*, chap. 3, pp. 31–33, discusses this period. It says nothing about a deal to occupy the city for only three days, or about a lack of fighting; it says simply that Feng decided to attack Hsüchow. Li T'ai-fen, p. 15, says the same thing. *Jihchi*, I, Chüan 3, pp. 76–77, admits that there was a vigorous struggle with many casualties.

65. Liu Kuang-yen, p. 102, says Ts'ai had 3,130 men. Liang, p. 550, says that "while the government troops numbered several tens of thousands of

well-fed and well-equipped troops, the men led by Ts'ai were hungry and numbered less than 5,000 men."

66. Yu Hui-yüan, p. 67.

67. *NCH*, Mar. 11, 1916, p. 672. Wen, *Pien* 3, pp. 63–70, has a good brief account of the warfare in south Szechwan. He describes the struggle for Hsüchow as hard-fought.

68. *NCH*, Mar. 18, 1916, pp. 733–34.

69. Kao, p. 34. T'ao, *Pei-yang*, II, 172, says that Feng's men were the first to occupy another town, Nach'i, after the departure of the rebels, and that it was for this that Feng was rewarded. This is incorrect; the reward was for the taking of Hsüchow.

70. Yu Hui-yüan, p. 67.

71. *Ibid.*, p. 79.

72. Ts'ai, 4th ts'u, Chün-cheng wen-tien, chung, pp. 24b–25. The exact date of this wire is not clear. It is dated only by the character "tung" (冬), which is used to indicate the 2nd of a month. However, the wires in this collection are arranged chronologically, and this wire falls between a wire dated simply Mar. 1916 and another dated Mar. 31, 1916. It therefore seems safe to assume that the wire in question was sent on Mar. 2. This would not contradict T'ao Chü-yin's assertion in *Pei-yang*, II, 189, that Feng twice sent men to Ts'ai sometime before the middle of April. However, Li Chien-nung, *Chung-kuo*, p. 465, quotes at length from Ts'ai's telegram and specifically dates it Apr. 20.

73. *NCH*, May 6, 1916, p. 249.

74. T'ao, *Pei-yang*, II, 190.

75. Ts'ai, 4th ts'u, Chün-cheng wen-tien, chung, p. 31.

76. *NCH*, May 13, 1916, p. 313. There had been so little suggestion that Feng had anything to do with the revolutionaries that the *NCH* described this as a "sensational report."

77. *KMCKMS*, Appendix, p. 4. NCH, May 27, 1916, pp. 435–36, in a despatch dated May 16, reported Feng's return to Chengtu from Hsüchow.

78. *WSH*, p. 280.

79. Kao, p. 35. Li Chien-nung, *Political History*, p. 344, says Ch'en Shu-fan was forced to declare independence by his subordinates, among whom was Feng Yü-hsiang. This not only is factually incorrect, but also is an incorrect translation of Li's Chinese text. Indeed, the entire passage is translated carelessly. Li, in the Chinese text, specifies that Ch'en Shu-fan, a Defense Commissioner in Shensi, declared his independence on May 9. The translation says Shensi declared independence on May 9. Actually, Ch'en did not maneuver to get the entire province to declare independence until May 16. As far as Feng is concerned, the Chinese text is also clear. See Li Chien-nung, *Chung-kuo*, pp. 464–65.

80. *KMCKMS*, Appendix, p. 4. It is possible Feng did not leave Szechwan until late July or in August. *KMCKMS*, chap. 3, pp. 36–37, gives the text of a statement Feng made just before he and Ch'en left the province. The statement is dated July 17, 1916. The same statement, with the same date, is in Li T'ai-fen, pp. 19–20. However, the implication of the first reference cited in this note is that Feng left in June. Moreover, *NCH*, June 30, 1916, p. 726, reports that Ch'en Huan left Chengtu on June 26. Kao, p. 36, notes

that Ch'en left Chengtu on June 25. Therefore there seems no doubt that Ch'en left at the end of June, and that there is some error in *KMCKMS*; either Feng did not leave when Ch'en did, or the date is too late. In any event, Feng departed in the summer of 1916.

81. *WSH*, pp. 288–93.

82. *WSH*, p. 298.

83. Li T'ai-fen, p. 22.

84. *WSH*, p. 299.

85. *WSH*, p. 299. It is very possible that Lu Chien-chang knew about the plans for a restoration, and perhaps he foresaw that this would give Feng an opportunity to regain his command. Lu had close enough connections with the pro-restoration group that later, when they saw that they were losing the war, Lei Chen-ch'un, one of Chang Hsün's associates, entrusted Lu Chien-chang with a secret letter that was part of an attempt to escape the anti-restoration forces. See Wen-i pien-she she, chap. 4, p. 14.

86. *Feng Yü-hsiang ko-ming shih*, Pien 3, p. 2.

87. Feng himself, in *WSH*, p. 297, says his dismissal was the work of Fu Liang-tso and Hsü Shu-cheng, Vice-Ministers of War, who disliked him because he did not give them gifts, and because of his revolutionary activities in Szechwan, all of which is very doubtful. T'ao, *Tu-chün*, p. 39, asserts that Tuan Ch'i-jui wanted to make Ch'en Huan tuchün of Kansu, and that Ch'en wanted to take Feng's brigade without Feng. This is possible, but as the same writer has pointed out in *Pei-yang*, III, 12–13, Tuan had little use for Ch'en Huan after the latter had not only declared Szechwan independent but also severed all relations with their mutual patron, Yüan Shih-k'ai. *Feng Yü-hsiang ko-ming shih*, Pien 3, pp. 1–2, says that Feng disobeyed some of Tuan Ch'i-jui's orders, and that as a result Tuan lost confidence in him. Tuan thus decided to disband the 16th Mixed Brigade, but was persuaded by Lu Chien-chang to preserve the brigade by simply replacing the commander. Fuse, pp. 30–31, gives the same explanation, but he took it directly from *Feng Yü-hsiang ko-ming shih*.

88. Ts'ai, 4th ts'u, Chün-cheng wen-tien, chung, p. 24b.

89. Hsieh Kuan-lan, No. 41, p. 6.

90. *Feng Yü-hsiang ko-ming shih*, Pien 3, p. 1. Feng, in *WSH*, pp. 296–97, relates that during an interview with Fu Liang-tso the latter said "You have three regiments of men. We will have to cut that down a little." Normally a mixed brigade consisted of between five and six thousand men; Feng already had close to 10,000.

91. *WSH*, p. 302; Li T'ai-fen, p. 22. Fuse, p. 31, says that Feng and his officers secretly planned means by which Feng could recover his command.

92. Chang Hsün, in a statement made after the defeat of the restoration, asserted that they had been planning it for several years. See Lo Chia-lun, VII, 75. This volume contains many documents and newspaper articles relative to the pre-restoration maneuvering. For details on the meetings and intrigues of the time, see T'ao, *Tu-chün*.

93. To be precise, the announcement was made on the evening of June 30, to be effective from July 1. See Wen, Pien 3, p. 80.

94. T'ao, *Tu-chün*, pp. 46–50. In Lo Chia-lun, VII, 75, is a wire from Chang Hsün in which he says that Tuan Ch'i-jui, "although he did not reveal

his attitude, did not reject the idea" of a restoration. Pp. 1 and 50 are also relevant.

95. *Feng Yü-hsiang ko-ming shih*, Pien 3, pp. 3–4.

96. *WSH*, pp. 306–7. Feng wrote that he mortgaged his house in Peking for 5,000 yüan.

97. *WSH*, p. 307.

98. *WSH*, pp. 308–9.

99. Fuse, p. 33, says that Feng and Yang shared formal control over the brigade after Feng returned. Li T'ai-fen, p. 23, says that Yang was made a staff adviser at general headquarters, presumably Tuan Ch'i-jui's headquarters. This seems more reasonable, and highlights the fact that Yang was not opposed to Tuan, whose only reason for agreeing to the return of Feng was that the brigade would not obey Yang.

100. For the text of this proclamation, see *KMCKMS*, chap. 4, p. 44. Wen, Pien 3, p. 81, says that Feng Yü-hsiang was the first to announce that he was marching toward Peking, but *KMCKMS*, which includes most such documents, makes no mention of this.

101. Specific details about these battles are in *KMCKMS*, chap. 4, pp. 44–46, and *WSH*, pp. 309–12. Wen, Pien 3, pp. 79–82, discusses the military operations of the anti-restoration war, but gives only a few details about Feng and his men specifically.

102. *NCH*, July 28, 1917, p. 193.

103. Li Chien-nung, *Chung-kuo*, p. 501. The English translation of this passage in *Political History*, p. 373, is garbled. It says that Li Shun was transferred *to* Kiangsi, and does not mention Ch'en Kuang-yüan, although it then refers to "these three provinces."

104. T'ao, *Pei-yang*, IV, 7, 12. Note 1 on p. 12 gives the positions these three men held under Feng Kuo-chang.

105. Li Chien-nung, *Chung-kuo*, p. 507.

106. T'ao, *Tu-chün*, p. 168.

107. *NCH*, Jan. 5, 1918, p. 16, carried such a report, which was attributed to a "Chinese source, usually reliable." T'ao, *Pei-yang*, IV, 71, says that Lu came to Nanking when Feng was there.

108. *WSH*, p. 322. Feng does not mention the presence of Lu Chien-chang.

109. Two of Feng's former subordinates, in separate interviews with this writer on Taiwan in the spring of 1959, stated that Lu determined Feng's policy at this time, although neither could or would explain what the aims of that policy were.

110. Hsieh Kuan-lan, No. 41, p. 6.

111. T'ao, *Pei-yang*, IV, 71.

112. *Ibid.*, p. 92. There is no proof of T'ao Chü-yin's assertion that the conquest of Anhwei was an important factor in Lu Chien-chang's plans at this time. In fact, lack of information obscures a number of events in which Lu played an important part. However, it is significant that Ni Ssu-ch'ung was very concerned with the threat Lu posed, although this concern became acute only in Feb. 1918, at the time of Feng's Wuhsüeh declarations. See Hsieh Kuan-lan, No. 41, p. 6.

113. Li Chien-nung, *Chung-kuo*, p. 510. The English translation is again in error on p. 380, when it states that all these wires were sent on Nov. 14.

114. *Ibid.*, p. 513.
115. *Ibid.*, p. 514. The English translation, p. 382, is again in error. It says that Tuan Ch'i-jui was made Minister of War. The Chinese original states that it was Tuan Chih-kuei.
116. *Ibid.* The English translation omits mention of the independence of the Hupeh militarists.
117. *Ibid.* Li says Tuan Ch'i-jui took advantage of the threat to Hupeh to send men into the province to urge war against the South. The implication is that Tuan sent men to Wang Chan-yüan, and that Wang was convinced. The *NCH*, Jan. 19, 1918, p. 115, reported that "it is understood that the Military Governors of Kiangsi and Hupeh ... have telegraphed President Feng Kuo-chang urging resumption of hostilities...."
118. Fei, pp. 74–75.
119. Hsieh Kuan-lan, No. 41, p. 6.
120. *NCH*, Feb. 9, 1918, p. 302.
121. *NCH*, Mar. 2, 1918, p. 487. *KMCKMS*, chap. 5, p. 54, says that Feng was ordered to attack Southern forces in the rear of Changsha.
122. *NCH*, Feb. 2, 1918, p. 235.
123. *NCH*, Feb. 16, 1918, p. 371. This news report is the only reference to the obstacle presented by low water. All subsequent accounts interpret the disembarkation of the brigade as a planned part of the Wuhsüeh incident that followed. However, this news report was written before the Wuhsüeh declarations and referred to all ships, not just Feng's. There seems to be no reason why it should not be accepted as correct. It thus raises the question of whether Feng originally planned to stop at Wuhsüeh.
124. *WSH*, p. 333, contains a quotation from the wire and a general description of it, but the date of the wire is given as Jan. 14, which is incorrect. The entire text of the wire is in *KMCKMS*, chap. 5, pp. 55–57.
125. *WSH*, pp. 333–34. This, too, is incorrectly dated as Jan. 18. Actually, it was sent Feb. 18. The complete text of this wire is in *KMCKMS*, chap. 5, pp. 58–61.
126. *NCH*, Mar. 2, 1918, p. 487.
127. Li T'ai-fen, pp. 31–32; T'ao, *Tu-chün*, p. 176.
128. T'ao, *Tu-chün*, p. 176.
129. *NCH*, Mar. 23, 1918, p. 686.
130. For example, U.S. Department of State, "Biography of Feng Yü-hsiang," p. 2.
131. Separate interviews with two of Feng's former subordinates, Taiwan, 1959.
132. *NCH*, Mar. 23, 1918, p. 687.
133. Foreign observers at the time noted the deterrent effect on Anhwei troops; see *NCH*, May 11, 1918, p. 334.
134. T'ao, *Tu-chün*, p. 175; *NCH*, Feb. 23, 1918, p. 418.
135. *NCH*, Apr. 13, 1918, p. 81.
136. *NCH*, Apr. 27, 1918, p. 199; June 1, 1918, p. 509.
137. Li T'ai-fen, p. 33. *NCH*, June 1, 1918, p. 514, carried a report on Feng's fighting in Hunan. It said Feng had issued a circular telegram saying that he had to fight because he was being attacked, and in any event the be-

havior of the enemy troops toward the people was so brutal as to warrant his opposition.

138. *NCH*, June 22, 1918, p. 684; T'ao, *Tu-chün*, p. 191.

139. Hsieh Kuan-lan, No. 41, p. 7. Reports at that time also specifically attributed the murder to Hsü, and said that Tuan Ch'i-jui "is only mildly blamed for condoning the rash act of his brilliant, strong supporter." This from *NCH*, June 22, 1918, p. 685. See also *NCH*, June 29, 1918, p. 744.

140. *NCH*, June 22, 1918, p. 684.

141. The exact date of the appointment is not clear. *WSH*, p. 340, says that he received the appointment while still en route to Ch'angte, which, it will be recalled, he occupied on June 22. Evidently the appointment was originally temporary, and was made permanent on Nov. 4, 1918; see T'ao, *Tu-chün*, pp. 191, 210.

Chapter Four

1. Ch'eng, p. 12; *KMCKMS*, chap. 1, p. 2.

2. *WSH*, p. 182. Compare these requirements with the standard army specifications described in *CYB, 1914*, p. 318.

3. Interview with one of Feng's former officers, Taiwan, 1959. With regard to leaves, see also Feng, *Feng Yü-hsiang hsün-ling*, Chüan 3, pp. 21–22.

4. Someone knowledgeable about technical military matters could probably infer a great deal about the level of theory and practice in Feng's army from the orders in Feng, *Feng Yü-hsiang chün-shih*, particularly Chüan 3.

5. *WSH*, pp. 381–82.

6. *WSH*, pp. 314–15, explains that the Big Sword Unit was set up in late 1917. Li T'ai-fen, p. 21, alludes to the unit's existing at the time of the battle at Hsüchow, in 1916.

7. Chien, *Wo so*, p. 39.

8. *WSH*, p. 170.

9. Li T'ai-fen, p. 21.

10. *WSH*, p. 294.

11. *WSH*, pp. 285–86.

12. Feng, *Feng Yü-hsiang hsün-ling*, Chüan 1, p. 18.

13. *WSH*, p. 286.

14. *WSH*, pp. 380, 385. See also Feng, *Feng Yü-hsiang hsün-ling*, Chüan 1, pp. 5–6.

15. *NCH*, Aug. 9, 1919, p. 341.

16. *WSH*, p. 381. See also Feng, *Feng Yü-hsiang hsün-ling*, Chüan 1, pp. 5–6.

17. Chien, *Wo so*, p. 41. Feng, *Feng Yü-hsiang hsün-ling*, Chüan 7, contains orders relating to physical education, with pp. 1–10 relating specifically to the Ch'angte period.

18. Ch'eng, p. 20, says that of the men entering Feng's army, 60 per cent were illiterate, 30 per cent knew some characters, and 10 per cent could read and write. Feng, in *WSH*, p. 382, says: "Ninety-five per cent of the officers and men under me came from poor families, and they did not get an education while they were young."

19. *WSH*, p. 170. Feng, *Feng Yü-hsiang hsün-ling*, Chüan 1, pp. 17–18, lists

an order commanding that a specified rate of progress be made in mastering these 800 characters.

20. *WSH*, pp. 382–83.

21. *WSH*, p. 383.

22. Li T'ai-fen, p. 22; Ch'eng, p. 61.

23. Jonathan and Rosalind Goforth, p. 147; *WSH*, p. 383; Ch'eng, pp. 25–26.

24. *WSH*, p. 384; Ch'eng, p. 26; Broomhall, pp. 21–22.

25. *NCH*, Aug. 9, 1919, p. 342.

26. *WSH*, p. 383.

27. *WSH*, p. 227. Ch'eng, pp. 9–11, quotes or paraphrases over twenty of the sayings from Feng's booklet.

28. *WSH*, p. 325.

29. *WSH*, p. 368.

30. Interview with one of Feng's former subordinates, Taiwan, 1959.

31. Aho, pp. 180–81.

32. This estimate is based on the fact that in the winter of 1919 there were about 1,000 men enrolled as catechumens. See Aho, p. 180. In addition, the rate of conversion implied in other missionary reports makes this estimate appear conservative. See Jonathan and Rosalind Goforth, pp. 141–42. Moreover, a few years after Feng's brigade left Ch'angte, his forces—then much expanded—were reported to be about 50 per cent Christian. Since the men of the 16th Mixed Brigade had been exposed to Christian teachings the longest, it is probable that by that time the percentage of Christians among them was larger than this figure.

33. *WSH*, p. 306. One of Feng's former officers said in an interview on Taiwan in 1959 that this was one of the main reasons Feng encouraged his men to become Christians.

34. Jonathan and Rosalind Goforth, p. 142.

35. Li T'ai-fen, p. 10, states: "Feng used Christianity as a tool to control and discipline his troops." This is the most forthright statement on this question to be found in a Kuominchün source.

36. *NCH*, Mar. 23, 1918, p. 690; Apr. 13, 1918, p. 81.

37. *WSH*, pp. 191–92; Chien, *Wo so*, p. 2; interview with one of Feng's former officers, Taiwan, 1959.

38. Li T'ai-fen, p. 35.

39. *WSH*, pp. 284–85.

40. Ch'eng, p. 48.

41. Fuse, p. 372.

42. Li T'ai-fen, p. 21.

43. This was the impression given by one of Feng's former officers during an interview on Taiwan in 1959.

44. There is no question that Feng was an extraordinary speaker, despite the fact that his voice was unusually high for a man of his great size. I have spoken with many individuals who heard him speak, both Chinese and foreigners, pro-Feng and anti-Feng. Almost without exception they remarked on his ability. See Chien, *Wo so*, pp. 2, 9.

45. *WSH*, pp. 186–87.

46. Feng, *Feng Yü-hsiang hsün-ling*, Chüan 1, pp. 9–10.

47. *Ibid.*, pp. 12–14, is one example.
48. Chien, *Wo so*, p. 7. Fuse, p. 378, says that Feng did employ his brother-in-law, but stresses that it was only because he was competent, and that otherwise Feng would not have accepted him.
49. *WSH*, pp. 282–83.
50. *WSH*, pp. 187–88.
51. *WSH*, pp. 211–13; *KMCKMS*, Appendix, p. 3.
52. Interview with one of Feng's former officers, Taiwan, 1959.
53. *WSH*, p. 172.
54. *WSH*, pp. 172, 229.
55. *WSH*, pp. 173, 176. See also Feng, *Feng Yü-hsiang hsün-ling*, Chüan 1, pp. 19–22.

56. *NCH*, Aug. 9, 1919, p. 341.   57. Ch'eng, p. 48.
58. *WSH*, p. 294.   59. Li T'ai-fen, p. 21.
60. *Ibid.*, p. 35; *WSH*, p. 384.   61. Chien, *Wo so*, p. 6.
62. Aho, p. 178.
63. Li T'ai fen, pp. 33–34; Aho, p. 178.
64. *WSH*, p. 375. With regard to this figure and to much of the information about Feng during the Ch'angte period, it is not clear whether the data in question refer to the city of Ch'angte or the three hsien over which Feng had jurisdiction.
65. *NCH*, June 14, 1919, p. 704.
66. *WSH*, p. 376; Ch'eng, p. 18.
67. *WSH*, pp. 375–76.
68. Ch'eng, p. 18, says that Feng "even had women detectives, to check gambling in the homes."
69. *WSH*, pp. 343, 375. The passage on p. 343 is difficult to interpret. All sources agree that Feng abolished prostitution, and on p. 375, as elsewhere, Feng flatly asserts that he did. Yet on p. 343 he speaks of the brothels sending representatives to his headquarters, on his demand, to obtain some kind of certificate. This would seem to imply regulated and legalized prostitution.
70. *WSH*, pp. 359–60, 377–79.
71. *NCH*, Mar. 9, 1918, pp. 556–57.
72. *Ibid.*, pp. 556–57; Mar. 23, 1918, p. 690; Apr. 13, 1918, p. 81; Apr. 27, 1918, p. 199.
73. Feng, *Feng Yü-hsiang hsün-ling*, Chüan 3, pp. 15–21, 34–35.
74. *NCH*, Mar. 22, 1919, p. 768.
75. *NCH*, July 31, 1920, p. 293.
76. *Ibid.*, p. 287.
77. *NCH*, July 10, 1920, p. 108.
78. Chien, *Hsi-pei*, pp. 6–7; *WSH*, p. 371.
79. *WSH*, p. 373.
80. *WSH*, pp. 369–70.
81. *WSH*, pp. 343–44, 346–50.
82. *NCH*, June 7, 1919, p. 628; June 14, 1919, p. 704. *WSH*, p. 351.
83. Chien, *Hsi-pei*, p. 6.
84. *WSH*, pp. 352–56, describes the events of this time in some detail. However, there are ambiguities in the account, and except for the incident of Feng's posting guards in front of Japanese shops, it is not confirmed else-

where. Chien Yu-wen's account, cited in note 83 above, is not firsthand; he was not with Feng at that time. It is possible that Feng was not as intransigent toward the Japanese as his account suggests.

85. Close, p. 84, wrote: "Wu [P'ei-fu] and Feng [Yü-hsiang] would not allow Chang [Ching-yao]'s maladministrators and extortioners in the territory occupied by their troops, and virtually created a little independent kingdom in their neighborhood where justice and order were maintained."

Chapter Five

1. Ch'ang, p. 61. For similar estimates of Chang's personality and policies, see *WSH*, p. 388; *NCH*, July 3, 1920, pp. 45–46, and Jan. 15, 1921, p. 119.

2. *NCH*, July 10, 1920, p. 108.

3. *WSH*, p. 391.

4. *Jihchi*, I, Chüan I, pp. 3–14; Chüan 2, pp. 1–10. On almost every page there is some self-criticism or concern for character deficiencies.

5. *Jihchi*, I, Chüan 2, p. 10.

6. *Ibid.*, p. 3.

7. *WSH*, p. 407, says $100,000 was taken. *NCH*, Feb. 5, 1921, p. 332, quotes a Chinese newspaper's report that Feng took $200,000. Ch'eng, p. 31, asserts that Feng did not take the money, but detained the train until the government promised to remit $100,000. There is a gap in Feng's diary covering this period.

8. T'ao, *Pei-yang*, VI, 33–34; *WSH*, p. 415; Ch'eng, p. 33; *NCH*, Apr. 30, 1921, p. 298; May 7, 1921, p. 370; May 14, 1921, p. 443. Feng's diary has no entries for the period from Apr. 6 to Oct. 16.

9. Pye, pp. 150–51. See also T'ao, *Pei-yang*, VI, 33–34, and *NCH*, May 14, 1921, p. 443.

10. *CYB, 1923*, p. 890.

11. The *Weekly Review of the Far East*, July 30, 1921, p. 427.

12. *NCH*, June 25, 1921, p. 868.

13. *WSH*, p. 420.

14. *NCH*, Aug. 20, 1921, p. 534, summarizes the relations between Ch'en Shu-fan and Kuo Chien from 1916 to 1921. See also *NCH*, Aug. 27, 1921, p. 608.

15. For Feng's description of Kuo, see *WSH*, pp. 425–26. For a description by foreigners, see *NCH*, Sept. 24, 1921.

16. One of Feng's former officers informed me in an interview on Taiwan in Apr. 1959 that Feng's main reason for murdering Kuo Chien was his treatment of Lu Chien-chang.

17. *WSH*, p. 426. See also Li T'ai-fen, p. 49, and T'ao, *Pei-yang*, VI, 37.

18. *WSH*, p. 424.

19. *NCH*, Sept. 24, 1921, p. 927.

20. Kao, p. 82. Ch'ang, p. 62, asserts that Feng poisoned Yen Hsiang-wen at a dinner party, but no evidence is offered; indeed, there is a factual error in the same sentence that charges Feng with the murder. This source has many errors, and is clearly bent on blackening Feng's reputation.

21. *WSH*, pp. 432–33.

22. T'ao, *Pei-yang*, VI, 37. Chang Yün-chia, p. 96, asserts that Feng absorbed much of the Ching Kuo Chün into his own forces, and Li T'ai-fen, p.

54, seems to agree. It is certain that Feng would have liked to do this, but it is difficult to see how he could have. *KMCKMS* does not mention any such absorption, nor does Feng himself. The only evidence for such a statement seems to be Hu's subsequent support of Feng, especially his cooperation in Feng's seizure of Peking in 1924. Nevertheless, Hu remained an independent commander.

23. *WSH*, pp. 430–32.
24. *NCH*, Mar. 18, 1922, p. 733.
25. Ch'eng, p. 34.
26. Li T'ai-fen, p. 57.
27. *WSH*, pp. 433–34.
28. *Jihchi*, I, Chüan 2, p. 46.
29. *WSH*, p. 437. See also Feng, *Feng Yü-hsiang hsün-ling*, Chüan 16, p. 1.
30. Li T'ai-fen, pp. 58–59.
31. Ch'eng, p. 34.
32. *NCH*, Mar. 18, 1922, p. 733.
33. *NCH*, June 24, 1922, p. 868.
34. *NCH*, Feb. 11, 1922, p. 362.
35. *NCH*, Mar. 18, 1922, p. 733.
36. The report in *NCH*, Feb. 11, 1922, p. 362, justifies this inference.
37. Broomhall, p. 50.
38. *NCH*, Mar. 18, 1922, p. 733.
39. Ching-chih t'u-shu-kuan, *Feng Yü-hsiang*, p. 6.
40. *NCH*, Feb. 18, 1922, p. 469; the article was written by Rodney Gilbert.
41. For events leading up to the First Chih-Feng War, see Chang Tzu-sheng, *Jen-hsü*, pp. 2–19. Ching-chih t'u-shu-kuan, *Chih-Feng*, pp. 1–25, has many of the telegrams exchanged between Wu and Chang, and on pp. 26–28 is a summary description of the war of telegrams. Wen, Pien 3, pp. 115–16, briefly summarizes both the long-range and immediate causes of the war. Li Chien-nung, *Chung-kuo*, pp. 556–65, covers the war from beginning to end.
42. All the works cited in note 41 above contain descriptions of the hostilities, but perhaps the clearest brief account, which includes a comparison of the two sides at the beginning of the war, is Wen, Pien 3, pp. 116–32.
43. *Jihchi*, I, Chüan 3, pp. 39–40.
44. For a list of the units under Feng's command, see Chang Tzu-sheng, *Jen-hsü*, p. 22.
45. *Jihchi*, I, Chüan 3, pp. 40–42.
46. The battle on this front is described in Chang Tzu-sheng, *Jen-hsü*, pp. 37–40. See also Impey, *Chinese Army*, p. 10, and *CYB, 1923*, p. 575.
47. Impey, *Chinese Army*, p. 20.
48. T'ao, *Pei-yang*, VI, 117–18.
49. *Ibid.*, p. 118.
50. Kao, p. 94.
51. *NCH*, May 13, 1922, pp. 443–44. *NCH*, May 27, 1922, p. 594, carries a report summarizing the events of the revolt of the Chao brothers and the subsequent fighting with Feng. See also Chang Tzu-sheng, *Jen-hsü*, p. 47. For Feng's account, see *WSH*, pp. 446–47; *KMCKMS*, chap. 6, pp. 78–79, also describes events from Feng's point of view. Both accounts are correct in their essentials, although both omit the fact that Wu P'ei-fu tried to put all the blame for the revolt on Chao Chieh and to keep Chao T'i in office.
52. *NCH*, May 20, 1922, p. 514.
53. T'ao, *Pei-yang*, VI, 119.
54. *WSH*, p. 451. Ting, p. 23.
55. *Jihchi*, I, Chüan 3, p. 49.
56. Wen, Pien 2, p. 167. *NCH*, Aug. 5, 1922, p. 372, carries a report from

326

NOTES TO PAGES 112–14

Kaifeng stating that "great numbers of recruits are being mobilized throughout the province."

57. T'ao, *Pei-yang*, VI, 164. Some sources give a much higher figure. However, by late 1923 there were many references to Feng's troops as numbering about 30,000, so T'ao's figure is probably right for late 1922.

58. Broomhall, p. 61.

59. The visitor was Robert Gailey of the Peking YMCA. The event is described in a personal letter written by Ernest T. Shaw from China, Oct. 29, 1922, a copy of which Mr. Shaw kindly showed me.

60. Ch'eng, p. 42.

61. Yu Tinn-hugh, p. 497.

62. *Jihchi*, I, Chüan 3, pp. 49, 61.

63. *KMCKMS*, chap. 7, pp. 81–83; *WSH*, pp. 454–55.

64. *NCH*, June 10, 1922, p. 735.

65. *Ibid.* This article reports the sum of $3,000,000. Fuse, p. 51, says that it amounted to slightly over 1,300,000 yüan. Of course, most sums reported by any sources in this period are not clear because the writers seldom indicate what currency they are talking about.

66. Ch'eng, p. 40.

67. *CYB, 1923*, pp. 264–99, traces the history of monetary problems in China and describes conditions in 1922.

68. See, for example, two articles on this question in *NCH*, July 1, 1922, pp. 6–8.

69. The two articles cited in note 68 discuss the problem in terms of debasement. These articles elicited a letter from Lansing W. Hoyt, American Trade Commissioner, who maintained that "the fact that China is flooded by 25 billion 10-cash pieces clearly shows that the depreciation is primarily due to superabundance." This is in *NCH*, July 8, 1922, p. 109. *CYB, 1923*, p. 270, echoes Mr. Hoyt's approach. The latter source refers to a general discussion of the situation produced by the indiscriminate minting of copper coins written by Donald McColl which appeared in *CYB, 1921–22*, pp. 289 ff.

70. *NCH*, June 10, 1922, p. 735.

71. *NCH*, Nov. 18, 1922, p. 438, has the following report from Kaifeng: "Finance has been stabilized. There may be two opinions about this, but everyone will concede that the provincial bank has been given a new lease on life under Feng. When he came, he found that the depredations of Chao [T'i] had robbed the bank of its reserves and left it with a debt of $1,000,000. The dollar notes were worth only 50 per cent, and the 1,000 cash notes could be bought for 300 cash." But in August a report came from Huaich'ing (now called Ch'inyang) that presented a different picture. It appeared in *NCH*, Aug 26, 1922, p. 590, and said: "The value of copper cash is steadily on the decrease. A Mexican dollar, which last May sold for 1,480 cash, now sells for 1,900 cash, so the local Chinese who only deal in cash find that for them all commodities have risen in price. Salt has increased from 76 cash per catty to 100 cash. All cereals have advanced more or less around 25 per cent. Recently 500,000 Honan paper $1 bills were brought in and an order issued that all taxes were to be paid henceforth in paper bills. When the paper money was brought in an equal amount of silver was taken away." It would seem that Huaich'ing was well out of Feng's domain since, as will be de-

scribed in the text, Feng's control was largely limited to the area east of Kaifeng, and Huaich'ing is to the west, not far from Wu P'ei-fu's headquarters at Loyang. However, such an inference is complicated by a report from Huaich'ing in *NCH*, June 24, 1922, p. 876, which says the new magistrate was a former officer in Feng's army, but goes on to describe just the type of reforms that Feng was implementing in the areas under his control. Therefore it is probable that Huaich'ing was at that time under Feng's jurisdiction.

72. *NCH*, Oct. 21, 1922, p. 142. *Jihchi*, I, Chüan 3, p. 4, tells of a similar practice when Feng was tuchün of Shensi.

73. *WSH*, p. 457. *NCH*, Oct. 21, 1922, p. 142, does not mention the sums requested, but notes that "in response to the heavy demands of Wu P'ei-fu there has been scarcely any appropriation. . . ."

74. *NCH*, Nov. 25, 1922, pp. 504–5. See pp. 504–7 of the same issue for two articles on the "disgraceful" state of affairs in Honan.

75. *The Weekly Review*, Nov. 18, 1922, p. 428.

76. The issues of the *NCH* throughout 1922, especially in the latter half of the year, contain numerous articles reporting the extent and destructiveness of banditry in Honan. *NCH*, Nov. 11, 1922, p. 363, reports alleged plans by Honan bandits to seize the American Minister to China, who planned a trip through the province. Feng briefly discusses the problem in *WSH*, p. 455.

77. *NCH*, Nov. 11, 1922, pp. 360, 361.

78. *The Weekly Review*, Sept. 9, 1922, p. 60.

79. *NCH*, Sept. 2, 1922, p. 663. See also *NCH*, Sept. 23, 1922, p. 870; Nov. 11, 1922, p. 361; Dec. 30, 1922, p. 850.

80. *NCH*, June 10, 1922, p. 735. Also *NCH*, July 22, 1922, p. 231; Nov. 18, 1922, p. 438; and Li T'ai-fen, p. 71.

81. *WSH*, p. 452; *NCH*, June 10, 1922, p. 735.

82. *NCH*, Nov. 18, 1922, p. 438.

83. *NCH*, Oct. 21, 1922, p. 145.

84. *WSH*, pp. 452–53; T'ao, *Pei-yang*, VI, 163.

85. Ch'eng, p. 41.

86. *NCH*, Nov. 18, 1922, p. 438; June 9, 1923, p. 662; June 22, 1922, p. 231.

87. *NCH*, June 10, 1922, p. 735.

88. *NCH*, July 22, 1922, p. 231. Also *NCH*, June 10, 1922, p. 735, and June 24, 1922, p. 876.

89. *NCH*, June 24, 1922, p. 876. Also *NCH*, June 10, 1922, p. 735; Oct. 21, 1922, p. 143; Nov. 18, 1922, p. 438.

90. *The Weekly Review*, Oct. 8, 1922, p. 314; *NCH*, Oct. 21, 1922, p. 145.

91. *KMCKMS*, Appendix, p. 9.

92. Dailey, "Banditry in China," *The Weekly Review*, Jan. 6, 1923, p. 210.

93. *The Weekly Review*, Feb. 24, 1923, p. 510.

94. In *The Weekly Review*, Feb. 24, 1923, p. 510, there is an allusion to "when Commissioner Ling resigned," so his resignation was sometime before that date. Presumably Ling left when Feng did.

95. *NCH*, Dec. 30, 1922, p. 850. Also *NCH*, Nov. 25, 1922, p. 509.

96. For the deterioration of conditions in Kueite, see *NCH*, Jan. 6, 1923, p. 14.

97. T'ao, *Pei-yang*, VI, 162.
98. *WSH*, p. 457.
99. Rodney Gilbert, in *NCH*, Nov. 11, 1922, pp. 360–61, asserted that Ts'ao's adherents effected Feng's transfer, and that Wu P'ei-fu did not particularly want Feng to leave, but thought that Feng wanted to go.
100. *The Weekly Review*, Nov. 11, 1922, p. 394.
101. T'ao, *Pei-yang*, VI, 164.

Chapter Six

1. For details on this aspect of the Nanyüan program, see *WSH*, p. 464, and Li T'ai-fen, pp. 80–81.
2. For details on this aspect of the program, see *WSH*, p. 462, and Li T'ai-fen, pp. 79–80.
3. Li T'ai-fen, p. 81.   4. *Ibid.*; *NCH*, Oct. 13, 1923, p. 89.
5. *Jihchi*, I, Chüan 5, pp. 72–73.   6. Li T'ai-fen, p. 81.
7. *Ibid.*, p. 80.   8. *Ibid.*, pp. 83–84; Broomhall, p. 67.
9. Li T'ai-fen, p. 84.
10. *Ibid.*, p. 83; Broomhall, p. 68; Ch'eng, pp. 60–61; *NCH*, Mar. 1, 1924, p. 322.
11. *Jihchi*, I, Chüan 4–5, *passim*.
12. Li T'ai-fen, p. 83; *WSH*, p. 469.
13. Li T'ai-fen, p. 83.
14. Broomhall, pp. 65, 68.
15. Miner Journal, Feb. 28, 1924; Mar. 26, 1924.
16. *Jihchi*, I, Chüan 4–5, *passim*.
17. *Jihchi*, I, Chüan 5, p. 68.
18. *Ibid.*, p. 11.
19. *WSH*, pp. 469–70.
20. *Jihchi*, I, Chüan 4, p. 48; Chüan 5, pp. 55–56. Broomhall, p. 67.
21. Ch'ang, p. 64.
22. T'ao, *Wu P'ei-fu*, p. 80.
23. *CYB, 1924–25*, pp. 1179–80, summarizes these alignments.
24. T'ao, *Wu P'ei-fu*, pp. 78–85; Li Chien-nung, *Chung-kuo*, pp. 591–95.
25. *CYB, 1924–25*, pp. 914–19, summarizes the various campaigns by regions.
26. *NCH*, Apr. 28, 1923, p. 221; May 5, 1923, p. 290.
27. *WSH*, p. 460; *NCH*, Aug. 18, 1923, p. 455. *The Weekly Review*, Nov. 4, 1922, p. 356, quoted a report that Feng was to receive $300,000 per month.
28. *NCH*, May 5, 1923, p. 290.
29. *NCH*, May 12, 1923, pp. 362–63.
30. The precise date when Hsüeh Tu-pi was approved as director of the octroi is not clear. *CYB, 1924–25*, p. 1182, says it was Apr. 1, 1923. But in *NCH*, Apr. 28, 1923, p. 218, there is a brief report datelined Apr. 21 that says the question was to be discussed by the cabinet that afternoon. T'ao, *Pei-yang*, VI, 237–38, says it was on June 2. Calendars of events in issues of *Tung-fang tsa-chih* of that time allude to Li's refusal to sign the mandate in early June, but they do not indicate the date of the original cabinet decision.

31. *NCH*, June 9, 1923, p. 649. The sequence of events is detailed in Li Chien-nung, *Chung-kuo*, pp. 594–99, and T'ao, *Pei-yang*, VI, 232–38.

32. Kao, pp. 122–23; *NCH*, June 9, 1923, p. 649.

33. T'ao, *Pei-yang*, VI, 240; wire to the Secretary of State from American Minister Schurman, June 9, 1923, 893.00/5033. See also the report of an interview by the dean of the diplomatic corps with Li Yüan-hung on the afternoon of the police strike, 893.00/5090. *NCH*, June 16, 1923, p. 722.

34. Pye, pp. 162–65, analyzes Li Yüan-hung's ouster in terms of the shifting alignment within the Chihli clique.

35. There are many reports in the *NCH* from its own Western correspondents about the revulsion of feeling against Ts'ao, Feng, and others as a result of their ousting Li. In addition, *NCH*, June 23, 1923, p. 797, carries a summary of Chinese press views that states: "There is no doubt at all that the Chinese people have never been so deeply stirred before as they are now by the shameful but clumsy tactics adopted by the leaders of the Chihli faction in forcing President Li Yüan-hung from his office. For the past week, the Chinese press has been full of caustic comments regarding the latest political coup, and the Chinese public organizations have been holding meetings to discuss ways and means to meet the situation." It is hardly necessary to add that the reference to the "Chinese people" means the politically articulate Chinese, especially in Peking.

36. The letter is in *NCH*, July 14, 1923, p. 87.

37. Feng told an interviewer: "I had no wish that the President [Li Yüan-hung] should leave, no desire, no thought about his doing so." This is in *NCH*, Aug. 18, 1923, p. 455. Somewhat earlier, in *NCH*, June 23, 1923, p. 795, it was reported that Feng, who was "very sensitive to foreign opinion," was urgently trying to discover how foreigners regarded Li's ouster.

38. *WSH*, p. 482, contains three lines describing "division commanders and brigade commanders going en masse to demand pay from Li Yüan-hung." Li was "not fundamentally a brave man," and he fled. There is no mention of Feng's participation. In *Jihchi*, entries for the first ten days of June 1923 are simply omitted, but in the entry for May 17, 1923 (*Jihchi*, I, Chüan 4, p. 53), Feng notes that he will absolutely oppose a change of Presidents. *KMCKMS*, chap. 7, p. 90, disposes of Li's ouster in one sentence, which attributes the key role to Wang Huai-ch'ing, and does not mention Feng's participation. Feng's ex-subordinates whom I asked about this affair flatly denied that Feng took any part in it.

39. Chien, *Wo so*, p. 31. Chien's explanation is apparently the source of Fuse's comments, pp. 59–60. Shortly after Li left office, Feng explained to an interviewer that he had resigned with Wang Huai-ch'ing because President Li had disclaimed responsibility for paying the army, thus "practically making the troops the possession of their individual generals. . . . If the army is not a national army, I would rather have nothing to do with it." This, he said, is why he resigned. See *NCH*, Aug. 18, 1923, p. 455.

40. *WSH*, pp. 455, 460.

41. *Jihchi*, I, Chüan 4, pp. 1–58 *passim*. Fuse, p. 56, wrote that after leaving Honan Feng was very humble toward Ts'ao K'un in an obvious attempt to curry favor with him.

42. *NCH,* Mar. 1, 1924, p. 320.

43. On July 6, 1923, Feng's nominee, Hsüeh Tu-pi, became director of the Peking Octroi Administration, and Feng received $100,000 per month from this source, according to *NCH,* Oct. 27, 1923, p. 227. However, the same source reports that in Oct. 1923 the cabinet informed Feng that the octroi revenues must revert to their original uses, and that arrangements would be made for Feng to receive a similar monthly allotment from surplus salt revenues, to which Feng agreed. But it is doubtful that this came to pass. I have found no other confirmation of it, and an article in *NCH,* June 14, 1924, p. 409, states that Feng was still receiving $100,000 per month from the Octroi Administration, and notes that under Hsüeh Tu-pi's administration the octroi revenues had increased substantially. In Aug. 1923, Feng was still complaining that his men had not been paid for 13 months, according to *NCH,* Aug. 18, 1923, p. 454. However, Ts'ao K'un did not become President until August, and I find no later reports of Feng's complaining about not being paid. Feng himself, in *WSH,* pp. 460–61, states that he had difficulty obtaining funds, but that by mid-1923 he finally obtained a total of $150,000 per month from the octroi revenues and the Peking-Suiyuan Railway. Therefore, this was apparently his minimum regular income in late 1923 and early 1924. *Jihchi,* I, Chüan 5, p. 20, indicates that Feng still controlled the octroi through Hsüeh Tu-pi as of Jan. 1924. Feng's monthly bill to the government was much higher than the minimum regular income noted above. For his one division and three mixed brigades, he asked for $360,000 per month. This figure is included in a listing of the government's monthly expenses in *NCH,* Dec. 29, 1923, p. 873.

44. *CYB, 1925–26,* p. 1201.

45. *Jihchi,* I, Chüan 4, p. 138; *CWR,* Dec. 22, 1923, p. 138. Ch'ang, p. 63, states that Feng beat his first wife frequently, and·implies strongly that he kicked her to death. Ch'eng, p. 58, states that she died of meningitis, although the date he gives, 1922, is incorrect. On the same page, Ch'eng also says that Mrs. Feng learned to read after her marriage, and was baptized a Christian when the army was in Ch'angte. There is very little information about the first Mrs. Feng.

46. *Jihchi,* I, Chüan 5, p. 31. *CWR,* Feb. 23, 1924, p. 468, reported that the "engagement" of Feng and Li Te-ch'üan was announced at a luncheon party. Perhaps this error was due to the fact that a Chinese wedding can be simply the public announcement of betrothal at such a luncheon or other party, although foreign journalists in China presumably knew this. Conceivably the foreign press was intentionally misled because Feng's wedding followed so soon upon his first wife's death.

47. *Miner Journal,* Feb. 28, 1924.

48. The background of the war is lightly sketched in "Fighting Begins," p. 4, and is more completely described in Li Chien-nung, *Chung-kuo,* pp. 648–49. An excellent brief summary of the origins of the war, the issues involved, the personalities of the antagonists, and the origins of the Shanghai problem is in a report prepared by consul John K. Davis at Nanking for the Secretary of State, Sept. 15, 1924, 893.00/5635. For the present summary description, these accounts were supplemented by information from *Who's Who in China* (3d ed.), pp. 157–59, 582–83.

49. For an analysis of the alliance between Chang Tso-lin and Lu Yung-hsiang, see Pye, pp. 128–41.

50. Impey, "Flood, Famine, and Civil War," p. 150.

51. *WSH*, pp. 497–98, indicates that Wu was not prepared, and *CYB*, *1925–26*, p. 1130, also describes the Chihli party as "badly prepared." Li Man-k'ang, May 16, 1960, p. 4, says that Wu's military arrangements could not be made in such a short time.

52. Miner Journal, Oct. 25, 1924.

53. Wen, Pien 3, pp. 182–83.

54. The U.S. chargé in Peking reported to the Secretary of State, Sept. 2, 1924, that the Peking government had raised $3,000,000 during the preceding few days, and that $1,000,000 had been given to Feng. See *Papers Relating to the Foreign Relations of the United States*, p. 365. Li Man-k'ang, No. 71, p. 9, quotes Wu as saying that he first gave Feng $100,000 for expenses, and then raised it to $150,000. Feng, in *WSH*, pp. 495–96, says he paid $100,000 for equipment, but does not say where he obtained it.

55. *Jihchi*, I, Chüan 5, p. 108; *WSH*, p. 495.

56. *WSH*, p. 499.

57. Impey, "Flood, Famine, and Civil War," p. 152; *NCH*, Oct. 11, 1924, p. 49. The quotation is from *NCH*, Oct. 18, 1924, p. 90. For other reports about Feng's reluctance to support Wu, see "New Political Line-up," p. 330; *NCH*, Sept. 27, 1924, p. 486; MacNair, p. 56; "General Feng's Coup," p. 268. Feng himself, in *WSH*, p. 492, says that he opposed the war, although by itself this would not be sufficient evidence because his account of this period is unreliable.

58. *WSH*, p. 498.

59. This meeting is described in *Jihchi*, I, Chüan 5, p. 103, in the entry for Sept. 10, 1924. *WSH*, pp. 489–90, also contains an account of the meeting, but there Feng says it occurred a few days after Sept. 10.

60. *WSH*, pp. 492–93; *Jihchi*, I, Chüan 5, pp. 107, 111, 113.

61. *KMCKMS*, Appendix, p. 10; *WSH*, p. 500; *Jihchi*, I, Chüan 5, p. 118.

62. *Jihchi*, I, Chüan 5, p. 120; *WSH*, p. 504.

63. *WSH*, pp. 505–6, describes the steps in the occupation of Peking. See also Dailey, "Is Feng a Traitor," pp. 364–70.

64. These proclamations are translated into French in Wieger, pp. 102–4. The proclamation to the population of Peking is translated into English in Dailey, "Is Feng a Traitor," pp. 366–68. *Kuo-min-chün chia-tzu*, section 2, contains Chinese texts of two of the proclamations, as does Li T'ai-fen, p. 116.

65. *Kuo-min-chün chia-tzu*, section 2; Kao, p. 155.

66. Wu's activities after the coup and the military aspects of his defeat are discussed in "Shih-shih shu-p'ing," pp. 4–5. See also Wen, Pien 3, pp. 197–98, and Impey, "Chinese Progress," p. 104.

67. A copy of this agreement, translated into English, is in *CYB*, *1925–26*, pp. 631–33.

68. Johnston, pp. 390–91; *CYB*, *1925–26*, p. 844; *NCH*, Nov. 22, 1924, p. 314. *NCH*, Dec. 13, 1924, p. 440, contains a report of an interview with P'u-i in which he describes his expulsion from the Forbidden City.

69. On the day following the coup, for example, the American chargé in Peking cabled that the coup was "formulated and executed" by Feng, Hu

Ching-i, and Sun Yo. *Papers Relating to the Foreign Relations of the United States*, p. 384.

70. *WSH*, p. 492; also pp. 493, 502–5.

71. For example, *KMCKMS*, chap. 8, pp. 1–4, emphasizes that Feng was caught up in a new wave of revolution, and that his connections with the Kuomintang were very close. This work generally stresses Feng's revolutionary past. The other extreme is manifested by Weale, p. 207.

72. *Jihchi*, I, Chüan 5, pp. 1–120 *passim*.

73. Dailey, "Is Feng a Traitor," p. 371, quotes Feng's justification. Ch'eng, pp. 73–74, reports the explanation Feng gave him shortly after the coup; there is not a single allusion to Sun Yat-sen or his ideas.

74. Wen, *Pien* 2, p. 29, asserts that Feng, Sun, and Hu were helped by Kuomintang agents.

75. T'ao, *Pei-yang*, VI, 163, summarizes the early relations between Wu and Feng.

76. *WSH*, p. 443, describes the incident but says that it was meant to express the idea that "between friends, water is sufficient." The gift was reported in *NCH*, Apr. 15, 1922, p. 148, with some apparent misgivings that it would be accepted by Wu in the spirit in which it was given. *NCH*, Nov. 1, 1924, p. 173, interprets the gift as a sign of Feng's disapproval of Wu's drinking. Kotenev, *Soldier*, pp. 114–15, has the same interpretation. Mao, "T'an Feng Yü-hsiang," asserts that in northern China such a gift had an insulting implication.

77. *WSH*, p. 458.

78. This statement appears in Dailey, "Significance of Banditry," p. 210. Dailey wrote this article shortly after having talked personally with Wu and his officers, and therefore presumably had good grounds for making the statement. Ting, pp. 23–24, asserts that Feng's execution of Pao was the beginning of the split between Wu and Feng.

79. T'ao, *Pei-yang*, VI, 164, asserts that after Feng's dismissal as Honan tuchün, he "became Wu's secret enemy." Two of Feng's officers whom I interviewed in Taiwan in 1959 said that Feng's being forced to leave Honan was the main cause of the split between him and Wu.

80. *NCH*, Dec. 6, 1924, p. 396; Frederick Mayer to the Secretary of State, Oct. 29, 1924, 893.00/5690. Also see *NCH*, Nov. 8, 1924, p. 217, which reported that "Japanese sources as far apart as Tokyo and Dairen reported it as expected, before it occurred." Weale, pp. 262–63, says that the coup was reported in Tokyo newspapers at least two days before it occurred. A translated article from the *Peking and Tientsin Times*, Nov. 18, 1924, sent in a despatch from G. C. Hanson, consul at Harbin, to the Secretary of State, Dec. 8, 1924, 893.00/5904, said that news of the impending coup actually reached Tokyo on the afternoon of Oct. 17.

81. *Peking and Tientsin Times*, Nov. 12, 1924, translated in a despatch from G. C. Hanson, consul at Harbin, to the Secretary of State, Dec. 8, 1924, 893.00/5904.

82. Fuse, p. 70.

83. "Pei-ching," Oct. 25, 1924, p. 1.

84. Jefferson Caffery, U.S. chargé at the Tokyo embassy, to the Secretary of State, Oct. 22, 1924, 893.00/5765.

85. Information about this railroad agreement is in a memorandum from the Japanese Ambassador to the Secretary of State, July 16, 1925, 893.77/2361, and the many documents from the Japanese embassy to the Secretary of State, July 17, 1925, 893.77/2362. A message from the American group of the Chinese consortium to the Secretary of State, May 5, 1926, 893.77/2428, includes the contract between Chang and the Japanese; the Chinese requested that the contract not be made public because of the political situation at that time. Notification of the American group of the consortium was dated Mar. 24, 1926.

86. "Go Hai-fu."

87. Bisson, p. 42.

88. *Who's Who in China* (3d ed.), p. 380.

89. Matsumuro Takayoshi, a Japanese army officer, participated in the last stages of the Peking coup, and thereafter served as an adviser to Feng Yü-hsiang. His role is described in the text. I had three interviews with Mr. Matsumuro in Tokyo in 1959. He informed me that Huang Fu was the middleman. In addition, Rihachiro Banzai, who was associated with the Japanese military in China from 1912 to 1924, and was once a military adviser to Wu P'ei-fu and Ts'ao K'un, wrote in *Zoku tai-shi kaikoroku*, p. 832, that Huang Fu was the man who was persuaded by the Japanese to convince Feng to attempt the coup. The long description of the coup written by Rodney Gilbert in *NCH*, Dec. 6, 1924, p. 396, derived largely from confidential information given to Gilbert by Banzai. See the personal letter from Frederick Mayer to J. V. A. MacMurray, Nov. 26, 1924, 893.00/5949, and the report by C. E. Gauss, American Consul General at Tientsin, to the Secretary of State, Dec. 10, 1924, 893.00/5909. The same facts appear in a long article by H. G. W. Woodhead in the *Peking and Tientsin Times*, Nov. 22, 1924. All these reports, of course, say that Huang Fu was the first Chinese approached in the matter.

90. This conclusion is based on several points. (1) Rumors of defection circulated in Peking long before the Second Chih-Feng War actually began. (2) A report in *NCH*, Dec. 6, 1924, p. 396, asserts that the "Anfu leaders who work closely with the Japanese freely admit that Feng's defection was arranged for many months before the war actually started." (3) *NCH*, Nov. 15, 1924, p. 259, reports that Tuan Ch'i-jui's subordinates said that Feng's participation in Wu's defeat was arranged "prior to Chinese New Year's." That would mean before Feb. 4, 1924. (4) *NCH*, July 19, 1924, p. 86, carried a story that reportedly came "from a number of independent sources in almost identically the same form." The story says that Chang Tso-lin, Lu Yung-hsiang, Tuan Ch'i-jui, and Sun Yat-sen had secured the cooperation of Feng Yü-hsiang in attempting a coup planned for Sept. 1924. (5) Fuse Katsuji, who is better informed about the coup than many observers, says that behind-the-scenes maneuvers of the Kuomintang facilitated the alliance of Feng, Hu Ching-i, and Sun Yo. See Fuse, p. 69. This would mean that the plans for the coup preceded the agreement between Feng, Hu, and Sun. Huang Fu may have been the Kuomintang representative Fuse had in mind. (6) *Jihchi*, I, Chüan 5, p. 85, reveals that on July 29, 1924, Suzuki Teiichi and Itagaki Seishiro visited Feng, and that Nomura Kichisaburo met with him on Aug. 1. Suzuki and Itagaki were Japanese army officers who later became well known

during the war in Manchuria, and Admiral Nomura also became famous, notably as the Japanese ambassador to the United States at the time of the Pearl Harbor attack. There is no indication of what took place in their meetings with Feng; it is certainly possible that these meetings had no connection with the coup. Nevertheless, this sudden contact between Feng and Japanese officers is suggestive; if we assume their meetings were related to the coup, it would follow that Huang Fu came to an agreement with Feng sometime before their visit, for they would hardly have visited Feng without prior assurance that their proposals would be favorably received.

91. Matsumuro interview. Mr. Matsumuro was very emphatic on this point. He asserted that Hayashi Yasakichi told him that Feng had received a check for 1,500,000 yen drawn on the Yokohama Species Bank. But Mr. Matsumuro was also told that Feng had demanded 3,000,000 yen. In view of this, a passage in Lynn, p. 174, acquires significance. "In some quarters," Lynn wrote, Chang Tso-lin "was believed to have paid $1,400,000 to Feng Yü-hsiang through a YMCA secretary to turn on Wu P'ei-fu. This statement was even openly admitted in a circular by Li Ching-lin during the Li-Feng War of 1925–26." The admission to which Lynn refers was doubtless the circular telegram issued by Li Ching-lin in Dec. 1925, which denounced Feng and listed all of his alleged betrayals, murders, and other crimes. The wire, which is translated in Weale, pp. 249–50, contains the line: "It was only last year that he [Feng] sold his chief, ex-President Ts'ao K'un, for a sum of 1,400,000 dollars." The most striking feature of these reports is the similarity of the sums cited. It should also be noted that whereas Lynn attributed the payment of the money to Chang Tso-lin, the circular telegram of Li Ching-lin, as translated by Weale, does not mention Chang; it simply says that Feng was bought for that amount. NCH, Dec. 6, 1924, p. 396, also cites a figure, but it is much larger than that quoted by Mr. Matsumuro: "The estimated total cost of the deal was $20,000,000, of which $5,000,000 was to be paid over to the conspirators on the eve of the coup and the remainder whenever it resulted in Wu P'ei-fu's complete collapse and removal from the political field." The same source says that the funds were provided by a great Japanese corporation in Manchuria, and that the company was to be repaid by the Chinese government to be established after the coup.

92. Rihachiro Banzai, in Zoku tai-shi kaikoroku, p. 832, asserts that he learned that Ts'ao K'un was going to get help from the United States in order to maintain his position. He obtained documentary evidence of this, and fearing that such U.S. involvement would threaten Japanese interests, he turned it over to Dohihara Kenji. The latter persuaded Huang Fu to show it to Feng. It is not clear what type of American assistance was to be rendered, nor why news of it should have been so effective in persuading Feng.

93. Perhaps the best proof of this is that Tuan actually did head the government established late in Nov. 1924. In addition, Matsumuro declared that Huang Fu and Tuan hoped to organize a government together. Fuse, p. 75, says that the plan was for Tuan to take over the government. Chang Tso-lin told an interviewer three days after the coup, on Oct. 26, that "the Peking government will be taken over by Marshal Tuan Ch'i-jui." This is from NCH, Nov. 1, 1924, p. 175. Note that this was before Chang Tso-lin

had left Manchuria to confer with Feng and Tuan in Tientsin, where they were presumably to decide on the new government.

94. *WSH*, pp. 506–7.

95. *NCH*, Sept. 20, 1924, p. 450.

96. *Jihchi*, I, Chüan 5, p. 119; *WSH*, p. 502.

97. Wieger, pp. 104–5.

98. That Tuan Ch'i-jui was the one who brought about an understanding between Feng and Chang Tso-lin is asserted by Fuse, p. 69, and by Ting, p. 60. Dailey, "Is Feng a Traitor," p. 370, asserts that Feng had arranged with Li Ching-lin, commander of the Second Fengtien Army, that Lin would desert Chang Tso-lin when Feng deserted Wu P'ei-fu. Lynn, pp. 173–74, relates the same story. Both writers report this as fact, not rumor.

99. Ting, p. 55.

100. *WSH*, p. 502.

101. *NCH*, Dec. 6, 1924, p. 396.

102. Impey, "Chinese Progress," p. 104.

103. *Jihchi*, I, Chüan 5, pp. 80–147; II, Chüan 6, pp. 1–57 *passim*.

104. Matsumuro interview.

105. Matsumuro interview.

106. Although Matsumuro's statement seems implausible, it is worth noting that a description of the coup (attributed to a prominent Japanese whom I have identified as Kihachiro Banzai) reported in *NCH*, Dec. 6, 1924, p. 396, asserts that the "whole scheme, according to this authority [Banzai], was conceived and very largely worked out by a Japanese Major General resident in China." At the time of the coup, Matsumuro was apparently a major; Hayashi Yasakichi, Japanese military attaché, was a major general.

107. Matsumuro interview.

108. "Hyo Gyoku-sho no kinkyo."

109. Matsumuro interview. According to *NCH*, Dec. 6, 1924, p. 396, the Japanese were angry because Feng had seized Peking instead of attacking Wu P'ei-fu. On this basis, they refused to give Feng the remainder of the payment promised him. According to this source, it was after this that Feng, seeing that he had already lost Japanese support, ousted P'u-i.

110. *NCH*, Apr. 2, 1921, p. 10. See also the following issues of *NCH*: Oct. 23, 1920, p. 220; Nov. 27, 1920, p. 617; Feb. 12, 1921, p. 428; Mar. 12, 1921, p. 648; Mar. 19, 1921, p. 720; Apr. 9, 1921, pp. 76, 83.

111. Johnston, pp. 324–32.

112. *NCH*, Mar. 22, 1924, pp. 436–37. *Chia-tzu Ch'ing-shih* contains documents and facsimiles on a restoration plot in early 1924; however, it has been suggested that this publication was designed to whitewash Feng's action. See also the enclosures in the despatch from J. V. A. MacMurray to the Secretary of State, Aug. 21, 1925, 893.00/6636.

113. Johnston, pp. 413–14.

114. *Papers Relating to the Foreign Relations of the United States*, pp. 390–91.

115. *NCH*, Nov. 29, 1924, p. 353.

116. *NCH*, Feb. 14, 1925, p. 255, carries a long article describing Li's operations in a very insinuating fashion, and states unequivocally that pieces of the palace collection had been and were being sold.

117. Weale, p. 216.

118. It is probably impossible to settle conclusively the question of whether Feng stole palace treasures. All the Kuominchün officers whom I interviewed denied that anything was taken, although this cannot be considered very strong evidence because of their high regard for Feng, and the fact that an admission that anything was taken would imply their complicity. Also, objects could have been taken without their knowledge. Mao I-heng, who served with Feng after the coup, in *O-Meng*, p. 210, says that Lu Chunglin told him that warfare at Nankow in 1926 used up the 14,000,000 yüan that had been obtained from the sale of the palace treasures. But Mao's book is not completely reliable, so this must be viewed skeptically. If objects were taken from the palace, it is possible that someone else took them, and, indeed, that they were taken prior to the coup. For example, a year before the coup it was reported that many valuable items had been stolen from the palace, presumably by eunuchs employed by the imperial family. Over 1,000 eunuchs were subsequently dismissed; see *NCH*, July 21, 1923, p. 157. Even a few objects from the collection appearing on the market would have been enough to start rumors that Feng had taken them. It must be remembered that nobody has maintained that Feng took all of them, although this is sometimes implied by the bald phrase that he stole the palace treasures. In any event, in later years rumors and allegations periodically cropped up about others' having stolen them. For example, *CWR*, Oct. 13, 1934, p. 233, describes charges that I P'ei-chi, former director of the palace museum, together with other officials stole at least $50,000,000 worth of the palace treasures. See also *CWR*, Sept. 10, 1932, p. 46; *CWR*, Jan. 13, 1934, pp. 275–76; *CWR*, May 12, 1934, p. 416. Thousands of cases of the palace treasures were successively shipped to several places in China to prevent their seizure by the invading Japanese, and today many pieces from the collection—indeed, the bulk of it—are in central Taiwan.

119. Wieger, p. 11.

120. Houn, pp. 152, 213, n. 3. See also Li Chien-nung, *Chung-kuo*, pp. 654–55.

121. MacNair, p. 59; *NCH*, Nov. 29, 1924, p. 347

122. Li T'ai-fen, p. 142. Wieger, pp. 118–19, has the wire in French translation.

Chapter Seven

1. *NCH*, May 19, 1923, p. 433. Li T'ai-fen, p. 88, indicates that Feng tried to resign this appointment shortly after receiving it. His resignation was not accepted, and Feng simply did nothing.

2. Dailey, "Feng Yü-hsiang's Next Move," p. 337, and "Feng Yü-hsiang: Colonist," p. 213.

3. E. F. Stanton, American vice-consul at Kalgan, wrote a fairly detailed report on agricultural development in the Northwest under Feng. This report, dated May 2, 1925, is 893.61/31. See also *NCH*, Sept. 19, 1925, p. 380.

4. Chang Yu-i, II, 656.

5. *Jihchi*, II, Chüan 6, pp. 14, 17, 20–21, 24. *NCS*, Apr. 19, 1925, p. 2, contains a copy of the regulations for immigrants to the northern territories. See also *NCS*, Apr. 18, 1925, p. 5, and Apr. 21, p. 3.

6. *NCH,* Sept. 19, 1925, p. 380.
7. A despatch by E. F. Stanton, vice-consul at Kalgan, June 12, 1925, 893.911/210.
8. Chang Yu-i, II, 656.
9. *Jihchi,* II, Chüan 6, p. 21; see also p. 24.
10. For a description of the New Village, see Miner, "Works of Peace," and Li T'ai-fen, p. 151.
11. *NCH,* Sept. 19, 1925, p. 380.
12. *WSH,* pp. 523–24; Wieger, p. 55; Fenn, p. 11.
13. For Feng's requests for American investment, see the despatch from American Minister Schurman to the Secretary of State, Jan. 29, 1925, 893.00/6061; the confidential report from Vice-Consul E. F. Stanton to the American legation, July 10, 1925, 811.503193/21; and another despatch from Stanton, Aug. 13, 1925, 893.00/6583.
14. Wieger, p. 227; *NCH,* July 25, 1925, p. 41.
15. *Jihchi,* II, Chüan 6, pp. 80–81.
16. Interview with Matsumuro Takayoshi, Nov. 1959.
17. "Hyo Gyoku-sho no kinkyo."
18. Mao, *O-Meng,* pp. 9–10.
19. Interview with Matsumuro Takayoshi, Nov. 1959.
20. *NCH,* Aug. 15, 1925, p. 165.
21. *Jihchi,* II, Chüan 6, p. 110.
22. *Ibid.,* pp. 19, 22.
23. For Feng's policies toward the Peking-Suiyuan Railway, see "Hyo Gyoku-sho no kinkyo"; *NCH,* Mar. 28, 1925, p. 514, and May 16, 1925, p. 266; Dailey, "Feng Yü-hsiang: Colonist," p. 213; and Mao, *O-Meng,* p. 3. Two despatches from E. F. Stanton, vice-consul at Kalgan, treat this subject: Apr. 22, 1925, 893.00/6213, and Sept. 22, 1925, 893.00/6686.
24. *NCH,* July 18, 1925, p. 18.
25. Report from E. F. Stanton, vice-consul at Kalgan, to the Secretary of State, Mar. 6, 1925, 893.512/315. See also 893.512/312, 893.512/356, and 893.512/381. Document 893.00/7306 includes a long article by Rodney Gilbert from the Mar. 9, 1926, issue of the *North China Daily News,* which discusses the harshness of Feng's economic exploitation. *NCS,* Oct. 20, 1925, p. 4, reports on the capital tax and the profit tax.
26. Despatches from E. F. Stanton, vice-consul at Kalgan, to the American legation, July 8, 1925, 893.797/52, and July 14, 1925, 893.797/53.
27. *NCH,* Mar. 28, 1925, p. 514.
28. *WSH,* p. 524.
29. *WSH,* pp. 530–31; Li T'ai-fen, pp. 155–56; *NCS,* Sept. 23, 1925, p. 8.
30. *NCH,* Apr. 11, 1925, p. 51, and May 16, 1925, p. 266; *NCS,* July 2, 1925, p. 8; report from E. F. Stanton, vice-consul at Kalgan, Aug. 10, 1925, 893.516/233.
31. *Jihchi,* II, Chüan 6, p. 24. See also Li T'ai-fen, p. 153.
32. *NCH,* Mar. 28, 1925, p. 514; Li T'ai-fen, p. 153. *CYB, 1925–26,* p. 585, quotes an article in the *Peking and Tientsin Times* of Apr. 6, 1925, by a reporter who bought opium in Kalgan himself to prove that it was easily obtained. He wrote that "a tax has to be paid when the opium is bought, the receipt for the tax being called a 'fine-receipt.' " The accuracy of this story

is indirectly confirmed by Mrs. Christian Hannestad, who at that time was living in Kalgan. In an interview with Mrs. Hannestad in Yokohama in Nov. 1959, she told me that she had once pointed out to Mrs. Feng that, Feng's prohibitions notwithstanding, "opium had never been so cheap in Kalgan." According to Mrs. Hannestad, Mrs. Feng was shocked, and the "next day there was no opium to be found in Kalgan." It is difficult to believe that opium was being sold openly without Feng's knowledge. In view of his search for sources of revenue, the story quoted in the *CYB* seems credible. And even if sales did cease immediately, which seems doubtful, this would tend to confirm that the opium trade was under Feng's control in the first place.

33. Ch'eng, pp. 78–79; Mrs. Hannestad interview; Li T'ai-fen, p. 151.

34. *NCH*, May 16, 1925, p. 266, reported that Feng instituted a tax on brothels. Moreover, in my interview with Mrs. Hannestad she declared, "Feng could not stand sin!" and proceeded to illustrate by relating how Feng had once had an officer beaten for visiting a brothel. When I pointed out that this incident confirmed the existence of brothels, Mrs. Hannestad speculated that some remained open through the negligence or corruption of those charged with enforcing Feng's order to close them. This may have been the case, but it seems more likely that some remained open by paying taxes. Feng's beating of the officer would not have been inconsistent with such an arrangement because Feng certainly would not have sanctioned whoring on the part of his own men.

35. Ch'eng, p. 18.

36. Li T'ai-fen, p. 150; Ch'eng, pp. 79–80.

37. Speer, pp. 195–96.

38. Mrs. Hannestad interview.

39. Li T'ai-fen, p. 152; Ch'eng, p. 80; *NCS*, July 30, 1925, p. 8; Nov. 6, 1925, p. 8; Dec. 4, 1925, p. 8; and May 13, 1926, p. 6.

40. Stanton, p. 34.

41. Impey, "Kalgan the Key," p. 190.

42. Wen, Pien 2, pp. 19–20.

43. Ting, pp. 107–8; Li T'ai-fen, p. 131.

44. Report from American Minister Jacob Gould Schurman, Jan. 2, 1925, 893.00/5901. For a general survey of the disposition of troops immediately after the Second Chih-Feng War, see Ho Hsi-ya.

45. Li T'ai-fen, p. 157, contains a list of the divisions with the names of the commanders, as does *KMCKMS*, chap. 9, pp. 49–50. In *WSH*, p. 522, Feng briefly describes his forces in mid-1925. Wen, Pien 2, pp. 32–34, describes the organization of the First Kuominchün as of Sept. 1925, and says the total number of men was only 90,000. All other estimates are well over 100,000.

46. *Jihchi*, II, Chüan 6, p. 15.

47. Shyu, p. 11, provides a chart showing the positions these men held in 1925, their birthplaces, and their backgrounds. Also see pp. 12–13.

48. *Jihchi*, II, Chüan 6, *passim*, esp. pp. 25, 34, 42.

49. For a detailed account of the expansion of the Second Kuominchün, with a unit breakdown of the army as it was in mid-1925, see Wen, Pien 2, pp. 35–44.

50. Geoffrey, p. 68.
51. For details on the expansion of the Third Kuominchün, see Wen, Pien 2, pp. 44–47.
52. E. F. Stanton, vice-consul at Kalgan, sent a despatch to American Minister J. V. A. MacMurray, Dec. 11, 1925, 893.00/7024, describing the work in the Kalgan mint. See also *CYB, 1926–27*, p. 1051, and Li T'ai-fen, p. 156.
53. The major "false start" was the contact the Russians made with Wu P'ei-fu. See Tsai, pp. 4–5; Wilbur and How, pp. 139–40; and Mao, *O-Meng*, p. 157.
54. *WSH*, pp. 470–71, 525.
55. Wieger, p. 15.
56. Wilbur and How, pp. 336–37.
57. The *NCH* of Dec. 26, 1925, reported on p. 552 that "in February of this year it became generally known in diplomatic circles that General Feng Yü-hsiang had entered into some kind of written agreement with the Reds." MacNair, p. 60, accepts this estimate of when a preliminary agreement was made. There are several independent reports that Russian supplies were enroute to Feng before Apr. 21, which, according to the captured documents translated by Wilbur and How, was the date when serious talks between Feng and the Russians began. A report in the *NCH*, May 9, 1925, p. 221, said that Feng had been receiving Russian goods since Apr. 10. Another report on the same page of that issue said that several tons of Russian arms and other supplies bound for Kalgan had been seen in Urga (present-day Ulan Bator) on Apr. 19. Roy Chapman Andrews, an American explorer who was camped 95 miles from Kalgan on Apr. 20, saw 90 motor cars loaded with ammunition going from Urga to Kalgan; see Andrews, *On the Trail of Ancient Man*, pp. 253–54. If Feng was in fact receiving Russian aid before Apr. 21, what are we to make of the statement of his chief Russian adviser that has been interpreted to mean that the agreement between Feng and the Russians was made in late April? One possibility is that the document is a forgery; the authenticity of these documents has long been questioned, a problem discussed by Wilbur and How, pp. 8–37. However, it is also possible, indeed I think probable, that the document and the statement are both trustworthy. One need only assume there was an earlier, perhaps tentative, agreement providing for the supplies that, according to the above-mentioned reports, were on the way to Kalgan in April. The agreement referred to in the document, in all probability, was simply a second, more significant one negotiated by the 35-man Russian mission that arrived in April to deal with Hu Ching-i, only to find that he had died on Apr. 10. When they turned their attention to Feng—if this interpretation is correct—they had to negotiate a firmer pact providing for the large-scale aid and the Russian advisers that had been intended for Hu. Such an interpretation, incidentally, accords with the fact that both the *NCH* article and the passage in MacNair cited above refer to a preliminary and a later agreement. For Feng's version of how his association with the Russians came about, see *WSH*, pp. 525–26. He does not discuss the question in his diary.
58. In an interview in Nov. 1959, Mrs. Christian Hannestad told me a story that might have some bearing on Feng's rapprochement with the Russians. Mrs. Hannestad, who was the wife of a missionary doctor in Kalgan,

gave Feng daily English lessons during the first part of 1925. (Feng confirms this in his diary.) She related how a German businessman in Kalgan, a Mr. May, claimed to have served at Feng's request as an intermediary between him and the Russians. According to Mrs. Hannestad, May considered himself the prime mover in Feng's obtaining Russian aid. In the absence of other evidence, the story does not sound very credible. I pass it on simply as an interesting fragment that may fit into a pattern of facts uncovered by others.

59. "Jen Te-chiang's Letter to Frunze on Alliance with Feng Yü-hsiang," Wilbur and How, p. 337.

60. Ibid., p. 339.

61. "Letter to Karakhan on Feng Yü-hsiang," Wilbur and How, p. 342.

62. "Soviet Report on the Political Attitude of Feng Yü-hsiang and First Kuominchün Officers," Wilbur and How, p. 365.

63. "Ya-en's Report on the Kalgan Soviet Group," Wilbur and How, pp. 356–57.

64. "Jen Te-chiang's Letter," Wilbur and How, pp. 338, 340.

65. "Letter to Karakhan," Wilbur and How, p. 341.

66. Ibid., pp. 341–42.

67. "Jen Te-chiang's Letter," Wilbur and How, p. 337.

68. Allen, p. 64.

69. Wen, Pien 2, p. 34. Wen estimates that by August Feng had as many as 80,000 infantry rifles. A Russian adviser stated in early Dec. 1925 that Feng's army had only 59,000 rifles. "Record of a Meeting at the Soviet Embassy in Peking," Wilbur and How, p. 349.

70. Ibid.

71. Ibid., pp. 344–47.

72. "Ya-en's Report," Wilbur and How, p. 355.

73. Ibid.

74. Ibid., pp. 355–56.

75. NCH, Oct. 17, 1925, p. 90, says 600 students were enrolled, with about 5,000 applicants still waiting. Kotenev, Soldier, p. 19, also says 600, although he may well have obtained his information from the NCH article. Allen, p. 117, says about 1,000.

76. Allen, pp. 124–26.

77. "Record of a Meeting," Wilbur and How, p. 347.

78. Li T'ai-fen, p. 180; Ch'eng, p. 89; NCH, July 18, 1925, p. 18.

79. Jihchi, II, Chüan 6, passim. On p. 54 is the account of Feng's distributing over 300 copies of Sun's lectures.

80. Dailey, "Soviet Red Bear," p. 4.

81. Jihchi, II, Chüan 6, p. 74.

82. Ibid., pp. 67ff. See also a despatch from E. F. Stanton, vice-consul at Kalgan, to the American legation in Peking, July 7, 1925, 893.00/6497.

83. Allen, pp. 61–63. According to Allen, this play was presented early in June, just a day or two after the news of the May 30th Incident reached Kalgan.

84. NCH, July 4, 1925, p. 514.

85. NCH, Aug. 29, 1925, p. 248. The NCH story was taken from an interview with Feng that appeared in a German newspaper. Feng's diary for the second half of 1925 shows that a number of foreign journalists traveled to Kalgan to interview him. See also Wieger, pp. 205–6, 220–21.

86. Wieger, pp. 215–16; *KMCKMS*, chap. 9, pp. 40–44; *NCH*, July 11, 1925, p. 517.

87. *NCH*, Dec. 19, 1925, p. 510; Ch'eng, pp. 81–82.

88. Ch'eng, pp. 84–85.

89. *NCH*, Dec. 19, 1925, p. 510.

90. Auxion de Ruffe, p. 53, describes Feng as "leading the anti-foreign movement."

Chapter Eight

1. Telegram from Minister Jacob Gould Schurman to the Secretary of State, Mar. 18, 1925, 893.00/6090.

2. Wen, Pien 3, pp. 206–12; Fuse, pp. 122–27; Li T'ai-fen, p. 216.

3. *NCH*, Jan. 2, 1926, p. 8. Miner Journal, Dec. 5, 1925, states that Kuo's "young wife was a student in the sub-freshman and junior college departments of our college, and she and Gen. Feng's wife are friends. I think she became a Christian, but she did not join the church." Mao, *O-Meng*, p. 11, asserts that the plot originated with the wives. Many other sources allude to such a possibility, which is somewhat substantiated by the fact that Mrs. Kuo was executed with her husband when the revolt failed.

4. Feng's explanation of the plot in *WSH*, pp. 542–43, asserts that when Kuo Sung-ling arrived in Japan he was mistaken for a representative of Chang Tso-lin who was due to arrive to "acknowledge the Twenty-One Demands, in return for which Japan would supply Fengtien the weapons with which to attack the Kuominchün." According to Feng, Kuo, as a loyal Chinese, was disturbed by this and confided in Han Fu-chü that if Fengtien attacked the Kuominchün he would turn against Chang Tso-lin. This explanation is echoed in *KMCKMS*, chap. 9, p. 62. Although this story is not convincing, it is interesting that in early December, about two weeks after the revolt began, a "story was current in Mukden that in return for a promise to settle in their favor the dispute regarding land ownership in Manchuria, which was one of the terms agreed to in the famous Twenty-One Demands of ten years ago, the Japanese are supplying Chang Tso-lin with extra artillery and munitions to the extent of ten million yen." This is from Weale, pp. 247–48. In any event, regardless of Kuo's original motives, it is probable that he and Han did discuss the plot in Japan. Han Fu-chü returned to China about Nov. 6. Five days later, one of Feng's officers who had been on a trip to the Soviet Union returned to China. When I interviewed this officer on Taiwan in 1959, he said the arrangements with Kuo Sung-ling had been made by the time he returned. Such arrangements could hardly have been proposed and agreed upon in five days. And there is no indication that Feng and Kuo had any negotiations before the beginning of October, when Han left China for Japan.

5. For various versions of the agreement, see Ma, pp. 55–56; Wen, Pien 3, p. 212; Li T'ai-fen, p. 221; Allen, p. 142; Fuse, pp. 123–24; *WSH*, p. 543.

6. Li T'ai-fen, pp. 239–41. Feng's wire is translated in Wieger, p. 261.

7. Telegram to the Secretary of State from Minister J. V. A. MacMurray, Dec. 7, 1925, 893.00/6825.

8. Kotenev, *New Lamps for Old*, p. 230; Auxion de Ruffe, p. 167.

9. Li T'ai-fen's account of the revolt, pp. 215–52, includes many of the communications sent by Kuo during the revolt, as well as other relevant

documents. See *CYB, 1926–27*, pp. 1025–28, for a good summary. See also the despatch from Jacob Gould Schurman to the Secretary of State, Feb. 8, 1926, 893.00/7124, and the confidential report from M. S. Myers, consul at Mukden, to Minister J. V. A. MacMurray, June 13, 1928, 893.00/10135. Document 893.00/6980 includes many newspaper clippings regarding Kuo's revolt.

10. Despatch from C. E. Gauss, American consul at Tientsin, to Minister J. V. A. MacMurray, Dec. 14, 1925, 893.00/6929.

11. A detailed account of the battle at Tientsin is in Impey, *Chinese Army*, pp. 47–52. See also Li T'ai-fen, pp. 242–43.

12. Allen, pp. 188–89.

13. For Feng's telegram of resignation, see Li T'ai-fen, pp. 262–63. See also *NCH*, Jan. 9, 1926, pp. 45–46, and Jan. 16, 1926, p. 89.

14. Despatch from E. F. Stanton, vice-consul at Kalgan, to Minister J. V. A. MacMurray, Jan. 6, 1926, 893.00/7083.

15. Telegram from Minister J. V. A. MacMurray to the Secretary of State, Jan. 9, 1926, 893.00/6920. In this wire MacMurray cited a report from Stanton to the effect that Feng could not count on the loyalty of his subordinates. But two weeks later, on Jan. 21, 1926, Stanton reported to MacMurray on the proceedings at a conference of Kuominchün leaders on Jan. 19 at P'ingtich'uan, where Feng had gone prior to leaving the country. During the conference, Feng pointed out that his departure should facilitate an understanding with Wu P'ei-fu. This report is 893.00/7121.

16. *NCH*, Oct. 23, 1926, p. 150; despatch from vice-consul E. F. Stanton to Minister J. V. A. MacMurray, Mar. 25, 1926, 893.00/7380.

17. Li T'ai-fen, pp. 267–72, has a detailed account of the fighting in Honan, and a number of relevant telegrams and other documents. For the activities of the Red Spears in the Honan campaign, see *CYB, 1926–27*, p. 1030.

18. Vice-consul E. F. Stanton to Minister J. V. A. MacMurray, Mar. 12, 1926, 893.00/7315. See also *NCS*, Feb. 18, 1926, p. 1.

19. *NCS*, Feb. 27, 1926, p. 8, reports that Huang Fu asked Sun Ch'uanfang to join Feng against Wu, but that Sun refused. *Jihchi*, II, Chüan 6, p. 143, says that Sun was willing to oppose Wu in some ways, but would not use military force against him.

20. For details on the *Oleg* trips, see "Soviet Plot," document 23; telegram from the commander-in-chief of the U.S. Asiatic Fleet to the chief of naval operations, Mar. 28, 1926, 893.00/7245; despatch from C. E. Gauss, Consul General at Tientsin, to Minister J. V. A. MacMurray, Mar. 16, 1926, 893.00/7337; *NCH*, Mar. 20, 1926, p. 516, and Mar. 27, 1926, p. 567. The information about the role of the French officials in warning Fengtien is in a despatch from Samuel Sokobin, consul at Mukden, to Minister MacMurray, May 3, 1926, 893.113/970.

21. *NCH*, May 8, 1926, p. 242.

22. For the rationale behind Lu Chung-lin's political maneuvers before abandoning Peking, see Allen, pp. 207–9. For the military dispositions around Peking, see Li T'ai-fen, pp. 280–84. *NCS*, Apr. 11, 1926, p. 1, carries a long story on the attempt to arrest Tuan, and the invitation extended to Wu.

23. For the determination of the allies to destroy the Kuominchün, see the

wire from Minister J. V. A. MacMurray to the Secretary of State, Apr. 3, 1926, 893.00/7274. *NCH,* Mar. 27, 1926, p. 599, carries a long account of the role of Japan in the conflict.

24. Despatch from E. F. Stanton to Minister J. V. A. MacMurray, July 7, 1926, 893.00/7546. See also *NCS,* June 23, 1926, pp. 1 and 5, and July 10, 1926, p. 8.

25. For the Soviet attitude toward Feng in the spring of 1926, and for details on the supplies given to the First Kuominchün by the Soviet Union, see Wilbur and How, pp. 365–66; "Soviet Plot," pp. 218–28; attaché's report, May 13, 1926, 893.00/7482; despatch from E. F. Stanton to Minister J. V. A. MacMurray, May 28, 1926, 893.00/7500; Minister MacMurray's report on political conditions during June 1926, dated July 30, 1926, 893.00/7602; despatch from Stanton to MacMurray, July 7, 1926, 893.00/7546. For Russian participation in the fighting, see three despatches from Stanton to MacMurray: Mar. 2, 1926, 893.00/7286, June 4, 1926, 893.00/7499, and July 28, 1926, 893.00/7586.

26. Li T'ai-fen, pp. 295–98; despatch from E. F. Stanton to Minister J. V. A. MacMurray, May 28, 1926, 893.00/7500.

27. For descriptions of the Kuominchün retreat, see *NCH,* Oct. 30, 1926, p. 209; Allen, pp. 222–23; Li T'ai-fen, p. 229; attaché's report, Oct. 7, 1926, 893.00/7936. This period was also described to me by a participant.

28. *NCS,* Aug. 5, 1925, p. 1, reported that the Kansu opium tax amounted to over twenty million dollars a year. *CYB, 1926–27,* p. 632, gives the same figure for 1924–25.

29. For detailed accounts of the plot against Lu Hung-t'ao and of Liu Yü-fen's seizure of Li and Pao, see Yin, shang pien, chap. 3, sections 3–4, and chap. 4, section 2, and Li T'ai-fen, pp. 186–88. See also *NCH,* Jan. 2, 1926, p. 8, and Jan. 9, 1926, p. 54.

30. *NCH,* July 17, 1926, p. 106, gives a rough demarcation between Muslim and Chinese areas in Kansu.

31. Yin, shang pien, chap. 5, sections 2–3. This source says that the conference was called "in December," and the context indicates that it was Dec. 1925. However, in Feng, *Feng Yü-hsiang hsün-ling,* Chüan 14, pp. 1–2, there is an order from Feng to Liu Yü-fen dated Jan. 9, 1927, ordering Liu to call a provincial conference to institute measures designed to centralize military and political control in Liu's hands. The general aims of the conference were the same as those described in Yin. This would seem to suggest either that there was an error in dating or that Liu's first conference yielded so few results that Feng thought he would try again.

32. For a detailed description of the various battles, tactics, personnel, etc., see Yin, shang pien, chap. 5, section 4, through chap. 11, section 2.

33. *NCH,* July 17, 1926, p. 106; July 25, 1926, p. 151; Sept. 11, 1926, p. 489; Nov. 20, 1926, p. 348.

34. *NCH,* Jan. 8, 1927, p. 10. For Kuominchün administrative policies in Kansu, see Li T'ai-fen, pp. 188–92.

35. *Jihchi,* II, Chüan 7, p. 1, gives the date of Feng's departure as Mar. 20. *KMCKMS,* Appendix, p. 12, gives the same date, and other sources agree. Fuse, p. 138, gives Mar. 16 as the date of departure. I have accepted Fuse's date because Kuominchün as well as newspaper sources all indicate that Feng

arrived in Urga on Mar. 22, and it seems that more than two days were required to make this trip across more than 600 miles of steppe. Indeed, a week was required for Feng to make the return trip from Urga to Wuyüan in Aug. 1926.

36. *WSH,* pp. 555–71, describes Feng's stay in Mongolia. See also *Jihchi,* II, Chüan 7, pp. 2–18.

37. *WSH,* p. 566, indicates that it was in Mongolia that Feng decided to join the Kuomintang. *Jihchi,* II, Chüan 7, p. 25, however, says that it was on May 10, 1926, shortly after his arrival in the Soviet Union, that he resolved to enter the Kuomintang and work for the national revolution. Doubtless Feng recognized at the outset of his journey from China that circumstances had conspired to make his joining the party virtually inevitable.

38. *WSH,* pp. 579–85; *Jihchi,* II, Chüan 7, pp. 24–57. For Radek's speech about Feng and the text of Feng's speech to the students of Sun Yat-sen University, see Li T'ai-fen, pp. 302–4.

39. *WSH,* pp. 576–600; *Jihchi,* II, Chüan 7, pp. 24–57. Mao, *O-Meng,* is primarily a record of the trip to Mongolia and then to Moscow. It contains many details about Feng's visit, but not all of them are reliable.

40. *Jihchi,* II, Chüan 7, pp. 36–54; *WSH,* p. 577; Mao, *O-Meng,* p. 201.

41. "Soviet Plot," pp. 224–27. Fuse, pp. 170–71, said that the Russians made Feng's joining the Kuomintang the first condition for giving him aid.

Chapter Nine

1. The oath is in Li T'ai-fen, pp. 310–11. See also my p. 298.

2. Lo Chia-lun, XV, 702–3; *NCH,* Oct. 23, 1926, p. 150; Li T'ai-fen, p. 305; a report from E. F. Stanton, vice-consul at Kalgan, after a visit to Suiyuan, Nov. 23, 1926, 893.00/7994.

3. This series of dates is from Kao, pp. 222–24.

4. Despatch from Lewis Clark, vice-consul at Kalgan, to Minister J. V. A. MacMurray, Jan. 14, 1927, 893.00/8247.

5. There are various interpretations of the fact that Han and Shih joined Yen Hsi-shan. One of Feng's subordinates informed me that the two men not only decided to leave Feng, but tried to persuade others to defect. Others think it was simply a tactical move. Feng said that when he asked Han about his intentions, Han said that he was sorry and would thereafter obey Feng completely, a remark that implies that the move was far more than tactical. Kao, p. 229, says that Yen ordered Han Fu-chü to go to south Shansi in an attempt to get him away from Feng's requests to return to the Kuominchün.

6. Lo Chia-lun, XV, 704–5; *WSH,* pp. 608, 619–33.

7. E. F. Stanton, vice-consul at Kalgan, to Minister J. V. A. MacMurray, Nov. 23, 1926, 893.00/7994.

8. *Jihchi,* II, Chüan 7, p. 85.

9. *Ibid.,* p. 79.

10. Fuse, pp. 186–87; *Jihchi,* II, Chüan 8, p. 79.

11. I have asumed that the strategy that had the Kuominchün march south to Shensi, and then east from T'ungkuan, was decided in consultation with Kuomintang leaders, perhaps even before Feng's return; Li Ming-chung and Liu Chi might have represented Feng in such decisions.

However, Feng indicates in *WSH*, p. 619, that whether the Kuominchün should fight its way back through Suiyuan and Chahar was discussed, and that a note from Li Ta-chao suggested going south. Fuse, pp. 172–73, says that Feng was in favor of fighting back to Peking from the west until Li Shih-tseng, in Peking, informed Feng of the formidable strength of Fengtien, information that would seem to have been superfluous given Feng's firsthand knowledge of that strength.

12. For the beginnings of the siege, see *WSH*, p. 634. For reports on conditions in the besieged city, see *NCH*, Oct.-Dec. 1926, pp. 205, 248, 339, 485, 617; and Feb. 5, 1927, p. 184. Bertram, p. 161, alleged that 35,000 people died of starvation during the siege. There are some indications that civilians were permitted out of the city, although certainly the entire population was not released, and it is unclear just who was permitted to go and why. According to Wales, p. 175, Chi P'eng-fei claimed that "food inside the city became scarce, and the civilians were all sent out, leaving only Yang's two divisions of troops inside." *Jihchi*, II, Chüan 7, p. 100, says that reports received by Feng from the front showed 30,000 *lao-pai-hsing* died of starvation during the siege.

13. *NCH*, Oct. 23, 1926, p. 155, describes the attitude of the Red Spears. One of Feng's officers explained to me that if Sian had fallen, the defending officers would surely have been killed.

14. *KMCKMS*, chap. 11, pp. 140–41.

15. The raising of the siege is briefly described in Chang Tzu-sheng, *Chancheng shih*, shang, pp. 68–70.

16. *Jihchi*, II, Chüan 7, p. 89.

17. Feng, *Feng Yü-hsiang chün-shih*, Chüan 2, p. 4; see Chüan 1, pp. 2–4, for other orders relating to the relief of Sian. See also *WSH*, pp. 642–48.

18. *WSH*, pp. 633–42, 652, 656.

19. Meng Po-ch'ien, pp. 19–20; *WSH*, p. 631.

20. Li T'ai-fen, p. 361; *WSH*, pp. 619, 630–31.

21. Feng, *Feng Yü-hsiang chün-shih*, Chüan 6, p. 2.

22. Meng Po-ch'ien, pp. 19–20; *NCH*, Sept. 25, 1926, p. 584.

23. Feng, *Feng Yü-hsiang chün-shih*, Chüan 4, p. 1, and Chüan 6, pp. 4–5.

24. *Ibid.*, Chüan 6, pp. 1–2, 5.

25. *WSH*, p. 631; *Jihchi*, II, Chüan 8, p. 36.

26. Feng, *Feng Yü-hsiang hsün-ling*, Chüan 3, pp. 39–40.

27. *Jihchi*, II, Chüan 8, p. 27.

28. *Ibid.*, Chüan 8, p. 28.

29. *WSH*, pp. 656, 719–20.

30. *Jihchi*, II, Chüan 7, p. 82. *NCH*, Jan. 1927, pp. 96 and 147, carries stories about anti-Christian activities in Sian, although the Kuominchün is not specifically accused of supporting such behavior.

31. Feng, *Feng Yü-hsiang chün-shih*, Chüan 6, pp. 7–9; *Jihchi*, II, Chüan 8, p. 26; *WSH*, pp. 654-55.

32. Meng Po-ch'ien, pp. 17–18; *KMCKMS*, chap. 11, pp. 142–44; Li T'ai-fen, pp. 322–24, 361.

33. Feng, *Feng Yü-hsiang hsün-ling*, Chüan 14, pp. 4–5; *WSH*, pp. 671–75, 698; Li T'ai-fen, pp. 418-19.

34. *Jihchi*, II, Chüan 8, p. 25. Feng, *Feng Yü-hsiang chün-shih*, Chüan

1, p. 11, contains an order dated Mar. 21, 1927, in which Feng says that unless Chiang Kai-shek sends supplies the situation will be critical.

35. Professor C. Martin Wilbur kindly provided me with a note he took from document 441/22 in the Kuomintang Archives, titled "Kuo-min cheng-fu chün-shih wei-yüan-hui ching-li-chu min-kuo shih-liu-nien ssu-yüeh fen-chün fei shou chih pao-kao shu." In this report, the breakdown of *regular* expenses shows 600,000 yüan budgeted for Feng, and the same amount as actually paid out. The breakdown of extraordinary military expenses indicates that Feng received 130,000 yüan for "bedding and clothing."

36. *Jihchi*, II, Chüan 8, p. 17; *NCH*, Jan. 8, 1927, p. 10.

37. Chien, *Hsi-pei*, p. 13. *WSH*, p. 676, says that only 100,000 yüan of money was printed.

38. Feng, *Feng Yü-hsiang chün-shih*, Chüan 1, p. 11, and *Feng Yü-hsiang hsün-ling*, Chüan 4, pp. 21–22; *Jihchi*, II, Chüan 7, p. 112; Mao, *O-Meng*, pp. 228ff; *NCH*, Jan. 22, 1927, p. 96; *WSH*, p. 648; despatch from Lewis Clark, vice-consul at Kalgan, to Minister J. V. A. MacMurray, Dec. 20, 1926, 893.00/8115.

39. Feng, *Feng Yü-hsiang hsün-ling*, Chüan 4, pp. 21–22, is an order from Feng to his troops to economize on ammunition; he said it cost one yüan for each ten bullets shipped from Kulun to Ninghsia. The order includes elaborate recommendations about how to train troops to be frugal with ammunition. No precise figures on the amount and cost of the supplies seem to be available.

40. Despatch from J. V. A. MacMurray to the Secretary of State, Jan. 10, 1928, 893.00/9767.

41. *NCH*, May 14, 1927, p. 274; *Jihchi*, II, Chüan 8, p. 12.

42. The battle arrangements for Feng's troops are in Lo Chia-lun, XV, 706–9, and Chang Tzu-sheng, *Chan-cheng shih*, hsia, pp. 17–18.

43. A despatch from F. P. Lockhart, consul at Hankow, to Minister J. V. A. MacMurray, June 30, 1927, 893.00/9298, includes a detailed description of the military aspects of the Honan campaign. See also Chang Tzu-sheng, *Chan-cheng shih*, hsia, pp. 18–19; Lo Chia-lun, XV, 696–701; T'ang, *Inner History*, pp. 277–79.

44. Li T'ai-fen, pp. 348–49.

45. *NCH*, June 18, 1927, p. 495. T'ang, *Inner History*, p. 278, stresses the heavy Wuhan casualties, and gives a figure of 13,000 killed and wounded out of a total of 70,000 men. Professor C. Martin Wilbur kindly gave me a copy of his notes on Wang Ching-wei's report on the Chengchow Conference, "Wang Ching-wei pao-kao," in which Wang mentions the figure of 14,000.

46. "Wang Ching-wei pao-kao."

47. Li T'ai-fen, pp. 343–45.

48. "Wang Ching-wei pao-kao"; T'ang, *Inner History*, pp. 282–84; Roy, pp. 474–75; Lo Chia-lun, XV, 710–11.

49. The still controversial relations between Russians, Chinese Communists, Left Kuomintang, and Chiang Kai-shek are described in many works, particularly Isaacs. Holcombe, pp. 214–16, describes the activities of labor and peasant associations that alienated the Left Kuomintang.

50. T'ang, *Inner History*, pp. 282–83; Isaacs, p. 255; Fuse, pp. 194–95.

Moreover, Feng's wires to Wuhan after his conference with Chiang Kai-shek imply that anti-Russian and anti-Communist measures were discussed at Chengchow.

51. On June 15, three days after the end of the Chengchow Conference, the Comintern representative M. N. Roy submitted to the Politbureau of the Chinese Communist Party a proposal that included support for Feng Yü-hsiang in the campaign against Peking; see North and Eudin, p. 346. Moreover, the surprise and dismay expressed by Russian leaders when Feng joined Chiang Kai-shek seems not to have been adulterated by any fore-knowledge of Feng's anti-Communist views.

52. "Wang Ching-wei pao-kao." Wang Wei-lien, pp. 41–44, describes the many ways in which Feng showed himself to be openly hostile to Chiang Kai-shek.

53. For Chiang's campaign during May, see Chang Tzu-sheng, *Chan-cheng shih*, hsia, pp. 42–43.

54. Lo Chia-lun, XV, 790–91.

55. Mao, *O-Meng*, p. 245, says it was 2,000,000 yüan per month.

56. Lo Chia-lun, XV, 711.

57. A translation of the joint wire is in *NCH*, July 2, 1927, p. 1.

58. Misselwitz, pp. 123–25; Isaacs, p. 256.

59. North and Eudin, p. 114. See also Isaacs, pp. 252–56.

60. Misselwitz, p. 123.

61. Minister J. V. A. MacMurray to Secretary of State, July 18, 1927, 893.00/9346, and June 17, 1927, 893.00/9287. Naval attaché's report, July 14–Aug. 4, 893.00/9406, discusses negotiations between Chiang and Chang during July and August. One of Fengtien's demands is said to have been that Chiang sever relations with Feng.

62. Li T'ai-fen, pp. 379–80. *Jihchi*, II, Chüan 8, p. 60. Feng's purge of Communists was described briefly by Sun Lien-chung to Professor C. Martin Wilbur, who kindly permitted me to see his notes of that description.

63. F. P. Lockhart, consul at Hankow, reported to the Legation on June 30, 1927, 893.00/9298, that all Kuomintang political workers were sent home from the Kuominchün immediately after the Chengchow conference in early June.

64. Li T'ai-fen, pp. 380–81, 384, 418–19.

65. *CWR*, Jan. 14, 1928, p. 185.

66. Li T'ai-fen, p. 384.

67. The change in tone and content can be seen, for example, in Feng, *Feng Yü-hsiang chün-shih*, Chüan 6, by comparing the orders issued in late 1926 and early 1927 with those after July 1927. Something similar can be seen in appropriate series of orders in Feng, *Feng Yü-hsiang hsün-ling*.

68. Li T'ai-fen, p. 419. For more of Feng's ideas about Communism, see Li T'ai-fen, pp. 381–83; Fuse, pp. 208–12; *Jihchi*, II, Chüan 8, pp. 68f.

69. Feng, *Chiu i-ch'i*, p. 3. The rest of the booklet is devoted to the movement. The order to start the New Life Movement is in Feng, *Feng Yü-hsiang hsün-ling*, Chüan 10, pp. 20–21, and the oath is on both p. 21 and p. 23.

70. Li T'ai-fen, pp. 384–88.

71. *Ibid.*, pp. 369–73. A detailed description of the Chin Yün-ngo affair

348

NOTES TO PAGES 235–41

in English is in a despatch from F. P. Lockhart, consul at Hankow, to the American legation in Peking, Sept. 30, 1927, 893.00/9585. Between July 1927 and June 1928, there were several petty warlords besides Chin who were dissatisfied with their lot in Feng's sphere, and were crushed by Feng. See *KMCKMS*, chap. 13, pp. 35–36; *NCH*, May 1928, pp. 223 and 312; Li T'ai-fen, pp. 369, 395–96.

72. For Feng's views on the military situation during the second half of 1927, see Feng, *Feng Yü-hsiang chün-shih*, Chüan 1, pp. 18–20, 22–32, 35–77; Chüan 2, pp. 13–51.

73. Chang's telegram is translated in *NCH*, Oct. 8, 1927, pp. 45–46. For Yen-Chang relations leading up to this, see C. Y. W. Meng, "General Yen Now Mobilizes"; memorandum by John Magruder, American military attaché at Peking, July 25, 1927, 893.00/9430; *NCH*, Aug. 27, 1927, p. 354, and Sept. 17, 1927, p. 471.

74. For a sketch of the plans for Kuominchün participation in the Northern Expedition discussed at Kaifeng, see Lo Chia-lun, XVIII, 5–6.

75. For the distribution of units in the northern alliance at the beginning of the Northern Expedition, see Chang Tzu-sheng, *Chan-cheng shih*, hsia, pp. 56–59. For Feng Yü-hsiang's summary evaluation of the Fengtien troops under Chang Hsüeh-liang, Chang Tsung-ch'ang, and Sun Ch'uan-fang, see *Feng Yü-hsiang chün-shih*, Chüan II, pp. 67–68. The American military attaché in Peking surveyed the relative strength of the various military groupings in late 1927 in a memorandum of July 25, 1927, 893.00/9430, and another of Nov. 8, 1927, 893.00/9711.

76. Lo Chia-lun, XVIII, 3–10; Chang Tzu-sheng, *Chan-cheng shih*, hsia, pp. 52–56.

77. The military events of the Northern Expedition are covered in various sources. Chang Tzu-sheng, *Chan-cheng shih*, hsia, pp. 59–69, gives a summary description. Lo Chia-lun's Vols. XII–XXI contain many relevant documents; Vol. XIX has documents on the Tsinan incident. Kuominchün activities are stressed in *KMCKMS*, chap. 13, pp. 58–70, and Li T'ai-fen, pp. 474ff.

78. Lo Chia-lun, XX, 1450–51.

79. Minister J. V. A. MacMurray, in a despatch dated Apr. 14, 1928, 893.00/9864, wrote that the obvious desire of the Peking regime was to defeat and drive out Feng, but to come to some compromise with Shansi and Nanking. In a despatch to the Secretary of State on Feb. 6, 1928, 893.00/9806, MacMurray described a conversation with Chang Tso-lin's vice-minister for Foreign Affairs in which the latter explained the Ankuochün's attitude toward the various groups in the southern coalition.

80. Despatch from Norman Armour, chargé d'affaires, June 8, 1927, 893.00/9148; memorandum by Nelson Johnson of telephone conversation with the Chinese minister, May 11, 1928, 893.00/9940; telegram from Minister MacMurray to the Secretary of State, May 31, 1928, 893.00/10015.

Chapter Ten

1. F. F. Liu, pp. 63–70, discusses the military reorganization of October 1928, and its power implications.

2. There is abundant and varied evidence that warlordism continued into the Nationalist period, but a single source that describes the situation

well, on the basis of questionnaires filled in by many consular officials scattered throughout China, is the despatch sent by Mahlon F. Perkins to the Secretary of State, Aug. 24, 1928, 893.00/10226. See also *NCH*, Sept. 8, 1928, p. 397, for a description of the financial districts into which the country had to be divided.

3. Fuse, pp. 255–57; "Summary of events and conditions in the Nanking consular district during July 1928," by J. Hall Paxton, Aug. 17, 1928, 893.00 P.R. Nanking/3. Li T'ai-fen, p. 493, summarizes the differing views of Feng and Yen on disbandment procedures.

4. Fuse, pp. 352–53.

5. The chief participants are listed in Lo Chia-lun, XXIV, 1.

6. *Ibid.*, pp. 1–80, contains various documents on the Disbandment Conference. A report from Ernest B. Price to the American legation at Peking, Feb. 6, 1929, 893.00 P.R. Nanking/9, contains a detailed description of the conference, and the breakdown of committee membership.

7. Shyu, pp. 38, 56.

8. Misselwitz, p. 161; "Marshal Feng and His 6 A.M. Interviews," pp. 382, 384; *CYB, 1929–30*, p. 1185; *NCH*, Feb. 16, 1929, p. 267.

9. Li T'ai-fen, pp. 495–500; Misselwitz, pp. 163–66; "Marshal Feng and His 6 A.M. Interviews," pp. 382–83.

10. Li T'ai-fen discusses Feng's reforms in Honan on pp. 440–47, in Shensi on pp. 447–52, and in Kansu on pp. 452–56. See also "Chinese Affairs: A Weekly Survey of Important Events Relating to China," International Relations Committee, No. 7, July 21, 1928, 893.00 Weekly Survey/3, pp. 6–8; Chen, p. 9; *NCH*, Mar. 24, 1928, pp. 467, 476, and May 5, 1928, p. 181.

11. Chien, *Hsi-pei*, pp. 11–12; Fuse, pp. 220–21; *NCH*, Mar. 10, 1928, p. 386.

12. *NCH*, Jan. 21, 1928, p. 90; report from Walter K. Adams, consul at Hankow, to the American legation in Peking, Mar. 19, 1928, 893.00/9888; Snow, pp. 230–31.

13. Report from F. P. Lockhart, Consul General at Hankow, to the American legation in Peking, Apr. 5, 1928, 893.00/9929.

14. Feng, *Feng Yü-hsiang hsün-ling*, Chüan 15, pp. 18–19, and Chüan 16, pp. 10–11.

15. Feng's educational measures are described in Li T'ai-fen, pp. 444, 449–50, 454–55. See also *NCH*, Mar. 24, 1928, p. 476, and Feng, *Feng Yü-hsiang hsün-ling*, Chüan 16, pp. 8–9.

16. Zung, pp. 523–25, is an account of the Rural Training Institute by one of the participants. Holcombe, pp. 254–55, has a brief description of Feng's model village. See also Li T'ai-fen, p. 441, and a memorandum about Feng's work in Honan by J. H. Reisner, included in a despatch from J. V. A. MacMurray to the Secretary of State, Jan. 10, 1928, 893.00/9767.

17. J. Lossing Buck, pp. 213–14.

18. Both quotations and some of the other data are from a detailed evaluation of famine conditions in Honan in a report from J. V. A. MacMurray to the Secretary of State, Dec. 20, 1928, 893.48L/97. Another despatch from MacMurray to the Secretary of State, Jan. 30, 1929, 893.48L/109, includes a breakdown by district of conditions in Honan in early Feb. 1929. *NCH*, Nov. 24, 1928, p. 301, outlines the plans for immediate relief formulated by the Famine Committee for Honan, Shensi, and Kansu. The compo-

sition and organizational affiliation are not indicated, but it was probably organized by Feng and other Chinese; foreign famine organizations felt little confidence in its recommendations, and regarded its statements skeptically. For more on famine conditions in Shensi and Honan, see *NCH*, Mar. 1929, pp. 348, 393, 446; Jan. 14, 1930, p. 49; and July 29, 1930, p. 156.

19. *NCH*, Aug. 3, 1929, p. 167.

20. *NCH*, July 29, 1930, p. 156.

21. Despatch from Walter A. Adams, consul at Hankow, to the American legation in Peking, Nov. 12, 1928, 893.00 P.R. Hankow/9; *NCH*, Oct. 20, 1928, p. 87.

22. Yin, hsia, chap. 1, sections 1 and 2; *NCH*, Oct. 20, 1928, p. 87, and Dec. 8, 1928, pp. 389–90.

23. *NCH*, Sept. 29, 1928, p. 539.

24. For the Muslim revolt in Kansu, Yin, hsia, gives a detailed account from the Kuominchün point of view. Reports from American foreign-service personnel contain some information; see especially the despatch from Walter A. Adams to the American legation, Nov. 12, 1928, 893.00 P.R. Hankow/9; despatches from F. P. Lockhart to the legation, July 6, 1929, 893.00 P.R. Hankow/24, Aug. 23, 1928, 893.48/203, Apr. 1, 1929, 893.48/210, and Apr. 26, 1929, 893.48/211. *NCH* periodically printed letters from missionaries in Kansu and other reports, and although some of the missionaries were prone to exaggeration, they give much information: Sept. 29, 1928, p. 539; Oct. 20, 1928, p. 87; Dec. 1928, pp. 389–90, 435; Mar. 1929, pp. 343, 476; Oct. 5, 1929, p. 9.

25. Letter from V. G. Plymire to the American Consul General at Hankow, Feb. 28, 1929, enclosed in a despatch to the American legation from F. P. Lockhart, Apr. 1, 1929, 893.48/210. Punctuation and spelling have been corrected.

26. Despatch from Walter A. Adams to the American legation in Peking, Jan. 30, 1929, 893.48L/114; despatch from F. P. Lockhart to the American legation, July 1, 1929, 893.00 P.R. Hankow/24; *NCH*, Dec. 8, 1928, pp. 389–90; Mar. 9, 1929, p. 393; June 1929, pp. 346, 427, 512; Aug. 3, 1929, p. 167; Jan. 1930, pp. 92, 136; Howard, p. 17.

27. *NCH*, June 1, 1929, p. 346.

28. *NCH*, Jan. 28, 1930, p. 136.

29. For the origins and development of the Kwangsi clique, see report from J. Hall Paxton, vice-consul at Nanking, to the Department of State, Apr. 10, 1928, 893.20/80, report by Douglas Jenkins, Consul General at Canton, Nov. 1, 1924, 893.00/5902; memorandum from Ernest B. Price enclosed in despatch from J. V. A. MacMurray to the Secretary of State, Dec. 17, 1928, 893.00/10271.

30. The events leading up to the Nanking-Kwangsi rupture are described in MacNair, pp. 164–67. See also Fuse, pp. 308–11, and report from J. V. A. MacMurray to the Secretary of State, Mar. 18. 1929, 893.00 P.R./17.

31. Interview with one of Feng's ex-subordinates, Taiwan, May 1959.

32. Chung-kuo ch'ing-nien, p. 55; "The Case of Chiang Kai-shek Versus Feng Yü-hsiang," p. 9; telegrams from J. V. A. MacMurray to the Secretary of State, Mar. 29, 1929, 893.00/10358, and Apr. 16, 1929, 893.00/10389; *NCH*, Apr. 20, 1929, p. 89.

33. Feng, *Feng Yü-hsiang hsün-ling,* Chüan 20, p. 5.
34. "Hyo Gyoku sho."
35. Despatch from Ernest B. Price, consul at Tsinan, to the American legation in Peking, Nov. 6, 1928, 893.00 P.R. Tsinan/6.
36. Despatch from J. V. A. MacMurray to the Secretary of State, Nov. 12, 1928, 893.00 P.R./12.
37. Despatch from E. F. Stanton to J. V. A. MacMurray, May 6, 1929, 893.00 P.R. Tsinan/14, includes a detailed description of the Japanese withdrawal, and of the activities of Feng and Chiang.
38. Despatch from Leroy Webber to J. V. A. MacMurray, June 1, 1929, 893.00 P.R. Chefoo/18, said that the Chinese public felt Chiang should not have ejected Feng from Shantung, and that a victory by Feng over Chiang would be popular, and listed the reasons why Feng was regarded as "an idol of the public."
39. Chung-kuo ch'ing-nien, pp. 59–63; *CYB, 1929–30,* pp. 1208–10. See also "The Case of Chiang Kai-shek Versus Feng Yü-hsiang," pp. 10, 41.
40. *CYB, 1929–30,* pp. 1210–11.
41. *NCH,* May 25, 1929, p. 295.
42. Telegram from J. V. A. MacMurray to the Secretary of State, May 24, 1929, 893.00/10455, gives the complete text of Feng's message to the American legation.
43. Ma, pp. 140–41, reports remarks of Han Fu-chü that imply that he resented the poverty imposed upon him and the other commanders by Feng.
44. Chien, *Hsi-pei,* p. 49.
45. For an estimate of Feng's military strength in May, and a list of the defectors from his army, see the despatch from Ernest B. Price to J. V. A. MacMurray, June 8, 1929, 893.00/10501. For an evaluation of Feng's position in May, and the effect of the defections, see the despatch from F. P. Lockhart to J. V. A. MacMurray, June 5, 1929, 893.00 P.R. Hankow/23.
46. *CYB, 1929–30,* p. 1212.
47. *Ibid.,* p. 1213.
48. *NCH,* June 15, 1929, p. 418.
49. Despatch from J. V. A. MacMurray to the Secretary of State, July 9, 1929, 893.00/10508; *NCH,* June 22, 1929, p. 462; MacNair, pp. 171–72.
50. Ma, p. 137. Louella Miner, Mrs. Feng's old teacher, visited the Fengs in August, and they asked her to go abroad with them as counselor and friend. Miss Miner understood that they planned to go to the United States. See Miner Journal, Aug. 20, 1929.
51. Despatch from Walter A. Adams to J. V. A. MacMurray, Aug. 20, 1929, 893.00/10535, reports on Feng's conversations with Left Kuomintang members about ousting Chiang and bringing Wang Ching-wei to power. See also a wire from J. V. A. MacMurray to the Secretary of State, Aug. 21, 1929, 893.00/10530. Six months earlier, *NCH,* Mar. 23, 1929, p. 473, reported that Feng sent a long telegram to Wang Ching-wei, who was then abroad, asking him to return to China to take his proper place as the head of the party. For more on this earlier period, see a wire from J. V. A. MacMurray to the Secretary of State, May 21, 1929, 893.00/10450, in which he appraises the developing anti-Chiang coalition.
52. *NCH,* Sept. 28, 1929, p. 474.

53. Chung-kuo ch'ing-nien, p. 70.

54. Ma, p. 138, asserts that Yen took the lead in the anti-Chiang move-ment even at this stage. On p. 141, Ma indicates that Yen hoped Feng and Chiang would destroy each other. Fuse, p. 322, claims that Feng planned to invade Shansi, and then bide his time and build up his strength to challenge Nanking. See also the analysis in the despatch from Ernest B. Price to J. V. A. MacMurray, June 8, 1929, 893.00/10501.

55. See, for example, Ware, p. 154, in which he describes the antipathy for the southerners that he observed in the North, and the northerners' con-sequent sympathy for Feng Yü-hsiang and Yen Hsi-shan.

56. For speculation that the peace was negotiated, see the despatch from F. P. Lockhart to Mahlon F. Perkins, Dec. 3, 1929, 893.00 P.R. Hankow/29, and the despatch from Walter A. Adams to Mahlon F. Perkins, Dec. 19, 1929, 893.00 P.R. Nanking/20. Chung-kuo ch'ing-nien, p. 74, lists several reasons for the defeat of the Kuominchün, and mentions no negotiations.

57. For the conflict between China and the USSR over the Chinese Eastern Railway, see Tang, pp. 199-241, and especially pp. 234-35, which relate to November 1929.

58. NCH, March 4, 1930, p. 333.

59. Chung-kuo ch'ing-nien, pp. 136-53; CYB, 1931, pp. 552-56.

60. Lee, p. 321. NCH, July 8, 1930, p. 43, describes the take-over of the Tientsin Customs.

61. Not all of the anti-Chiang units were in the northern coalition. In fact, the distribution of military power was both complex and ambiguous. For a breakdown of Chinese armies into pro-Chiang, anti-Chiang, and un-certain, see Chung-kuo ch'ing-nien, pp. 132-36.

62. Ibid., pp. 153-79, discusses the reasons for the formation of the En-larged Conference, the scope of its membership and aims, and the view-points of the participating factions.

63. Despatch from M. S. Myers to J. V. A. MacMurray, June 6, 1929, 893.00 P.R. Mukden/25.

64. MacNair, pp. 177-78; NCH, Sept. 23, 1930, p. 462.

Chapter Eleven

1. Feng, *Feng Yü-hsiang shih-ko*, pp. 5-32, contains a number of poems written in 1931.

2. Letters written by Louella Miner during 1931 and 1932 provide many details about Feng's activities during those years. It was Miss Miner who provided Feng with the books mentioned. Other information in the para-graph comes from Louella Miner's letters of Jan. 8, 1932; Aug. 29, 1932; and Oct. 6, 1932. Other glimpses of Feng's life at T'ai Shan are given in Chin, No. 13.

3. See, for example, the summary of a long statement issued by Feng immediately after his arrival in Kalgan. It is in "Feng Yü-hsiang and Hu Han-ming [sic] Become Vocal." Also see C. Y. W. Meng, "Chinese Leaders."

4. *CWR*, Apr. 1, 1933, p. 168.

5. *CWR*, Apr. 22, 1933, p. 289.

6. Feng, *Ch'a-ha-erh*, Pien I, pp. 67-68. English translations, abbreviated

and mistaken in detail, may be found in *CYB, 1934,* p. 363, and *CWR,* June 10, 1933, pp. 56–57.

7. Feng, *Ch'a-ha-erh,* Pien I, p. 87; Meng Po-ch'ien, p. 91; "Marshal Feng Shows No Sign," p. 183.

8. Feng, *Ch'a-ha-erh,* Pien I, pp. 90–101, gives a detailed breakdown of the composition of the People's Anti-Japanese Allied Army, indicating the number of men and guns in each unit.

9. *NCH,* June 7, 1933, p. 367; Aug. 2, 1933, p. 166.

10. Bisson, pp. 63–64; *NCH,* July 19, 1933, p. 86.

11. The Political Branch of the French Police in the International Settlement at Shanghai seized various papers, reports, and miscellaneous material in raids on Communist premises in that city. The police report mentioned in the footnote on p. 273 describes some of this material, including a report that mentioned a secret society called "The Chinese Grand League Against Fascism." This society, which appeared in June 1934, was said to have been organized at Tientsin, by Feng Yü-hsiang, Hsü Ch'ien, Li Chi-shen, Chi Hung-chang, Cheng Ying-chi, Fang Ting-ying, Fang Tseng-wu [Fang Chen-wu?], and Hsu Hwei-lieh. The secretary-general was called Lao Wu. It is clear that the society was opposed to Chiang Kai-shek and the Nanking government, but there is no information about its specific policies or, indeed, whether it ever functioned.

12. *Kuo-min-chün ko-ming shih* is one such book. Not only is its political orientation to the left, but the terminology employed—"ruling class," "feudal society" when referring to traditional China, "international capitalism," etc.—implies that the book was written or influenced by a leftist, although, of course, such terminology is by no means limited to Communists. The same orientation is apparent in the preface of *Feng Yü-hsiang tu Ch'un-ch'iu Tso-chuan cha-chi,* which was signed by Feng, but, of course, may have been written by someone else. This seems likely because the preface contains a strong denunciation of the past, an attitude not typical of Feng. *Ch'a-ha-erh* has similar traits. An interesting feature of these books is that they have both Chinese and English titles. Why English?

13. For details about Feng's life at T'ai Shan during 1934 and 1935, see the letters of Louella Miner for those years. See also "Marshal Feng in Retirement," p. 89.

14. Feng, *Chao Wang-yün,* p. 12.

15. Feng, *Feng tsai Nan-ching pao-kao chi (1),* pp. 1–19.

16. *Ibid.,* pp. 21–32.

17. Feng, *Feng tsai Nan-ching ti-erh nien,* pp. 137, 265–66; *CWR,* Dec. 19, 1936, p. 83.

18. Feng, *Feng tsai Nan-ching ti-erh nien,* contains many of the speeches Feng gave, and indicates the variety of speaking engagements he fulfilled. Also see R. Y. Lo, p. 276.

19. Interview with a former subordinate of Feng's, Taiwan, 1959.

20. Several informants have told me of hearing Feng speak in support of the war effort. Mr. Ho Ch'eng, who was once assigned to guard Feng during a speaking engagement, stressed that Feng's speeches were so effective that people stripped rings from their hands to donate to the nation's war chest.

21. The general public and journalists interpreted Feng's foreign assign-

ment as a move by the government to remove an annoying critic. However, Mr. K. C. Wu, who was at that time a high official in the Nationalist government, assured me in a telephone interview on July 3, 1964, that Feng personally requested the assignment to the United States.

22. A copy of this letter was shown to me in Berkeley, California, on June 12, 1961, by Mr. Richard Lindheim. A notation on the copy indicated that the letter had been published in the Sept. 21 issue of *The Chinese World*.

23. This and most of the other information in the paragraph was told to me in the interview with Dr. and Mrs. Lowdermilk.

24. Personal interview in Taipei in 1959 with Mr. Chang Yüan-hsi, a member of the technical staff that accompanied Feng on his trip to the United States.

25. Interview with Walter Lowdermilk.

26. Feng, "Why I Broke with Chiang," p. 523. Feng reviewed his differences with Chiang in an open letter dated Feb. 8, 1948, in Chung-kuo Kuomin-tang, pp. 153–56. See also *The New York Times*, Oct. 11, 1947, p. 8; Dec. 14, 1947, p. 28; Dec. 23, 1947, p. 5; Jan. 15, 1948, p. 14.

27. Rohrbough, p. 50.

28. Chung-kuo Kuo-min-tang, p. 162.

29. For reports of Feng's claim that the Chinese Communists were not practicing Communism, see *The New York Times*, Oct. 11, 1947, p. 8, and Dec. 23, 1947, p. 5. Feng recommended American aid to the moderate groups in "Why I Broke with Chiang," p. 525.

30. *The New York Times*, Jan. 10, 1948, p. 7.

31. Rohrbough, p. 50.

32. Press release issued by Feng Yü-hsiang in New York on Jan. 14, 1948. A mimeographed copy of this press release was kindly shown to me by Mr. Richard Lindheim of Berkeley, California.

33. *The New York Times*, Sept. 5, 1948, p. 28, and Sept. 6, 1948, p. 1. See also Li Te-ch'üan, "An Open Letter," p. 12, and Chung-kuo Kuo-min-tang, *passim*, for accounts of Feng's death.

34. *The New York Times*, Sept. 6, 1948, p. 6, reported that Feng's daughter-in-law raised the possibility that Feng was the victim of his own motion-picture hobby. She said that he had some personal movies and a quantity of film of his travels through the United States on board with him.

35. The book is *Feng Yü-hsiang shih-ko*, published by the Hsin Wen I Publishing Society, Shanghai, in 1957.

36. The occasion and ceremonies were described in a news release of the China News Service, which was kindly sent to me by Howard Boorman.

Chapter Twelve

1. It is, of course, impossible to be very definite about the influence that novels had on Feng's development, although it seems reasonable to believe that they had some effect. One is reminded of the discussion on pp. 178–82 of *The Lane of Eternal Stability*, where the author, K. C. Wu, discusses the effect on many young Chinese of *The Romance of the Three Kingdoms* and the *Water Margin Novel*, which he translates as *Tales of the Marshes*. Ac-

cording to Wu, reading these two novels taught Chinese youth ways of deceit, treachery, and cruelty; "a generation of cynics and opportunists was brought into being." (p. 180.)

2. Feng, *Feng Yü-hsiang chün-shih*, Chüan 4, pp. 18–19.

3. Interview with one of Feng's former officers, Taiwan, 1959.

4. Wilbur and How, p. 352.

5. Chow, pp. 360–61.

Annotated Bibliography

Aho, Ilma Ruth. "A Record of the Activities of the Finnish Missionary Society in Northwest Hunan, China, 1902–1952." M.A. thesis. University of California, Berkeley, 1953.

Allen, Genri. Zapiski volontera (Notes of a volunteer). Translated from the English by Oleg Ordynets. Leningrad, preface dated 1927 by the translator. This book purports to be a diary of a Canadian officer who served as instructor in Feng's army during 1925–26. However, it was probably written by Feng's chief Russian adviser, who used the pseudonym "Henry A. Lin." Some events are incorrectly described and incorrectly dated, perhaps deliberately. Nevertheless, it is a valuable source.

Altree, Wayne. "A Half-Century of the Administration of the State Railways of China," in Papers on China (mimeographed), Vol. 3. Cambridge, Mass., Harvard University, 1949.

Andrews, Roy Chapman. On the Trail of Ancient Man: A Narrative of the Field Work of the Central Asiatic Expeditions. New York, 1930.

Andrews, Roy Chapman, with chapters by Walter Granger, Clifford H. Pope, and Nels C. Nelson, and summary statements by G. M. Allen et al. The New Conquest of Central Asia: A Narrative of the Explorations of the Central Asiatic Expeditions in Mongolia and China, 1921–1930. New York, 1932.

Auxion de Ruffe, [Reginald] d'. Is China Mad? Translated from the French by R. T. Peyton-Griffin. Shanghai, 1928. This book exemplifies the view that warlord struggles were comic-opera wars. The author is extremely prejudiced against the Chinese.

Backhouse, E., and Bland, J. O. P. Annals and Memoirs of the Court of Peking. New York, 1914. On pp. 188–208 is a translation of Yang-chou shih-jih chi (The diary of ten days at Yangchow) that differs markedly from the one by Lucien Mao listed below under Wang Hsiu-ch'u.

Baker, John Earl. Explaining China. London, 1927.

Bales, W. L. Tso Tsung-t'ang: Soldier and Statesman of Old China. Shanghai, 1937.

358   ANNOTATED BIBLIOGRAPHY

Bertram, James. First Act in China: The Story of the Sian Mutiny. New York, 1938.
Bisson, T. A. Japan in China. New York, 1938.
Boorman, Howard L., ed. Men and Politics in Modern China: Preliminary 50 Biographies—I. New York, 1960.
Brandt, Conrad. Stalin's Failure in China, 1924–27. Cambridge, Mass., 1958.
Broomhall, Marshall. Marshal Feng: A Good Soldier of Christ Jesus. London, 1924. This volume, by the editorial secretary of the China Inland Mission, stresses Feng's devotion to Christianity and his exemplification of the highest Christian principles. The work is imprecise in dating, etc.
Buck, J. Lossing. "The Big Swords and the Little Swords Clash," CWR, XLVI, No. 7 (Oct. 13, 1928), 213–14.
Buck, Pearl. "Chinese War Lords," The Saturday Evening Post, CCV, No. 43 (Apr. 22, 1933), 3–5, 76–77.
"The Case of Chiang Kai-shek versus Feng Yü-hsiang," CWR, XLIX, No. 1 (June 1, 1929), 8–10, 41.
Chang Chuang-an. Fu-pi hsiang-chih (Detailed record of the restoration [of 1917]). Peking, 1917.
Chang Tzu-sheng. Jen-hsü cheng-pien chi. English title: The Civil War of China in 1922. Shanghai, 1924. This book contains two essays. The first is an excellent summary of the First Chih-Feng War, and the second deals with Li Yüan-hung's resumption of office.
———. "Kuo-min ko-ming-chün pei-fa chan-cheng chih ching-kuo" (The Northern Expedition of the National Revolutionary Army), Tung-fang tsa-chih (Eastern miscellany), XXV, No. 15 (Aug. ,10, 1928), 21–32; No. 16 (Aug. 25, 1928), 25–38; No. 17 (Sept. 10, 1928), 41–66.
———. Kuo-min ko-ming-chün pei-fa chan-cheng shih (History of the Northern Expeditionary War of the National Revolutionary Army), ed. by Wang Yün-wu and Li Sheng-wu. Shanghai, 1933. A reprint in two small volumes of the Tung-fang tsa-chih articles listed above.
Chang Yu-i. Chung-kuo chin-tai nung-yeh shih tzu-liao (Materials relating to recent Chinese agricultural history). 2 vols. Peking, 1957. The first volume, compiled by Li Wen-chih, deals with the period from 1840 to 1911.
Chang Yün-chia. Yü Yu-jen chuan (Biography of Yü Yu-jen). Taipei, 1958. A chatty and superficial biography, but it has some interesting material on the Ching Kuo Chün and on the relief of the siege of Sian.
Ch'ang Jen. "Feng Yü-hsiang ti chuan-pien" (The changeability of Feng Yü-hsiang), Hsien-tai shih-liao (Materials of current history), III (1934), 57–78. This essay argues that Feng was treacherous and opportunistic throughout his career.
Chen Tsung-hsi. "Honan After a Year of Feng's Administration," CWR, XLVI, No. 1 (Sept. 1, 1928), 9.
Ch'en Hsiao-wei. "Feng Yü-hsiang chih 'Ch'e niao-fen' miao-yü" (Feng Yü-hsiang's ingenious illustration about avoiding bird droppings), Jo-ting-lu

sui-pi (Notes from the hut at Jo-ting), No. 1, Hong Kong, 1939, pp. 116–17.

Ch'en, Jerome. Yuan Shih-k'ai (1859–1916). Stanford, Calif., 1961.

Ch'en Shou-yi. Chinese Literature: A Historical Introduction. New York, 1961.

Ch'eng, Marcus. Marshal Feng—The Man and His Work. Shanghai, preface dated 1926. Ch'eng was Chaplain General in Feng's army when he wrote this book, which praises Feng inordinately. However, it contains much factual information, particularly on Feng's reform programs.

Chia I-chün, comp. Chung-hua min-kuo ming-jen chuan (Biographies of famous men of the republic). Peiping, 1932–33.

Chia-tzu Ch'ing-shih mi-mou fu-p'i wen-cheng (Documents pertaining to the 1924 Ch'ing restoration plot). Peking, 1929.

Chien Yu-wen, under the pseudonym "Ta-hua-lieh-shih" (Tovarich). Hsi-pei tung-nan feng (Winds from the northwest and the southeast). Shanghai, 1935. This book was kindly loaned to me by Chien Yu-wen, who informed me that he was the author. The first part deals with anecdotes and stories about Feng and his army.

——. Wo so jen-shih ti Feng Yü-hsiang chi hsi-pei chün (What I know about Feng Yü-hsiang and the Northwestern Army). N.p., n.d. A brief laudatory biography of Feng.

Ch'ien Tuan-sheng. "The Role of the Military in Chinese Government," *Pacific Affairs*, XXI, No. 3 (Sept. 1948), 239–51.

Chin Tien-jung. "Wo yü Feng Yü-hsiang ti i-tuan yüan-yüan" (Experiences I shared with Feng Yü-hsiang), *Ch'un Ch'iu* (Spring and Autumn), No. 13 (Jan. 16, 1958), pp. 11–13; No. 14 (Feb. 1, 1958), pp. 10–11; No. 15 (Feb. 16, 1958), pp. 4–6. These contain parts 3–5 of an anecdotal account of experiences with Feng at T'ai Shan in the early 1930's. Some of the material is simply lifted from Feng's writings.

The China Weekly Review, published in Shanghai, contains many useful articles about Chinese politics. It bore this title after June 23, 1923, before which it was known as *Millard's Review, The Weekly Review of the Far East*, and *The Weekly Review*.

The China Yearbook, edited by H. G. W. Woodhead, was published about once a year from the beginning of the Republic, first in London, then in Tientsin, then in Shanghai. It contains much useful information, especially in the issues of the mid-1920's, when warlordism was rampant.

Chinese Communist Party. Biographies of Kuomintang Leaders. Yenan, 1945. Originally published for Communist Party workers; mimeographed for private distribution by the Committee on International and Regional Studies, Harvard University, Feb. 1948.

Ching-chih t'u-shu-kuan (Ching-chih library). Chih-Feng ta-chan shih (History of the Chihli-Fengtien War). N.p., 1922.

——. Feng Yü-hsiang ch'uan-chuan (Complete biography of Feng Yü-hsiang). N.p., 1922. Deals largely with Feng in Shensi in 1921.

————. Ts'ao K'un li-shih (History of Ts'ao K'un). N.p., 1923.
Chow, Tse-tsung. The May Fourth Movement: Intellectual Revolution in Modern China. Cambridge, Mass., 1960.
Chung-kuo ch'ing-nien chün-jen she (Society of Young Chinese Military Men). Fan Chiang yün-tung shih (History of the anti-Chiang movement). N.p., 1934.
Chung-kuo Kuo-min-tang ko-ming wei-yüan-hui (Revolutionary committee of the Kuomintang of China). Feng Yü-hsiang chiang-chün chi-nien ts'e (Volume in memory of Marshal Feng Yü-hsiang). Hong Kong, n.d.
Chung-kuo li-shih yen-chiu hui (Chinese historical research association). Chung-kuo t'ung-shih chien-pien (Short, comprehensive history of China). Peking, 1950.
Close, Upton (pseud. of Josef Washington Hall). In the Land of the Laughing Buddha: The Adventures of an American Barbarian in China. New York, 1924.
Clubb, O. Edmund. Twentieth Century China. New York, 1964.
Dailey, Charles. "The Real Significance of Banditry in China," The Weekly Review, XXIII, No. 6 (Jan. 6, 1923), 207–11. Discusses the relationship between banditry and warlordism, and quotes extensively from accounts by bandit captives.
————. "Is Feng a Traitor or Patriot—Details of the Capture of Peking," CWR, XXX, No. 12 (Nov. 22, 1924), 364–71.
————. "Feng Yü-hsiang's Next Move," CWR, XXXI, No. 12 (Feb. 21, 1925), 336–37.
————. "Feng Yü-hsiang: Colonist," CWR, XXXII, No. 8 (Apr. 25, 1925), 212–13.
————. "Soviet Red Bear Shows His Teeth," CWR, XXXIII, No. 1 (June 6, 1925), 4–5.
————. "Feng Yü-hsiang and the Peking-Suiyuan Railway Debts," CWR, XXXIV, No. 7 (Oct. 17, 1925), 159–60.
————. "Christian General at the Crossroads," CWR, XLII, No. 3 (Sept. 17, 1927), 65–66.
Fairbank, John King, and Liu Kwang-ching. Modern China: A Bibliographical Guide to Chinese Works, 1898–1937. Cambridge, Mass., 1950.
Favre, B. Les Sociétés secrètes en Chine: Origine, rôle historique, situation actuelle. Paris, 1933.
Fei Ching-chung (using the pseudonym "Wu-ch'iu-chung-tzu"). Tuan Ch'i-jui. Shanghai, 1921.
Feng Yü-hsiang. "What China Needs Today," The Living Age (Jan. 16, 1926), pp. 131–35. A mid-1925 statement of Feng's political position. The same document is printed as an appendix in Marcus Ch'eng, Marshal Feng —The Man and His Work.
————. Chiu i-ch'i hsin sheng-ming (The New Life Movement of September 17). N.p., 1927.

———. Fan kuo-lien t'iao-ch'a-t'uan pao-kao shu (Refutation of the Lytton Report). Shanghai, 1932.

———. Feng Yü-hsiang jih-chi (Feng Yü-hsiang's diary). 2 vols. Peiping, 1932. The diary is largely devoted to summaries of Feng's speeches to his troops and other groups; there is much repetition. Some political comments were deleted from the original diary before publication, making it a less valuable source than one might expect. The first entry is Nov. 25, 1920, and entries continue through 1927.

———. Ch'a-ha-erh k'ang-Jih shih-lu (The anti-Japanese campaign in Chahar). Shanghai, 1933. Although the title page indicates that this is part of Feng's collected works, it is doubtful that he wrote anything except the preface. The volume contains many documents—wires from Feng, wires from other commanders, etc.—pertaining to the anti-Japanese campaign in Chahar.

———. Feng Yü-hsiang chün-shih yao-tien hui-pien (Important telegrams of Feng Yü-hsiang concerning military affairs). Shanghai, 1933. Most of the telegrams relate to 1927–28. A good source for Feng's ideas on training men, military strategy and tactics, and political indoctrination of his troops.

———. Chao Wang-yün nung-ts'un hsieh-sheng chi (Chao Wang-yün's drawings of village life). Tientsin, 1934. Feng wrote the poems that accompany Chao Wang-yün's sketches in this book.

———. Feng Yü-hsiang hsün-ling hui-pien (Feng Yü-hsiang's military and political orders). Shanghai, 1934. A valuable collection. Most of the military orders date from 1919–20; the exact dates are not given. The political orders date largely from 1927–28, and most bear exact dates.

———. Feng Yü-hsiang tu Ch'un Ch'iu Tso Chuan cha-chi (Feng Yü-hsiang's annotations on the Ch'un Ch'iu and Tso Chuan). Shanghai, 1934.

———. Feng tsai Nan-ching chiang-yen chi (Feng in Nanking—collected speeches). N.p., 1936. Most of these speeches were delivered in the first half of 1936.

———. Feng tsai Nan-ching pao-kao chi (1) (Feng in Nanking—collected reports 1). N.p., 1936. Four reports delivered by Feng to Kuomintang party organs.

———. Feng tsai Nan-ching pao-kao chi (Feng in Nanking—collected reports). Nanking, 1937.

———. Feng tsai Nan-ching ti-i nien (Feng in Nanking—the first year). N.p., 1937. Includes speeches, lectures, telegrams, poems, and various other materials, including a chronology of Feng's activities from Nov. 1, 1935, to Oct. 31, 1936.

———. Feng tsai Nan-ching ti-erh nien (Feng in Nanking—the second year). Kueilin, 1938. A chronology of Feng's activities from Nov. 1, 1936, to Aug. 14, 1937, together with copies of speeches, wires, reports, etc., sent to the government and private groups. A detailed and varied source for Feng's

activities in the late 1930's. It also includes a long account of the Luanchow rebellion.

———. Hua Ai-kuo, comp. Feng fu-wei yüan-chang k'ang-chan yen-lün chi
(Vice-Chairman Feng's collected speeches on the war of resistance). N.p.,
1940. Contains speeches delivered mainly between Oct. 1938 and the end
of 1939.

———. Wo-ti sheng-huo (My life). Shanghai, 1947. This autobiography
covers the years from Feng's birth to 1928, and is a very valuable source.

———. Wo-ti tu-shu sheng-huo (My life of study). Shanghai, 1947. Feng's
account of his attempts at self-education to 1911.

———. "Why I Broke With Chiang," The Nation (Nov. 15, 1947), pp. 522–
25. This article, written while Feng was in the United States, denounces
Chiang Kai-shek for his dictatorial and corrupt government.

———. "Farewell to America," Far East Spotlight, IV, No. 3 (Sept. 1948), 5.

———. Wo so jen-shih ti Chiang Chieh-shih (The Chiang Kai-shek I knew).
Shanghai, 1949. Feng's highly critical recollections of Chiang Kai-shek.

———. Feng Yü-hsiang shih ko hsüan chi (Selected poems by Feng Yü-
hsiang). Shanghai, 1957.

———. Kuo-min-chün ko-ming shih (Revolutionary history of the Kuominchün). Shanghai, n.d. Although the title page indicates that this is one of
Feng's works, he almost certainly did not write it. It is a valuable book,
however, not only for its detailed treatment of Feng's career from 1912,
but also for its many documents and illustrations.

Feng Yü-hsiang, Madame: see Li Te-ch'üan.

"Feng Yü-hsiang and Hu Han-ming [sic] Become Vocal—Announce Political
Programs," CWR, LXII, No. 12 (Nov. 19, 1932), 503–4.

Feng Yü-hsiang ko-ming shih (The revolutionary history of Feng Yü-hsiang).
Shanghai, 1928.

"Feng Yü-hsiang Orders Suppression of Communism," CWR, XLIII, No. 7
(Jan. 14, 1928), 185.

"Fengtien Opens Attack on Chihli Forces," CWR, XXX, No. 5 (Oct. 4, 1924),
164, 166–67.

Fenn, H. C. "The New Map of China," CWR, XLII, No. 1 (Sept. 3, 1927),
10–12.

Feuerwerker, Albert. China's Early Industrialization: Sheng Hsuan-huai
(1844–1916) and Mandarin Enterprise. Cambridge, Mass., 1958.

"Fighting Begins Between Chekiang and Kiangsu," CWR, XXX, No. 1 (Sept.
6, 1924), 4–8.

Finch, Perry. Shanghai and Beyond. New York, 1953.

Fitzgerald, Charles Patrick. Revolution in China. New York, 1952.

Fuse Katsuji. Shina kokumin kakumei to Fu Gyoku-sho (The Chinese national revolution and Feng Yü-hsiang). An important account of Feng and
his army by a Japanese journalist who spent five years in China.

Gale, Esson M. Salt for the Dragon: A Personal History of China, 1908–1945. East Lansing, Mich., 1953.

"General Feng's Coup and What It Has Produced," *CWR*, XXX, No. 9 (Nov. 1, 1924), 267–69.

Geoffrey, C. C. "The Red Spears in China," *CWR*, XXXX, No. 3 (Mar. 19, 1927), 68.

Gillin, Donald G. "Portrait of a Warlord: Yen Hsi-shan in Shansi Province, 1911–1930," *The Journal of Asian Studies*, XIX, No. 3 (May 1960), 289–306.

Goforth, Jonathan. A Chinese Christian Army. Shanghai, n.d. A pamphlet describing several incidents showing the extent to which Feng's army was truly Christian. It was kindly lent to me by one of Dr. Goforth's daughters, Mrs. Robert Moynan.

Goforth, Jonathan and Rosalind. Miracle Lives of China, Grand Rapids, Mich., 1931. This book, also lent to me by Mrs. Moynan, contains one chapter about Feng.

"Go Hai-fu ni taisuru teikoku no taido ni tsuite" (Concerning the attitude of Japan toward Wu P'ei-fu), despatch from the military attaché at the Japanese legation in China, Feb. 1924, in *Mitsu dai nikki* (Confidential great daily records), V, No. 11 of Shina (1924).

Grube, Wilhelm, and Mueller, Herbert. Feng-Shen-Yen-I: Die Metamorphosen der Goetler. Leiden, 1912.

Han Min (pseud.), ed. Tang-tai Chung-kuo jen-wu chih (Biographies of personages of contemporary China). Shanghai, 1939. This book, containing over 300 brief sketches of military and political leaders of republican China, was kindly lent to me by Mr. Yu Tinn-hugh.

Hervey-Saint-Denys, Marquis d'. Six Nouvelles nouvelles traduites pour la première fois du chinois. Paris, 1892.

Hewlett, Meyrick. Forty Years in China. London, 1944.

HHKM: Hsin-hai ko-ming.

Ho Hsi-ya. "Chia-tzu ta-chan hou ch'uan-kuo chün-tui chih t'iao-ch'a" (Investigation of the nation's military after the 1924 war), *Tung-fang tsa-chih* (Eastern miscellany), XXII, No. 1 (Jan. 10, 1925), and No. 2 (Jan. 25, 1925).

Ho Shih-chun. Jou Lin Wai Che: Le Roman des lettres: Etude sur un roman satirique chinois. Paris, 1933.

Holcombe, A. N. The Chinese Revolution: A Phase in the Regeneration of a World Power. Cambridge, Mass., 1931.

Houn, Franklin W. Central Government of China, 1912–1928: An Institutional Study. Madison, Wisc., 1957.

Howard, H. P. "Famine and 'Mohammedan' Banditry Again Devastating Kansu," *CWR*, XLIX, No. 1 (June 1, 1929), 17.

Howell, E. B., trans. "The Restitution of the Bride" and Other Stories from the Chinese. New York, 1926.

———, trans. "The Inconstancy of Madam Chuang" and Other Stories from the Chinese. New York, n.d.

Hsieh Kuan-lan. "Feng Yü-hsiang wei-shem-ma yao sha Hsü Shu-cheng?" (Why did Feng Yü-hsiang want to kill Hsü Shu-cheng?), *Ch'un Ch'iu*, No. 40 (Mar. 1, 1959), pp. 12–13; No. 41 (Mar. 16, 1959), pp. 6–9, 20; No. 42 (Apr. 1, 1959), pp. 11–13; No. 43 (Apr. 16, 1959), pp. 11–13.

Hsieh Pao-chao. The government of China (1644–1911). Baltimore, 1925.

Hsin-hai ko-ming (The Revolution of 1911), ed. Ch'ai Te-kung and six others. Shanghai, 1956. Vol. VI of the series Chung-kuo chin-tai-shih tzu-liao ts'ung-k'an (Modern Chinese historical materials series), under the general editorship of Chung-kuo shih-hsüeh hui (Chinese Historical Society).

"Hsin-hai Luan-chou ping-pien chi" (The Luanchow revolt in the Revolution of 1911), in *HHKM*, pp. 331–33.

Hu Ngo-kung. "Hsin-hai ko-ming pei-fang shih-lu" (The true account of the North during the Revolution of 1911), in *HHKM*, pp. 271–328.

Hua Ai-kuo: see under Feng Yü-hsiang.

Hugh, Albert Y. "Significance of Secret Societies in Chinese Life," *CWR*, XLII, No. 2 (Sept. 10, 1927), 38–39.

Hummel, Arthur W., ed. Eminent Chinese of the Ch'ing Period (1644–1912). 2 vols. Washington, D.C., 1943–44.

Hundhausen, Vincenz. The Oil Vendor and the Sing Song Girl: A Chinese Tale in Five Cantos. Translated from the German by Fritz Ruesch. Peking; the date is cut from the title page, but the translator's introduction is dated 1938.

"Hyo Gyoku-sho no kinkyo" (Feng Yü-hsiang and the present situation), despatch from the military attaché at the Japanese legation in China, Feb. 1925, in *Mitsu dai nikki* (Confidential great daily records), V, No. 8 (1925).

"Hyo Gyoku-sho tai Sainan jiken oyobi tonichi ni kansuru ken" (Regarding Feng Yü-hsiang and the Tsinan Incident, and his intention to come to Japan), despatch from the military attaché at the Japanese legation in China, July 18, 1928, in *Rikushi mitsu ju dai nikki* (Confidential important daily records of the military academy), VII, No. 12 of Joho (1928).

Impey, Lawrence. "Flood, Famine and Civil War in North China," *CWR*, XXX, No. 5 (Oct. 4, 1924), 150–53.

———. "Will Winter Force a Stalemate in the War?," *CWR*, XXX, No. 8 (Oct. 25, 1924), 238.

———. "Chinese Progress in the Art of War," *CWR*, XXXI, No. 4 (Dec. 27, 1924), 101–4.

———. "Kalgan the Key to the North China Political Situation," *CWR*, XXXII, No. 7 (Apr. 18, 1925), 188–91.

———. The Chinese Army as a Military Force. Tientsin, 1926. Impey was attached to Wu P'ei-fu's staff headquarters during the Second Chih-Feng

War, and his book is largely based on that experience. He has short, somewhat superficial chapters on various aspects of the Chinese military. His concluding chapter is a sketch of the fighting between the Kuominchün and Li Ching-lin's troops in late 1925 in the vicinity of Tientsin.

Isaacs, Harold R. The Tragedy of the Chinese Revolution. Rev. ed. Stanford, Calif., 1951. First edition 1938; second, revised edition 1961.

Jihchi: Feng Yü-hsiang, *Feng Yü-hsiang jih-chi.*

Johnston, Reginald F. Twilight in the Forbidden City. New York, 1934.

Jowe, Peter S. "Chinese Militarism and the People," *The Weekly Review of the Far East,* XVII, No. 4 (June 25, 1921), 169–71.

———. "Illegal Military Taxes Undermining China's Position," *CWR,* XXX, No. 13 (Nov. 29, 1924), 391–92.

———. "Who Sells the Guns to China's War Leaders?," *CWR,* XXXII, No. 7 (Apr. 18, 1925), 192–98.

Kao Yin-tsu. Chung-hua min-kuo ta-shih chi (Record of major events of the Chinese republic). Taipei, 1957.

KMCKMS: Feng Yü-hsiang, *Kuo-min-chün ko-ming shih.*

Kotenev, Anatol M. New Lamps for Old: An Interpretation of Events in Modern China and Whither They Lead. Shanghai, 1931.

———. The Chinese Soldier: Basic Principles, Spirit, Science of War, and Heroes of the Chinese Armies. Shanghai, 1937.

Kuo Hsiao-ch'eng. "Chih-li ko-ming chi" (Record of revolution in Chihli), in *HHKM,* pp. 268–71.

Kuo-min-chün chia-tzu ko-ming (The Kuominchün revolution of 1924). N.p., 1936. This account of the 1924 Peking coup is written from the Kuominchün point of view. I was provided with a handwritten copy of the original through the courtesy of the custodian of the Kuomintang historical archives in Taiwan.

Kuo-shih hsin-wen pien-chi-pu (National affairs news editorial board). Peiching ping-pien shih-mo chi (A complete record of the soldier mutinies in Peking). Peking, 1912.

Lee, Edward Bing-shuey. "What Is Going On in the North?," *CWR,* LV, No. 9 (Apr. 26, 1930), 321.

Li Chien-nung. Chung-kuo chin-pai-nien cheng-chih shih (The political history of China for the last one hundred years). Taipei, 1957. An English translation of the 1948 edition was published by D. Van Nostrand Co. in 1956 as *The Political History of China, 1840–1928.* A number of passages examined closely for this study proved to be translated obscurely or incorrectly.

Li Man-k'ang. "Min shih-san-nien ti-erh tz'u Chih-Feng ta-chan chen shih" (The curious history of the Second Chih-Feng War in 1924), *Ch'un Ch'iu,* No. 69 (May 16, 1960), pp. 2–4; No. 70 (June 1, 1960), pp. 2–4; No. 71 (June 16, 1960), pp. 8–11. A sympathetic discussion of Wu P'ei-fu's activities during the Second Chih-Feng War. Not very valuable.

Li T'ai-fen. Kuo-min-chün shih-kao (Draft history of the Kuominchün). N.p., 1930. Li, a professor, was associated with Kuominchün educational programs from about 1925. His book contains a great deal of material about the organization of the Kuominchün, detailed accounts of important battles, including maps, and biographical data about Feng's subordinates. Many documents are quoted in full or in part, notably Feng's circular telegrams and speeches. Despite frequent errors in dates and other details, this is a very valuable source.

Li Te-ch'üan (Mme. Feng Yü-hsiang). "An Open Letter from Madame Feng Yü-hsiang," Far East Spotlight (Nov. 1948).

Liang Ch'i-ch'ao. "Hu-kuo chih i-hui ku-t'an" (Reminiscent chat about the National Protection War), in Tso Shun-sheng, ed., Chung-kuo chin-pai-nien shih tzu-liao hsü-pien (More material on Chinese history of the past one hundred years). Taipei, 1958.

Ling Yüeh. "Luan-chou kuang-fu chi-shih" (The truth about the Luanchow revolution). This is a handwritten manuscript by a participant in the Luanchow rebellion. It consists of forty pages and was probably written in 1936, although internal evidence suggests the possibility that it was written a few years later. The copy in my possession is a handwritten copy of the original, and was provided to me through the courtesy of the custodians of the archives of the Committee for the Compilation of Kuomintang Historical Materials. The manuscript describes those events of the Luanchow revolt in which the author took part, and alludes briefly to other aspects of the revolt.

"The Lion and the Unicorn," CWR, XXX, No. 5 (Oct. 4, 1924), 148.

Liu E (Liu T'ieh-yün). The Travels of Lao Ts'an. Translated from the Chinese and annotated by Harold Shadick. Ithaca, N.Y., 1952.

Liu, F. F. A Military History of Modern China, 1924–1949. Princeton, 1956.

Liu Kuang-yen. Ts'ai Sung-p'o. Hong Kong, 1958. A simplistic biography; eulogizes Ts'ai Ao.

Liu-yün-chü-shih (pseud.), comp. Ming-chi pai-shih hui-pien (Compilation of informal history of the Ming period). N.p., n.d. 16 ts'e, 2 han. The 10th ts'e contains the "Record of the Massacre at Chiating," and the 16th ts'e contains the "Diary of Ten Days at Yangchow," the two works that Feng said turned him against the Manchus.

Lo Cheng-wei. "Luan-chou ko-ming chi-shih ch'u-kao" (First draft of the true history of the Luanchow rebellion), in HHKM, pp. 330–60.

Lo Chia-lun, ed. Ko-ming wen-hsien (Records of the revolution). Taipei, 1953–

Lo Kuan-chung. Romance of the Three Kingdoms. Translated by C. H. Brewitt-Taylor. 2 vols. Tokyo, 1959.

Lo, R. Y. "Marshal Feng in Nanking," CWR, LXXIX, No. 8 (Jan. 23, 1937), 276.

Lynn, Jermyn Chi-hung. Political Parties in China. Peking, 1930. Lynn, whose Chinese name was Lin Chi-hung, was an adviser to Wu P'ei-fu, Chang Tso-lin, Tuan Ch'i-jui, and other leading men of the time. This book consists of articles originally written from day to day for serial publication in the North China Standard. It covers in some detail the complex struggles and relationships of the period from 1912 to 1930. Although the book is neither lucid nor exact, it contains a great deal of information.

Ma Po-yuan. Wo so chih-tao ti Kuo-min-chün yü Kuo-min-tang ho-tso shih (What I know about the history of cooperation between the Kuominchün and the Kuomintang). N.p., 1931.

MacMurray, John V. A., comp. and ed. Treaties and Agreements With and Concerning China, 1894–1919. 2 vols. New York, 1921.

MacNair, Harley Farnsworth. China in Revolution: An Analysis of Politics and Militarism Under the Republic. Chicago, 1932. This is still one of the most complete studies of the warlord period.

Mao I-heng. O-Meng hui-i lu (Recollections of Russia and Mongolia). Hong Kong, 1954. Mao was associated with Feng Yü-hsiang in 1925, and accompanied Feng to Moscow. His comments on Feng and Feng's relations with the Russians are important. However, much of the material in the book is questionable. Mao builds up his own role in the Northwestern Army and as an adviser to Feng. He has a tendency to gossip, and on some points is vague and evasive. Finally, he wrote this book "to help the battle against Communism," and it shows. Despite all these shortcomings, there are no other sources as detailed as this on Feng's experiences in Moscow.

———. "T'an Feng Yü-hsiang" (Chatting about Feng Yü-hsiang), Lun Yü (Discourse), No. 3 (May 6, 1957), p. 8.

"Marshal Feng and His 6 A.M. Interviews," CWR, XLIV, No. 12 (Aug. 18, 1928), 382–84.

"Marshal Feng Continues to Embarrass Government," CWR, LXV, No. 2 (June 10, 1933), 56–57.

"Marshal Feng in Retirement—Now Known as 'The Kind,'" CWR, LXX, No. 3 (Sept. 15, 1934), 89.

"Marshal Feng Shows No Sign of Leaving Kalgan," CWR, LXV, No. 5 (July 1, 1933), 183.

Meng, C. Y. W. "General Yen Now Mobilizes," CWR, XLII, No. 6 (Oct. 8, 1927), 153.

———. "Chinese Leaders Oppose the Recommendations of the Lytton Report," CWR, LXII, No. 9 (Oct. 29, 1932), 378–79.

Meng Po-ch'ien. Hui-shang jen-tao (Return to the human way). Hong Kong, 1953.

Michael, Franz. "Military Organization and Power Structure of China During the Taiping Rebellion," Pacific Historical Review, XVIII, No. 4 (Nov. 1949), 469–83.

Michael, Franz, and Taylor, George E. The Far East in the Modern World. New York, 1956.

Mif, P. Heroic China: Fifteen Years of the Communist Party of China. New York, 1937.

Miner, Louella. Journal. Louella Miner worked for many years in China as an educator and missionary under the auspices of the American Board of Commissioners for Foreign Missions. Li Te-ch'üan was one of her students, and Miss Miner became a friend of the Feng family after Li's marriage to Feng Yü-hsiang. This friendship continued until Miss Miner's death, in the 1930's. During those years, Miss Miner wrote hundreds of letters to friends, relatives, and organizations in the United States. She frequently wrote long letters, duplicated them, and sent them to various people, retaining one copy for her files. These she called her Journal. The letters have not been published, but many are in the library of the American Board of Commissioners for Foreign Missions, in Boston. It is through the courtesy of the American Board that I have been able to use them.

——. "Works of Peace in Marshal Feng's Army," The Chinese Recorder, LVII, No. 3 (Mar. 1926), 183–86.

Misselwitz, Henry Francis. The Dragon Stirs: An Intimate Sketchbook of China's Kuomintang Revolution, 1927–29. New York, 1941.

Mitarevsky, N., ed. World-Wide Soviet Plots, as Disclosed by Hitherto Unpublished Documents Seized at the U.S.S.R. Embassy in Peking. Tientsin, n.d.

"The New Political Lineup and Its International Significance," CWR, XXX, No. 11 (Nov. 15, 1924), 329–31.

The North China Herald and Supreme Court and Consular Gazette, Shanghai, is an excellent source for warlordism, especially in establishing chronology.

North, Robert C., and Xenia J. Eudin. M. N. Roy's Mission to Moscow; the Communist-Kuomintang Split of 1927. Documents translated by Helen Powers. Berkeley, Calif., 1963.

Northrop, F. S. C. The Meeting of East and West: An Inquiry Concerning World Understanding. New York, 1946.

Ou, Itai. Le Roman chinois. Paris, 1933.

Papers Relating to the Foreign Relations of the United States: 1924, vol. 1. Washington, D.C., 1939.

"Pei-ching cheng-chü ti pien-hua" (Transformation of the Peking political situation), Tung-fang tsa-chih (Eastern miscellany), XXI, No. 20 (Oct. 25, 1924), 1–3; No. 21 (Nov. 10, 1924), 1–4.

Pei-p'ing t'e-pieh shih tang-wu chih-tao wei-yüan-hui (Party affairs management committee of the Peiping special municipality). Feng Yü-hsiang ti tsung chien-ch'a (Comprehensive investigation of Feng Yü-hsiang). Peking, 1929.

Pelliot, Paul. "Le Kin Kou K'i Kouan," *T'oung Pao*, XXIV, No. 1 (1925–26), 54–60.

Piry, A. Théophile. Erh-Tou-Mei, ou Les Pruniers merveilleux: Roman chinois traduit et accompagné de notes philologiques. Paris, 1880.

Powell, Ralph L. "The Rise of Yüan Shih-k'ai and the Pei-yang Army," in Papers on China (mimeographed), vol. 3. Cambridge, Mass., Harvard University, 1949.

———. The Rise of Chinese Military Power: 1895–1912. Princeton, 1955.

Pratt, John T. War and Politics in China. London, 1943.

Pye, Lucian Wilmot. "The Politics of Tuchünism in North China, 1920–1927: An Aspect of Political and Social Change in Modern China." Ph.D. dissertation, Yale University, 1951.

Rohrbough, Edward. "Christian General Feng Acts," *CWR*, CIV, No. 2 (Dec. 13, 1947), 50.

Roy, M. N. Revolution and Counter-Revolution in China. Calcutta, 1946.

"Shih-shih shu-p'ing: tung-pei chan-cheng ti sheng-fu chüeh-ting le" (Discussion and comment on current events: determination of success or failure in the northeastern war), *Tung-fang tsa-chih* (Eastern miscellany), XXI, No. 21 (Nov. 10, 1924), 4–5.

Shyu, Nae-lih. "Feng Yü-hsiang and the Kuominchün, 1924–1928." M.A. thesis, University of Washington, 1960. Particularly useful for its information about the background of Feng's officers.

Snow, Edgar. Red Star Over China. New York, 1944.

Sonoda Ichiki. Fen-sheng hsin-Chung-kuo jen-wu-chih (A record of personages of New China by provinces). Translated from the Japanese by Huang Hui-ch'üan and Tiao Ying-hua. Shanghai; n.d., but Fairbank and Liu say 1930. Excellent for the warlord period.

The Soviet in China Unmasked: Documents Revealing Bolshevistic Plans and Methods, Seized in the U.S.S.R. Embassy, Peking, April 6, 1927. Shanghai, 1927.

"Soviet Plot in China," *The Chinese Social and Political Science Review*, XI, No. 3 (July 1927), 153–92; No. 4 (Oct. 1927), 193–272. Contains translations of 32 documents seized in the April 1927 raid on the Soviet embassy in Peking.

Spector, Stanley. "Li Hung-chang and the Huai-chün." Ph.D. dissertation, University of Washington, 1953. University Microfilms Publication 7200, Ann Arbor, Mich., 1954.

Speer, Robert E. "Lu Taifu" Charles Lewis, M.D.: A Pioneer Surgeon in China. New York, n.d. This work, consisting largely of excerpts from letters written by Dr. Lewis and his associates, not only contains material on the warlords, but also has interesting comments on the level of medical understanding in China, and on the effects of warlordism on the common people.

Stanton, Edwin F. Brief Authority: Excursions of a Common Man in an Uncommon World. New York, 1956.
Strong, Anna Louise. "Chang and Feng and Wu," Asia, XXVI, No. 7 (July
1926), 596–601, 649–51.
Su-lien yin-mou wen-cheng hui-pien (Collection of documentary evidence of
the Soviet Russian conspiracy). Peking, 1928.
Tai-shi korosha denki hensankai (Commission for the compilation of bio-
graphical memoirs of those who rendered service regarding China). Tai-shi
kaikoroku (A record looking back on China). 2 vols. Tokyo, 1936. Zoku tai-
shi kaikoroku (supplement). 2 vols. Tokyo, 1941–42.
Tan, Chester C. The Boxer Catastrophe. New York, 1955.
Tang, Peter S. H. Russian and Soviet Policy in Manchuria and Outer Mon-
golia, 1911–1931. Durham, N.C., 1959.
T'ang Leang-li. China in Revolt: How a Civilization Became a Nation.
London, 1927.
———. The Inner History of the Chinese Revolution. New York, 1930.
T'ao Chü-yin. Wu P'ei-fu chiang-chün chuan (Biography of Marshal Wu
P'ei-fu). Shanghai, 1941.
———. Tu-chün t'uan-chuan (A chronicle of the group of warlords). Shang-
hai, 1948. A history of political events and machinations from the death of
Yüan Shih-k'ai to the Anhwei-Chihli War. Somewhat gossipy, but useful.
———. Pei-yang chün-fa t'ung-chih shih-ch'i shih-hua (Historical talk about
the period when the Peiyang warlords held sway). 6 vols. Peking, 1957–58.
Teng Chih-ch'eng. "Hu-Kuo-Chün chi-shih" (An account of the activities of
the National Protection Army), Shih-hsüeh nien-pao (Historical annual),
II (1935), 1–22. A comprehensive account of the National Protection Army
from its beginnings through the war against Yüan Shih-k'ai and through
the subsequent warfare in Szechwan and Yunnan. A good source for warlordism in Szechwan.
Ting Wen-chiang. Kuo-min chün-shih chin-chi (Recent military affairs in the
republic). Peking, 1926.
Ting Wen-chiang, Weng Wen-hao, and Tseng Shih-ying. Chung-hua min-
kuo hsin ti-t'u (New atlas of the Republic of China). Shanghai, 1934. A
good atlas for the warlord period. Many place-names have been changed
since it was published, and it is therefore much easier to use than later
maps.
"To Be Paid 'When the War Is Over,'" CWR, XXXVII, No. 5 (July 3, 1926),
114.
Tretiakov, S. A Chinese Testament: The Autobiography of Tan Shih-hua
as told to S. Tretiakov. New York, 1934.
"Ts'a-p'ing" (Notes and comment), Tung-fang tsa-chih (Eastern miscellany),
XXIII, No. 4 (Feb. 25, 1926), 1–4.
Tsai Ho-shen. "Istoria Opportunisma v Kommunisticheskoi Partii Kitaia"

(The history of opportunism in the Communist Party of China), *Problemy Kitaia* (Problems of China), No. 1 (1929), pp. 1–77.

Ts'ai Ao. Ts'ai Sung-p'o hsien-sheng i-chi (Collected works of Ts'ai Sung-p'o [Ts'ai Ao]). Shaoyang, 1943.

United States Department of State, Division of Biographic Information. "Biography of Feng Yü-hsiang." Nine typewritten pages, dated Apr. 14, 1948.

Verbrugge, R. Yuan Che-k'ai: Sa Vie, Son Temps. Paris, 1934.

Vinacke, Harold M. "Military Power and Constitutional Development in China," *The Weekly Review of the Far East*, XVII, No. 8 (July 23, 1921), 377–79; No. 9 (July 30, 1921), 437–40.

Wales, Nym. Red Dust: Autobiographies of Chinese Communists. Stanford, Calif., 1952.

Waley, Arthur. The Opium War Through Chinese Eyes. London, 1958.

Wang Ching-wei. "Wang Ching-wei pao-kao Cheng-chou hui-i ching-kuo" (Wang Ching-wei's report on the experiences of the Chengchow Conference). June 13, 1927. This report was copied from the draft minutes of the 28th meeting of the Central Political Council. An English translation was supplied to me by Professor C. Martin Wilbur.

Wang Hsiu-ch'u. "A Memoir of Ten Days' Massacre in Yangchow." Translated by Lucien Mao, in the *T'ien Hsia Monthly*, IV, No. 5 (May 1937), 515–37.

Wang Wei-lien. "Wu-han cheng-fu yü Feng Yü-hsiang" (The Wuhan government and Feng Yü-hsiang), *Hsien-tai shih-liao* (Contemporary historical materials), I (1934), 40–44.

Ware, H. D. "The Phlegmatic North Wants a Dictator," *CWR*, XLIX, No. 4 (June 22, 1929), 154.

Weale, B. L. Putnam (pseud. of Bertram Lenox Simpson). *The Vanished Empire*. London, 1926.

"The Week in the Far East," *CWR*, XXXII, No. 1 (Mar. 7, 1925), 23–25.

Weisshart, Herbert. "Feng Yü-hsiang: His Rise as a Militarist and His Training Programs," in Papers on China (mimeographed), vol. 6. Cambridge, Mass., Harvard University, 1952.

Wen-i pien-she she (Society of literary translations). Fu-p'i shih-mo chi (A record of the restoration from beginning to end). Shanghai, 1917.

Wen Kung-chih. Tsui-chin san-shih-nien Chung-kuo chün-shih shih (History of Chinese military affairs for the past thirty years). Shanghai, 1932.

Werner, E. T. C. Myths and Legends of China. London, 1922.

Who's Who in China. 3d ed. Shanghai, 1925. In almost every issue of *The China Weekly Review* there are one or two biographical sketches of prominent Chinese. In 1925 many of these were assembled in this volume. It is helpful, though not always reliable.

Wieger, P. Leon. Le Feu aux poudres. Hopei, 1925. Vol. VI in the series "La Chine moderne."

Wilbur, C. Martin, and How, Julie Lien-ying, eds. Documents on Communism, Nationalism, and Soviet Advisers in China, 1918–1927: Papers Seized in the 1927 Peking Raid. New York, 1956.

Wilhelm, R., ed. The Chinese Fairy Book. Translated by Frederick H. Martens. New York, 1921.

Williams, S. Wells. The Middle Kingdom. 2 vols. New York, 1913.

Woodhead, H. G. W. The Truth About the Chinese Republic. London, 1925.

Wright, Mary Clabaugh. The Last Stand of Chinese Conservatism: The T'ung-chih Restoration, 1862–1874. Stanford, Calif., 1957.

WSH: Feng Yü-hsiang, Wo-ti sheng-huo.

WTTSSH: Feng Yü-hsiang, Wo-ti tu-shu sheng-huo.

Wu Ching-tzu. The Scholars. Peking, 1957.

Wu, K. C. The Lane of Eternal Stability. New York, 1962.

"Xenanskie 'Krasnye Piki'" (The "Red Spears" of Honan), Materialy po Kitaiskomu voprosu (Materials on the Chinese question), No. 10 (1928), pp. 167–75.

Yang Hsien-yi and Yang, Gladys. The Courtesan's Jewel Box: Chinese Stories of the Xth–XVIIth Centuries. Peking, 1957.

Yin Tso-ch'üan. Kuo-min-chün ju-Kan ko-ming chan-shih (History of the revolutionary war of the Kuominchün in Kansu). Kansu, 1929. The first portion of this work deals with the Kuominchün in Kansu in 1926, and the second portion deals with 1928. It is written from the viewpoint of the Kuominchün. I used a hand-copied version obtained through the courtesy of the director of the Kuomintang Historical Archives, Taiwan.

Young, John, comp. Checklist of Microfilm Reproduction of Selected Archives of the Japanese Army, Navy, and Other Government Agencies, 1868–1945. Washington, D.C., 1959. Mimeographed.

Yu Hui-yüan. Chung-hua min-kuo tsai ts'ao shih (History of the reestablishment of the Chinese Republic). Shanghai, 1917.

Yu Tinn-hugh. "A History of the Chinese Northwestern Army," CWR, XLVII, No. 12 (Feb. 16, 1929), 492–97; No. 13 (Feb. 23, 1929), 528–32.

Yu Yün-lung. "Hu-kuo shih-kao" (Draft history of the National Protection movement), Chin-tai shih tzu-liao (Materials for modern history), No. 4 (1957), pp. 41–104. This work, originally published in Kunming in 1950, should be used with the following work by Yü Yung-shun.

Yü Yung-shun. "Kuan-yü 'Hu-kuo shih-kao' ti chi-ko wen-ti" (Several questions about the "Draft History of the National Protection Movement"), Chin-tai shih tzu-liao (Materials for modern history), No. 5 (1958), pp. 109–16. A criticism of Yu Yün-lung's work listed above.

Zoku tai-shi kaikoroku: see under Tai-shi korosha denki hensankai.

Zung, G. S. "Marshal Feng and Rural Reconstruction," The Chinese Recorder, XIX, No. 8 (Aug. 1928), 523–25.

Glossary

The following list does not include place names, and also excludes the names of a few well-known persons mentioned only incidentally in the text. It does include all those mentioned in the text who had anything to do with Feng Yü-hsiang or who were related in some way to warlordism in modern China. Courtesy names are given only for those few people who were better known by them than by their original names.

An-kuo-chün　安國軍
Chang Chao-chia　張兆鉀
Chang Chien-kung　張建功
Chang Chih-chiang　張之江
Chang Chih-kung　張治公
Chang Ching-chiang (Chang Jen-chieh)　張靜江
Chang Ching-yao　張敬堯
Chang Fa-k'uei　張發奎
Chang Fu-lai　張福來
Chang Hsüeh-liang　張學良
Chang Hsün　張勳
Chang Huai-chih　張懷芝
Chang Jen-chieh (Chang Ching-chang)　張人傑
Chang Shao-tseng　張紹曾
Chang Tso-lin　張作霖
Chang Tsung-ch'ang　張宗昌
Chang Wei-hsi　張維璽
Chao Chieh　趙傑
Chao Heng-t'i　趙恒惕
Chao T'i　趙倜
Chao Wang-yün　趙望雲
Ch'en Chiung-ming　陳烔明

Ch'en Huan (Ch'en I)　陳宧
Ch'en I (Ch'en Huan)　陳宧
Ch'en Kuang-yüan　陳光遠
Ch'en Shu-fan　陳樹藩
Cheng Chin-sheng　鄭金聲
Cheng Shih-ch'i　鄭士琦
Ch'eng Shen　程慎
Chi Hung-ch'ang　吉鴻昌
Ch'i Hsieh-yüan　齊變元
Chia Te-yao　賈德耀
Chiang Hung-yü　蔣鴻遇
Chiang Chieh-shih (Chiang Kai-shek)　蔣介石
Chiang Teng-hsüan　姜登選
Chien Yu-wen　簡又文
Chin Yün-ngo　靳雲鶚
Chin Yün-p'eng　靳雲鵬
Ching-kuo-chün　靖國軍
Ching-shen shu　精神書
Ch'u Yü-p'u　褚玉璞
Fan Chung-hsiu　樊鍾秀
Fang Chen-wu　方振武
Feng Chi-shan (Feng Yü-hsiang)　馮基善

Feng Huan-chang (Feng Yü-hsiang)　馮煥璋

Feng Kuo-chang　馮國璋

Feng Yu-mou　馮有茂

Feng Yü-hsiang　馮玉祥

Fu Liang-tso　傅良佐

Han Fu-chü　韓復榘

Han Yu-lu　韓有祿

Hayashi Yasakichi　林弥三吉

Ho Ch'i-kung　何其鞏

Ho Chien　何健

Ho Feng-lin　何豐林

Ho Ying-ch'in　何應欽

Hsiang-chün　湘軍

Hsiao Yao-nan　蕭耀南

Hsiung Pin　熊斌

Hsü Ch'ien　徐謙

Hsü Shih-ch'ang　徐世昌

Hsü Shu-cheng　徐樹錚

Hsüeh Tu-pi　薛篤弼

Hu Ching-i　胡景翼

Hu Han-min　胡漢民

Huai-chün　淮軍

Huang Fu　黃郛

Huang Hsing　黃興

Huang Shao-hsiung　黃紹雄

I P'ei-chi　易培基

Jen Yu-min　任右民

K'an Chao-hsi　闞朝璽

Ku Chen　顧震

Ku Meng-yü　顧孟餘

K'ung Fan-chin　孔繁錦

Kuo Chien　郭堅

Kuo-min-chün　國民軍

Kuo Sung-ling　郭松齡

Li Ch'ang-ch'ing　李長清

Li Chi-shen　李濟琛

Li Ching-lin　李景林

Li Hung-chang　李鴻章

Li Lieh-chün　李烈鈞

Li Ming-chung　李鳴鐘

Li Shih-tseng (Li Yü-ying)　李石曾

Li Shun　李純

Li Te-ch'üan　李德全

Li Tsung-jen　李宗仁

Li Yü-ying (Li Shih-tseng)　李煜瀛

Li Yüan-hung　黎元洪

Li Yün-lung　李雲龍

Liang Ch'i-ch'ao　梁啟超

Liang Shih-i　梁士詒

Ling Ping　凌冰

Ling Yüeh　凌鉞

Liu Chen-hua　劉鎮華

Liu Chen-nien　劉珍年

Liu Chi　劉驥

Liu Hei-ch'i　劉黑七

Liu I-ch'ing　劉一清

Liu Ju-ming　劉汝明

Liu Po-chien　劉伯堅

Liu Yü-fen　劉郁芬

Liu Yün-feng　劉雲峰

Lo Wen-kan　羅文幹

Lu Ch'eng-wu　陸承武

Lu Chien-chang　陸建章

Lu Chung-lin　鹿鍾麟

Lu Hung-t'ao　陸洪濤

Lu Ti-p'ing　魯滌平

Lu Yung-hsiang　盧永祥

Lung Yün　龍雲

Ma T'ing-hsiang　馬廷勤

Matsumuro Takayoshi　松室孝良

Men Chih-chung　門致中

Meng Po-ch'ien　孟伯謙

Ni Ssu-ch'ung　倪嗣冲

Niu Yung-chien　鈕永建

Okura Kihachiro　大倉喜八郎

Pai Ch'ung-hsi　白崇禧

P'an Chü-ying　潘矩楹

Pao Te-ch'üan　鮑德全

Pao Yü-hsiang　包玉祥

Pao Yü-lin　鮑毓麟

Pei-yang-chün　北洋軍

Pei-yang ta-chen　北洋大臣

P'eng Shou-hsin　彭壽莘

P'u-i 溥儀

Shang Chen 商震

Shao Li-tzu 邵力子

Shih Ching-t'ing 石敬亭

Shih Ts'ung-yün 施從雲

Shih Yu-san 石友三

Sun Chien-sheng 孫諫聲
 (sometimes 孫建聲)

Sun Ch'uan-fang 孫傳芳

Sun I-hsien (Sun Yat-sen)
 孫逸仙

Sun Liang-ch'eng 孫良誠

Sun Lien-chung 孫連仲

Sun Yo (or Yüeh) 孫岳

Sung Che-yüan 宋哲元

Ta-tao-tui 大刀隊

Tai K'an 戴戡

T'an Yen-k'ai 譚延闓

T'ang Sheng-chih 唐生智

Teng Yen-ta 鄧演達

Ts'ai Ao 蔡鍔

Ts'ai Yüan-p'ei 蔡元培

Ts'ao Jui 曹銳

Ts'ao K'un 曹錕

Tseng Kuo-fan 曾國藩

Tuan Ch'i-jui 段祺瑞

Tuan Chih-kuei 段芝貴

tuchün 督軍

tupan 督辦

tutu 督都

tut'ung 都統

Wan Fu-lin 萬福麟

Wang Chan-yüan 王占元

Wang Ch'eng-pin 王承斌

Wang Chin-ming 王金銘

Wang Ching-wei 汪精衛

Wang Ch'ung-hui 王寵惠

Wang Huai-ch'ing 王懷慶

Wang K'e-min 王克敏

Wang Shih-chen 王士珍

Wang Shih-ch'ing 王石清

Wu Chih-hui (Wu Ching-heng)
 吳稚暉

Wu Ching-heng (Wu Chih-hui)
 吳敬恒

Wu Hsin-t'ien 吳新田

Wu P'ei-fu 吳佩孚

Yang Hu-ch'eng 楊虎城

Yang Kuei-t'ang 楊桂堂

Yang Yü-t'ing 楊宇霆

Yen Hsi-shan 閻錫山

Yen Hsiang-wen 閻相文

Yü Shu-te 于樹德

Yü Yu-jen 于右任

Yüan Shih-k'ai 袁世凱

Yüeh Jui-chou 岳瑞洲

Yüeh Wei-chou 岳瑞洲

Yüeh Wei-chün 岳維峻

Index

Agreements. *See* Treaties and agreements

American Red Cross, 24

An-Chih War. *See* Chihli-Anfu War

Andrew, G. Finlay, 252

Anfu clique, 12, 99, 101, 107f, 124, 131n, 138–45 *passim*, 186n; leaders of, 64, 72

Anhwei Army, 2ff, 6, 31, 33–34

Anhwei-Chihli War. *See* Chihli-Anfu War

Anhwei clique. *See* Anfu clique

Ankuochün, 235–39 *passim*

Arms Embargo Agreement, 30

Bandits, 36, 50–51, 55, 90–91, 91n; and warlords, 18f, 160, 161–62, 193, 307n35; in Shensi, 103–5; in Honan, 114–15, 117; in Shantung, 130, 254. 257. *See also* Red Spear Society; White Spear Society; White Wolf

Bauer, Max, 254

Big Sword Unit, 76, 78, 95

Book of the Spirit, 80

Boorman, Howard, 281n

Borodin, Mikhail, 163, 199, 219–20, 228–29

Buck, Pearl, 20, 24

Buddhism, 82n, 116, 143

Chahar, 151–59 *passim*

Chang Chao-chia, 195–96, 208

Chang Chien, 119n

Chang Chien-kung, 46f, 47n

Chang Chih-chiang, 112, 149, 184, 187, 196

Chang Chih-kung, 221

Chang Chih-tung, 4

Chang Ching-chiang, 227n

Chang Ching-yao, 57, 60, 96, 97–98

Chang Fa-k'uei, 221, 263f

Chang Fu-lai, 117f

Chang Hsüeh-liang, 181, 205, 236, 243n, 266–67, 269, 276

Chang Hsün, 11, 65f, 109n, 124, 145

Chang Huai-chih, 69

Chang Shao-tseng, 45f, 125

Chang Tso-hsiang, 243n

Chang Tso-lin, 10, 19, 146, 180, 205, 236, 250; and Chihli-Anfu War, 12, 107; and Northern Expedition, 14, 206, 238; war with Feng Yü-hsiang, 23, 155, 171, 177, 178–80, 189–90, 194, 230; and England, 29–30; and First Chihli-Fengtien War, 108–10, 124, 130, 140; and Second Chihli-Fengtien War, 130ff, 135, 139, 141–44; conferred with Feng Yü-hsiang, 136, 147; and Japan, 140f, 178, 183–84, 296; and control of Peking, 148, 150; raided Russian embassy, 164n; organized Northeastern bloc, 177;

and Kuo Sung-ling revolt, 181–85; and Wu P'ei-fu, 186, 188f; and Yen Hsi-shan, 205, 235; and Sun Ch'uan-fang, 218; and Nanking, 229–30; mentioned, 20, 69, 137, 148, 251, 266, 288

Chang Tsung-ch'ang, 24, 178n, 186, 188, 218, 234–37 passim, 255–58 passim

Chang Wei-hsi, 204, 208

Ch'angte, 72–96

Chao Chieh, 110–11

Chao Heng-t'i, 217

Chao T'i, 100, 110–17 passim

Chao Wang-yün, 273

Charitable organizations, 24, 151, 158, 185n, 197, 249, 252, 258

Ch'en Chiung-ming, 20, 288

Ch'en Huan, 55ff, 60–63 passim

Ch'en I. See Ch'en Huan

Ch'en Kuang-yüan, 67

Ch'en Shu-fan, 62, 64, 68, 101–7 passim, 115, 317n79

Cheng Chin-sheng, 44

Cheng Shih-ch'i, 178n

Ch'eng, Marcus, 175

Ch'eng Shen, 100, 110

Chengchow Conference, 225–26, 228, 233

Chi Hung-ch'ang, 273n

Ch'i Hsieh-yüan, 131n, 132, 178n

Chiang Hung-yü, 59

Chiang Kai-shek, 226, 232, 253, 266, 273n, 276; and Communists, 14, 219, 224, 230, 271n; war with Yen-Feng alliance, 21n, 261–67; and Feng Yü-hsiang, 197, 225, 229, 255–59 passim, 268–82 passim, 292; and rift in Kuomintang, 203, 219, 233; and Northern Expedition, 217–20, 224, 227–28, 230, 233–38; and Hsüchow Conference, 226–28; offices of, 233–36 passim, 241, 243n; and disbandment, 243; and Japanese invasion,

269–71; warlord characteristics of, 291–94

Chiang Teng-hsüan, 178n

Chicherin, Georgi, 200

Chien Yu-wen, 81n

Chih-An War. See Chihli-Anfu War

Chih-Feng Wars. See Chihli-Feng-tien Wars

Chihli-Anfu War (1920), 12, 97–101 passim, 107f, 142, 179n

Chihli-Anhwei War. See Chihli-Anfu War

Chihli clique, 19, 21, 97, 104; leaders in, 12, 67; factions in, 101, 124–29 passim, 139; and Feng Yü-hsiang, 108–9, 111, 117–18; areal control in 1924, 131n; and Japan, 140–41

Chihli-Fengtien Wars: First (1922), 12, 23, 107–9, 118, 124, 138f; Second (1924), 12, 21, 26, 130–47, 160f, 167, 179n; results of Second, 177–81 passim

Chin Yün-ngo, 234–35

Chin Yün-p'eng, 108

China International Famine Relief Commission, 151, 249, 252

Chinese Communist Party, 13, 30, 163, 240, 271, 293; and Kuomintang, 13f, 29, 164, 217f, 224–29, 233, 290; and Chiang Kai-shek, 14, 219, 268; and Feng Yü-hsiang, 209–10, 215, 230–31, 273, 279–82 passim

Ching Kuo Chün. See Nation Pacifying Army

Ching-shen shu. See Book of the Spirit

Ch'ing government. See Manchu government

Ch'iu Pin, 129n

Christianity, 52–54, 106–7, 128, 322-n32; and military discipline, 81–83, 88, 112, 169, 174–76, 213f, 269, 285–88 passim. See also Missionaries

Chu Teh, 282
Chu Tzu-su, 43
Ch'u Yü-p'u, 236, 238
Communist International, 163, 198,
    220, 228
Communist Party of China. *See* Chinese Communist Party
Confucianism, 3–4, 54, 80, 169–70,
    283–86
Customs, 154, 180

Disbandment Conference, 242–43

Education and schools, 78–80, 115ff,
    122, 130, 159, 199f, 210, 246–47
Eighth Mixed Brigade, 112
Eleventh Division, 97, 102, 109, 112
Empress Dowager, 5, 284

Famine, 23–24, 196, 248, 248n, 251–
    52
Famine Relief Commission, 151, 249,
    252
Fan Chung-hsiu, 238
Fang Chen-wu, 259, 271, 273
Favorable Treatment, Treaty of,
    66n, 136, 145
Feng-Chih Wars. *See* Chihli-Fengtien Wars
Feng Kuo-chang, 11f, 19, 61, 64–73
    passim, 123
Feng Yü-hsiang: and Wu P'ei-fu, 12,
    114, 117–18, 133–48 *passim*; war
    with Chiang Kai-shek, 15–16, 259–
    67; war with Chang Tso-lin, 21n,
    23, 177–92, 194; foreign advisers
    of, 29, 144–45, 165, 167, 198–99,
    201, 216; birth and childhood, 31–
    33, 37–38, 309n2; acquired name,
    32, 39n, 309n4; as young soldier,
    33–37; and Boxer Rebellion, 34;
    wives and children of, 35, 129, 130,
    277n, 278n; in Manchuria, 36–37;
    and Society for the Study of the
    Military Arts, 44–45; and Luan-

chow Revolt, 44–48; and Second
Revolution of 1913, 50; and White
Wolf, 51; and Hung-hsien monarchy, 56–63; and battle for Hsüchow, 57–60; and restoration of
P'u-i, 63–67; at Pukow, 68–69, 71;
Wuhsüeh declarations of, 70–71,
117; occupied Ch'angte, 72–73;
wrote *Book of the Spirit*, 80; treatment of foreigners, 94–95; relations with the public, 93–94, 112,
118–19; poetry of, 99, 268, 273–74,
282; robbed train, 100; and Chao
T'i, 100, 110–11, 113; killed Kuo
Chien, 102; and the First Chihli-
Fengtien War, 108–9; shot Pao Te-
ch'üan, 111; and banditry in Honan, 114–15; on dignity of labor,
121–22; fostered cult of common
people, 123, 210, 285, 293; nationalism of, 123, 284; ousted Li Yüanhung, 124–28, 329n35; death of,
130n, 280–81, 282, 294; and Peking coup d'etat of 1924, 133–47;
and ousting of P'u-i, 136, 145–47;
and Matsumuro Takayoshi, 144–
45, 155, 167n, 256; and Kuomintang, 150, 170–73, 198–99, 215,
224–25, 230–34, 290–91; and Mongols, 151–52, 190, 191; political orientation of, 169–76, 201–2, 201n,
209–16, 230, 279, 290–91, 295–99;
Confucianism of, 169–70, 283–86;
and Sun Yat-sen's ideas, 170–71;
and anti-imperialism, 172–76, 290;
organized northwestern bloc, 177–
78, 178n; and Kuo Sung-ling revolt, 181–85, 341; and murder of
Hsü Shu-cheng, 186n; in Mongolia, 198–99; health of, 202; and
Northern Expedition, 217–39 *passim*; and Nanking-Wuhan split,
220, 224–33; and battle for Honan,
220–24; and Chiang Kai-shek, 229,
276–77; and Chinese Communists,

230–33, 273, 282, 294; and his own New Life Movement, 232; and Chin Yün-ngo, 234–35; extent of control in 1928, 240–41; and control of Shantung, 241–42, 254–59; end of career, 242; and disbandment, 242–43; and Red Spear Society, 247; revolt against, 249–52; and Kwangsi warlord revolt, 254; and Liu Chen-nien, 257; and Yen Hsi-shan, 261f; at T'ai Shan, 269, 273; in United States, 277–81; on United States' China policy, 279; evaluation of career of, 283–94; philosophy of government of, 285–87; and social revolution, 289, 291; and New Culture Movement, 288–89; Wuyüan Oath of, 203, 209, 232, 295–96; variation of name of, 309n4; and death of Yen Hsiang-wen, 324n20

—personality and characteristics: ambition of, 33, 86, 172, 286–87; opportunism of, 56, 62, 73; eloquence of, 84–85, 322n44; simplicity of dress and habits, 86n, 244, 269; daily schedule of, 99; ingenuity of, 235n

—education: 36–42; elementary, 37–38, 310n33; books he read, 38–43, 122–23, 138; shortcomings of, 42, 197–98; self-education of, 44, 269, 273; by Russians, 197–202 passim

—army of: established personal army, 49–52; recruiting practices in, 50, 74–76, 87, 112; physical condition of, 51, 77–78, 120; training methods and devices in, 63, 74–90, 120–23, 124; size of, 64, 74, 90, 97, 112, 122, 160–61, 243n, 271; military skills of, 76–77; education in, 78–80; indoctrination of, 80–83, 88, 122, 123, 170, 173–74, 209–16, 231–32; Christianity in, 81–83, 88, 112, 122, 174–75; discipline and

loyalty in, 83–87, 89, 160–61, 213; Feng's rapport with troops, 84–85; important features of, 89–90, 166n; relations with masses, 93–94; regional characteristic of, 161; armaments of, 163, 166n, 167, 191, 206, 209; advisers in, 164–69, 167n; medical care in, 184–85n; defections from, 261

—official positions of: early promotions of, 35, 36, 49, 50; commander 14th brigade, 7th division, 51; Sixteenth Mixed Brigade, 63, 66, 70, 318n87; Defense Commissioner of Ch'angte, 72–73; tuchün of Shensi, 97, 109; tuchün of Honan, 97; commander 11th division, 97; Inspecting Commissioner of the Army, 117; Marshal, 129; Tupan of Northwestern Defense, 149; tupan of Kansu, 159n, 194; resignation of, 187, 197; Second Army Group, 220; Chairman of Honan, 226; Vice-Chairman of Executive Yuan, 241; Minister of War, 241; member of State Council, 266; Minister of Home Affairs, 269; Vice-Chairman of the Military Affairs Commission, 274

—as civil administrator: at Ch'angte, 90–96; in Shensi, 103–7; in Honan, 112–17; in Chahar-Suiyuan, 151–59; in Kansu-Shensi-Honan, 244–49; premises of, 284–89, 293–94

—reforms of: opium, 91–92, 105, 116; at Ch'angte, 91–93; prostitution, 92, 158, 245–46, 338n34; public works, 92–93; gambling, 92, 116; ephemerality of, 98n, 107, 117; in Shensi, 105, 107; education, 115–16, 122, 159, 246; footbinding and queues, 116, 245; colonization and development, 151–56; in northwest, 157–59; eleemosynary institutions, 158, 197, 258;

limits of, 247–49; motivation behind, 283–86
—and Japan: at Ch'angte, 95; and Peking coup d'etat of 1924, 139–45, 146; attitude toward, 109, 145, 154–55, 290; in North China, 179; in Shantung, 255–56; and People's Anti-Japanese Allied Army, 270–73, 274, 275; on the Japanese invasion, 274–75; and the anti-Japanese war, 276; and May 30th Incident, 290
—revenues of: dearth of, 99, 126–28; from land tax, 104; in Honan, 113–14, 248–49; and octroi, 126, 128, 330n43; various sources of, 132, 154, 156–57, 191, 205–6, 216, 257, 272; from opium, 157–58, 193, 246, 337n32; in Kansu, 193, 196, 251
—and Christianity: 81–82, 94, 106, 174–75, 213f, 269, 285, 288; adoption of, 52–54; anti-Catholic, 94; rumored abandonment of, 169
—and Russians: aid from, 29, 150, 163–69, 191, 202, 206, 216, 230, 339–40; Feng in the U.S.S.R., 199–202; view of Russians' role in China, 228–29, 291
Feng Yü-hsiang, Mrs. (Feng's first wife), 35, 129. For second wife, see Li Te-ch'üan
Feng Yu-mou, 31–32
Fengtien Army, 72, 108, 124, 135, 143, 167, 181, 221–24; and disbandment, 243n. See also Ankuochün; Chang Hsüeh-liang; Chang Tso-lin; Chihli-Fengtien Wars
Fifth Kuominchün. See Kuominchün
First Army Group, 236f, 243n, 260
First Chih-Feng War. See Chihli-Fengtien Wars
First Kuominchün. See Kuominchün
Footbinding, 116, 245, 284

Foreigners, relations with, 94–95, 105–6, 154, 157, 168, 172–76, 290
Fourth Army Group, 237, 243, 243n
Fourth Kuominchün. See Kuominchün
Fu Liang-tso, 67

Gailey, Robert, 86n, 327n59

Han Fu-chü, 50, 155, 181–82, 204–5, 239n, 254, 261, 344n5
Han Yu-lu, 195–96
Hayashi Yasakichi, 141, 144f, 154
Ho Ch'i-kung, 199n, 227n
Ho Chien, 253
Ho Feng-lin, 131n
Ho Ying-ch'in, 235, 242
Ho-Umetsu Agreement, 274
Hodges, Paul, 307n54
Honan, 97, 100, 112–17, 187–88, 206–7, 220–24, 226, 244–49 passim
Hsi-liang, 43
Hsiang-chün. See Hunan Army
Hsiao Yao-nan, 188
Hsü Ch'ien, 138, 199, 199n, 201, 225
Hsü Shih-ch'ang, 35, 43, 124
Hsü Shu-cheng, 69, 72, 186n
Hsüan-t'ung emperor. See P'u-i
Hsüchow (Szechwan), battle of, 57–60
Hsüchow Conference, 226–28, 229, 233
Hsüeh Tu-pi, 126–27, 262
Hu Ching-i, 103n, 104, 133–35, 137–44 passim, 160, 161–62, 178n
Hu Han-min, 227n
Hu Lin-i, 41
Hu Shih, 119n
Huai-chün. See Anhwei Army
Huang Fu, 136, 142–47 passim, 227n
Huang Hsing, 314n14
Hunan Army, 2–3, 6
Hung-hsien monarchy, 10, 54–63

Japan, 76, 88, 95, 123, 137, 141, 154–

55; in Shantung, 13, 140, 241, 255, 258; and Chang Tso-lin, 19, 143–44, 178, 183–84; and Chinese warlords, 29, 69, 147, 155; and 1924 Peking coup d'etat, 139–45, 146f; and U.S.S.R., 178–79, 190; encroachments in North China, 179, 269–70, 274. *See also* Manchuria; Shantung; Tsinan Incident; Twenty-one Demands
Jen Yu-min, 199*n*

Kalinin, Mikhail, 200
K'an Chao-hsi, 177*n*
Kansu, 159*n*, 193–97, 244–52 *passim*
Karakhan, Leo, 164f
Kiangnan arsenal, 180
Koo, V. K. Wellington, 119*n*
Ku Huan-chang, 39*n*
Ku Meng-yü, 225
Kuang-hsü emperor, 42
K'ung Fan-chin, 196
Kuo Chien, 102, 104
Kuo Sung-ling, 181–86, 190, 341
Kuominchün, 135, 143, 148, 159–63
—First, 135, 159–63 *passim*, 208, 214; Russians in, 164–69, 191, 209, 230; evaluation of, 166*n*; indoctrination in, 173–74, 209–15, 230–32, 295–99; Christianity in, 174–76, 214; war with Chang Tso-lin and allies, 180–97; medical care in, 184*n*; in Kansu, 193–97; disintegration of, 193, 204–5; and battle for Honan, 220–24; revolt against in Kansu, 249–52. *See also* Feng Yü-hsiang; Northwest Army; Second Army Group
—Second, 161–62, 177–84 *passim*, 247; in Honan, 187–88, 206–7. *See also* Hu Ching-i; Yüeh Wei-chün
—Third, 158*n*, 161f, 177, 184, 188, 207. *See also* Sun Yo
—Fourth, Fifth, Sixth, *and* Seventh, 160*n*

Kuominchün Political Catechism, 295–99
Kuomintang: reorganization of, 12–13, 30, 163–64, 217; alliance with Chinese Communist party, 13–14, 29, 290; absorbed warlords, 14, 15, 236–37, 236*n*, 240–43, 292–93; split in, 14, 203, 219–20, 224–30, 233–34, 240; and Second Revolution of 1913, 50; and Hung-hsien monarchy, 54–63; and Peking coup d'etat of 1924, 137–38, 146; and Feng Yü-hsiang, 146, 150, 166–72 *passim*, 176, 197–99, 260, 290–94; and reorganization of government, 149*n*, 241; and Russians, 163–64, 202; and Northern Expedition, 203, 216–20, 236*n*; and Kuominchün, 206, 209–16, 290–99; and Yen Hsi-shan, 235; military elements in, 240–41; flag of, 245*n*; and Kwangsi clique, 253–54; Third National Congress of, 260, 263; expelled Wang Ching-wei, 265; war with Chinese Communist Party, 268, 277, 280; ousted from Hopei, 274; corruption in, 277, 294; mentioned, 103*n*, 202, 292. *See also* Left Kuomintang; Enlarged Conference of the Kuomintang; Revolutionary Committee of the Kuomintang; Chiang Kai-shek; Northern Expedition
Kwangsi clique, 11, 15, 240f, 252–54, 258, 260

Labor movement, 13f, 217, 231, 240
Lach, Donald, 273*n*
Left Kuomintang, 203, 209, 214, 217–19, 226–29 *passim*, 233, 263, 266. *See also* Kuomintang
Left Route Reserve Army, 49
Lei Chen-ch'un, 318*n*85
Lenin, 199, 201
Lewis, Charles, 159

Li Ch'ang-ch'ing, 194f,
Li Chi-shen, 240, 242, 243n, 253, 260, 282
Li Ching-lin, 23, 136n, 178–89 *passim*
Li Hung-chang, 2ff, 31
Li Lieh-chün, 172, 227n
Li Ming-chung, 50, 86–87, 109, 112, 118, 149, 203, 227n
Li Shih-tseng, 146–47, 227n
Li Shun, 67f, 71
Li Te-ch'üan, 129–30, 175, 199n, 269, 277n, 281, 281n, 294
Li Tsung-jen, 233, 237–43 *passim*, 253
Li Yüan-hung, 10f, 64–65, 117, 119n, 120, 124–29, 139, 329$n35$
Li Yün-lung, 206
Liang Ch'i-ch'ao, 41, 55
Liang Shih-i, 108
Lin (adviser to Feng Yü-hsiang), 198–99, 201
Linch'eng Incident, 130–31
Ling Ping, 116f, 246
Ling Yüeh, 46
"Little Hsü." *See* Hsü Shu-cheng
Liu Chen-hua, 207, 209
Liu Chen-nien, 245n, 257f,
Liu Chi, 199n, 203
Liu Fang, 53
Liu I-ch'ing, 56, 60
Liu Ju-ming, 50, 204
Liu K'un-i, 4
Liu Ming-ch'uan, 31
Liu Po-chien, 210
Liu Yü-fen, 159n, 194–96, 204
Liu Yün-feng, 59f, 62
Lo Chia-lun, 277n
Lo Wen-kan, 125
Lowdermilk, Walter Clay, 277f
Lowdermilk, Mrs. Walter Clay, 277n, 278n
Loyang faction. *See* Chihli clique
Lu Ch'eng-wu, 186n

Lu Chien-chang, 35, 48–52 *passim*, 56, 62–73 *passim*, 101f, 186n, 318-$n85$
Lu Chung-lin, 136, 149, 189f, 193, 259, 262
Lu Hung-t'ao, 194
Lu Ti-p'ing, 253
Lu Yung-hsiang, 131n, 132, 142, 147, 178n, 179n
Luanchow revolt, 44–48, 214, 311$n76$
Lunacharsky, A. V., 200
Lung Yün, 243n

Ma T'ing-hsiang, 250
MacMurray, J. V. A., 161n, 186n
MacNair, Harley F., 273n
Manchu government, 1–8, 44–47, 136
Manchuria, 29, 36–37, 43, 137n, 269. *See also* Japan
Manning (American mining man), 156
Mao Tse-tung, 281n, 282
Matsumuro Takayoshi, 144–45, 155, 167n, 256
May Fourth Movement, 13, 95, 284
May Thirtieth Incident, 154, 157, 168, 172, 179, 214, 290, 296–98 *passim*
Men Chih-chung, 262n
Mencius, 170
Mencius, 41, 109n
Meng Po-ch'ien, 271n
Miner, Louella, 130n
Ming Army, 31
Ming-tzu-chün. *See* Ming army
Missionaries, 82–83, 93ff, 122, 130. *See also* Christianity
Mongolia, 198–99
Mongols, 151–52, 190f
Mott, John R., 53
Muslims, 196n, 214, 249–52

Nanking, 229–30, 240, 241–42, 253

Nankow Pass, battle of, 190–93, 204
Nation Pacifying Army, 103n, 104, 107
National Protection Army. See Hung-hsien monarchy
National Revolutionary Army, 12–15 passim, 215n, 216–20, 233–36 passim, 242–43, 306n28. See also Northern Expedition
Nationalism, 12f, 30, 123
XNew Culture Movement, 288–89
XNew Life Movement, 232, 275
Newspapers, 119n, 151–52, 152n
Ni Ssu-ch'ung, 68f, 71, 71n
XNien Rebellion, 31
Ninghsia, 153n, 262n
Nishihara Loans, 26, 29, 69, 140, 279
Niu Yung-chien, 247n
XNorthern Expedition, 9–14 passim, 23f, 193, 199–206 passim, 216–41 passim, 250–57 passim, 262n, 293
Northwest Army, 160. See also Kuominchün
Northwestern Bank, 157
Northwestern Route Army of the Party Safeguarding and National Salvation Forces, 260

Octroi, 126n, 126–27, 128f, 330n43
Okura Kihachiro, 140, 154f
Oman, Charles M., 184n
Opium, 91–92, 116, 131n, 193, 196, 284, 337n32; and warlord revenues, 24, 26, 101, 105, 157–58, 246, 251

Pai Ch'ung-hsi, 227n, 233, 240, 243n, 253
Pai Ya-yü, 311n69
P'an Chü-ying, 45
Pao Te-ch'üan, 111, 118, 139
Pao Yu-hsiang, 194
Pao Yü-lin, 239n
Paoting faction. See Chihli clique

Peasant associations, 13, 162, 215, 217, 226, 231, 240. See also Red Spear Society
Peiyang Army, 4–12 passim, 16–22 passim, 35–36, 40–45 passim, 61–67 passim
Pei-yang ta-chen, 4n, 35
Peking, 148, 150; coup d'etat of 1924, 133–47, 200, 333–34
Peking Union Medical College, 184n
P'eng Shou-hsin, 132
People's Anti-Japanese Allied Army, 270–73, 274f
People's Republic of China, 281
People's Republic in Fukien, 273n
Personal armies: of Feng Yü-hsiang, 120–24 passim, 160–75 passim, 184n, 191, 206–16 passim, 231–32, 261, 271; formation of, 49–52. See also Eleventh Division; Second Army Group; Sixteenth Mixed Brigade. For others, see Anhwei Army; Hunan Army; Peiyang Army; Warlord armies
Pritchard, Earl, 273n
Progressive party, 54–63
Prostitution, 92, 158, 245–46, 338n34
P'u-i, 10f, 24, 63–67, 109, 136–37, 137n, 145–49 passim, 318n85

Radek, Karl, 200
Railways, 43–45 passim, 65, 140–41, 178–84 passim, 220–27 passim, 234–38 passim, 257f, 266; Peking-Hankow, 26, 115, 134, 181, 220–24 passim, 235f, 248; Peking-Suiyuan, 153–56 passim, 191f, 238
XRed Spear Society, 91n, 162, 188, 206f, 247
Regency government, 137, 147–48
Regional armies. See Personal armies
Regionalism, 1–8 passim, 15, 98n, 207, 250, 253, 305n1

Reorganizationists, 263f, 266
Restoration of monarchy. See P'u-i; Hung-hsien monarchy
Revolution of 1911, 5, 8, 19, 42–46 passim, 66f, 77
Revolutionary Committee of the Kuomintang, 280, 282
Right Wing Guards Army, 34f, 40
Rockefeller Foundation, 224
Roy, M. N., 220
Russians, 203, 220, 229, 271n; aid to Feng Yü-hsiang, 155, 157, 163–69, 177–79, 191, 194, 202, 206, 216, 339n57, 58; advisers in the Kuominchün, 191, 199, 286–87; instructed Feng Yü-hsiang, 197–202 passim, 214; reliance on Feng Yü-hsiang, 224–25, 228
Russo-Japanese War (1904–5), 7, 19, 41

Salvation Army, 185n
Sangurskii (adviser to Feng Yü-hsiang). See Wusmanoff
Schurman, Jacob Gould, 153
Second Army Group, 203, 220, 225, 232, 237f, 243n
Second Kuominchün. See Kuominchün
Second Revolution of 1913, 50
Seventh Kuominchün. See Kuominchün
Seventh Mixed Brigade, 112
Shang Chen, 204ff
Shantung, 26, 91n, 130, 140–41, 180–83 passim, 204, 241–42, 254–59
Shao Li-tzu, 254
Shaw, Ernest T., 86n
Shensi, 62, 97–109 passim, 208, 244–49 passim, 317n79
Shih Ching-t'ing, 255
Shih Shih-lun, 39n
Shih Tsung-yün, 44, 46f, 311n66
Shih Yu-san, 50, 204f, 261, 344n5
Shun (legendary sage king), 109n

Sian, siege of, 206–9, 345n12
Simpson, B. Lenox, 265n
Sino-Japanese War (1894–95), 4
Sixth Route Patrol Defense Corps, 63f
Sixteenth Mixed Brigade, 51–52, 55, 63–66, 68–72 passim, 74–96, 97–102 passim, 381n87
Sixth Kuominchün. See Kuominchün
Society for the Study of Military Arts, 44–45, 46
Southwest Political Council, 272
Soviet Union. See Russians
Ssu-ma Kuang, 41
Stalin, Joseph, 200, 226, 228
Stelle, Elizabeth, 130n
Suiyuan, 151–59 passim, 205
Sun Chien-sheng, 43, 46, 312n77
Sun Ch'uan-fang, 24–25, 131n, 132, 179ff, 188, 218, 233–37 passim, 257
Sun Fo, 225
Sun Liang-ch'eng, 50, 204, 208–9, 237, 254–59 passim, 265
Sun Lien-chung, 50, 204
Sun Tzu, 41
Sun Wen. See Sun Yat-sen
Sun Yat-sen, 71, 103n, 119n, 163, 201, 246, 279f, 298–99; and Protect the Constitution Movement, 11, 67; death, 14, 217; and Feng Yü-hsiang, 137–38, 169–72 passim, 199n, 210, 214, 230f, 266; Will of, 213, 295
Sun Yo, 133–42 passim, 160, 162, 178n, 180n, 187n, 188
Sung Che-yüan, 112, 271ff
Szechwan. See Hsüchow

Tai K'an, 55
T'ai Shan, 269, 273
Taiping Rebellion, 2ff, 31, 53
T'an Yen-k'ai, 98, 225
T'ang Sheng-chih, 217–18, 219–33 passim, 236n, 253f

Tangar, sack of, 251
Tangku Truce, 270
Tao-kuang emperor, 2
Taxation, 24–26, 104, 114–17 passim, 156–57, 206, 248–50, 257, 308n61. See also Octroi
Teng Yen-ta, 225
Third Army Group, 237, 243n
Third Kuominchün. See Kuominchün
Three Principles of the People, 170, 210–13 passim, 228, 298
Tong, Y. L., 259, 262
Treaties and agreements, 30, 35, 66n, 136, 145, 270, 274
Trotsky, Leon, 200
Ts'ai Ao, 55–64 passim
Ts'ai Yüan-p'ei, 119n, 227n
Ts'ao Jui, 184
Ts'ao K'un, 12, 19, 57–62 passim, 69–72 passim, 96–101 passim, 108, 117–43 passim, 189
Tseng Kuo-fan, 2f, 41, 43, 123, 284, 292
Tsinan Incident, 237, 255–58 passim
Tso Tsung-t'ang, 31
Tuan Ch'i-jui, 10ff, 19, 35, 63–72 passim, 123, 137–50 passim, 159, 189n; and Nishihara loans, 26, 29, 69; and Hsü Shu-cheng, 186n
Tuan Chih-kuei, 69
Tuchün, 10n, 149n. See also Warlord armies; Warlordism; Warlords
T'ung-Chih Restoration, 284
T'ung Meng Hui, 46, 311n69
Tupan, 10n, 149n
Tutu, 10n
Tut'ung, 149n
Twenty-fifth Mixed Brigade, 112
Twenty-one Demands, 88, 123, 140, 296

USSR. See Russians
United States of America, 142, 155, 277–81

Voroshilov, Kliment, 200

Waley, Arthur, 39
Wan Fu-lin, 243n
Wang, C. T., 119n
Wang Chan-yüan, 67, 69, 71, 108
Wang Ch'eng-pin, 133
Wang Chin-ming, 44, 46f, 311n66
Wang Ching-wei, 217, 224–28 passim, 234, 263–66, 294
Wang Ch'ung-hui, 119n, 125
Wang Huai-ch'ing, 47, 126f, 132
Wang Hsiu-ch'u, 43
Wang Shih-chen, 69
Wang Shih-ch'ing, 44
Warlord armies: wars between, 12, 15, 22–23, 67, 131, 131n; loyalty in, 17, 261; recruitment of, 17–18, 50, 75, 307n34; forced labor in, 18; absorption of enemy troops, 18, 87, 160–61, 220; medical care in, 23, 184n; foreign advisers in, 29–30; sources of arms, 30; corporal punishment in, 85; North-South antagonisms, 98n; casualties in, 185n, 224, 307n54
Warlord period, 1, 8–16, 240–41
Warlordism: early phase, 9–13; second phase, 13–14; third phase, 14–16, 240–41; definition of, 20; characteristics of, 20–30, 111, 186, 287; and murder, 21, 186n, 194, 257; character of wars in, 21, 22–23; and foreign involvement, 22, 29–30; in Shantung, 26, 91n, 204, 256f; effects of, 30
—social effects of: looting, 17, 27–28, 251; famine, 23–24, 251–52; suffering of populace, 23–39, 30, 161n, 196n, 207; taxation, 24–26, 104, 117, 157, 248–50; exploitation of railroads, 26, 154, 156, 191; confiscation of vehicles and animals, 26–27, 132n; Kansu ravaged, 196; civilian deaths, 207

Warlords: 16–20; definition of, 1, 16;
in Kuomintang, 15, 233–34, 240–
43; and bandits, 18f; training of,
19–20; origins of, 19; and government, 19; characteristics of, 20f,
56; use of murder, 21, 102, 194;
alliances of, 21–22; confiscate vehicles and animals, 26–27, 132n;
and foreign powers, 29, 190; values of, 56; disposition of power in
1924, 131n; sources of arms, 163;
retire to Tientsin, 189n; and Nanking government, 240, 241–42,
253; in Shantung, 256–57, 259
—revenues of: 15, 24–26, 99–100,
252–53; exploit railroads, 25–26,
26n, 154, 156, 191, 255; opium, 26,
101, 105, 131n, 193, 251; issue currency, 26, 157, 190–91, 216; taxes,
26, 104, 114, 117, 128, 156–57;
magnitude of, 113. See also Taxation
—territorial domains of: 18, 177n,
307n30; in January 1927, 208; in
May 1927, 222–24; in 1928, 240–
41; in Kansu, 195
Washington Conference, 106, 108
Weale, Putnam, 265n
Western Hills faction, 266
Whampoa Academy, 168
White Spear Society, 162
White Wolf, 50–51, 55, 114,
314n15
Wu Chih-hui, 227n
Wu Hsiang-chen, 316n47

Wu Hsin-t'ien, 101, 104
Wu P'ei-fu, 19f, 29, 60, 72, 195, 234,
288, 296; and Chihli-Fengtien
Wars, 12, 107–20 passim, 124–48
passim, 160f; and Chihli-Anfu
War, 96–101 passim, 107, 142,
179n; and Honan, 186–90 passim,
206, 217–21 passim
Wuhan-Nanking split, 203, 210, 220,
224–33. See also Kuomintang
Wuhsüeh Declarations, 70–71, 117
Wusmanoff (adviser to Feng), 201,
216
Wuyüan Oath, 203f, 209, 232, 295–
96

Yang Hu-ch'eng, 207
Yang Kuei-t'ang, 63, 65f
Yang Yü-t'ing, 178n, 179f, 236
Yangtze tuchüns, 69, 71, 143f, 147
Yen Hsi-shan, 15–21 passim, 119n,
191f, 204f, 229f, 235–43, 259–67
passim, 288; and battle for Honan,
223–24
Yen Hsiang-wen, 101, 102–3, 324n20
Yü Shu-te, 225
Yü Yu-jen, 103n, 199, 201, 225f
Yüan dynasty, 106n
Yüan Shih-k'ai, 4–11, 17–22 passim,
34, 40f, 45–64 passim, 263, 287f.
See also Hung-hsien monarchy
Yueh Jui-chou, 44
Yüeh Wei-chün, 158n, 162, 178n,
180n, 181, 188
Yui, David Z. T., 119n